An International Antitrust Primer

An International Antitrust Primer

A Businessman's Guide
to the International Aspects
of United States Antitrust Law
and to Key Foreign Antitrust Laws

Earl W. Kintner and Mark R. Joelson

Macmillan Publishing Co., Inc.
New York

Collier Macmillan Publishers
London

Macmillan Publishing Co., Inc.
866 Third Avenue, New York, New York 10022

Collier-Macmillan Canada, Ltd.

Library of Congress Cataloging in Publication Data

Kintner, Earl W
  An international antitrust primer.

  Bibliography: p.
  1. Trusts, Industrial—United States—Law.
2. Trusts, Industrial—Law. 3. Investments, Foreign
—Law and legislation—United States. I. Joelson,
Mark R., joint author. II. Title.
KF1649.K53   343'.73'072   74–84
ISBN 0–02–364380–3

Printing: 1 2 3 4 5 6 7 8   Year: 4 5 6 7 8 9 0

foreword

This fifth book in my series of Macmillan Publishing Co., Inc., primers for businessmen, lawyers, and students on the antitrust and trade regulation laws is co-authored by my law partner Mark R. Joelson. He and my law partner Jack L. Lahr, who is co-author of the sixth and last book in this series, have agreed to share with me the burden of future revisions of all of the books as such become necessary.

E. W. K.

preface

In moving toward an international economy, we are in the midst of an evolutionary process with consequences for business that will be no less profound than those of the industrial revolution in Europe and the United States during the nineteenth century. It is already accepted that activity on a nationwide basis is no longer the final stage to which a typical business firm may aspire as it progresses from local, to state-wide, to regional, and then national operation. Particularly since 1945, enterprises in the advanced economies of North America, Western Europe, and Japan have increasingly tended to seek capital, labor, and management, as well as markets, outside the territory of their home countries.

The acceleration of the trend toward multinational business activity can be seen in current statistics on foreign direct investment—the book value of equity and long-term debt held in foreign firms by domestic companies. Between 1945 and 1973 American investment in foreign firms rose from $8 billion to $107.3 billion. During the same period foreign investment in American companies rose from $2.5 billion to $17.7 billion. The prognosis is one of continuing increase in the magnitude of multinational investment and trade and a concomitant partial integration of national economies.

In order to deal effectively with the challenges and opportunities presented by this trend toward the multinationalization of investments, markets, and production, the businessman must be able to recognize and assess at an early stage the considerations inherent in the conduct of a given multinational business operation that distinguish it from his national business activity. While the businessman cannot have all the necessary knowledge himself, he must be able to identify the special problems, to know which specialist to call upon, to evaluate properly the recommendations he receives, and to formulate plans that give due allowance to all the applicable special considerations.

Of all the special disciplines affecting multinational business planning, none is more pervasive than the law, and few bodies of law are more pervasive than the antitrust and trade regulation laws. These laws reach into every sector of the economy. Dealings with suppliers and customers, relationships with competitors and consumers, transfers of technology, imports, exports, pricing—all, and more, are affected by the laws designed to ensure that competition is free and fair.

Here in the United States, a number of statutes and judicial decisions, as well as rules and guidelines of the Department of Justice and Federal Trade Commission, are pertinent to the manifold problems of maintaining fair competition in domestic and foreign commerce. These are of concern both to the American businessman and to foreign firms who deal or wish to deal in the U.S. market. Moreover, abroad, foreign nations and supranational organizations have their own complicated competition laws and guidelines that may affect the American businessman's foreign ventures and the conduct of his foreign competitors. It is the objective of this book to attempt to pull together, for the benefit of both the American and the foreign businessman, the most important aspects of this mass of information and to present them in a concise and easy-to-understand manner.

This book is primarily concerned with U.S. antitrust law. There are several reasons for this choice of emphasis. First, our years of experience in dealing with the U.S. antitrust laws have made us keenly aware of the numerous problems these laws may create for American and foreign businessmen. The U.S. antitrust laws are the most comprehensive and vigorously enforced in the world. If the business generalist is to avoid violating these laws he must have some familiarity with their basic provisions. Moreover, even if an American businessman is not one of the many engaged in foreign trade or investment, it may well be that some of his competitors or suppliers are involved in such multinational activity. A regional firm may, for example, be concerned about practices associated with its import competition. Today every American businessman needs a basic understanding of the various facets of the U.S. antitrust laws in order to develop the ability to detect legal transgressions of competitors or suppliers before he suffers irreparable damage.

As trade has continued to internationalize and the dynamic growth of foreign economies has led foreign firms to look increasingly to the United

States for trade and investment, the foreign businessman or lawyer too has developed more than a passing interest in the U.S. antitrust laws. Once viewed abroad perhaps as a severe but remote disease that foreigners were unlikely to contract, "American antitrust" is now recognized by the astute international-minded foreign businessman as a discipline that he cannot ignore unless he is prepared to ignore the American market also. We hope that this book, therefore, will be of assistance to the foreign, as well as the American, businessman and lawyer.

Antitrust or, as it is often called abroad, the "law of competition" is, of course, not a phenomenon restricted to the United States. It is an important, and expanding, regimen for many of the major trading nations of the world. As we shall see, the U.S. antitrust laws have served as the model for the competition laws of many foreign nations. Therefore, an understanding of the provisions of U.S. laws will frequently facilitate an understanding of these foreign laws. Moreover, once the reader has achieved an understanding of the provisions of the U.S. antitrust laws, he will be better able to discern and evaluate the contrasting provisions and philosophies of the foreign antitrust laws discussed in Chapter 11.

The first chapter of this book is a short introduction to the development of antitrust law around the world. The second chapter summarizes the pertinent U.S. antitrust laws, so that the reader can have this general background as he turns to the application of those laws in particular contexts. The third chapter explains when U.S. law can be applied to international transactions. In the fourth chapter, we consider the distinct and often thorny procedural and practical problems posed in the application of U.S. antitrust law in the international setting. These problems can be particularly troublesome where action is sought to be taken against a foreign firm or where considerations of foreign law and comity are concerned. The fifth chapter deals with contracts, combinations, and conspiracies in foreign commerce. In the sixth chapter, special antitrust problems arising in the course of "vertical" dealings, those with suppliers or customers, are examined. The seventh chapter discusses the application to international commerce of two important statutes enforced by the Federal Trade Commission, one being the FTC Act itself and the other the Robinson–Patman Act.

In the eighth chapter American antitrust as applied to mergers, acquisitions, and joint ventures is examined. Another area of major current interest in the field, the licensing of patents, know-how, and trademarks, is reviewed in Chapter 9. Chapter 10 explores several of the key exemptions to the U.S. antitrust laws that are pertinent from the international viewpoint. The last two chapters focus upon the most important foreign antitrust laws and upon the probable future course of developments in international antitrust.

A word about what this book is *not* designed to do is necessary. Although the major premises of the antitrust laws of the nations under consideration have been considered and the leading cases examined, many refinements and allusions to case law have necessarily been omitted. This book is not a comprehensive treatment of every phase of American or foreign antitrust or competition law. A work of many volumes would be inherent in that task. Our intention, to the contrary, is to simplify the subject matter, to the extent consistent with accuracy, and thus to provide a readily usable primer for the alert business executive. It is our hope also that the general practitioner who counsels businessmen will find the primer helpful.

Nor is this book designed to enable the businessman to be his own antitrust lawyer. This would be folly, particularly because the laws in question are extensive, subtle in their nuances, and subject to continual legislative amendment or change in judicial interpretation. But if the businessman can be made aware of the nature of these laws and how they generally bear on his activities, he will be in a position to consult a specialist *before* irretrievable action is taken and, in this manner, to shape his activities intelligently and lawfully.

E. W. K.

M. R. J.

acknowledgment

The authors are deeply appreciative of the significant contributions made to this book by many persons. We gratefully acknowledge the assistance of our associate Joseph P. Griffin and of Katherine Drew Hallgarten, both of whom made substantial research and editorial contributions to this work as a whole. Bruce V. Bordelon, Dr. Cornelis Canenbley, Alan Diamond, Fred Klein, Walter Niemasik, Jr., Elisabeth M. Pendleton, and Merle F. Wilberding also provided valuable research assistance.

Our associate William B. Sullivan contributed heavily to the design of Chapter 10, as did Peter J. Vaghi to the design of Chapter 12. Other of our associates, Eugene J. Meigher, I. C. Waddey, Jr., Mark J. Mathis, and David L. Cohen, provided valuable contributions to the design of Chapters 8, 9, 5, and 6, respectively. The authors appreciate the insights into the workings of the Webb–Pomerene Act offered by William A. Bailey, formerly of the Federal Trade Commission staff. We must express our gratitude to Dr. Alfred Gleiss of Stuttgart, Germany, who was kind enough to share with us some of his insights into the competition law of the European Economic Community. We are also grateful to Mr. William J. Brown of London, England, and to Mrs. Michiko Ariga of Japan for their comments with regard to the United Kingdom and Japanese law segments of this book. Finally, we thank Janice Bardley for her skill and patience.

E. W. K.

M. R. J.

contents

An International Antitrust Primer

chapter 1

International Antitrust: Overview of Antitrust Development Around the World

Every modern businessman realizes that antitrust laws are not uniquely American phenomena. In fact, every country in noncommunist Europe except Turkey has some type of restrictive business practices legislation presently on the books or under consideration. Moreover, Argentina, Australia, Brazil, Canada, Chile, Colombia, Israel, Japan, Mexico, New Zealand, Pakistan, the Philippines, South Africa, and Thailand also have legislation concerning anticompetitive behavior. An analysis of each of these laws, in addition to those of the U.S. and the European Common Market, is beyond the scope of this book. However, the businessman confronted with the task of complying with these complex and sometimes conflicting laws around the world should be relieved to learn that none of them currently carry penalties such as death, loss of an ear, imprisonment on bread and water, or lifelong banishment, which were the penalties for violations of some earlier antitrust laws.

The greater and initial portion of this book is a relatively detailed discussion of U.S. antitrust law as applied to international transactions, with the second portion focusing upon the antitrust and competition laws of some other major trading nations, and upon the probable future course of developments in international antitrust. Before turning to the discussion of

1

U.S. law, however, it may prove useful background to review briefly the historical origins of the worldwide patchwork of antitrust laws.

No one is certain as to the earliest antecedents of the concept that governmental action is needed to protect free enterprise from anticompetitive practices. Aristotle is quoted as saying: "It is best to have property private. In this manner industry will be increased, as each person will labor to improve his own property." By 50 B.C. Roman legislation prohibited profiteering and joint action to influence the corn trade. Two hundred and fifty years later Diocletian issued an edict, backed up by the death penalty, which forbade concealment of foodstuffs, and hence the artificial creation of scarcity. The Roman constitution of Zeno, promulgated in 483 A.D. protected consumers against artificial increases in the price of all foodstuffs and other articles in everyday use. After the decline of Rome there came a long period of economic and political instability, war, and reduced trade, which was not conducive to either flourishing economies or anticompetitive business activity. It was not until the tenth century that merchants, who were the principal targets of the early Roman competition laws, began to show enthusiasm for the re-establishment of combinations and monopolies. In response to this re-emergence of anticompetitive conduct, England, France, and several of the Italian city-states, by the end of the thirteenth century, enacted statutes prohibiting specified restrictive practices, such as combinations of fishmongers for the joint purchase and sale of fish or price fixing by ore traders.

From the time of the Magna Carta, English common law judges began to develop principles concerning "restraint of trade." These doctrines proscribed monopolies and covenants not to compete as unlawful restrictions on the freedom of the individual. In 1349 a statute was enacted providing that merchants who overcharged for victuals must pay to the injured party double the sum charged. These statutes and common law principles were incorporated into the jurisprudence of England's American colonies and, later, into the laws of the newly independent United States. Moreover, the American colonists' hostility to the practices of the trade monopolies chartered by the English crown was so great that several newly formed states wrote prohibitions against monopolies into their constitutions. These constitutional provisions and other laws were designed to put an end to unjustified privilege and to insure a permissive, diversified, and decentralized way of life.

The industrial revolution began and flourished under these state constitutional provisions and laws favoring free play of market forces, unrestricted freedom of contract, freedom to enter any line of business, and economic individualism. The economic, political, and social climate of laissez faire that prevailed in America from revolutionary times until the late nineteenth century (becoming known in the post-Civil War era as Social Darwinism) encouraged individuals to seek the rewards of technological progress through unrestrained competition and the survival of the economically fittest. As the pace of technological improvements in banking, communications, production, and transportation quickened, emphasis was increasingly placed upon efficiencies and economies of scale. Mass production required heavy fixed investments, which in turn meant that only well-financed enterprises could enter the industry in question. It was the large-scale enterprises that were able to attract the necessary amount of financing. Moreover, the obvious economic advantages of control of sources of supply, means of production, and marketing outlets encouraged integration on the part of the firms large enough to gain entry into the market. The competition in the prevailing atmosphere of freedom of contract and laissez-faire economics became more and more fierce, as existing firms fought for capital, customers, and raw material. This cutthroat competition and accompanying predatory practices often resulted in the destruction of the weakest members of the industry, and either formation of combinations among the surviving competitors or establishment of a monopoly by the sole survivor. Consequently, the individual entrepreneur and the small partnership were steadily replaced by the corporation, the trust, and the cartel as the customary forms of business organization.

As big business began to alter the lives of individual Americans, protests against its abusive power mounted. The traditional common law "restraint of trade" doctrines and remedies were obviously incapable of controlling a ferocious brand of competition practiced by the "robber barons." Small businessmen complained of being driven out of business or of being denied an opportunity to enter business. Farmers agitated against the railroad rebate system and price discrimination between the long and short haul. Labor organizations began to demand government control of large business as a method of obtaining better wages and working conditions, as well as of preventing anti-union activities. Consumers and the public rebelled against the rising prices, deteriorating quality, unfair and deceptive practices, and politically dangerous concentrations of power. As the trend toward combination in order to avoid "ruinous" competition intensified, so did the demand for public supervision or regulation of big business. Outrageous abuses in the railroad and petroleum industries led to the formation of the Grange movement and other groups which entered politics in order to obtain government regulation of business.

By 1887 forces in America seeking government control of predatory business practices had gained enough political power to obtain enactment of the first federal statute for the regulation of business—the Interstate Commerce Act. The Act outlawed the pool, the rebate, and the short-haul discrimination and created the first strong federal regulatory agency, the Interstate Commerce Commission. Small businessmen, labor, and agrarian groups quickly organized an attempt to extend this pattern of regulation from the railroads to all trusts and monopolies. In 1888 both major American political parties promised business reform in their election platforms, and Benjamin Harrison, the newly elected president, lost no time in requesting legislation to curb "dangerous conspiracies" and monopolies. The author of the first antitrust bill to be introduced, Senator John Sherman, summed up the public's mood thusly:

> The popular mind is agitated with problems that may disturb social order, and among them all none is more threatening than the inequality of condition, of wealth, and opportunity that has grown within a single generation out of the concentration of capital into vast combinations to control production and trade and to break down competition. These combinations already defy or control powerful transportation corporations and reach State authorities. They reach out their Briarean arms to every part of our country. They are imported from abroad. Congress alone can deal with them, and if we are unwilling or unable there will soon be a trust for every production and a master to fix the price for every necessity of life.

The final version of Senator Sherman's bill passed both houses of the U.S. Congress with only one dissenting vote and was signed by President Harrison on July 2, 1890. The scope and application of the Sherman Antitrust Act are discussed in subsequent chapters.

The antimonopoly movement intensified after the passage of the Sherman Act, in part because the authorities made reluctant use of the new statute. The severe depression of the early 1890's caused a clamor for tighter antitrust enforcement which was only partially silenced by the enactment of the Wilson Tariff Act in 1894 and the "trust-busting" activities of Presidents Theodore Roosevelt and William Howard Taft. By 1912 all the major political parties were calling for remedial legislation to strengthen and expand government control of business. Consequently, within the following six years three new antitrust laws were enacted, the Clayton and Federal Trade Commission Acts of 1914 and the Webb–Pomerene Act of 1918. These laws will be discussed in later chapters.

The emphasis of this legislation, like that of the Sherman Act, was primarily negative. These laws were "antitrust" and "antimonopoly" and were intended to eliminate the flagrantly anticompetitive activities of the period. The assumption underlying them was that the public interest is best protected from evils of monopoly and predatory behavior by the maintenance of a competitive economy free from limitations based upon corporate self-interest. The unrestrained interaction of market forces would dictate the best course of development of the nation's resources and would insure a prosperous economy. Moreover, free competition was thought to be the best method of preserving the Jeffersonian ideal of an economy made up of many independent small businessmen. Congress was also attempting to establish minimum ethical standards for the conduct of business in order to insure that an ethical businessman would not suffer by being forced to compete with an unscrupulous one.

These beliefs were not confined to the boundaries of the United States. Canada had experienced a very similar trend toward concentration and monopoly and had reacted in a similar manner. In fact, fourteen months before the Sherman Act was enacted in the United States, Canada enacted an Act for the Prevention and Suppression of Combinations Formed in Restraint of Trade, which imposed criminal penalties for anticompetitive behavior. Moreover, just as in America, the first legislation did not quell the demand for government control of business. Therefore, in 1910 Canada enacted the Combines Investigation Act to toughen its antitrust laws.

Outside North America the years 1889 to 1918 passed without any comparable initiation of legislation designed to regulate anticompetitive business practices. Because of historical national rivalries and the ever-present danger of war, each government and national business community believed that it had an overriding common interest in maintaining the economic strength and stability of its own country. Powerful industry was considered to be a prerequisite for victory in war. Therefore, governments encouraged the development of strong national business forces even if that entailed creation of cartels or monopolies, and protected local business from foreign competition by means of high tariffs. It was not uncommon for the leaders of business and government to consult and collaborate so closely that their aims became interchangeable. When cartels and monopolies were criticized, it was only for stratifying society in terms of wealthy employers and underpaid, mistreated wage earners or for being less efficient forms than centralized economic planning in a socialist system. Eventually, a few countries did become concerned about financial chaos and unemployment caused by the predatory practices of cartels and monopolies. Between 1920 and 1934 Bulgaria, Denmark, Germany, Norway, Portugal, Romania, and Yugoslavia all enacted some type of anti-restrictive practices legislation. Outside of Europe, Argentina, Australia, Mexico, and South Africa followed suit. However, most of this legislation was little enforced or was abandoned as, first, the Great Depression of the 1920's and 1930's and then World War II spread around the globe.

After World War II the United States forcefully advocated strong antitrust laws. The military occupation authorities in Germany and Japan quickly imposed American-style antitrust laws in order to prevent the re-emergence of large, politically powerful prewar cartels. Around the world, other countries and supranational groups began to enact or resuscitate restrictive business practices legislation. This activity has continued and intensified up to the present day. The most significant of these foreign antitrust laws are discussed in Chapter 11. The prospects for future developments in international antitrust law are discussed in Chapter 12. As noted, the scope of this book precludes an examination of the precise origins and contents of each nation's antitrust laws. However, there are certain common origins and patterns for these various laws that are worth noting.

The widespread post-World War II enactment of laws designed to curb cartels and monopolies can be attributed to several factors. First, American pressure against restrictive practices was exerted through reconstruction aid programs and treaty negotiations. Second, as a result of postwar investigations conducted by several governments into the wartime activities of cartels, many countries gained a new awareness of the power of cartels and of the willingness of the latter to place corporate self-interest above national interest. Moreover, the tremendous productivity and industrial growth of the United States during World War II were generally attributed in large part to its competition policy. Therefore, other nations enacted similar legislation in hopes that fair competition would increase their productivity, help to control postwar inflation, and reduce barriers to international trade.

Nearly all the present foreign antitrust laws contain provisions relating to restrictive agreements and to the conduct of firms in a "dominant" position, including both oligopolists and monopolists. Other practices that frequently are the subject of prohibition are resale-price maintenance, excessive or illegal prices, discrimination, improper refusal to sell, coercion, and tying arrangements. Many countries require that certain types of restrictions be reported to the government before implementation and be publicly registered. The possibility of receiving discretionary exemptions from legal prohibitions is also common. Although all countries hold that their laws apply to the activities of foreigners within their borders, only Germany, the European Common Market, and the United States have made forceful assertions that their laws apply also to activity conducted outside their territory that produces a detrimental effect within the territory.

The essentially negative character (implicit in the word *antitrust*) of the U.S. and Canadian legislation enacted at the turn of the century is often absent from the post-World War II statutes of other nations. Indeed, foreign lawyers often consider the term *antitrust law* inappropriate and insist upon using terms such as *competition policy*. The distinction lies primarily in the goal set for the legislation. Rather than concentrating on limiting market power, enforcing standards of fair business conduct, and reducing the power of large business enterprises, the most recent, "positive" laws concentrate on promoting and obtaining economic growth and performance, channeling the use of natural resources, and encouraging the development of small business. In this context, therefore, attempting to understand the law by reliance only upon the text of the statute can be hazardous because similarly worded laws may be the product of considerably different cultural traditions, political pressures, economic objectives, and perceptions of what is practicable. For example, although some of the antitrust laws of the United States and the European Common Market are textually very similar, the Common Market authorities attach much more importance to the goal of integrating their nine national economies into a single economy capable of competing effectively with the United States and Japan, than they attach to the goal of limiting market power.

In addition to these problems of varying goals, one should also keep in mind the fact that questions regarding restrictive practices legislation sometimes become embroiled in larger issues of foreign economic policy. Solutions to problems created by balance-of-payments deficits, the need for access to foreign markets, tariffs, consumer protection, treaty obligations, and commitments made to international organizations may influence the scope and content imparted to an antitrust law at any given time. In short, each modern antitrust or competition law can be fully understood only if one has some feeling for its appropriate political, economic, and social, as well as legal, perspective.

With this general background, we begin our detailed examination of the applicable laws by turning to the U.S. antitrust laws, as they apply to the businessman engaged in multinational commerce.

chapter 2

Survey of the Pertinent U.S. Antitrust and Trade Regulation Laws

Laws have been called the "wise restraints that make men free." This characterization is certainly true with respect to the American antitrust and trade regulation laws. These laws are essentially conservative in nature. Their purpose and design is to maintain free competition in the economy by applying restraints that assure that the competitive struggle is fairly waged. Thus, they seek to prevent coercive practices and the development of giant aggregations of economic power through unfair means. In summary, the antitrust and trade regulation laws seek to prevent conduct that impairs or destroys competition.

The Sherman Act

The basic antitrust law is the Sherman Act. Its passage in 1890 resulted from concern aroused by the "vast accumulation of wealth in the hands of corporations and individuals, the enormous development of corporate organization, the facility for combination which such organizations afforded, the fact that the facility was being used and that combinations known as trusts are being multiplied, and the widespread impression that their power had been and would be exerted to oppress individuals and injure the public generally."

The wording of the Sherman Act's two substantive sections reflects these

8

broad policies in very general terms. Section 1 declares: "Every contract, combination in the form of trust or otherwise, or conspiracy, in restraint of trade or commerce among the several States, or with foreign nations is declared to be illegal." Section 2 is scarcely more specific: "Every person who shall monopolize, or attempt to monopolize, or combine or conspire with any other person or persons, to monopolize any part of the trade or commerce among the several States, or with foreign nations, shall be deemed guilty of a misdemeanor. . . ."

In Section 1 Congress indicates the kind of joint conduct which is prohibited only in terms of the very general phrase *restraint of trade*. It was left to the courts to impart content to this phrase in the process of deciding specific cases. Initially, the Supreme Court was split on the proper interpretation of the statute. The language of Section 1 itself is sweeping in the extreme. It declares every contract, combination, or conspiracy in restraint of trade to be illegal. If read literally, this language would outlaw many useful business arrangements, such as sales contracts extending over a period of time or covenants not to compete incident to the sale of a business. When first faced with the task of interpreting this language, the Supreme Court, by a five-to-four vote, adopted just such a literal interpretation. Every restraint of trade was declared illegal. The phrase *restraint of trade* was given its ordinary English meaning, thereby making every contract a restraint. Because contracts always limit the rights of the contracting parties, necessarily restraining their exercise of full freedom in trading, this early approach carried grave implications for subsequent enforcement.

Almost immediately, however, the courts began to withdraw from this literal and unjustifiable reading of Section 1, a reading that had, fortunately, only been applied in price-fixing cases. In 1898 a circuit court of appeals in *United States* v. *Addyston Pipe & Steel Company* considered the legality of an agreement among manufacturers of cast iron pipe to fix prices in areas where they competed and to divide markets to avoid the rigors of competition. Judge Taft, who became both president of the United States and chief justice of the Supreme Court, wrote the opinion for the court. While recognizing that the case could be disposed of by applying Section 1 literally, he went on to test the legality of the agreements by reference both to common law rules and to what subsequently developed into the "rule of reason."

At common law, Judge Taft stated, "no conventional restraint of trade can be enforced unless the covenant embodying it is merely ancillary to the main purpose of a lawful contract, and necessary to protect the covenantee in the enjoyment of the legitimate fruits of the contract, or to protect him from the dangers of an unjust use of those fruits by the other party." The classic example of the sort of valid ancillary restraint to which Judge Taft was referring is the seller's limited covenant not to compete contained in the contract of sale of a going business. In such a case the valid main purpose of the contract is the sale of the business. But because the seller may possess the good will of the business personally, the value of what the purchaser obtains could be significantly decreased if the seller were to open a competing business. For example, suppose Smith, the owner of Smith's Bakery in Charlottesville, Virginia, sold the business to Allen. If Smith were to open a new bakery next door to the one now owned by Allen, it would be likely that he would get all the old bakery's business. To protect himself from such a fate, Allen might get Smith to promise not to open a bakery in Charlottesville for five years. As this restraint of trade is limited to the legitimate purpose of maintaining the value of the bakery and is ancillary to a valid main contract, it is not illegal.

A corollary to this proposition is that any ancillary restraints must be limited to protection of a legitimate value. If Smith had promised not to open a bakery anywhere for five years, the agreement would have been invalid. Allen's only legitimate fear is that Smith will open a competing bakery in Charlottesville; if Smith opened a bakery in Elizabethtown, Kentucky, it could not hurt Allen. Hence, this broader promise goes further than necessary to protect Allen and is to that extent invalid.

Extending this approach, Taft stated the common law rule with respect to restraints of trade. That rule was that only those restraints which were "unreasonable" were illegal. As stated by an English court:

> We do not see how a better test can be applied to the question whether this is or [is] not a reasonable restraint of trade than by considering whether the restraint is such only as to afford a fair protection to the interests of the party in favor of whom it is given, and not so large as to interfere with the interests of the public. Whatever restraint is larger than the necessary protection of the party requires can be of no benefit to either. It can only be oppressive. It is, in the eye of the law, unreasonable. Whatever is injurious to the interest of the public is void on the ground of public policy.

This approach has had a lasting effect on the development of antitrust law. Only those restraints of trade which are unreasonable have been held to violate the law. And, in judging reasonableness, courts have often looked at the relationship between the legitimate value being protected and the breadth of the restraint. Only those restraints designed for and limited to protecting such values have been upheld.

Returning to the facts of the *Addyston* case, the court held that the agreements to fix prices and divide markets were plainly illegal. Far from being ancillary to a valid main contract, the restraints themselves were the main purpose of the contract. The only purpose of the agreements being to suppress competition, a finding of illegality necessarily followed. This was particularly so because there was no redeeming business justification.

In 1911 the Supreme Court itself adopted the rule of reason in the famous *Standard Oil* case. Henceforth only those restraints of trade that were unreasonable would be considered violations of the Sherman Act. At the same time, the Court expressed its conclusions as to the meaning and interrelationship of Sections 1 and 2.

> In other words, having by the 1st section forbidden all means of monopolizing trade, that is, unduly restraining it by means of every contract, combination, etc., the 2d section seeks, if possible, to make the prohibitions of the act all the more complete and perfect by embracing all attempts to reach the end prohibited by the 1st section, that is, restraints of trade, by any attempt to monopolize, or monopolization thereof, even although the acts by which such results are attempted to be brought about or are brought about be not embraced within the general enumeration of the 1st section.

This language, although hardly memorable in itself, is the real starting point of modern antitrust law. Under both Section 1 and Section 2 only those acts or practices that are found to be unreasonable are to be illegal. Further, the two sections are to be regarded as complementary methods of accomplishing the same goal, that goal being the prevention of monopoly. With this general purpose and this general rule of legality in mind, we can turn to other major problems arising under the Sherman Act.

The Sherman Act was enacted under the power of Congress "to regulate Commerce with foreign Nations, and among the several States. . . ." As courts have held that in enacting this law Congress exercised all the power it possessed, the scope of the Act is coterminous with congressional regulatory power. The determination of just what activities are in interstate or foreign commerce and, accordingly, within the regulatory power of Congress has occupied lawyers and courts continually for the past eighty years. In Chapter 3 we will consider the question of what activities in foreign commerce are within the scope of the Sherman Act and the other antitrust laws. Here, to complete the picture, let us take a brief look at the concept of "interstate commerce" that has developed for purposes of applying the Sherman Act.

In the late nineteenth century a very narrow definition of the concept was employed. At that time interstate commerce was thought to consist only of the actual movement of goods across state lines. Neither the production of goods by the manufacturer prior to shipment nor the retail sale of the goods by the local dealer after he had received them were thought to be a part of interstate commerce. The first change in this approach came in the famous antitrust case against the meat-packing industry, *Swift & Company* v. *United States.* That case involved an agreement among meat packers on the prices they would pay when purchasing livestock. The packers contended that the purchase of livestock at a stockyard was not in interstate commerce. Accordingly, they argued that their price-fixing conspiracy was beyond the reach of the Sherman Act. The Supreme Court replied:

[c]ommerce among the states is not a technical legal conception, but a practical one, drawn from the course of business. When cattle are sent for sale from a place in one state, with the expectation that they will end their transit, after purchase, in another, and when in effect they do so, with only the interruption necessary to find a purchaser at the stockyards, and when this is a typical, constantly recurring course, the current thus existing is a current of commerce among the states, and the purchase of the cattle is a part and incident of such commerce.

The *Swift* case thus gave birth to what has come to be called the flow-of-commerce approach. Briefly, it provides that anything happening in the flow of interstate commerce, though it happens wholly in one state, is in interstate commerce. The first seventy years of this century have witnessed the steady expansion of the number of activities found to be in the flow of interstate commerce. The intrastate sale of goods at retail is often found to be in the flow of commerce, against the contention that the goods have come to rest on the retailer's shelves and have thereby ceased to be in interstate commerce. Today there is no longer any doubt that the manufacture of goods prior to shipment across state lines is in the flow of commerce. Indeed, acts relating to the intrastate procurement of supplies necessary for manufacturing have been held to be within the flow of commerce. At the retail end of the shipment even long storage in one state prior to sale in that state has not served to withdraw the commodities from interstate commerce.

Even more significant than the flow theory in bringing within the reach of the Sherman Act what had long been thought to be purely local activity is the concept that any activity that *affects* interstate commerce is covered by the Sherman Act. In one important case cloth came from outside Massachusetts to jobbers located in Boston. These jobbers, in turn, sent the cloth to stitching contractors, also located in Boston, for the performance of certain work. The cloth was then returned to the jobbers and eventually shipped out of the state. The Supreme Court held that the stitching contractors were in interstate commerce and that their boycott therefore violated the Sherman Act. As the Court put it: "If it is interstate commerce that feels the pinch, it does not matter how local the operation which applies the squeeze."

Section 1 of the Sherman Act relates only to contracts, combinations, or conspiracies. Purely individual conduct is beyond the reach of this statute. A whole body of law has been built up in the effort to determine what is a contract, combination, or conspiracy and to establish what will prove the existence of such agreements. Chapter 5 will deal with this topic. For the moment it is enough to note the requirement of multiple actors and to remind the reader that individual conduct may be attacked under other statutes, such as the Clayton Act and the Federal Trade Commission Act, as well as Section 2 of the Sherman Act.

The Sherman Act can be enforced both civilly and criminally. The possible imposition of criminal penalties for antitrust violations provides an accurate indicator of the importance with which we in America view the preservation of free competition. It also acts as a special deterrent to those who would willingly engage in restraining trade.

As we noted earlier the Sherman Act is extremely general. This led to an early attack on its constitutionality as a criminal statute. The defendant argued that the statute was so vague that it provided no meaningful standards by which to judge whether particular conduct was legal or illegal. No businessman, it was argued, could tell what a court would find to be an unreasonable restraint of trade. Mr. Justice Holmes summarily rejected this contention and stated: "[t]he law is full of instances where a man's fate depends on his estimating rightly, that is, as the jury subsequently estimates it, some matter of degree." Notwithstanding this early ruling that the criminal proscriptions of the Sherman Act were not unconstitutionally vague, the fact is that conduct which is today considered legal may tomorrow be illegal. The body of antitrust law is constantly growing and evolving as new practices threaten our competitive structure. Indeed, an impossible dilemma would be posed for businessmen if every action could lead to criminal penalties. Fortunately, the government enforcement agencies have recognized this difficulty, and the criminal provisions of the Sherman Act are usually invoked only against conduct, such as price fixing, that has been clearly held illegal for a substantial period of time by the courts.

As we observed, Section 1 prohibits only unreasonable restraints of trade. Theoretically, a defendant should have the opportunity to show that the practices attacked are reasonable in view of business conditions and that they do not in fact substantially and adversely impair existing competitive conditions. But to allow this is to encourage every antitrust case to become a welter of detail in which the statute's purposes are likely to be lost. To avoid this undesirable result the courts have in the course of time designated certain conduct that is unreasonable in itself. To engage in the types of conduct that have been so labeled is to commit per se violations of the antitrust laws. Among the types of conduct that have been held to violate the statute per se are price-fixing agreements, group boycotts, and agreements to divide markets. We shall have more to say about each of these violations and others in succeeding chapters.

The Wilson Tariff Act

Sections 73–76 of the Wilson Tariff Act of 1894, although enacted as part of a tariff statute, are antitrust provisions. The purpose of these provisions was to punish efforts to abuse the import laws of the United States through agreements or conspiracies between importers and other persons. The year of enactment was 1894, only four years after the passage of the Sherman Act. Senator Morgan of Alabama, who introduced the antitrust amendments to the tariff bill, pointed out that under the tariff bill as it then stood there were opportunities for the formation of trusts, which the earlier Sherman Act was designed to prevent. For example, under the tariff bill at that time a tax was to be put on sugar, which would discriminate in favor of its being imported raw, and then refined in the United States, instead of its being refined abroad and imported in that condition into the United States. Senator Morgan expressed the fear that such a tariff provision would encourage the growth of the already existing sugar trust in an unwonted fashion, unless the bill were amended to guard against the abuse of the power that would inure to that, and other trusts, because of other similar tax provisions.

Section 73 of the Act makes illegal, contracts and combinations between two or more persons or corporations, either of which "is engaged in importing any article from any foreign country into the United States," with intent to restrain trade, or "to increase the market price in any part of the United States of any article or articles imported or intended to be imported into the United States, or of any manufacture into which such imported article enters or is intended to enter." As Senator Morgan stated, it "leaves any *individual* in the United States, no matter what the extent and amount of his capital may be . . . perfectly free to import any amount of goods he pleases from any country he wishes and sell them at any price that he can; but it prevents the *combination* of one person who may be importing with another person *for the purpose of importing goods with the intent of affecting the market.*"

Section 74 of the Act grants the federal district courts jurisdiction to enjoin violations of Section 73. Section 75 provides for all necessary parties to be brought before the court in an injunctive proceeding. Section 76 of the Act, which has seldom been invoked, provides for forfeiture of articles "imported into and being within the United States or being in the course of transportation from one State to another . . . ," when "owned under any contract or by any combination, or pursuant to any conspiracy" in restraint of trade in violation of Section 73.

Specific discussion of the Wilson Tariff Act in judicial decisions is meager. In nearly all cases decided to date allegations of violation of the Wilson Tariff Act have been coupled with allegations of violations of the Sherman Act, and the former is treated as a specific application of the latter to importers. In *United States* v. *Sisal Sales Corp.* several American corporations, a Mexican corporation, and certain individual officers and agents organized to deal in sisal, the fiber that is used in making twine. Sisal was a plant found primarily in Mexico, and the object of the plan was to control and monopolize the purchase, importation, and sale of sisal in the United States. The government sought an injunction, alleging that this conduct was in violation of both the Sherman Act and the Wilson Tariff Act. The Supreme Court held that the allegations were sufficient to state a cause of action under both statutes. As to the Wilson Tariff Act, the Court declared:

> Moreover, appellees are engaged in importing articles from a foreign country and have become parties to a contract, combination and conspiracy intended to restrain trade in those articles and to increase the market price within the United States. Such an arrangement is plainly denounced by §73 of the Wilson Tariff Act, as amended.

A statement of the overlapping of the Wilson Tariff and Sherman Acts and the essentially reinforcing role of the Wilson Tariff Act is found in *Fosburgh* v. *California & Hawaiian Sugar Refining Co*. The Ninth Circuit Court of Appeals there stated: "The Wilson Act, as amended . . . is not more comprehensive in its scope than the Sherman Act, and serves only to make the law more specific in its application, as it relates to foreign commerce."

The language of Section 73 of the Wilson Tariff Act indicating that it is only an "intended" restraint of trade that is forbidden raises the question of whether a *specific* intent of some sort must be shown. Although there is little case law on this point, statements by courts in the *General Dyestuff* and *General Electric* "Carboloy" decisions, as well as the tendency to view the Sherman and Wilson Tariff Acts similarly, indicate that no specific intent to violate the law or restrain trade need be shown. It would appear to be sufficient to show that the party intended to enter into the challenged agreement, wherefrom restraint of trade was a foreseeable result. In the *General Dyestuff* case, the district court described the Wilson Tariff Act as a "statute which makes explicit the prohibitions of the Sherman Act in the field of foreign commerce." The court disregarded the indictment's failure specifically to allege unlawful intent in the Wilson Act count, stating that because the tenor of the complaint was that the *purpose* of the conspiracy was to restrain trade, the complaint satisfied the statute.

In another famous case involving General Electric, the "incandescent lamp" case, the court held that the Wilson Tariff Act was inapplicable despite a Dutch company's agreement not to sell for import into the United States. It relied on the fact that no proof had been made that either the Dutch firm or the other conspirators were engaged in *importing* glass bulbs. The court reasoned that the Dutch firm, Philips, had violated the Sherman Act because the latter covers *agreements* not to sell for import, but had not violated the Wilson Tariff Act, which requires that at least one of the conspirators be engaged in importing. The court distinguished this situation from those in *Sisal* and *General Dyestuff*:

It is plain that the appellees in the Sisal case were importers. The General Dyestuff case is on a demurrer to an indictment and the point is not raised. This ruling in favor of Philips on the Wilson Act charge, however, does not take the evidence as to the glass agreements out of the case. Its significance must still be examined in connection with the Government's charges against Philips for violations of §1 and §2 of the Sherman Anti-Trust Act.

Although this narrow judicial application of the Wilson Tariff Act has been criticized as unjustified, it illustrates the problems that lurk in a statute that was drafted with relatively limited objectives in mind. The statute has had little independent use and has, as we have seen, been utilized primarily to accompany Sherman Act allegations. One significant value of the Wilson Tariff Act is derived from its forfeiture provisions, which have been employed to compel foreign corporations to consent to U.S. jurisdiction. In most cases, such consent is granted and the forfeiture provision is not used.

The Clayton Act

The Clayton Act was enacted by Congress because of the sentiment that certain defects and omissions in the Sherman Act had to be remedied if the competitive system was to retain its resilience. Notwithstanding the sweeping and apparently all-inclusive prohibitions of the Sherman Act, new legislation was thought necessary both because of the judicial refusal to find certain conduct to be violative of the Act and because of the recognition of additional anticompetitive conduct that had not been considered detrimental before. For example, the recognition that the acquisition by one company of the stock of another could lead to dangerous oligopoly led to the prohibition of certain acquisitions by Section 7 of the Clayton Act. Similarly, a fear that predatory price discriminations by a company might drive its competitors out of business inspired Section 2 of the Clayton Act, which forbids certain price discriminations. In short, the Clayton Act patched up what were felt to be specific defects in the Sherman Act by proscribing certain conduct that had proved anticompetitive in practice. Its formulation is a reflection of the pragmatic approach that has guided antitrust philosophy in the United States. It has always been deemed better to cure newly discovered evils by applying repairs to the existing system than to transform the system radically.

The provisions of the Clayton Act that are most pertinent to international commerce are considered in detail in the later chapters. Section 2 of the Act, which was amended by the Robinson–Patman Act in 1936, prohibits discrimination in price, discrimination in the granting of allowances, services, and facilities, and certain brokerage payments. Section 3 governs product distribution arrangements and makes it unlawful to lease,

*FTC
Section
5*

r sale of products, whether patented or unpatented, "on
ement, or understanding that the lessee or purchaser
e or deal in the goods, wares, merchandise, machinery,
mmodities of a competitor or competitors of the lessor
e effect of such arrangement "may be to substantially
r tend to create a monopoly in any line of commerce."
ayton Act applies to mergers and acquisitions and is
its incipiency concentration in the economy that will
competition and monopoly. The original provision
was strengthened by the Celler–Kefauver amendments of 1950, so as to
cover asset as well as stock acquisitions.

Section 8 of the Clayton Act prohibits any person from serving at the
same time as a director of two or more corporations that are or have been
competitors. This provision was prompted by concern over the possibility
that a few individuals or groups could effectively control and eliminate
vigorous competition between corporations through the use of common
directorates and thus circumvent other sections of the antitrust laws.

The major substantive sections of the Clayton Act, dealing with price
discrimination, exclusive dealing, and mergers, were all designed to reach
in the incipiency acts or practices that may eventually lead to adverse
competitive effects. Except in the area of per se violations, the Sherman
Act is not deemed violated unless actual and substantial adverse competitive effects have already transpired and are proved. With the Clayton
Act, on the other hand, illegality can be found in conduct that has the
probable result of substantially lessening competition. This distinction between actual and potential competitive effects is of the utmost importance.
We shall return to it again as we explore the types of conduct that pose
international antitrust questions.

The Federal Trade Commission Act

Section 5 of the Federal Trade Commission Act forbids "unfair methods
of competition in commerce, and unfair or deceptive acts or practices in
commerce." Initially, therefore, reference must be made to the commerce
requirement.

In contrast to its interpretation of the Sherman Act, the Supreme Court
has held that Congress did not seek to exercise its full regulatory power
over commerce when it passed the Federal Trade Commission Act. The
Court indicated that although Congress could constitutionally regulate
matters merely *affecting* commerce, by its choice of the phrase *in commerce* in the Federal Trade Commission Act the legislature meant only to
regulate those acts and practices that are in the flow of commerce. This
1941 ruling by the Supreme Court appeared at first blush to be of tre-

mendous significance. Court and commission rulings since then, however, have made it clear that the commission's regulatory power extends to a great many activities that might be labeled intrastate. For example, practices relating to the intrastate retail sale of goods originating from out of the state were held to be in the flow of commerce and hence within the jurisdiction of the commission, although the goods had been warehoused prior to sale. Moreover, misleading or deceptive advertising is within the reach of the commission if it is conveyed across state lines, even if the sale to which it relates may be wholly intrastate.

Unfair methods of competition include acts or practices that violate the Clayton or Sherman Acts. Additionally, acts or practices that are for technical reasons beyond the scope of these acts may be reached by the commission under Section 5 if they have or are likely to have a substantial anticompetitive effect. But the same standards of proof required in actions under the Clayton and Sherman Acts may not be required under Section 5. Many practices forbidden by the Sherman Act are illegal only if they have an actual deleterious effect on competitive conditions. Section 5, though, would be violated if such an effect was the probable result of continued use of the practice. To use the phrase of the courts, the commission under Section 5 was authorized "to stop in their incipiency acts and practices which, when full blown, would violate" the Sherman and Clayton Acts.

At the same time that it laid down standards of conduct, the Federal Trade Commission Act created the agency to enforce those standards. The commission was created by Congress in the desire to establish an administrative agency "specially competent to deal with" the problems of unfair and competitively dangerous business practices "by reason of information, experience and careful study of the business and economic conditions of the industry affected." What was envisaged then was an expert federal agency to protect the competitive structure from the inroads of monopoly and to protect business from other unfair acts by competitors. By an amendment in 1938 the commission's purpose was broadened to include protection of the public from deceptive business acts.

The Webb–Pomerene Act

The Webb-Pomerene Act was intended to help American firms compete in foreign markets, especially against foreign cartels. The Act provides that an association entered into for the "sole purpose of engaging in export trade and actually engaged solely in such export trade, or an agreement made or act done in the course of export trade by such association" is not illegal, provided it is not in restraint of trade within the United States and is not in restraint of the export trade of any domestic competitor of such an export association. The Act also contains a provision prohibiting unfair methods of competition in export trade against competitors engaged in export trade.

Enforcement

The federal antitrust laws are enforced in three ways: by the Antitrust Division of the Department of Justice, by the Federal Trade Commission, and by private parties asserting damage and/or injunction claims. Each type of enforcing action has contributed to the development and effectiveness of the antitrust laws. This overlapping enforcement, however, complicates understanding of the role of each enforcer. There follows a brief summary of the relationships of the enforcement agencies to each other and of each of them to the laws.

The Antitrust Division of the Department of Justice is charged with the enforcement of the Sherman, Clayton, Webb–Pomerene, and the relevant portions of the Wilson Tariff Acts. As we observed earlier, liability under the Sherman Act may be either criminal or civil. Under the Clayton Act (with the exception of a few relatively obscure sections) only civil suits may be brought. The Wilson Tariff Act, in addition to forfeiture, provides for fines and/or imprisonment. Except with respect to per se violations of the Sherman Act, the Antitrust Division normally enforces the antitrust laws through civil suits, the aim of which is to have a court declare the practices in question unlawful and forbid the defendant company to engage in such practices in the future.

The Federal Trade Commission is the only agency entitled to enforce the provisions of the Federal Trade Commission Act. That Act, of course, is wholly civil in nature. In addition, the commisson has the right to enforce the Clayton and Webb–Pomerene Acts. The FTC, rather than the Justice Department, normally enforces the Robinson–Patman Act, which is part of the Clayton Act. Several other statutes related to the agency's functions are also enforced by the commission. Consultation is carried on between the FTC and the Antitrust Division to prevent collision or duplication where their jurisdiction is concurrent.

Formal commission enforcement usually takes the following form. The commission first files a complaint charging failure to comply with one of the relevant laws. After necessary preparation, hearings on this charge are held before an administrative judge appointed by the commission. An initial decision is then prepared by the judge. Appeal of such decisions to the full commission is allowed as a matter of right, and it is common procedure for either the commission staff counsel or the counsel for the respondent to make such an appeal. The ruling by the commission may be appealed to a court of appeals, although the presumed expertise of the commission as well as the relative finality of its findings of fact lend support for the agency's decision in the courts.

Finally, the antitrust laws are enforced by private parties. A provision of the Clayton Act permits a suit in the federal courts for three times the actual damages caused by anything forbidden in the antitrust laws. Court costs and attorneys fees are also allowed. Generally speaking, the "antitrust laws" in the context of private enforcement encompass the substantive provisions of the Sherman, Clayton, and Wilson Tariff Acts. Because treble damages are awarded, private suits have become increasingly popular and important in recent years. Further, under the Clayton Act any nonconsent judgments in antitrust actions brought by the United States (that is, government actions contested by the defendants) constitute prima facie evidence of antitrust violations. In addition, the statute of limitations regarding the bringing of private actions is tolled while the government suit is being litigated. This provision makes private suits an almost automatic aftermath of any successful government action. Private injunctive actions are also authorized by the Clayton Act.

We have limited our discussion of the pertinent U.S. laws to those that are in the realm of antitrust. This is the scope of the present volume. The multinational businessman should remember, however, that there are many other U.S. laws that relate to international commerce. Some are specifically designed to regulate international trade, such as those bearing on import duties and quotas, customs requirements, export controls, and certain types of trade practices such as dumping. Other laws govern particular commercial activities and, like the antitrust laws, apply across the board to both domestic and international commerce. Some of the areas thus regulated are hazardous substances, food and drugs, cosmetics, automotive safety, flammable fabrics, fair packaging and labeling, and consumer product safety. The antitrust laws are an important part of this evergrowing fabric of laws designed to regulate the commerce of the United States and, particularly in recent years, to protect the American consumer.

chapter 3

Subject Matter Jurisdiction: When Does U.S. Antitrust Law Apply?

In determining when the U.S. antitrust laws apply to activities in foreign trade and investment, it is necessary to consider two types of jurisdiction, that over the subject matter and that over the person. Jurisdiction over the person will be discussed in Chapter 4. In the present chapter it will be assumed that there is jurisdiction over the person (or firm) sufficient to hale him into a U.S. court, and the discussion will focus on the authority of the court and U.S. law to deal with the alleged antitrust transgression.

The Congress of the United States has "power," under Article 1, Section 8, Clause 3, of the Constitution "to regulate Commerce with foreign Nations." Congress has used this mandate over the nation's foreign commerce to enact much legislation, and it is amply reflected in the antitrust laws. The most important of these, the Sherman, Clayton, and Federal Trade Commission Acts, each have potential application to international transactions affecting U.S. commerce. The attributes and limitations of the latter two statutes, including their jurisdictional features, are examined in some detail in the succeeding chapters. Here, in studying the basic issue of the "extraterritorial" application of the U.S. antitrust laws, we will, for the sake of clarity, concentrate on the Sherman Act. This first of our antitrust laws has a broad jurisdictional sweep, and it was within its context that the question of extraterritoriality was presented and resolved in the early cases.

Section 1 of the Sherman Act declares illegal, "Every contract, combination in the form of trust or otherwise, or conspiracy, in restraint of trade or commerce . . . with foreign nations. . . ." Section 2 makes it a crime for any "person" to "monopolize, or attempt to monopolize, or combine or conspire with any other person or persons, to monopolize any part of the trade of commerce . . . with foreign nations. . . ." Included in the definition of *person* or *persons* are corporations and associations existing under the laws of either the various U.S. jurisdictions or the laws of any foreign country.

Foreign Trade or Commerce to Which the Sherman Act Applies

In general terms, *trade or commerce with foreign nations* consists of the export from the United States or the import into this country of goods, and of transportation to or from the United States. But such commerce may extend even farther, because, in the words of Chief Justice Marshall, the Constitution authorizes the Congress to enact laws regulating "every species of commercial intercourse between the United States and foreign nations." By its very nature foreign commerce may involve activity abroad, as well as at home. It may encompass acts of U.S. citizens in foreign countries as well as in the United States, and acts of aliens in this country, as well as in their own and other countries. As we shall see, it is now settled law that the Sherman Act was intended to apply even to acts of aliens in foreign countries in certain circumstances. But the Act applies to the activities of none of the "persons" here described, no matter where their activities in foreign commerce take place, unless those activities have an anticompetitive effect on U.S. trade or commerce—an effect that restrains that trade.

Although Congress intended that the Sherman Act should have the indicated broad applicability to our foreign commerce, an added factor, the comity between nations under principles of international law, places certain practical limitations on the reach of this and of our other antitrust laws. If each nation were to apply its national laws with full sweep, whatever the impact on the vital concerns of other nations, severe international collisions and friction would be generated. Thus, when the application of our antitrust laws in the context of foreign commerce also touches on the interests of foreign nations, considerations of foreign policy and relationships may temper the scope of the law and the result.

Let us now consider the varying factual contexts in which the courts have been faced with restraints bearing on U.S. foreign commerce and their response to the basic question of whether our antitrust laws may be applied.

Locale of the Offending Acts

In the first Supreme Court case involving the extraterritorial reach of the U.S. antitrust laws, the famous *Banana* case in 1909, Mr. Justice

Holmes spoke of the "general and almost universal rule . . . that the character of an act as lawful or unlawful must be determined wholly by the law of the country where the act is done." Stating that, "All legislation is prima facie territorial," Justice Holmes declared that it would be "an interference . . . with the authority of another sovereign, contrary to the comity of nations" for another jurisdiction to apply its own laws to acts done outside its jurisdiction. This is an expression of the "limited territorial" principle of national jurisdiction.

In light of later cases that limit the scope of the decision in *Banana,* it is important to be aware of the facts in that case. American Banana Co. sued the United Fruit Co. alleging monopolization and restraint of the banana trade in violation of the Sherman Act. Both parties were U.S. corporations, and the acts complained of took place outside the United States, in territory over which Costa Rica claimed sovereignty. The plaintiff's main allegation was that the defendant had induced the Costa Rican government to confiscate plaintiff's banana plantation, which defendant later bought, and halted the construction of his railroad that would be used for export shipments. The acts complained of, which were performed outside the United States—the moves by Costa Rica upon plaintiff's plantation and railroad—were not unlawful where committed and were performed by the foreign sovereign. As Justice Holmes stated, "it is a contradiction in terms to say that, within its jurisdiction it is unlawful to persuade a sovereign power to bring about a result that it declares by its conduct to be desirable and proper. . . . It [the sovereign] makes the persuasion lawful by its own act." Dismissal of the complaint was upheld on the grounds that the Court lacked jurisdiction under the Sherman Act over acts allegedly induced by the defendant but performed by a foreign sovereign in a foreign country.

Despite Justice Holmes' broad statements about territorial jurisdiction, it is now well established that the Sherman Act is applicable to acts committed overseas, if they have an intended substantial effect on U.S. commerce. The result in the *Banana* case can, however, be justified because no such effect on our commerce was established in that case and because, as indicated, the acts complained of had been committed by the foreign sovereign itself, not simply the private corporation. The classic statement defining the extent to which our antitrust laws may be applied abroad was made many years later by Judge Learned Hand in the landmark *Alcoa* case, which we shall examine later. It is "settled law," he said, "that any [nation] may impose liabilities, even upon persons not within its allegiance, for conduct outside its borders that has consequences within its borders which the [nation] reprehends; and these liabilities other [nations] will ordinarily recognize." This statement expresses the "objective territorial" principle of jurisdiction, as distinguished from the "limited territorial" principle mentioned in the *Banana* case.

Thus, even if a combination is formed in a foreign country, or if a contract is executed in a foreign country where it is legal, if it affects substantially and adversely the foreign commerce of the United States, it is still potentially within the scope of the Sherman Act. This point is illustrated in *United States* v. *American Tobacco Co.,* a 1911 case involving agreements between American and British corporations that divided world markets in the tobacco trade. The American company agreed essentially to limit its business to the United States, its dependencies, and Cuba, and the British company agreed to limit its business to the United Kingdom, except for leaf purchases. Another British company, jointly owned by the two, was to take over the export business of both. The lower court ruled that the British companies were not liable, because their contracts had been entered into in England where they were lawful. The Supreme Court reversed this dismissal, reasoning that, the locale of the agreements notwithstanding, "the history of the combination [was] so replete with the doings of acts which it was the obvious purpose of the [Sherman Act] to forbid. . . . " that the defendants were liable, "including the foreign corporations insofar as by the contracts made by them they became cooperators in the combination. . . . " The district court in the *Timken* case in 1949 likewise observed that, "Nor does the fact that the cartel agreements were made on foreign soil relieve defendant from responsibility. . . . They had a direct and influencing effect on trade in tapered bearings between the United States and foreign countries."

Because the basic test is in terms of the impact on U.S. commerce, activity abroad or at home that seeks to restrict the availability of foreign goods for import into the United States is subject to our antitrust laws. In *United States* v. *Sisal Sales Corp.,* for example, violation of both the Sherman and the Wilson Tariff Acts was charged against an alleged combination to eliminate competition in the importation into the United States of sisal, an important Mexican plant used to make twine. The Supreme Court, distinguishing *Banana* on several grounds, upheld the sufficiency of the complaint because it was alleged that the conspirators "by their own deliberate acts, here and elsewhere, . . . brought about forbidden results within the United States."

Efforts to restrain shipping and other transportation between the United States and foreign countries are also subject to the U.S. antitrust laws. Thus the Sherman Act was deemed applicable in an early case in which foreign shipping companies and an American firm were charged with allocating passenger traffic between the United States and Europe. Moreover, in the *Pacific Seafarers* case in 1968 the Sherman Act was held applicable by the United States Court of Appeals to an alleged attempt by American shipping lines to destroy the American plaintiff firm's business of carrying Agency for International Development–financed cargoes between Taiwan and South Vietnam. The Federal Maritime Commission and the district court had disclaimed jurisdiction, apparently because the trade in question involved goods owned by foreigners and shipped by foreigners to foreigners, between foreign ports. (We will learn more about the role of the FMC in Chapter 10.) The court of appeals conceded that prior cases under the Sherman Act had involved "either exports or imports of goods, or transportation to or from United States ports." It concluded, however, that the facts in this case justified an extension of precedent because of the "nexus" to American commerce provided by the nationality of the parties and the AID-related transportation service being rendered. The court held:

> In the case before us . . . since there is an indentifiable, distinctive market for American-flag shipping service where the American characteristic is dominant—a market defined as involving the transportation of AID-financed cargoes, which has a definite nexus with significant interests of the United States—the Sherman Act is applicable to a conspiracy to exclude newcomers from the trade.

This concept of a "nexus" to American commerce has been extended to cover a suit by a Swiss corporation against a French corporation alleging violations of the U.S. antitrust laws. The Swiss company alleged that the French company had conspired to fix prices for and had monopolized the transportation of various chemical commodities from the United States to other countries. The American court held that it had jurisdiction over the dispute despite a Franco-Swiss treaty that required suits between nationals of France and Switzerland to be brought in the courts of the defendant's nation. The court stated:

> . . . a long standing public policy of the United States is involved which enjoys an overriding public interest and violations of which carry penal sanctions. In view of this and regardless of whether the Franco-Swiss treaty covers such an action, we are of the view that comity between nations does not require dismissal.

It is obvious therefore that the locale of the acts leading to the violation of our antitrust laws is not the decisive factor. Whether acts take place at home or abroad, the main question is their effect on U.S. trade.

The Nationality of the Wrongdoers

It is apparent from the foregoing that the antitrust laws can be applied with full force to activities carried on abroad by American firms and persons which have the effect of impairing our foreign commerce. This is not surprising because international law would be expected to place few obstacles to the jurisdiction of a nation over its own citizens, wherever they may be. As was observed by the court in a case arising under Section 5 of the Federal Trade Commission Act, *Branch* v. *FTC* (although the principle is not limited to §5 cases), "Congress has the power to prevent unfair trade practices in foreign commerce by citizens of the United States, although some of the acts are done outside the territorial limits of the United States."

What is more striking, and also demonstrated in some of the cases just discussed, is that the courts have sustained the application of the antitrust laws with respect to the activities abroad of *foreigners*. Thus the applicability of the U.S. antitrust laws has not been made to turn on the nationality of the alleged wrongdoer. Once again, the *effect* on U.S. commerce of the challenged activity has been the controlling consideration.

Is the imposition of such liability upon aliens compatible with principles of international law? By "international law" we do not mean an explicit set of enforced international rules because these have not been attained, but rather the standards of conduct, based largely on custom or practices, that have come to be accepted principles or norms in relationships between nations. The answer to this question depends on which of two conflicting theories of jurisdiction the particular nation subscribes to. Under the American view described by Judge Hand in the *Alcoa* case and subscribed to by Germany and the European Communities, jurisdiction exists under the objective territorial principle if the conduct has an intentional or at least foreseeable effect on commerce that is not merely insubstantial or remote. The opposing view argues that the "effects" test is appropriate only in those limited cases, such as homicide, where the effect of the extraterritorial act is direct physical injury in the other jurisdiction, and that, therefore, the objective territorial principle was never meant to apply to antitrust cases.

For illustration, let us look more closely at the landmark decision of Judge Hand in the *Alcoa* case. Aluminum Company of America (Alcoa) and another of the defendants, Aluminum Limited (Limited), a Canadian corporation, were charged with conspiring with foreign producers to restrain interstate and foreign commerce. Limited had been formed in Canada to take over properties of Alcoa that were outside the United States, but the companies later became wholly separated. Limited and a number of foreign corporations operated a cartel through the formation of a Swiss corporation. Production of aluminum by each shareholder in this company was tied to quotas agreed upon for each in accordance with the proportion of shares it held. The shareholders had agreed that imports into the United States should be included in the quota system. The trial court nevertheless held that Limited's acts abroad in this fashion did not violate the Sherman Act.

The United States Court of Appeals for the Second Circuit, speaking through Judge Hand, found that Alcoa had not joined in the cartel arrangement with the foreign companies, but that the alien corporation, Limited, had done so, and reversed the finding of no violation with respect to it. The court focused on the question of whether the Sherman Act and the

Constitution authorized imposition of liability by the United States on foreign persons or firms for acts committed by them abroad. Such acts, if they were not *intended* to affect U.S. commerce, were not within the coverage of the Sherman Act, the court reasoned. For, "when one considers the international complications likely to arise from an effort in this country to treat such agreements as unlawful, it is safe to assume that Congress certainly did not intend the Act to cover them." Moreover, the court postulated, if the agreement was intended to affect our commerce but *did not do so,* the law's application also was not justified. However, the court reasoned further that, if *both* intent and effect were established, the law could and should be applied. It did conclude in fact that, because the cartel agreements would clearly have been unlawful if made in the United States, they were unlawful although made abroad because the foreign cartel had both the intention to affect and an actual effect on U.S. imports. We will shortly be examining further this sometimes elusive concept of intent.

Effect on and intent to affect U.S. commerce, rather than the locale or nationality of the wrongdoers, have therefore been the keys to the American interpretation of the international reach of the U.S. antitrust laws. This is not to say, however, that locale or nationality are irrelevant. Where the questioned conduct takes place outside of the United States and is indulged in only by foreign nationals, for example, the need to keep our national antitrust enforcement internationally defensible will usually re-- quire that a truly substantial impact on our commerce be involved. In addition, as we shall see in Chapter 4, effective antitrust challenge in this setting may be inhibited by the practical difficulties of obtaining personal jurisdiction in our courts over the foreign nationals and by differing interpretations of the proper international reach of national law.

Defenses Offered

INTENT TO AFFECT U.S. TRADE OR COMMERCE

Because it is considered that persons, and especially foreigners, must have "intended" their conduct abroad to affect U.S. commerce before they may be held liable for violating our antitrust laws, it is important to note the definition of *intent* in this context. It is not a specific intent to violate the antitrust laws that is required or even a knowledge that the conduct in question would be so violative. Intent can be established simply in terms of the foreseeability of the consequences of an action With respect to a violation of Section 1 of the Sherman Act, for example, it is sufficient that there be the intent to enter into an agreement, the natural consequences of which would be to affect adversely U.S. commerce. Or to put it the other way around, the requisite intent can be imputed from the fact that the person who entered into the agreement knew or should have known that the effect would naturally follow from the carrying out of the agreement. In sum, the requirement of intent is not really a different one conceptually in the context of acts abroad by foreigners as compared to its application in the context of the purely domestic antitrust cases. In either setting a person is presumed to intend the natural consequences of his actions, and intent can be ascertained from the nature of the action. The difference is perhaps only one of emphasis; that is, with respect to the overseas acts of foreigners, because of the international sensitivities mentioned by Judge Hand, the presence and nature of the intent to impede our commerce will receive specific consideration so as to forestall charges that U.S. law is being applied "extraterritorially" and arbitrarily.

Another illustrative case on this point is the *General Electric* incandescent lamp case. It was alleged there that General Electric, N.V. Philips, a Dutch company, and others had entered into patent-licensing agreements containing territorial restrictions and into worldwide cartel agreements, furthering General Electric's incandescent lamp monopoly in the United States. Philips contended that, because it was a foreign corporation conducting its business abroad, the Sherman Act could be applied to it only if the government showed that it "willfully" intended to restrain U.S. trade and that its actions directly and substantially restrained such trade. The United States District Court for the District of New Jersey turned instead to the somewhat different guidelines expressed in the *Alcoa* case. It found that if Philips "did not know, it should have known, . . . [that its activities] were a substantial contribution to the scheme whereby the domination of General Electric over the United States market of incandesent electric lamps would be perpetuated and competition thwarted." The court also found that there had been a substantial deleterious effect upon United States trade. Although the court noted that "Philips was well aware of the United States anti-trust laws," it did not rely on this and indeed made it plain that a specific intent to violate the law or restrain trade was not a necessary element in holding Philips liable.

ALIENS AS CO-CONSPIRATORS BUT NOT DEFENDANTS

We saw that in *Alcoa* and in the *General Electric* case foreign participants in a conspiracy were brought before the U.S. court and subjected to liability for their roles. However, there have also been cases involving American and alien co-conspirators in which only the Americans were made defendants in the enforcement proceeding, with the aliens being named as co-conspirators but not joined as defendants. The question might then be posed whether it is proper and fair to permit a full adjudication of the matter against the American participants without bringing before the court their foreign accomplices.

Just such a contention was made by American corporate defendants in the *National Lead* case, which involved a worldwide market-division conspiracy. Judge Rifkind, the trial judge, first easily rejected the contention that the court lacked jurisdiction even to consider the conduct abroad by the foreign co-conspirators. He then rejected National Lead's (NL's) further contention that, because these foreigners were not before the court and amenable to its order, the court could not invalidate the challenged agreements. He put the pertinent principle succinctly in a footnote in the opinion:

> Were the rule advocated by NL allowed to operate in the field of restraints upon the foreign commerce of the United States, it would paralyze the enforcement of the law in all cases where one or more of the parties to the conspiracy was an alien corporation over whom the court could acquire no personal jurisdiction. The courts do not so readily permit a frustration of valid national policy.

The court ordered the agreements cancelled, and its decision was upheld by the Supreme Court on appeal. The nonjoinder of foreign conspirators in the United States proceedings is, therefore, no bar to consideration of the case and entry of a binding order against those who have been made defendants to the suit.

ACTS ACQUIESCED IN OR COMPELLED BY
FOREIGN LAW

We have observed in the early *Banana* case the ruling that conduct abroad that is directed by or performed by a foreign sovereign will not be deemed violative of the U.S. antitrust laws. Such an attitude is obviously necessary if the "comity" among nations is to be preserved. In the subsequent *Sisal* case, which we have also mentioned, a key allegation against the defendants was that they had obtained their monopoly over the interstate and foreign commerce in sisal by persuading the governments of Mexico and Yucatan to pass discriminatory legislation, forcing all other sisal buyers out of the market. The Supreme Court held the defendants liable in this situation, distinguishing *Banana* on the ground that, unlike in that case in which the injury had been inflicted solely by the foreign government at the instigation of the defendant, here the defendants had merely been "aided" by the discriminating legislation.

Banana and *Sisal* are early cases in the application of our antitrust laws to conduct overseas, and it is difficult to reconcile the two opinions completely. However, they and the later cases would seem to establish that (1) where the action complained of was performed *solely* by the foreign government (even if instigated by the private parties) or where action by the private parties was *directed* by foreign law, liability under the antitrust laws will not be imposed on the private parties, whereas (2) where the private parties commit other acts in furtherance of their wrongdoing, in addition to using the acts of the foreign sovereign or if their actions are merely permitted by, rather than directed by, the foreign sovereign, the involvement of the latter will not shield the private parties from antitrust liablity. Let us look at some of the pertinent cases in this regard.

In a 1962 Supreme Court private treble-damage case, *Continental Ore Co.* v. *Union Carbide Corp.,* it was alleged that the defendant's Canadian subsidiary, which had been appointed by the Canadian government as the exclusive agent to purchase and allocate vanadium for Canadian industries, had eliminated the plaintiff entirely from sales in the Canadian vanadium market. The trial court and court of appeals ruled that, even if the Canadian subsidiary's activities were such as to enhance a monopolistic plan affecting the United States, the company was acting as an arm of the Canadian government, so that its activities would not come within the purview of the Sherman Act. The Supreme Court disagreed. Noting the similarity of this case to *Sisal,* the Court emphasized that the Canadian subsidiary's anticompetitive activities had not been approved or directed by the Canadian government, and that the mere fact that the company was acting in a manner *permitted* by Canadian law did not insulate the activity from the Sherman Act. The Court stated, "There is nothing to indicate that [the Canadian law] in any way compelled discriminatory purchasing, and it is well settled that acts which are in themselves legal lose that character when they become constituent elements of an unlawful scheme."

Even where, as a practical matter, the foreign government approves the effects of private actions in its country that affect U.S. foreign trade, such approval cannot convert the private activity into an act of that government shielded by the doctrine of sovereign immunity. In the 1962 *Watchmakers of Switzerland* case in the United States District Court for the Southern District of New York, the defense of sovereign approval was urged unsuccessfully. In that case the United States alleged a conspiracy between several Swiss and American companies and trade associations, some of whom were named as defendants, and some as co-conspirators only, to impose unreasonable restraints on the foreign and domestic trade and commerce of the United States in violation of Section 1 of the Sherman Act, and Section 73 of the Wilson Tariff Act. The conspirators, who were manufacturers and sellers of Swiss watches and watch parts, and their trade associations had entered into successive private agreements, over a period of years, designed to protect the Swiss watch industry and prevent its expatriation. The basis of the complaint was an agreement known as the "Collective Convention," executed in Switzerland, which was intended to, and did, restrict unreasonably the manufacture of watches and watch parts in the United States, and restrain U.S. imports and exports of watches and watch parts for both manufacturing and repair purposes. Various other restrictive practices were charged. The Swiss government, indicating its approval of these private arrangements, passed legislation in aid of the Convention signatories. For example, any signatory who breached any of the Convention's provisions was, under Swiss law, subject to private sanctions provided in the Convention, and nonsignatories were subjected to certain price and other regulations.

Defendants claimed that the court should not assume jurisdiction over their activities because the American antitrust laws cannot be applied to acts of sovereign governments. In making this contention, they apparently relied on the fact that the agreements were entered into and became effective in Switzerland, and were sanctioned by Swiss law. The court responded that if "the defendants' activities had been required by Swiss law, this court could indeed do nothing." However, the challenged agreements in this case had been formulated privately without compulsion on the part of the Swiss government. Moreover, the facts that the private agreements were recognized and even approved of, as a practical matter, by the Swiss government were insufficient to "convert what is essentially a vulnerable private conspiracy into an unassailable system resulting from foreign governmental mandate. . . . In the absence of direct foreign governmental action compelling the defendants' activities," the court held, "a United States court may exercise its jurisdiction as to acts and contracts abroad, if . . . such acts and contracts have a substantial and material effect upon our foreign and domestic commerce."

Conversely, if the foreign government actually compels a person to act in a specified manner, and such act might otherwise violate our antitrust laws, such compulsion is a complete defense to an antitrust case based on the act compelled. Furthermore, the "act-of-state" doctrine prevents the court from inquiring into the validity of the law of the foreign nation under which the person acted. The application of these principles is illustrated by a 1970, private treble-damage action, *Interamerican Refining Corp.* v. *Texaco Maracaibo, Inc.* In that case, Interamerican, the plaintiff, alleged that there had been a concerted boycott designed to deny to Interamerican, Venezuelan crude oil required for its operations. Interamerican was a processor of low-cost Venezuelan crude oil, but was unable to obtain crude oil for processing in its bonded refinery in Bayonne, New Jersey, because of defendants' refusal to deal. One of the defendants, Amoco, claimed it was unable to obtain oil from its suppliers because the Venezuelan government had forbidden further sales that would, directly or indirectly, reach Interamerican. All suppliers refused to sell without the explicit permission of the Venezuelan government.

The District Court for the District of Delaware awarded summary judgment on the ground the defendants were compelled by Venezuelan regulatory authorities to boycott Interamerican, and thus had a complete defense to the action. In so ruling, the court referred to the "antitrust exception" in the case of acts of a foreign sovereign in its own jurisdiction.

The court reasoned that sovereignty includes the right to regulate commerce within the nation: "When a nation compels a trade practice, firms there have no choice but to obey. Acts of business become effectively acts of the sovereign. The Sherman Act does not confer jurisdiction on United States courts over acts of foreign sovereigns. By its terms, it forbids only anticompetitive practices of persons and corporations." Faced with this ruling, plaintiff sought an inquiry by the court as to the validity of the act of compulsion under Venezuelan laws. But the court declared that it could not undertake such an inquiry, because the act-of-state doctrine "based upon proper concepts of sovereignty and separation of powers commands that conduct of foreign policy reside exclusively in the executive."

In 1971, sixty years after the decision in *Banana* that refused to question the act of a Central American sovereign, the District Court for the Central District of California found the facts before it in *Occidental Petroleum Corp.* v. *Buttes Gas & Oil Co.* "strikingly similar" to those in *Banana* and refused to look behind the sovereign acts of three foreign powers that, it was alleged, had been induced by the defendants in an effort to deprive plaintiff of its Mideast oil rights. The court pointed out also that "inquiries by this court into the authenticity and motivation of the acts of foreign sovereigns would be the very sources of diplomatic friction and complication that the act of state doctrine aims to avert." This decision was affirmed by the court of appeals, and the Supreme Court denied further review.

In sum, the U.S. antitrust laws have a broad potential application to anticompetitive activity all over the world, whether carried on by U.S. citizens or by foreign nationals, so long as there is a significant intentional or foreseeable effect upon our interstate or foreign commerce. This great potential breadth of application, however, must in certain situations yield to considerations of international comity and, as we shall see in Chapter 4, also encounters practical limitations with respect to the matters of personal jurisdiction and enforcement of compliance with decrees.

chapter 4

Procedural and Related Considerations

In Chapter 3 we considered the applicability of the U.S. antitrust and trade regulation laws to activities carried on abroad, or, in other words, we dealt with a basic question of subject matter jurisdiction. For the purposes of that discussion we assumed that the parties were properly before the court, that is, that jurisdiction over the person of the defendants had been appropriately obtained in accordance with our Constitution, our statutes, and our rules of court. In this chapter we will turn to the practical question of how courts may obtain jurisdiction over the "person" of defendants, particularly foreign corporations and individuals, so that the U.S. antitrust laws that apply to their activities both in this country and abroad may be enforced. As we proceed we shall, in addition, look into the extent to which antitrust investigations and discovery may be carried on abroad in aid of a U.S. proceeding. We will learn how testimony and documentation may be obtained from outside the United States. We shall also consider the ways in which antitrust judgments, once obtained, can be enforced against the person and property of foreign defendants. Finally, we will review the special considerations that U.S. courts take into account in shaping antitrust decrees that involve foreign commerce. Our primary emphasis will be in terms of litigation in the federal courts, which are the arenas for antitrust enforcement by the Department of Justice and private litigants. We will, however, also examine some of the pertinent procedures employed by the Federal Trade Commission.

First, let us examine the mechanics of how cases and parties are brought before the courts. This will require us to turn to the concepts of jurisdiction over the person, venue, and service of process, in addition to another aspect of the question of subject matter jurisdiction.

Subject Matter Jurisdiction

There are actually a number of concepts embodied in the term *subject matter jurisdiction*. The aspect of *subject matter jurisdiction* referred to in this chapter is to be distinguished from the facet that we discussed in Chapter 3. There we were concerned with the territorial scope of coverage that Congress intended the antitrust laws to have. In this chapter on procedure, when discussing *subject matter jurisdiction* we are concerned with a second concept—which U.S. court has jurisdiction to entertain the particular matters that are sought to be litigated.

For the source of judicial power we look first at the Constitution. This document establishes the Supreme Court, provides for such "inferior" courts as Congress may ordain, and further provides that the judicial power of the United States:

> . . . shall extend to all Cases, in law and Equity, arising under this Constitution, the Laws of the United States, and Treaties made, or which shall be made, under their Authority;—to all Cases affecting Ambassadors, other public Ministers and Consuls; —to all Cases of admiralty and maritime Jurisdiction; —to Controversies to which the United States shall be a Party; —to Controversies between two or more States; —between a State and Citizens of another State; —between Citizens of different States; —between Citizens of the same State claiming Lands under Grants of different States, and between a State, or the Citizens thereof, and foreign States, Citizens or Subjects. [Art. III, Sec. 2]

Among the "inferior" courts established by Congress are the U.S. district courts, which are located in the judicial districts designated within each of the states, the District of Columbia, and Puerto Rico. In larger states there may be more than one district and district court. These district courts are granted subject matter jurisdiction over federal questions, over cases between citizens of "diverse citizenship," and there are also other pertinent statutory provisons, including Section 1337 of the Judicial Code, which confers jurisdiction with regard to cases "arising under any Act of Congress regulating commerce or protecting trade and commerce against restraints and monopolies." The district courts are, accordingly, the trial courts for actions brought by the Department of Justice or private parties to enforce the antitrust laws. These courts are empowered to enjoin violations of the law. They may also award damages and attorney's fees in private treble-damage suits brought by persons injured by "anything forbidden in the antitrust laws" and award actual damages for damage sustained by the United States itself. In criminal antitrust cases the courts may impose fines and even prison sentences.

1831608

Personal Jurisdiction

We turn now to the basic question of how the defendant is to be brought before the court, that is, when and how personal jurisdiction may be obtained over him. In the antitrust context, personal jurisdiction is not obtained simply because the defendant's conduct has allegedly violated our antitrust laws. The concept of personal jurisdiction has been described thus by Wright and Miller in *Federal Practice and Procedure*:

> Traditionally, notions of personal jurisdiction have been based on defendant's presence within the territorial jurisdiction of the particular court. However, this subject has undergone great doctrinal change in recent years and the earlier concept has given way to a broader and more refined application of the due process requirement; the current philosophy is that defendant must have sufficient contacts with the forum so that the maintenance of a suit against him in that locale does not offend American traditional notions of "fair play and substantial justice."

In *Hoffman Motors Corp.* v. *Alfa Romeo, S.p.A., et al.* an Italian company transacting business in the Southern District of New York was served by registered mail at its Italian headquarters and by personal service on its general manager in Italy (by an Italian attorney), pursuant to the Federal Rules of Civil Procedure and applicable statutes. The court rejected the argument that service of process in antitrust cases is limited to the United States. The court also found that the service was constitutionally valid, there having been at least minimal contacts by the Italian company with the district and service having been reasonably calculated to give the company actual notice of the U.S. proceedings.

The court's findings underlying its conclusions as to the propriety of venue and service of process are also an instructive application of the "minimal contacts" test that must be made for purposes of determining whether personal jurisdiction may be asserted:

> The activities of S.p.A. employees with regard to sales, promotion and warranties alone seem sufficient to meet the relatively minimal contacts necessary to constitute transacting of business. . . .

> But in addition to its direct activities S.p.A. has transacted business through Alfa Inc., its New York subsidiary. Alfa Inc. was an instrumentality used by its foreign parent to perform essential local operations. The parent completely controlled the subsidiary, setting its policies in Italy, appointing its own officers and employees as directors, officers and employees of the subsidiary and paying their salaries. Under such circumstances, the foreign corporate parent will not be permitted to hide behind its local instrumentality.

In sum, where a foreign corporation has business activities in the United States and adequate notice of the proceeding, it cannot validly complain about being subjected to personal jurisdiction and hence compelled to defend itself in the U.S. courts.

What Constitutes "Sufficient Contacts"

Foreign companies may be found to have sufficient contacts with the United States for jurisdictional purposes in a wide variety of factual situatons. We will discuss the most common situations in the next few pages.

ALIEN CORPORATIONS HAVING U.S. SUBSIDIARIES

As *Hoffman* also illustrates, alien corporations often carry on activities in this country through U.S. subsidiaries. Let us turn directly to the question of when personal jurisdiction may be obtained over the foreign parent by reason of its relationship with the U.S. subsidiary.

Continuous supervision maintained in New York by a British corporation over a U.S. company that it had formed and wholly owned was held a basis for asserting personal jurisdiction over the parent in the Supreme Court's decision in *United States* v. *Scophony Corp. of America.* Scophony Ltd. (British Scophony) engaged in a series of patent-licensing arrangements with three American corporations, including one which it controlled, Scophony of America. The patent-licensing arrangements had territorial and other restrictions that resulted in a charge of violation of the Sherman Act by British Scophony, American Scophony, and the others. The Court concluded that British Scophony was "found" in the Southern District of New York, within the meaning of Section 12 of the Clayton Act, inasmuch as, through key officials in New York, it exercised a continuing supervision over and intervention in the affairs of the American company.

In *Scophony* the parent company was itself adjudged to have sufficient activity in the district of suit to be subjected to the jurisdiction of its court. Where there are no such activities within the district by the parent, can merely the activity of the U.S. subsidiary subject the parent to the jurisdiction of the U.S. court? As a general rule, where the two act as distinct entities, such a result does not obtain, even if there are close commercial ties. But it was held in the 1955 *Swiss Watchmakers* case that "where the substance of corporate independence is not preserved and the subsidiary acts as an agent of the parent, this corporate separation has been found without significance." In that case the Switzerland Information Center, located in New York, was a jointly owned subsidiary of two of the alien defendants, FH and Ebauches. Having found that the "Information Center" was a "mere adjunct of its parent," the court regarded the subsidiary's acts in the New York district as those of the parents. The court seemed particularly impressed by the fact that the subsidiary, the Center, had "no independent business of its own." On the basis of this reasoning, the court ruled that the parents were "found" in the New York district, and that jurisdiction over them had been obtained by service upon their subsidiary, the Center, under Section 12 of the Clayton Act.

Scophony and *Swiss Watchmakers* can be compared to the factual situation in *O.S.C. Corp. & O.S.C. Corp. of California* v. *Toshiba America Inc. & Tokyo Shibaura Electric Co. Ltd.* where the Court of Appeals for the Ninth Circuit affirmed a lower court's holding that a Japanese parent company lacked sufficient minimum contacts with the district in which it was sued. The O.S.C. Corporations brought an antitrust action in California against Tokyo Shibaura Electric Co., a Japanese company and Toshiba America, Inc., a New York corporation which is a wholly-owned subsidiary of Tokyo Shibaura. Tokyo Shibaura makes and sells electronic calculators in Japan and sells the calculators to Toshiba America, Inc. in Japan. Toshiba America Inc. imports the calculators into the United States and sells them throughout the country, with the assistance of a branch office and warehouse in Los Angeles, California. The court rejected the O.S.C. Corporations' contention that Tokyo Shibaura, the parent, "transacts business" in Los Angeles because there was no contention that the corporate separateness between parent and subsidiary should be pierced and because:

1. Tokyo Shibaura has never registered to do business in California;
2. Tokyo Shibaura does not own or lease any property in California;
3. Tokyo Shibaura has no bank account in California;
4. Tokyo Shibaura has never sold its electronic calculators to either plaintiff and in fact it sells only to Toshiba [America Inc.] in Japan pursuant to letter of credit;
5. Tokyo Shibaura does not sell electronic calculators in California;
6. Tokyo Shibaura has no officer, director, employee or other representative in California for any business purpose;
7. Tokyo Shibaura has no agent, salesman or resident representative in California, nor has it any dealers or jobbers in California;
8. Tokyo Shibaura has not solicited any business in California; and
9. Tokyo Shibaura has no branch office, warehouse, or other place of business in California.

ALIEN CORPORATIONS HAVING U.S. PARENTS

It is also possible to attain jurisdiction and service with respect to foreign-based subsidiaries of American firms, although the former may have no property or activities here. Indeed, in *Swiss Watchmakers* such wholly owned foreign subsidiaries were reached through their American parents. The parents had permitted the subsidiaries to become parties to a Collective Convention in Switzerland under which anticompetitive practices were engaged in, and the parents had acquiesced in this program. They were considered in this way to have voluntarily subjected themselves to the "dominance" of their subsidiaries as to those anticompetitive practices. The court held on that basis that it had personal jurisdiction over the foreign subsidiaries by the effecting of service upon the American parents.

U.S. parent enterprises may also find themselves joined as parties to cases involving activities of their foreign subsidiaries that take place outside of the U.S. For example, in the *Quinine* cases of 1968 and 1970 several U.S. parent enterprises were charged together with their foreign subsidiaries and other foreign companies with allegedly engaging in a worldwide conspiracy to fix prices, allocate markets, and establish production quotas relating to cinchona bark, the source of quinine, and to quinine and quinine antimalaria drugs. The indictment in the criminal case stated that "each of these [U.S.] companies possessed and exercised control of the affairs of said subsidiaries and each had knowledge of the actions performed by such subsidiaries in furtherance of the offense alleged herein."

ALIEN CORPORATIONS ENGAGED IN CONTINUOUS
AND SYSTEMATIC ACTIVITY IN THE UNITED STATES

Of course, even if there is no U.S. subsidiary or U.S. parent of the foreign company, it may still be "found" in the United States. Many cases hold that the necessary minimum contacts for jurisdiction are not present if the only activity of the foreign company in the United States involves single, isolated, or occasional acts or transactions. Conversely, if the activity is continuous and systematic the necessary minimum contacts are present. For example, in the *Alcoa* case one of the defendants was a Canadian holding company (Limited) that maintained its "administrative" offices staffed by clerical and middle management personnel in Montreal and Geneva. The operations of the company were principally confined to owning the stock for a large number of aluminum industry companies located exclusively in the British Empire, Europe, and Asia; integrating the manufacturing and selling operations of these subsidiaries; and aiding in their financing. The U.S. court held that Limited was "present" and "actively and continuously engaged in transacting business" in New York City because of the following facts: (1) Limited maintained large offices in New York City at which executive officers carried out "executive duties" for the company; (2) Limited maintained large bank accounts in New York City; and (3) the executive offices had a permanent organization with a large staff and extensive equipment.

United States v. *De Beers Consolidated Mines, Ltd.* is an example of a factual situation that did not constitute continuous and systematic activity. The defendants were all interrelated alien companies who were accused of engaging in an unlawful conspiracy to restrain the foreign commerce of the United States in the sale of industrial and gem diamonds. Despite the following facts the court held that it lacked jurisdiction over the defendants: (1) the companies maintained ten bank accounts in New York City for the purpose of paying for advertising, publicity and purchases of machinery, tools, and supplies. The court stated, "[I]t does not appear that these bank accounts were used as a part of the main business of said defendants; at most, they were used to facilitate transactions within the district which, in their nature, were incidental to the main business of the defendants." (2) An elaborate and expensive advertising and publicity campaign was conducted for the defendants in the United States by a New York advertising agency. The court did not find this persuasive because, "[m]any of our large corporations advertise in all States of the Union, yet they do not thereby 'do business' in each State so as to subject themselves to suit in all States." (3) The advertising agency rendered other services to the defendants, including preparation of reports on U.S. government price regulations, reports on customer complaints, reports on union activities of diamond cutters in the United States, and providing office space for representatives of the defendants who occasionally visited the United States. As to these facts, the court said, "[I]t is not established that these defendants continuously conducted a substantial part of their main business here to the extent that it can be said that they were present in this jurisdiction." This case was decided before the *Scophony* case which was discussed earlier in this chapter and the result might well be different today in light of the willingness exemplified by *Scophony* of courts to find sufficient contacts.

The *De Beers* and *Alcoa* cases illustrate the careful case-by-case factual analysis that courts must make in order to determine whether the requisite "minimum contacts" are present. In many cases the courts cumulate a number of facts which in total amount to "minimum contacts" sufficient to satisfy due process notions.

CAUSING AN EFFECT IN THE UNITED STATES

Traditionally, "minimum contacts" must be proven on the basis of activity within the forum. However, in June 1973 a district court held that personal jurisdiction may be based on "causing an effect in the state by an act done elsewhere." The case involved a suit against a Danish joint stock company, Eskofot, alleging that it and its independent U.S. distributors conspired to eliminate Scriptomatic, a Delaware corporation, as a competitor and to monopolize the market for the sale of "table-top" offset duplicating equipment. In denying a motion to dismiss the suit for lack of personal jurisdiction, the court agreed with Eskofot's contention that "foreign manufacturers should not be compelled to face an antitrust charge in this court on the bare and perhaps unfounded allegations set out in a complaint." Therefore the court required a preliminary showing that "Eskofot had reason to engage in the conduct alleged in the complaint." Such a showing was made, in the court's opinion, by the following evidence: (1) the 1972 sales of Eskofot's products in the United States of over $1 million; (2) the "close" relationship between Eskofot and one of its American distributors; (3) a trans-Atlantic telephone call from the president of Eskofot to Scriptomatic's president in which the former threatened the latter with a $1 million patent infringement suit unless Scriptomatic sold all its rights to a new platemaker to Eskofot. This decision suggesting an "effects" test reflects a substantial departure from earlier case law and thus is not a representative decision.

SEIZED PROPERTY

Even if an alien company has no American subsidiaries or affiliates and does not engage in continuous and systematic activity, it still may be brought into an antitrust proceeding by means of actions to seize or forfeit its property. Section 6 of the Sherman Act provides:

> Any property owned under any contract or by any combination, or pursuant to any conspiracy (and being the subject thereof) mentioned in section one of this act, and being in the course of transportation from one State to another, or to a foreign country, shall be forfeited to the United States, and may be seized and condemned by like proceedings as those provided by law for the forfeiture, seizure, and condemnation of property imported into the United States contrary to law.

Section 76 of the Wilson Tariff Act contains a similar provision for imported goods.

These provisions have been used only three times in foreign antitrust cases. In 1907 the United States brought an action to seize 176 cases of cigarettes owned by a British tobacco company in connection with its suit against an American tobacco company. In 1928 there was a seizure of $100,000 worth of quinine imported into the United States in connection with a case against an international quinine cartel. The last use of these provisions was in 1930 in a case involving the importation of Norwegian sardines. The U.S. government seized several thousand cases of sardines, herring, and kippered snacks. In each of these three cases the property was returned as part of the resolution of the antitrust case.

Although these seizure and forfeiture provisions have been used seldom, they have, in the words of the former chief of the Foreign Commerce Section of the Antitrust Division:

> proved to be of considerable value at times as a lever to compel foreign corporations to consent to the jurisdiction or decree of an antitrust court. While the seizure method has not been used in recent years, it is always a potential threat against foreign corporations over which the Government is otherwise unable to obtain jurisdiction.

Venue in Civil Cases

Whereas the question of jurisdiction concerns a court's inherent power to hear a case, the concept of venue has reference to the particular geographic location at which the case may be brought and determined. The venue statutes enacted by Congress specify, in effect, in which judicial district (that is, in which district court) a particular antitrust or other case may properly be heard. An important purpose of these venue provisions is to protect the defendant from being compelled arbitrarily to defend a suit in a forum freely chosen by the plaintiff, which is inconvenient to the defendant.

Although the most convenient locale for a defendant is likely to be the district of his residence, this location may be very inconvenient for the plaintiff. The plaintiff's district of residence or other locales may have equal claims as the logical forum. The venue laws attempt to strike a fair balance of the various interests.

General Venue Statute for Civil Actions

The general venue statute for civil actions is Section 1391 of the Judicial Code. Subsection (a) deals with a common situation where venue problems arise, that is, where the plaintiff and defendant are not residents of the same state of the United States. It provides that if jurisdiction is founded *only* on diversity of citizenship, the case may be brought only in the judicial district where all plaintiffs or all defendants reside, or in the district in which the claim arose. Where jurisdiction is also founded on the federal antitrust laws, therefore, subsection (a) will be inapplicable.

Where jurisdiction is not founded solely on diversity of citizenship, the civil action may be brought, according to subsection (b), only in the judicial district where all the defendants reside, or in the district in which the claim arose, except as otherwise provided by law. Thus we see that although residence is an important factor in venue, the district where the claim arose may provide an equally logical situs and may, in fact, be the most convenient locale from the viewpoint of witnesses involved.

A corporation is deemed a citizen of the state in which it is incorporated and of the state where it has its principal place of business. However, under modern conditions a corporation's business activities will often extend well beyond those two locales. Taking this into account, Section 1391(c) of the Judicial Code expands the concept of "residence" in the general provisions of subsections (a) and (b) of Section 1391, and provides that there are three places where a corporation may be sued: in the judicial district in which it is (1) incorporated, or (2) licensed to do business, or (3) doing business.

It should be noted that Section 1391(c), as a corporation venue statute, supplements the more general venue provisions including Section 1391(b). Thus, in a 1972 private antitrust case, *Fox–Keller, Inc.* v. *Toyota Motor Sales, U.S.A., Inc.,* the court, finding that venue would not lie under Section 1391(c), treated the additional criterion of Section 1391(b), of where the "claim arose" as potentially applicable in assessing the propriety of the venue.

The general venue law gives the defendant "alien" no protection against an inconvenient suit. Section 1391(d) of the Judicial Code provides that an alien may be sued in a civil action in *any* district. We will examine the relationship between this general venue provision and the special antitrust venue provisions later in this chapter.

Special Antitrust Venue Provisions

There are special antitrust venue provisions for certain types of antitrust civil actions. The first thing to note about these provisions is that they are "liberalizing." Their provisions are intended to assist the plaintiff, that is, to make it more convenient for the plaintiff who has been injured by an antitrust violation to reach the defendant. Let us now see what these special antitrust venue laws provide, and how they relate to the general provisions.

As we have seen, Sections 4 and 4a of the Clayton Act authorize, respectively, private parties and the United States, where there is injury to business or property by reason of a violation of the antitrust laws, to bring suits for the damage incurred. For such cases the public interest in enforcement of the antitrust laws prompted the enactment of special, liberalizing venue provisions. The defendant may be sued in any district in which he "resides or is found or has an agent." Moreover, a provision in Section 12 of the Clayton Act declares that "any suit, action, or proceeding under the antitrust laws against a corporation may be brought not only in the judicial district whereof it is an inhabitant, but also in any district wherein it may be found *or transacts business. . . .* " (Emphasis added.)

The phrase *or transacts business* was added by Congress to the original language, following a number of restrictive court decisions as to when a corporation was "found" in a particular district. As was held in the Supreme Court's decision in *Eastman Kodak Co.* v. *Southern Photo Materials Co.,* the liberalizing language was intended to establish venue against a corporation "although not present by agents carrying on business of such character and in such manner that it is 'found' therein . . . if, in fact, in the ordinary and usual sense, it 'transacts business' therein of any substantial character."

**Relation of Special Antitrust Venue Provisions to
General Venue Provisions**

As we have seen, under Sections 1391(b) and (c) of the general
venue statutes, a domestic corporation may be sued in the district in "which
the claim arose" as well as where it is incorporated, licensed to do business,
or doing business. The question is raised whether this standard is displaced
by or is supplementary to the special antitrust venue provisions of Section
12 of the Clayton Act. The courts have, to date, tended to interpret the
liberal philosophy enunciated in the Supreme Court's decision in *Pure Oil
Co.* v. *Suarez* to mean that the general venue provisions of Section 1391
of the Judicial Code are available to supplement the special antitrust venue
statute in Section 12 of the Clayton Act. Under this view any action under the
antitrust laws against a domestic corporation may be brought in the judicial
district where it is an "inhabitant," where it may be "found," where it
"transacts business," or where the "claim arose."

The relationship between Section 1391(d) of the Judicial Code that
states that "an alien may be sued in any district" and the special antitrust
venue provisions appears to have been clarified by the decision of the U.S.
Supreme Court in the 1972 case of *Brunette Machine Works, Ltd.* v.
Kockum Industries, Inc. In that case an Alabama corporation that held a
U.S. patent on a machine that removes bark from logs brought a patent infringement suit in the District of Oregon against a Canadian corporation,
alleging that the latter had infringed the patent by assisting two American
manufacturers to make and sell similar machines. The Canadian corporation moved to dismiss the complaint on the ground of improper venue
because it contended that the special venue provision relating to patent
infringement litigation [28 U.S.C. §1400(b)] that provides that "any civil
action for patent infringement may be brought in the judicial district where the
defendant resides, or where the defendant has committed acts of infringement and has a regular and established place of business" was the *only*
venue provision that could be used and that its requirements were not
satisfied. The plaintiff argued that Section 1391(d) applies to all suits involving an alien, including patent infringement suits, and that therefore
venue in Oregon was proper. The Supreme Court unanimously agreed with
the plaintiff.

> We conclude that in §1391(d) Congress was stating a principle of
> broad and overriding application, and not merely making an adjustment
> in the general venue statute. . . . The principle of §1391(d) cannot be
> confined in its application to cases that would otherwise fall under the
> general venue statutes. For §1391(d) is properly regarded, not as a venue
> restriction at all, but rather as a declaration of the long-established rule
> that suits against aliens are wholly outside the operation of all the federal
> venue laws, general and special.

Although this case involved a patent infringement, most commentators believe that the Court's language is broad enough to cover antitrust cases.

The question of venue against an alien individual in an antitrust case was examined by a district court in *Hoffman Motors Corp.* v. *Alfa Romeo, S.p.A. et al.,* which we considered in another context earlier in this chapter. Mr. Rietz, a defendant and an Italian citizen who was a resident in New Jersey, claimed that venue in New York was improper as to him. He argued that, although Section 1391(d) laid venue for aliens in "any district," the more restrictive provision of Section 4 of the Clayton Act was exclusively applicable in an antitrust case against an individual. The court rejected his argument, noting the liberal congressional intent and concluding that "it may reasonably be assumed that Section 1391, at least with respect to aliens, is supplementary to the earlier venue provisions of the antitrust laws."

Although *Brunette* appears to permit venue against alien corporations and alien individuals in any district, it should be remembered that the due process test of "minimum contacts" must be met before an alien can be sued in any district. In the words of the court's opinion in the case of *Japan Gas Lighter Association* v. *Ronson Corp.,* "[o]f course, the alien defendant still is afforded some protection with regard to the fairness of locale by the requirements of constitutional jurisdiction and service. . ." and, "these latter requirements rather than venue become the operative constraints upon suing aliens. . . ."

Service of Process in Civil Cases

Procedure in the United States district courts in all suits of a civil nature is governed, with some few exceptions, by the Federal Rules of Civil Procedure. Rule 4 governs service of process. In this regard Rule 4 must be applied in the light of certain statutes, such as the clause in Section 12 of the Clayton Act that deals with process in antitrust cases. In addition, there are state laws on service of process, particularly "long-arm" statutes, providing for "extraterritorial" service, which are applicable in federal cases under certain circumstances.

A routine case may involve service of process on an individual defendant or corporate agent who resides within the state where the process-issuing court sits, and this is, of course, authorized. But in antitrust cases "extraterritorial" service is often necessary because the defendant is a corporation that is not resident within the state of suit and yet has engaged in activities within it sufficient to justify personal jurisdiction and venue. Rule 4 provides that service may be made in such case under either an applicable U.S. statute or under a state "long-arm" statute. It also provides a procedure for service in such cases, when necessary, to be effected in a foreign country.

The most important federal statute dealing with service of process in antitrust cases is, once again, Section 12 of the Clayton Act. It declares that "all process in such cases may be served in the district of which it [the defendant corporation] is an inhabitant, or wherever it may be found." *Inhabitant* as used in this provision is synonymous with *resident*. In short, this means that where a corporate defendant is doing business within the United States, there are no practical territorial limits upon service of the summons on it in an antitrust action because, wherever the suit is brought, the process can be served on the corporation's offices or agents. As to state "long-arm" statutes, Rule 4(e) of the Federal Rules provides that, "whenever a statute or rule of court of the state in which the district court is held provides . . . for service of a summons . . . upon a party not an inhabitant of or found within the state, . . . service may . . . be made under the circumstances and in the manner prescribed in the statute or rule." Such laws, which exist in many states, furnish a practical basis for obtaining proper service on nonlocal individual, as well as corporate, defendants in antitrust and other federal cases.

Because so much of the litigation with which we are concerned involves parties who do not reside in the United States, it is important to know how personal jurisdiction may be obtained over them. Rule 4 provides several alternative ways in which parties may be served in foreign countries. Such service overseas is permissible whenever a federal or applicable state statute authorizes service upon a party not an inhabitant of or found within the state in which the district court is held. Section 12 of the Clayton Act thus makes it possible to serve defendants overseas in private antitrust cases.

Rule 4(i) provides the following five alternative manners of service in the foreign country:

(A) in the manner prescribed by the law of the foreign country for service in that country in an action in any of its courts of general jurisdiction; or

(B) as directed by the foreign authority in response to a letter rogatory, when service [in the case of either (A) or (B)] is reasonably calculated to give actual notice. [a "letter rogatory" is a formal letter from the domestic court to the appropriate court of the foreign country requesting its aid in making service]; or

(C) upon an individual, by delivery to him personally, and upon a corporation or partnership or association, by delivery to an officer, a managing or general agent; or

(D) by any form of mail, requiring a signed receipt, to be addressed and dispatched by the clerk of the court to the party to be served; or

(E) as directed by order of the court.

In short, the Federal Rules of Civil Procedure provide ample means for making service of judicial process overseas.

Venue and Service for Nonresident Patentees

In 1952, Section 293 was added to the U.S. patent laws. It is designed to
assist a plaintiff to obtain personal jurisdiction and service of process over
foreign owners of U.S. patents who do not reside in the United States.
The section provides that nonresident patentees may file in the Patent
Office a written designation stating the name and address of a person
residing within the United States upon whom process or notice may be
served in proceedings affecting the patent or rights thereunder.

> If the person designated cannot be found at the address given in the
> last designation, or if no person has been designated, the United States
> District Court for the District of Columbia shall have jurisdiction and
> summons shall be served by publication or otherwise as the court directs.
> The court shall have the same jurisdiction to take any action respecting the
> patent or rights thereunder that it would have if the patentee were personally
> within the jurisdiction of the court.

This section is, in effect, a federal "long-arm" statute designed to broaden
a plaintiff's ability to bring foreign defendants within the reach of a federal
court. If a nonresident patentee neither has appointed an agent to receive
service of process nor has sufficient contacts with any other district, Section 293 may be invoked to obtain jurisdiction in the District of Columbia.
However, this does not mean that Section 293 is a special venue statute
that supersedes general jurisdiction and venue statutes by conferring exclusive jurisdiction and venue on the District of Columbia. Rather it
applies when jurisdiction cannot be asserted in any other district under the
usual service of process and "presence" rules.

In one recent case Section 293 was invoked in a civil patent antitrust
case against an English company that held U.S. patents on ampicillin and
other drugs. Service of process on the English company was made by
certified air mail to the corporate headquarters.

Procedure in Criminal Prosecutions

As we have seen earlier, liability under the Sherman and Wilson Acts
may be either criminal or civil. Under the Clayton Act (with the exception
of a few relatively obscure sections) only civil suits may be brought. As
a practical matter the Department of Justice normally enforces the antitrust laws through civil suits. When the criminal provisions of the Sherman
Act have been invoked, it has been against conduct of the type that is
known to be clearly illegal. Examples of the types of per se violations

where criminal actions may be brought are price-fixing conspiracies, group boycotts, and agreements to divide markets.

Despite the emphasis on civil remedies in antitrust enforcement, to complete the picture, brief mention should be made of the basic procedural aspects of criminal cases.

In antitrust criminal prosecutions, as in U.S. criminal prosecutions generally, U.S. district courts have original subject matter jurisdiction. As to venue, all criminal trials except impeachments are held, as provided in the U.S. Constitution, in the state where the crime was committed. If the crime was not committed in any state, the trial is to be held as otherwise provided in an act of Congress. In this connection Congress has provided that trials of offenses "begun or committed" outside any state or district are to be held where the offender or any one of two joint offenders is arrested or first brought into the jurisdiction of the United States. In the meantime, in order to meet the requirements of the appropriate statute of limitations defining the time within which an action may be commenced, an indictment or information may be filed in the district of the last known residence of the offender, or of any two or more joint offenders; if no such residence is known, filing is appropriate in the District of Columbia.

In reaffirmation of these established constitutional and statutory principles, Rule 18 of the Federal Rules of Criminal Procedure provides that, except as otherwise provided by statute or by "these rules," the prosecution shall be in a district in which the offense was committed, and the court is to fix the place of trial within the district "with due regard to the convenience of the defendant and the witnesses."

Of particular importance in antitrust conspiracy cases, where there may be no single locus of commission, is Section 3237 of the Criminal Code, which specifies that any offense begun in one district and completed in another, or committed in more than one district, may be prosecuted in any district where such offense was begun, continued, or completed.

Where a conspiracy is entered into in a particular district, venue lies in that district even though an overt act is committed in furtherance of it in another district or in a foreign country. In accordance with the general rule of law, applicable in antitrust cases, the appropriate U.S. court has jurisdiction over a person, whether a citizen or an alien, who commits a crime, wholly or partly, in the United States.

If the criminal violation of U.S. law takes place in another country, a citizen may likewise be prosecuted in the United States. The rule is otherwise as far as aliens are concerned. In order for a U.S. court to have jurisdiction in such a case there must have been a substantial effect within the territory of the United States, and the effect must have been the intentional or, at least, foreseeable, result of the extraterritorial conduct. In accordance with the general rule of law, the courts of the United States cannot, of course, exercise criminal jurisdiction as long as the alien remains on foreign soil. But if, after the commission of the act having a substantial effect within the United States, such alien enters the United States, thus coming under the courts' territorial jurisdiction, then he is subject to prosecution.

Discovery and Investigation Abroad

The institution and litigation of an antitrust lawsuit or administrative proceeding can entail considerable labor for all concerned. Often the attorneys for the parties must interview or depose numerous individuals; voluminous files, records, and documents must be found, read, and evaluated; legal issues, often numerous and complex, must be researched. When the case involves, either as defendants or as third-party sources of information, foreign companies, offices, or persons, the task becomes even more complex. Questions of extraterritoriality, foreign law, conflicts of law, and international comity become additional concerns and perhaps obstacles. In this section we will focus on the particular problems posed in the seeking of information from abroad.

Action by Justice Department

Antitrust investigations are initiated by the Justice Department on the basis of information it receives from a variety of sources, including complaints from the public, news stories in publications, and materials garnered by other federal agencies. Once the preliminary information indicates that a more far-reaching scrutiny is appropriate, two approaches of data collection are employed: voluntary and compulsory. Often the companies and persons involved decide to cooperate voluntarily with the government's investigation, which may be conducted by the Federal Bureau of Investigation or through inquiries from the Antitrust Division. If voluntary cooperation has not fulfilled its purpose or is otherwise inappropriate in a particular situation, the government will utilize its instruments of compulsory process. Where the suspected violation is serious enough to support criminal prosecution, grand jury proceedings involving the use of compulsory process may be instituted. For violations that may result in civil actions by the government, a Civil Investigative Demand (CID) authorized by the Antitrust Civil Process Act may be employed.

By use of its authority to issue a CID, the Justice Department is enabled, prior to filing of a suit, to examine and analyze the pertinent books, records, and other documents of a specified corporation or other legal entity (not a natural person) in order to determine whether the entity is or has been engaged in any civil antitrust violation. Essentially, the CID fills a void in the fact-finding process. Before its use was authorized, the government was compelled to rely on the voluntary cooperation of possible defendants or other readily available information to determine whether there was a sufficient basis to warrant the filing of a suit. Of course, after a civil suit has been filed, the government can avail itself of the extensive compulsory discovery authorized by the Federal Rules of Civil procedure. But these discovery rules are unavailable for purposes of determining in the first instance whether the filing of a civil antitrust suit is justified.

The Antitrust Civil Process Act does not, however, permit governmental review by CID of all documents of any company. The company must be "under investigation"; that is, it must be suspected of a violation of the civil antitrust laws. Further, the documents sought must be relevant to that investigation. Moreover, the penumbra of the Act does not go beyond the company being investigated. For example, if Company A is under investigation, the government cannot use the CID to examine Company B's books, no matter how pertinent to the matter. If a company fails to comply with a CID, the government may file a petition for enforcement in the appropriate federal district court. Where the company receiving the CID has objections to the demand, whether as to alleged unreasonableness, privileged matters, relevance, or insufficient specificity, it can challenge it by filing in the appropriate federal judicial district a petition to modify or set aside the CID. Of course, the compliance requirements are suspended during the litigation of a petition either by the company or by the government.

The Antitrust Civil Process Act, however, permits the demand to be served only at a place within the territorial jurisdiction of a U.S. court. Moreover, service must be made on a partner, executive officer, managing agent, general agent, agent authorized to receive service of process, or else at the principal office or place of business of the entity. This places limitations on the use of the CID to investigate foreign entities. On the other hand, it appears that the fact that documents are located in a foreign country will not affect the company's obligation to comply with the CID if it is properly served and the principal place of business is within the United States. Under the Act, the company must make the designated documents available for inspection and copying at the principal place of business.

Where a foreign company is validly served in the United States through an officer or agent, but has its principal place of business abroad, the method of production of the documents will probably be resolved, as a practical matter, by informal negotiation and agreement between the government attorney and counsel for the company involved. The government might inspect the materials abroad or they might be sent to the United States for review. The government has gone on record in stating that it stands ready to discuss any approach for production, so long as it is consistent with the objective of examining all relevant material. Where the company refuses to comply on any satisfactory basis, the federal court must have recourse to its contempt powers to insist on compliance. The contempt power will be exercised against corporate officials or agents over whom the court has jurisdiction.

Federal Court Procedures

The expansion of international commerce has resulted in an increase in litigation involving parties, witnesses, and evidence that are located within and/or subject to the laws of foreign jurisdictions. Some specific procedures have been adopted to deal with the exigencies of such situations, primarily in the context of the compulsory process available during litigation in the federal courts. These devices, provided by the statutes and the Federal Rules of Civil Procedure, are available to private litigants and to the Department of Justice *after* a suit has commenced.

Rule 45 of the Federal Rules of Civil Procedure provides for the issuance of subpoenas to compel testimony or production of documents, either for discovery or for trial. Such subpoenas may be directed to witnesses in foreign countries only in the limited circumstances provided by Section 1783 of the Judicial Code. Under the terms of this statute the person who is to be subpoenaed to appear as a witness or to produce documents must be either a citizen of the United States or a resident thereof. In a criminal case the person's testimony or document production must be necessary in the interest of justice. In a civil case, in addition to this showing of necessity, it must be shown that "it is not possible to obtain his testimony in admissible form without his personal appearance or to obtain the production of the document or other thing in any other manner." Service of the subpoena should be accomplished in accordance with the manner prescribed by the Rules for service of process in a foreign country, and all necessary travel and attendance expenses must be tendered to the subpoenee at the time service is made. After a failure to comply, the issuing court may issue an order to show cause and direct that the person's property within the United States be held as security for a possible fine of not more than $100,000.

The constitutionality of these statutes was upheld by the Supreme Court, on the ground that, "[t]he United States possesses the power inherent in sovereignty to require the return to this country of a citizen, resident elsewhere, whenever the public interest requires it, and to penalize him in case of refusal. . . ." The reasoning is that the United States still retains *in personam* jurisdiction over its nonresident citizens. This form of jurisdiction also allows the issuance of subpoenas to *aliens* who are at the moment in a foreign country but who reside in the United States. However, there is no authority to compel attendance or production by aliens who are residents of a foreign country at the time of the request.

The issuance of a subpoena is within the discretion of the court. In using its discretion, the court can impose whatever conditions it thinks proper and can order a deposition abroad in lieu of a personal appearance in the United States, if it determines that justice can be served in such manner. Rule 28(b) of the Federal Rules of Civil Procedure provides a number of methods for the taking of depositions in foreign countries. However, the deposition overseas will prove practicable only if the witness will voluntarily appear and testify or if the foreign jurisdiction is willing to compel his testimony or document production.

The courts have been cognizant of the burden imposed on persons whose testimony from abroad may be needed, so that, particularly in civil cases, the necessary information is usually secured by deposition or interrogatory in the foreign country.

Federal Trade Commission and Procedures

Under the Federal Trade Commission Act, the commission is empowered to make rules and regulations for the purpose of carrying out the provisions of the Act. These rules and regulations have the force and effect of law. The commission's investigative and discovery powers are set forth in these provisions, known as the Rules of Practice of the Commission.

Investigations by the Federal Trade Commission are originated by a variety of methods, including action on the commission's own initiative, complaints by the public, and requests from the Congress, government agencies, or officials. There are two basic forms of investigation, each with its own purpose and scope. One comprises general investigations of conditions in, or practices affecting, certain industries or segments of the economy. These are primarily undertaken to reveal information to the public, rather than to implement remedial processes. The other category of investigation stems from the regulatory functions of the commission, these investigations being undertaken to ascertain whether there have been violations of the statutes administered by the commission.

Various forms of compulsory process are available to the commission in the course of these investigations. Thus, corporations may be required to file special reports in response to specific questions directed by the commission. The commission may also direct "any corporation being investigated to grant access to files for the purpose of examination and the right to copy any documentary evidence. . . . " In addition, the commission or a member thereof can issue subpoenas *ad testificandum* and *duces tecum* to obtain oral testimony and documents with respect to matters under investigation. This ability to subpoena witnesses and documentation, and to hold depositions, is much broader than that afforded to the Justice Department during the investigatory stages. It has been firmly held that the FTC can gain enforcement of its subpoena to a witness even though such witness was not being investigated or proceeded against. The sole requirement is that the testimony or production of evidence sought be related to the matters under investigation.

The FTC must apply to the U.S. district courts when enforcement of its subpoenas is necessary. Under new authority granted the FTC in 1973, the commission is granted the power to initiate, to prosecute, to defend, or to appeal any court action in the name of the commission for the purpose of enforcing the laws subject to its jurisdiction through its own legal representative, "after formally notifying and consulting with and giving the Attorney General 10 days to take the action proposed by the Commission."

Where, as a result of an investigation, the commission has reason to believe that one or more of the statutes which it administers have been violated, it issues a complaint, initiating an administrative adjudicative proceeding. In the proceedings before the administrative law judge, discovery tools similar to those provided in the courts by the Federal Rules of Civil Procedure are available to the parties under the commission's Rules of Practice, including depositions, subpoenas, and requests for admissions.

There is no specific case law or authority dealing with the power of the Federal Trade Commission to conduct investigation and discovery proceedings abroad. The Federal Rules of Civil Procedure, which provide methods of obtaining information that is located abroad, are not applicable to proceedings conducted by administrative agencies like the FTC. However, the authority of the commission to issue rules that are comparable is well established, and the commission's investigatory and rule-making powers have been deemed by the courts to be extensive, as necessary to enable the agency to carry out its broad investigatory and adjudicative responsibilities.

By Section 6(h) of the Federal Trade Commission Act, the FTC is given the authority to investigate "trade conditions in and with foreign countries" where such conditions may affect the foreign trade of the United States. The scope of this investigatory authority has not been delineated by case law.

The FTC's Rules of Practice for Adjudicative Proceedings do make reference to situations in which depositions will be taken outside of the United States. Depositions often are so held in the course of proceedings, where the deponent is willing and his travel to the United States would be impractical. A more difficult question is the issuance of subpoenas by the commission to persons who are abroad. Section 9 of the FTC Act provides that subpoenas can be issued by the FTC to require the attendance of persons and the production of documents from any place *in the United States.* Read literally, this provision would mean that the FTC can only compel attendance or production at its proceedings when the person or information is located within the territorial United States. Such a rigid reading, however, would mean that one could avoid the subpoena power of the commission simply by removing himself and/or his evidence to a foreign country. In light of the commission's broad responsibilities and powers, it may well be that in a proper case the commission, with the aid of the courts, could compel compliance with its subpoena by a citizen or resident of the United States abroad under the standard of 28 U.S.C. §1783, previously discussed.

Discovery of Documents Located Outside the United States

One of the most controversial facets of multinational antitrust procedures is the area involving discovery of documents located outside the territory of the country where the forum court is located. Many countries and commentators have complained that U.S. courts have exceeded the bounds imposed by principles of public international law in several cases where they have sought documents located abroad. The U.S. federal courts believe that they have the authority to require the production of documents located in foreign countries where the court has *in personam* jurisdiction over the person or entity in possession or control of the material.

The first case to cause a major controversy was the *International Paper* case of 1947. In that case the United States government sought a court order against the International Paper Company (International), a New York corporation, ordering it to produce before a New York grand jury papers and documents held in Canada by two Canadian corporations, Canadian International Paper Co. (Canadian), a wholly owned subsidiary of International, and Canadian's wholly owned subsidiary, International Paper Sales Co., Inc. (Sales). Canadian and Sales moved for an order quashing the service of subpoenas, which had been served upon them as well as on their parent, because they were not "present" in New York and, thus, were not subject to the court's jurisdiction. The court held that the Canadian companies were "found" in New York because of several factors, including the fact that the companies had common officers, offices, and accounts with International.

The officers of Canadian also contended that they did not have control of the relevant documents because a quorum of the board of directors of Canadian, all residents of Canada, passed a resolution to the effect that the records of Canadian should in no case be allowed to be taken outside of Canada. The court rejected this contention because the papers sought belonged to the corporation and were in the possession of the corporation, therefore, "[t]he corporation may not evade complying with the subpoena by a resolution of this charter." The court then made the following frequently quoted statement of general principle:

> The fact that a corporation's records and documents are physically located beyond the confines of the United States does not excuse it from producing them if they are in its possession and the court has jurisdiction of the corporation. The test is control – not location of the records.

Five years later a grand jury investigation of an alleged worldwide oil cartel raised similar issues. Voluminous subpoenas were served on various oil companies and several of those companies moved to quash the subpoenas insofar as they called for the production of documents located in foreign countries. Several foreign governments complained to the U.S. Department of State that the subpoenas constituted an invasion of their sovereignty and the court reserved judgment on the subpoenas pending the oil companies showing:

1. "A good faith endeavor to gain consent from the foreign sovereign to remove the required documents."
2. "What, if any, interest the foreign sovereign has in the movant corporation, or in the investigation."
3. Proof of the foreign law by the opinion of experts or by other proper evidence.

The court also suggested that it would grant an order permitting the government to go to the oil companies' foreign offices to inspect documents.

Problems Created by Foreign Law and Principles of Comity

Despite these assertions of power the U.S. courts have recognized that there are situations in which it can be argued that it would be inappropriate for the court to exercise such authority. Such an argument has often been made in situations in which compliance with a production request would subject the subpoenee to criminal or civil sanctions under the law of the foreign jurisdiction where the records are located. For example, foreign laws may prohibit disclosure of business records and subject violators to a fine and/or imprisonment.

The U.S. courts have tended to be reluctant to order production of documents when this very act will constitute a criminal or quasi-criminal violation in a foreign country. This reluctance results from the principles of international comity, which dictate that the important policies of a foreign state be recognized, and also from understanding for the plight of the subpoenee who is caught between the conflicting demands of two sovereigns. Procedurally, this problem has been raised by a motion to quash the subpoena ordering production, or during contempt proceedings for noncompliance with the subpoena, or otherwise in the course of the hearings before the court or administrative agency that has issued the subpoena *duces tecum*.

As might be expected, the appropriate resolution of the issue and how it is implemented depend, in large part, upon the particular facts and circumstances of the case. Often the good faith attempt, or lack thereof, of the subpoenee to produce the documents has a significant effect on the final resolution of the issue. Thus, for example, to the extent a corporation interposes a blanket refusal to produce—as opposed to an actual production of a substantial number of documents and a detailed list of those segregated documents that it claims cannot validly be produced under the law of the foreign state—it jeopardizes its chances for a quashing of the subpoena or even a modification thereof.

In *First National City Bank* v. *IRS* the Internal Revenue Service was attempting to have produced certain records located at a foreign branch bank of City Bank. The latter resisted, arguing that production would violate the constitution and laws of the Republic of Panama, the situs of the branch office. The Court of Appeals for the Second Circuit rejected this argument because the foreign law relied on did not support the bank's contentions; that is, there was insufficient proof that the foreign laws proscribed the production. Further, the court reasoned that, when the foreign government licensed the branch office of the American bank, it must have contemplated that the bank would be required by U.S. law to furnish information from time to time to U.S. officials.

Yet the court did indicate that if, in fact, production would violate the foreign law, "we should agree that production of the Panama records should not be ordered." Accordingly, the circuit court remanded the case, with direction for a reinstatement of the subpoena and, in the event of non-compliance, further exploration into the demands of the foreign law.

In *Application of Chase Manhattan Bank* the government was seeking enforcement of a grand jury subpoena *duces tecum* which sought to direct the bank, a New York corporation, to produce records in the possession of a branch located in the Republic of Panama. Since the decision in *First National City Bank* v. *IRS,* a few years earlier, a new law had been enacted in Panama providing that: "The merchant furnishing a copy or reproductions of the contents of his books, correspondence and other documents for use in an action abroad, in compliance with an order of an authority not of the Republic of Panama, shall be penalized with a fine not greater than one hundred balboas." The bank presented evidence of this law and expert testimony that a violation would be equivalent to committing a misdemeanor under U.S. criminal law. At this juncture the district court concluded that production would constitute a violation of Panamanian law. Thus, the court stayed any further enforcement proceedings, permitting the government to petition the Panamanian authorities for permission to obtain the records and, at the same time, the court left the subpoena outstanding to insure that Chase Manhattan complied with its duty of cooperating with the government in any petition to the foreign authorities. The Second Circuit affirmed this approach by the trial court, citing the obligation of the U.S. courts "to respect the laws of other sovereign states even though they may differ in economic and legal philosophy from our own."

Chase Manhattan Bank and similar cases, involving foreign laws in the nature of criminal proscriptions, present the question of international comity in its clearest light because criminal strictures generally reflect the firmly held public policy of a foreign sovereign state. The problem is in a somewhat different posture where production of documents located in a foreign country will subject the person or entity not to criminal liability, but to possible civil liability under the law of the foreign state.

The leading case in this area is *United States* v. *First National City Bank,* decided in 1968, also by the Second Circuit. A federal grand jury had served a subpoena *duces tecum* on City Bank that required the production of documents located in the bank's offices in Germany. City Bank refused, asserting that compliance would subject it to civil liability and economic loss. Bank secrecy was not a part of the statutory law in Germany, so that no criminal sanctions attached to a breach. Bank secrecy was, however, in the nature of a traditional privilege flowing from the business relationship between bank and customer. The privilege could be waived by the customer, not by the bank, and breach of the privilege could subject the bank to liability in contract or tort.

The Second Circuit here rejected the proposition that the presence or absence of criminal sanctions by the foreign country should be determinative of whether obedience to the subpoena was required. It opined that international comity required that the result be based on more delicate considerations and a balancing test of the national interests of the respective countries. In this case the court had to balance American antitrust law, which it referred to as a cornerstone of U.S. economic policy, against German bank secrecy traditon. The court found it significant that the latter was nonstatutory, that it was merely a privilege that could be waived by the customer, and that any judicial enforcement of the privilege was left to the vagaries of private litigation. Another important factor was that neither the U.S. State Department nor the German government had expressed any interest in the matter. The court also gave little credence to the prediction of civil liability because of the remoteness of any compensable damages by the customer, the many defenses City Bank had in any suit, and the poor equitable position the customer had put itself in because it had adamantly refused to apply for an injunction as it was authorized to do under German law. After considering all these factors, the court thought the conclusion clear that City Bank could not validly oppose a subpoena *duces tecum* on the grounds that compliance would subject it to civil liability under the law of the foreign state.

This approach to asserted civil liability on the part of the company subpoenaed is a balanced and flexible standard which permits the courts to evaluate the national interests of the respective countries, as well as the implications for the individuals and companies concerned. Although this standard does not afford the convenience of a mechanical rule, it does offer a sound and reasoned basis for resolution of the sensitive questions of international comity and equity that such cases raise.

To synthesize, it is settled that a court that has personal jurisdiction over a party or witness has the power to order it to produce documents located in a foreign country even though production is a violation of the laws of the foreign sovereign. However, the existence of this power and the exercise of it must be maintained as clearly separate concepts. The rules governing the exercise of the authority are still evolving. The Second Circuit's 1968 opinion in *First National City Bank* is significant in rejecting "mechanical or overbroad rules of thumb." Under this approach the fact that foreign law inhibits production or disclosure is the starting point, not the final determinant. There must follow a precise analysis of the facts and circumstances of the particular case and a careful balancing of the national and private interests involved. The court will require a showing of a good faith attempt to secure the consent of the foreign sovereign to the requested discovery and proof by expert testimony or other evidence that the foreign law does in fact prohibit the requested discovery. It may be that this balancing approach that was developed with respect to possible civil liability will, as it is explored in new litigation, even be utilized in the context of potential criminal liability.

A case that is still pending at this writing illustrates the flexible approach presently being taken by courts and governments. In March 1970 the U.S. Department of Justice filed a civil antitrust suit against Bristol-Myers Co., Beecham, Inc., both of which are U.S. companies, and Beecham Group Ltd. [Beecham U.K.], a British company. Beecham, Inc., is a 90 per cent owned subsidiary of Beecham U.K. The government alleged that the three defendants combined and conspired to restrain and monopolize trade in ampicillin and other semisynthetic penicillin drugs by fraudulently procuring and enforcing Beecham U.K.'s U.S. patent covering ampicillin and by restraining the sale of drugs in bulk form or under other than specified trade names. Beecham U.K.'s motion to dismiss the complaint for lack of personal jurisdiction was denied on the ground that the court had jurisdiction under the statute quoted earlier in this chapter relating to non-resident holders of U.S. patents.

In November 1972 the court ordered Beecham U.K. to answer certain interrogatories relating to acquiring the U.S. patent and to its negotiation of agreements with Bristol-Myers. On December 5, 1972, an official of the United Kingdom Department of Trade and Industry (DTI), acting under Section 2 of the U.K.'s Shipping Contracts and Commercial Documents Act, issued an order to Beecham U.K. directing it not to comply with the American court's discovery order "so far as it relates to documents in the United Kingdom and to information to be compiled from such documents, [since the order] constitutes an infringement of the jurisdiction which, under international law, belongs to the United Kingdom."

The American court issued an order to show cause and held a hearing on why it should not enter an order against Beecham U.K. commanding it to obey the court's previous discovery order. The Department of Justice argued that "Beecham [U.K.] should be compelled to comply with the Court's previous order to furnish discovery on the merits, *despite any British government order to the contrary*," and that "even where compliance with a production or discovery order would involve, of necessity, a violation of the criminal or civil law of a foreign country or jurisdiction in which the documents or records are located—the courts of this country are not thereby deprived of jurisdiction to issue such a discovery order." (Emphasis added.)

In May 1973 the court issued an order, pursuant to Federal Rule of Civil Procedure 37(b), that those factual issues involved in the court's discovery order with which Beecham U.K. had failed to comply would be resolved against Beecham U.K. and for the plaintiffs, precluding Beecham U.K. from introducing at trial evidence in opposition to those claims. The court added:

> Beecham [U.K.] has failed to satisfy the Court that it has taken all affirmative steps required to achieve compliance with this Court's discovery orders. Although Beecham states generally that it protested the entry of the DTI Order, the Court notes, *inter alia,* that Beecham has made no effort to seek reconsideration, modification or review of the DTI Order and has made no effort to negotiate with the British government in order to achieve compliance with this Court's orders. It is further noted that Beecham has invoked the jurisdiction of the United States for its own protection, not only by securing patents in this country, but also by bringing an infringement suit and seeking the aid of the U.S. Tariff Commission. While these findings are not a prerequisite to the sanctions to be imposed under Rule 37(b), the Court deems them pertinent.

Subsequently, Beecham U.K. requested the DTI to lift the order barring compliance with the U.S. court's ruling. A new order was issued in August 1973 that modified the earlier order by removing all restrictions on discovery, except as "documents or information relate to any dealings between Her Majesty's Government or any public authority in the United Kingdom and Beechams." A letter from the DTI to Beecham U.K. accompanying the new order stated that the secretary decided to vary the original order after examination of the documents and added that "[h]e is concerned to give all possible help to the Court in this matter consistent with the maintenance of U.K. jurisdiction." Beecham U.K. filed as many interrogatory answers as it believed it could under the DTI order and the U.S. district court, noting that "Beecham [U.K.] has made a conscientious endeavor to complete discovery. . ." rescinded its May 1973 order that would have resolved factual issues against Beecham U.K.

Enforcement of Judgments Against Foreign Parties

A perplexing and yet vital aspect of international antitrust litigation is the question of how the Justice Department, the Federal Trade Commission, or a private plaintiff may obtain enforcement of a judgment or order in its favor against a foreign defendant. All the effort and expense devoted to the proceeding by the government or private plaintiff is for nought if compliance with a favorable decision cannot be achieved. In fact, the effectiveness of the entire U.S. antitrust policy rests on the ability to effectuate practically the relief granted by the courts. In this section we will consider the availability of, and the degree of success to be expected from, the various enforcement devices.

Enforcement of Judgments in the United States

There are three principal methods authorized by federal and state law for gaining compliance by defendants with judgments against them. These are attachment, garnishment, and contempt.

Attachment is a means by which the property of a defendant, real or personal, is placed in the custody of the law as security for compliance. If the judgment is for the defendant to engage, or to refrain from engaging, in certain action or conduct, the attachment of his property will usually induce his compliance. Where the judgment is for money damages, it can be satisfied out of a sale of the property with the net proceeds going to the judgment creditor.

Garnishment is a procedure for attaching an intangible asset that the judgment debtor is entitled to, such as a debt. The garnishment action is brought against the person or company owing the debt, known as the garnishee. Like attachment, garnishment can be utilized to compel certain conduct or, alternately, to satisfy a money award to the successful litigant.

Contempt is the third enforcement technique. Civil contempt, unlike criminal contempt, is not an offense against the dignity of the court but is essentially a remedial process used to bring about relief for the party in whose behalf the mandate of the court was issued. If and when the "contemnor" complies with the court order, the punishment will be terminated. The latter generally takes the form of a court-imposed fine which accumulates over the period that the order is not observed. It is also possible for the court to order imprisonment of an individual defendant until he agrees to comply with the judgment.

Postjudgment remedies are not the only recourse available to a plaintiff. Federal Rule of Civil Procedure 64 provides that at the commencement of and during the course of an action, all remedies allowing seizure of person or property for the purpose of securing satisfaction of an ultimate judgment are available to the extent authorized by the law of the state in which the district court is held, except if there is an applicable U.S. statute.

The property sought to be subjected to these remedies, whether before or after judgment, must be present within the territorial limits over which the court may exercise its power. When dealing with physical assets, this determination is not a difficult one. When seizure of wages or a debt is involved, certain specific rules come into play. A debt is thought to have its presence where either the creditor or the debtor resides. Moreover, even if both debtor and creditor reside outside of the jurisdiction, the debt may be deemed present therein if it arises from a contract made payable within the jurisdiction.

All fifty states recognize "foreign" attachment—the seizure of assets located within the jurisdiction belonging to a nonresident—in some form or another. This may involve a summary procedure with the defendant receiving neither notice nor hearing prior to the seizure of the property.

Despite the existence of such remedies, there are problems involved in their pursuit, and these may be dramatically compounded when the party acted against is a foreign entity. With foreign defendants it can be particularly important to seize assets early, before they can be shifted abroad. Some of the difficulties presented in connection with such relief were illustrated by the Supreme Court's decision in *De Beers Consolidated Mines Ltd.* v. *United States,* in which the corporate defendants were from South Africa, the Belgian Congo, Portugal, and Great Britain. The charge was that these parties were engaged in an unlawful conspiracy to restrain and monopolize the commerce of the United States with foreign nations in gem and industrial diamonds. Along with its complaint, the government sought a preliminary injunction restraining the defendants from withdrawing or disposing of their assets in the United States. As seizing the property was the only means of enforcing any potential decree of the court, the government argued that removal of the assets would cause irreparable injury to the United States.

The preliminary injunction was requested because the Federal Rules provided no suitable remedy. Rule 70 permitted seizure only after entry of a judgment. Rule 64, which permitted attachment at the commencement of an action where authorized by state law, was inoperative because the state in which the district court was situated had no such provision.

The Supreme Court observed that the injunction against a removal of property could not be justified by a need to safeguard a possible money judgment, because such a judgment was not being sought by the government. The injunction was being pressed instead on the theory that, *if* equitable relief were granted against defendants, and *if* they refused to comply, attachment of the property would be the sole effective means of compelling compliance. This, the Court felt, presupposed too much to justify an injunction, where the traditional provisional remedies were unavailable. The Court also expressed fear that to sustain this form of relief to promote antitrust policy would create a sweeping precedent that would engulf cases wholly unrelated to the antitrust laws. Therefore, the injunction was denied. This case serves to demonstrate the limitations of the remedies designed to secure the enforcement of judgments.

Problems may arise as to what assets are attachable. Suppose the defendant is a foreign-based corporation which has a wholly owned subsidiary doing business in the United States. Can the plaintiff attach the assets of the subsidary to either secure or satisfy a judgment? A few cases have held that a demonstration that a parent owns all the capital stock of a subsidiary and that the officers are identical would indicate that there was no real diversity of interest and render attachment permissible. Most decisions, however, find that ownership of stock and similarity of officers is not sufficient to "pierce the corporate veil." Generally, it must appear that the subsidiary was organized or utilized for an improper purpose and is under the actual control of the parent.

These are just some of the imponderables that are raised in connection with the enforcement of judgments and that may be magnified where a foreign defendant is concerned. Certainly possible problems in enforcement are among the factors weighed by the Justice Department and Federal Trade Commission when they evaluate the bringing of antitrust proceedings that will involve foreign parties. Where the circumstances are such that the U.S. courts will not have effective recourse against the agents or property of the foreign entity, even if the latter's contacts in the United States are sufficient to confer personal jurisdiction for purposes of instituting the case, the situation will be an uninviting one.

Enforcement of U.S. Judgments in Foreign Countries

There is an additional possibility for the American plaintiff armed with a money judgment against a foreign defendant who refuses to pay and is immune from execution in the United States. The plaintiff can consider instituting a new action in the courts of the foreign country that has adequate control over the defendant, in an attempt to enforce the judgment rendered in the United States. This procedure is vastly different from and more difficult than, for example, securing a judgment in California and thereafter bringing an enforcement action on the judgment in New York. The "Full Faith and Credit" clause of Article IV of the United States Constitution would govern that case. But the Constitution has no binding effect when a plaintiff gets a judgment in this country and attempts to enforce it by bringing an action on it in a foreign country.

Whether one country will give effect to another's judgments will vary from nation to nation, and often case to case. There are no principles of recognition which have met with anything like universal approval, for every country perceives every other country's system differently. What has developed is a maze of unilateral, bilateral, and multilateral arrangements for recognizing one another's judgments in an attempt to effectuate enforcement.

There are four general approaches taken concerning the effect to be given a foreign judgment:

1. A country may give it a "conclusive" effect, much the same as the effect New York would give under the "Full Faith and Credit" clause to a judgment rendered in California. This approach is very rare, however.
2. A country may conduct a full review of both the facts and the law of the underlying judgment—in effect, grant a new trial on the merits. This would permit a defendant to raise any defense in this proceeding, irrespective of whether it was litigated in the basic suit. This approach puts the plaintiff back in his original position; and often the plaintiff may justifiably feel that his situation has worsened because of the additional legal expenses, the practical difficulty in another country's applying U.S. antitrust law with all of its ramifications, and the apprehension (whether valid or not) that the foreign country's courts might be over-protective of the defendant.
3. The third possibility is that the foreign court will give the judgment prima facie weight, but the defendant may challenge it on the basis that it should not have been awarded in the original forum because of factors such as lack of jurisdiction, fraud on the court, clear mistake, or inconsistency with the law of the original forum. This may have the effect of a new trial on the merits.
4. The final approach turns on the concept of "reciprocity." Here Country A will apply conclusive effect to a judgment rendered in Country B if the latter accords the same treatment to a judgment from Country A.

Presently, the great majority of the significant nations act in accordance with the reciprocity rule. This has created numerous problems for enforcing American judgments abroad. The courts in foreign countries have had difficulty weaving their way through the tangled and confusing web of federal and state decisions in the United States in trying to determine what effect the United States gives their nations' judgments. As a result, although American courts have tended to grant conclusive effect to foreign judgments, the same treatment has not always been afforded in return. On the whole, except where a specific treaty or convention exists between the United States and the foreign country, enforcement of American judgments abroad tends to be difficult and largely impractical.

There is one additional problem, pertinent in the case of antitrust judgments, which may preclude enforcement in foreign courts, even where reciprocity exists as a general matter. Most countries will refuse to enforce another country's judgments that are either penal in nature or contrary to the public policy of the forum court. A U.S. antitrust judgment would often be viewed through foreign eyes as falling in one or both of these categories. Some countries also display a hesitancy to enforce judgments which would promote the economic policies of a foreign legislator. There are, therefore, many potential obstacles to the enforcement of U.S. antitrust judgments in foreign courts.

Considerations of Comity in Shaping Remedies

As we have already observed in a variety of contexts, antitrust litigation in the United States that concerns the nation's foreign commerce can present problems that are virtually "diplomatic" in nature, i.e., problems that touch on the relationship between the United States and another country or countries. These special international questions can also be raised, and in very sensitive fashion, when the litigation has been concluded and the sole remaining issue is the shaping of relief against the defendant. The problems are likely to be most severe where the defendant in question is a foreign party, where the judgment seeks to compel him to engage or refrain from engaging in particular conduct (as distinct from requiring him to pay money), and where the conduct is to be carried out in and/or will have some effect upon the foreign country.

The U.S. courts have recognized that, even with respect to regulating the conduct of U.S. nationals abroad, regard for the interests of foreign nations and their citizens may preclude certain orders. So far as foreign nationals are concerned, the courts have determined that, although personal jurisdiction permits issuance of injunctions against them, "[T]his power should be exercised with great reluctance when it will be difficult to secure compliance with any resulting decree or when the exercise of such power is fraught with possibilities of discord and conflict with the authorities of another country."

Perhaps the most graphic illustration of the problems that can ensue in this area is depicted by the 1952 decree of the United States District Court for the Southern District of New York in *United States* v. *Imperial Chemical Industries Ltd.* (ICI) and by its aftermath. The court had found that ICI and others had, with the aid of patent licenses, divided world markets in the chemical trade, in restraint of U.S. commerce and in violation of the Sherman Act. In the decree, Judge Ryan required compulsory licensing of all U.S. patents that were being licensed by the conspirators in furtherance of their scheme. With respect to the British corporation, ICI, and the patents that it held under British law, however, Judge Ryan sought to temper the relief by, instead of ordering compulsory licensing, directing ICI to grant immunity under the Britsh patents to parties who would otherwise be infringers. This action was rationalized with the theory that, on the basis of the personal jurisdiction the court had acquired over ICI, "we are merely directing ICI to refrain from asserting rights which it may have in Britain, since the enforcement of those rights will serve to continue the effects of wrongful acts it has committed within the United States affecting the foreign trade of the United States." Judge Ryan observed that the courts of Great Britain might not give full effect to this decree, but he felt that such doubt should not deter him from entering it.

The issue was joined when, shortly thereafter, another British company, British Nylon Spinners Ltd. (BNS), sued ICI in England for specific performance of a previous agreement under which ICI had agreed to grant BNS exclusive license rights under the pertinent British patents. BNS also sought a preliminary injunction restraining ICI from complying with the American judgment because this would damage BNS's exclusive rights. The British courts granted the injunctive relief to BNS and eventually also granted the specific performance of the agreement. They reasoned that comity did not require acceptance of a foreign decree which impaired British contract rights, especially where the injured party, in this case BNS, was not subject to the jurisdiction of the foreign court. The American judgment was viewed as an assertion of extraterritorial jurisdiction that British courts would not recognize. The British judges further observed, however, that a saving clause in the American judgment, to the effect that nothing in the order would operate against the company for action taken in complying with the law of a foreign government or instrumentality, precluded the situation from being one that would disturb the comity between the two countries.

This litigation offers a prime example of the imponderable difficulties that may arise when an effort is made by the United States to impose a particular pattern of conduct on a foreign-based entity with respect to its foreign activity. The U.S. court may not only encounter frustration in seeking to enforce compliance by the foreign entity, but also find that the form of relief has stirred up a hornet's nest abroad by adversely affecting other entities in the enjoyment of rights under foreign law or otherwise running afoul of foreign law or policy. Indeed, the controversy generated by the BNS case has persuaded U.S. courts to take even greater pains in considering the formulation of relief in such situations.

Also instructive is the *General Electric* "incandescent lamp" case, in which Philips, a Dutch corporation, was held liable for violation of the Sherman Act. The relief was carefully shaped as to Philips to meet the needs of the situation but not necessarily interfere with its foreign activities. Philips was enjoined from agreeing with any defendant or any other U.S.

manufacturer of lamps, lamp parts, or lamp machinery that (1) Philips would refrain from exporting to, or producing such products in, the United States or (2) that such defendant or other manufacturer would refrain from exporting such products from the United States to any other country. The court also ordered the defendants, including Philips, to dedicate to the public their U.S. patents on lamps and lamp parts. "As set forth in the opinion in this case Philips knowingly violated the U.S. antitrust laws. It is eminently appropriate that its U.S. patents be made available to the incandescent lamp industry as part of the program of restoring strong competitors, so long suppressed as a result of the conspiracy of which Philips was a part." The court declined, however, to order Philips to grant immunity from suit under its Dutch and other foreign patents.

With regard to visitorial rights included to help assure compliance, it was ordered that, as to Philips, this only be available for information located in the United States because of the jurisdictional impracticabilities involved. So far as removal of information from the United States was concerned, the court acknowledged that "[t]his is inherent in Philips' position as a foreign manufacturer." At one point the court remarked that "The effort has been made to insulate Philips against interference with its normal business abroad except where its activities would have an appreciable effect upon the commerce of the United States." Moreover, it was provided that "Philips shall not be in contempt of this Judgment for doing anything outside of the United States which is required or for not doing anything outside the United States which is unlawful under the laws of the government, province, country or state in which Philips . . . may be incorporated, chartered or organized or in the territory of which Philips . . . may be doing business." Philips was entitled, the court felt, to such "protection from being caught between the jaws of this judgment and the operation of laws in foreign countries where it does its business."

Foreign policy considerations led to the modification in 1965 of the final judgment in the *Swiss Watchmakers* case that we have previously discussed. The defendants had indicated they would appeal from this final judgment, but, at the request of the government, the judgment was modified. Among the grounds for the modifications was the fact that the Department of State had indicated to the Department of Justice that a resolution "on a basis consistent with United States antitrust laws" of this litigation, which involved foreign companies, would be advantageous from the standpoint of U.S. foreign policy. Since the entry of the judgment, the Swiss Confederation had issued official regulations on the subject of watch parts export permits, and the purpose of altering the judgment was to assure that the defendants were not compelled by the decree to undertake conduct contrary to the law of Switzerland.

Judge Cashin's remarks in connection with these modifications of the *Swiss Watchmakers* judgment indicated his keen awareness of what had transpired in the ICI–BNS litigation: "Moreover, these modifications will prevent any situation from arising such as has occurred in other litigation in the past when there was believed to be a possible conflict between a decree of a United States court and the sovereignty of a foreign nation. . . . In the main the modifications relate to peripheral areas of the judgment which might have been construed to have bearing upon the sovereignty of the Swiss Confederation."

This judicial desire to avoid collision with the interests of foreign nations does not mean, however, that the courts are unwilling to include in antitrust decrees provisions bearing on the conduct of defendants abroad. Particularly where it is the conduct of U.S. firms that is to be regulated, in which case the problems of comity are not so significant, the government and the courts are inclined to extend the scope of the relief to the fullest extent necessary to purge the unlawful situation and prevent its recurrence.

In the *National Lead* case the defendants were the two principal producers of titanium pigments in the United States, National Lead Co. and du Pont, plus Titan Co., which was wholly owned by National Lead. The court found that the defendants and foreign co-conspirators had, with the aid of patent license arrangements, agreed to divide the world trade in titanium pigments into exclusive territories, restraining U.S. commerce in violation of the Sherman Act. The court viewed the absence from the proceeding of the foreign conspirators a "practical limitation upon the scope of the court's decree," but not one that should prevent it from applying its mandate fully upon those who had been brought before it.

Accordingly, the unlawful agreements were canceled, with the domestic defendant companies enjoined from further performance or renewal of the agreements. The defendants were also ordered to grant to any applicant nonexclusive licenses at uniform reasonable royalties under the U.S. patents involved. Significantly from the "extraterritorial" viewpoint, defendants were "restrained from attempting to enforce any rights under any foreign patents owned by them or under which they are the exclusive licensees to prevent the exportation of titanium pigments from the United States to any foreign country."

A number of remedial antitrust decrees have had provisions directing firms to compete in foreign markets. In *United States* v. *Holophane Co.,* for example, the district court ordered Holophane, a Delaware corporation, to use "reasonable efforts" to compete in foreign markets, including the territories that had been allocated to its co-conspirators, a British and a French corporation, under agreements found to be in restraint of trade. The defendant was directed to establish new trademarks for foreign sales, if necessary for export, and also to try to employ distributors in the territories of the foreign co-conspirators. Further, Holophane was required to advertise at reasonable intervals in trade journals circulated in the foreign countries, in an effort to sell its products; it was also to respond in writing to persons who had previously sought information, or who in the future sought information, concerning the sale of the defendant's products, informing them of the availability of the products. Although the district court's decision and decree in other respects was affirmed unanimously by the Supreme Court, these detailed provisions for competition abroad by Holophane were affirmed only by an equally divided Court. Even the decree in *Holophane,* in any event, was careful to provide that the directions to the defendant should not be construed as requiring it to violate the valid patent, trademark, or trade-name rights of any person in the foreign country.

In the *Timken* decree, American Timken was ordered to publish advertisements in British and French trade journals advising potential purchasers of its products "of the nature of this judgment insofar as it concerns the removal of the restrictions which had previously prevented the sale of bearings in British and French Territory," and to give similar notice to all persons who had made inquiry of them as to the purchase of antifriction bearings for export.

International Treaties

Several attempts have been made to avoid possible international conflicts in the situations that we have discussed, including service of process, discovery, and enforcement of judgments. The United States has signed two multilateral treaties relating to these subjects. The earlier one, ratified by the United States in 1967, is the Convention on the Service Abroad of Judicial and Extrajudicial Documents in Civil or Commercial Matters. The more recent treaty, ratified by the United States in 1972, is the Convention on the Taking of Evidence Abroad in Civil or Commercial Matters. Fifteen nations have ratified the former and three nations have ratified the latter. Both Conventions are intended to provide minimum standards for international judicial cooperation and to facilitate such cooperation. The Civil Division of the United States Department of Justice performs certain tasks under the Conventions and each party country has such a "Central Authority" that performs similar functions. Because the Conventions merely establish minimum standards, any nation may have broader and more liberal provisions that remain unchanged and unrestricted by the Conventions. There have been about 400 requests annually by foreign parties for service of documents in the United States under the Convention on Service Abroad. There are no records on the number of requests made by Americans for service abroad because such requests are generally mailed directly abroad without passing through the United States Department of Justice.

A third Convention on the Recognition and Enforcement of Foreign Judgments in Civil and Commercial Matters has been drafted. However, at this writing it is mired in a complicated procedural impasse and has neither been ratified by the United States nor come into force by virtue of ratification by other nations.

Conclusion

Although, as we observed in Chapter 3, the antitrust laws of the United States have a very broad potential sweep in that they may be applied to conduct abroad and to the actions of foreign parties in proper circumstances, there may be serious practical obstacles to effective enforcement posed by the international setting. If the foreign corporation or individual is to be joined in the litigation and subjected to the final decree, the U.S. courts must properly have personal jurisdiction over the foreign national. Once a litigation has been instituted, the foreign location of a party, a witness, or documentary materials can render very difficult the conduct of discovery and the trial of the case.

Moreover, when a judgment has been obtained against a foreign-based party, there may be problems in bringing about compliance with that judgment. In situations where there is "leverage" upon the foreign party in the United States, either because it has agents in the country or else physical facilities or other assets subject to attachment, compliance is facilitated. Where, however, enforcement is dependent on the recognition given the U.S. antitrust decree in foreign countries, frustration may well be the result. The lack of settled procedures for according reciprocity on an international basis to national decrees is a basic obstacle, and this obstacle is compounded by the generally low level of understanding and sympathy for U.S. antitrust policy abroad.

These practical considerations, plus the awareness of the enforcement agencies and the courts of the principles of comity, are important factors that go into the determination of whether an antitrust suit involving foreign commerce should be filed; whether, if so, it is appropriate that foreign entities be joined as parties; and what the shape of any relief ultimately awarded should be.

chapter 5

Contracts, Conspiracies, and Monopolization in Foreign Commerce

In Chapter 3 we were concerned with whether certain practices in foreign trade substantially affect the interstate or foreign commerce of the United States so that our courts may have jurisdiction over them under our antitrust laws. We pointed out that, so long as the requisite effects on this country's trade or commerce are established, a great many transactions and practices in international commerce can be the subject of antitrust scrutiny and challenge. In this and succeeding chapters we will be discussing particular types of practices in international trade that violate our antitrust laws and examining the circumstances under which these violations come about.

The present chapter will deal with agreements among competitors and with the subject of monopolization, conduct encompassed by the express language of Sections 1 and 2 of the Sherman Act. Anticompetitive agreements such as price fixing, allocation of customers or territories, and boycotts are, as we shall see, proscribed in international commerce as well as in interstate commerce when they affect U.S. commerce. A number of the cases brought in the international setting and involving "cartels"—agreements among dominant world firms in an industry to divide up markets globally—have a distinctive flavor and reflect hard-core restraint of trade on a truly momentous scale.

Contracts, Combinations, and Conspiracies

Because Section 1 of the Sherman Act is addressed to "every contract, combination . . . or conspiracy, in restraint of trade . . . " one person acting alone cannot violate that statutory provision. An agreement, understanding, or concert of action between two or more parties is thus a prerequisite. As the Supreme Court stated as early as 1914: "An act harmless when done by one may become a public wrong when done by many acting in concert, for it then takes on the form of a conspiracy. . . ."

The terms *contract, combination,* and *conspiracy* can be differentiated but have often been used by the courts interchangeably to characterize a concert of action. *Contract* normally means a "formal agreement entered into by parties." *Combination* more generally refers to a "union of activity on the part of two or more persons." *Conspiracy* is usually defined in law as a "combination designed to accomplish an illegal purpose or to carry out a legal purpose by illegal means."

The existence of a "contract, combination . . . or conspiracy" is not dependent upon there being a written or even a "gentlemen's" agreement between the parties, but may be implied from a course of conduct. For instance, a violation of the Sherman Act was found where various associations of retail lumber dealers periodically circulated among their members a list containing names of wholesale lumber dealers reportedly selling direct to consumers. Although there was no explicit agreement on the part of the retailers to refrain from dealing with the wholesalers whose names appeared on the list, the Supreme Court found an unlawful combination and conspiracy to boycott the wholesalers because this was the evident purpose of the blacklists and because many of the retail dealers had in fact stopped purchasing from the listed wholesalers. This doctrine of *conscious adherence* was reiterated by the Supreme Court in 1948 in *Federal Trade Commission* v. *Cement Institute,* in which the Court stated: "It is enough to warrant the finding of a 'combination' within the meaning of the Sherman Act if there is evidence that persons, with knowledge that concerted action was contemplated and invited, give adherence to and then participate in a scheme."

The development of this rationale led to the question of whether proof of consciously parallel action is alone sufficient to establish the requisite combination or conspiracy. In the 1954 Supreme Court decison in *Theater Enterprises, Inc.* v. *Paramount Film Distributing Corporation,* the Supreme Court rejected this notion. It held that although uniform conduct or identical pricing may be *evidence* of a violation of Section 1 of the Sherman Act, their existence does not obviate the necessity of determining whether or not a conspiracy exists. The true test remains whether the conduct of the parties stemmed from an agreement, tacit or express, as distinct from independent decision. Nonetheless, as a practical matter, the line between a tacit agreement manifested by parallel conduct and consciously parallel conduct alone remains a thin one.

In the 1969 case of *United States* v. *Container Corporation of America,* the Supreme Court held that an agreement on the part of certain corrugated-container manufacturers who accounted for approximately 90 per cent of the shipments in a certain area to exchange price information concerning specific sales to identified customers constituted an unlawful combination or conspiracy in violation of Section 1 of the Sherman Act. Although characterizing the agreement as "somewhat casual," and notwithstanding the absence of any agreement to adhere to a price schedule, the Court nevertheless concluded: "Each defendant on receiving [a] request usually furnished the data with the expectation that it would be furnished reciprocal information when it wanted it. That concerted action is of course sufficient to establish the conspiracy, the initial ingredient of a violation of Section 1 of the Sherman Act."

The same reasoning that requires concerted action to constitute a violation of Section 1 of the Sherman Act leads to the conclusion that the officers and employees of a single corporation cannot combine or conspire among themselves or with the corporation in violation of Section 1, because a corporation can act only through its officers and employees. To hold otherwise would be to hold that a corporation can conspire with itself.

The principle that a corporation cannot conspire with its own officers or employees has been applied to charges of conspiracy between unincorporated divisions of a single corporation. Thus, the rule appears settled that agreements between a corporation and its officers or employees or between unincorporated divisions of a single corporation will not be found to constitute an unlawful conspiracy in violation of Section 1 of the Sherman Act.

The same reasoning has not been applied, however, to business activity between related corporations, even agreements between a parent corporation and a wholly owned subsidiary, known as intraenterprise conspiracy. The rationale has been that close affiliation between distinct entities does not immunize activity that would otherwise constitute unlawful conspiracy if engaged in by unrelated entities. In the *Timken* case, for example, agreements involving the Timken Roller Bearing Co., "British Timken," and "French Timken," the latter being foreign companies in which the former owned stock, were held unlawful divisions of markets. The court stated that "[t]he fact that there is common ownership or control of the contracting corporations does not liberate them from the impact of the antitrust laws."

Critics of the intraenterprise conspiracy doctrine find it particularly obnoxious in foreign commerce where valid business reasons, rather than restriction of competition, often dictate the formation of subsidiaries.

On this general subject the 1955 Report of the Attorney General's National Committee to Study the Antitrust Laws states:

> The substance of the Supreme Court decisions is that concerted action between a parent and subsidiary or between subsidiaries which has for its purpose or effect coercion or unreasonable restraint on the trade of strangers to those acting in concert is prohibited by Section 1. Nothing in these opinions should be interpreted as justifying the conclusion that concerted action solely between a parent and subsidiary or subsidiaries, the purpose and effect of which is not coercive restraint of the trade of strangers to the corporate family, violates Section 1. Where such concerted action restrains no trade and is designed to restrain no trade other than that of the parent and its subsidiaries, Section 1 is not violated.

In summary, Section 1 of the Sherman Act proscribes concerted activity among two or more parties in restraint of trade; when independent action gives way to concerted action, Section 1 may come into play.

The Rule of Reason and Per Se Violations

The prohibition of the Sherman Act is one very generally directed against "restraint of trade." Giving this concept a specific content was left for the courts to determine as they considered individual cases. Although the language of Section 1 condemns "every" agreement in restraint of trade, the Supreme Court established in the 1911 *Standard Oil* case the "rule of reason" as a limitation on the application of the statute. In brief, illegal restraints are those that are "unreasonably restrictive" of trade. The reasonableness of a restraint is evaluated in terms of its relationship to the attainment of legitimate objectives (as, for example, the seller's limited covenant not to compete, which is ancillary to the sale of a going business), the scope and impact of the restraint on others, and any other pertinent factors.

Nonetheless, the courts have, in the course of considering the various types of restrictive agreements, concluded that certain ones are inherently unreasonable, regardless of their context or justification. These restraints are called *per se* violations of the antitrust laws. Justice Black explained the concept as follows in 1958 in the case of *Northern Pacific Railway* v. *United States*:

> there are certain agreements or practices which because of their pernicious effect on competition and lack of any redeeming virtue are conclusively presumed to be unreasonable and therefore illegal without elaborate inquiry as to the precise harm they have caused or the business excuse for their use. This principle of *per se* unreasonableness not only makes the type of restraints which are proscribed by the Sherman Act more certain to the benefit of everyone concerned, but it also avoids the necessity for an incred-

ibly complicated and prolonged economic investigation into the entire history of the industry involved, as well as related industries, in an effort to determine at large whether a particular restraint has been unreasonable—an inquiry so often wholly fruitless when undertaken.

Among the types of conduct that have been held to violate the statute per se are price-fixing agreements, agreements to limit production or control supply, allocation of customers, group boycotts, and agreements to divide markets. We shall be considering these specific practices, among others, later in this chapter and the succeeding chapters.

The rule of reason and per se concepts are fully applicable whether the Sherman Act is being invoked in the context of international commerce or the more usual setting of interstate commerce. The rule of reason was, in fact, applied in *United States* v. *American Tobacco Co.* in 1911, the same year as the *Standard Oil* case, to condemn an international cartel arrangement. It was found that the purpose of the combination was from the beginning "to acquire dominion and control of the tobacco trade, not by the mere exertion of the ordinary right to contract and to trade, but by methods devised in order to monopolize the trade by driving competitors out of business. . . ." In a later case, *Timken Roller Bearing Co.* v. *United States,* a majority of the Supreme Court held that agreements dividing markets among the American Timken Comany and foreign firms in which it held an interest were violative of the Sherman Act. Justice Jackson, dissenting, expressed doubt, however, that it should be regarded as an "unreasonable restraint of trade" for an American industrial concern to organize foreign subsidiaries each limited to serving a particular market area. "If so [he stated], it seems to preclude the only practical means of reaching foreign markets by many American industries." Justice Jackson's reasoning was that, because the laws of many foreign countries restrict the operation in their territories of nondomestic corporations, the only way for Americans desiring to trade in those markets and to operate successfully may be by forming domestic subsidiaries. Thus, applying the rule of reason in foreign trade cases may call for the consideration of some market conditions that are nonexistent in interstate trade. As Justice Frankfurter, who joined in the dissent, expressed it, "the circumstances of foreign trade may alter the incidence of what in the setting of domestic commerce would be a clear case of unreasonable restraint of trade."

As we have seen, the majority of the Court was not persuaded in *Timken* that the agreements were necessitated by conditions in foreign countries, but found rather that competition would have been possible except for the restraints imposed by the co-conspirators themselves. The existence of foreign governmental barriers was offered as a defense in another conspiracy case, *United States* v. *Minnesota Mining & Manufacturing Co.* In the arrangement under scrutiny there, nine American competitors, who had controlled four fifths of the export trade in abrasives, combined to establish an export company under the Webb–Pomerene Act, as well as another American company with subsidiary manufacturing companies in foreign countries. The court found that the Webb–Pomerene exemption did not immunize this activity from the Sherman Act (see Chapter 10), and concluded that the combination of the major American competitors in jointly owning and operating foreign subsidiaries restrained the foreign commerce of the United States because of the limiting effect it had on U.S. exports. The court acknowledged that if foreign governmental barriers actually precluded U.S. exports into a particular area, a combination like the one in question would not "whatever else it may do . . . restrain foreign commerce in that area in violation of the Sherman Act." Here, as in *Timken,* however, the court determined that there were not in fact foreign governmental barriers justifying the arrangement under attack. The court accordingly held that the showing of the restrictive combination, together with a showing that in the absence of the combination there was a possibility of profitable American exports in reasonable volume, was proof of a violation of Section 1 of the Sherman Act.

Judge Wyzanski's opinion in *Minnesota Mining* includes suggestion of a theory that may be pertinent to the application of the Sherman Act in foreign trade, although application of this theory was not necessary in that case. The judge stated:

> It may very well be that even though there is an economic or political barrier which entirely precludes American exports to a foreign country, a combination of dominant American manufacturers to establish joint factories for the sole purpose of serving the internal commerce of that country is a *per se* violation of [the interstate commerce] clause of the Sherman Act. The intimate association of the principal American producers in day-to-day manufacturing operations, their exchange of patent licenses and industrial know-how, and their common experience in marketing and fixing prices may inevitably reduce their zeal for competition *inter sese* in the American market.

On this reasoning, the establishment of joint factories abroad by principal American competitors would be invalid per se because of an inevitable tendency to impair competition *in the American domestic market.*

International Cartels

One of the main thrusts of American antitrust enforcement involving foreign trade has been against private international agreements that limit imports into the United States or exports from the United States. The preservation of import competition is viewed by the government as an essential ingredient in the maintenance of our competitive system generally, and particularly as a stimulus to the more concentrated and complacent U.S. industries. Conversely, promotion of our exports is considered vital to the protection of our balance-of-payments posture and to the health of our national economy.

The division of markets among competitors on an international scale will, of course, restrain both imports into and exports from a particular nation and goes to the heart of international antitrust. It is this type of agreement that is most commonly associated with the phenomenon loosely called the international cartel. In the typical cartel case an agreement to allocate international markets is entered into by the dominant producers of a particular product in several countries. In essence, they allocate the world markets among themselves with each producer receiving one or more exclusive markets in which the others agree not to compete. Typically, the American firm agrees not to sell in certain foreign markets (inhibiting U.S. exports) and the foreign firms agree not to sell in the U.S. market (inhibiting U.S. imports), in restraint of the foreign commerce of the United States and violation of the Sherman Act.

A cartel arrangement was considered early in the history of the Sherman Act in the Supreme Court's decision in *United States* v. *American Tobacco Company* referred to previously. It will be recalled that, under the cartel arrangement, several corporations engaged in the tobacco trade, some of them American and two of them English, entered into agreements in England dividing world markets in that trade. American Tobacco agreed to limit its business to the United States, its dependencies, and Cuba. Imperial, one of the English companies, agreed to limit its business to the United Kingdom, except for leaf tobacco purchases. Further, the other English company, British–American Tobacco Company, with capital apportioned between American Tobacco and Imperial, was to take over the export business of both of those companies and operate in other countries. The Supreme Court held that the "assailed combination in all its aspects . . . including the foreign corporations insofar as by the contracts made by them they became co-operators in the combination—comes within the prohibitions of the 1st and 2nd sections of the anti-trust act. . . ."

In another leading case in the field, *United States* v. *National Lead Co.,* the dominant producers of titanium compounds divided the world market into exclusive territories for each of the parties. The Titanium Pigment Company, an American firm, was granted all of North America (defined to include also Central America and Panama). The Titan Co. A/S, a Norwegian company, was allocated the rest of the world except South America, in which both companies were allowed to operate. Neither company was allowed to sell any substance containing more than 2 per cent titanium in the other company's territory. Indeed, each company appointed the other company as its sole agent for the marketing of titanium products in the other company's territory. The result, in the words of the court, was that:

the parties had divided the world into trade areas or territories; that each party agreed not to trespass into the territory allotted to the other; and that commerce between the two territories in titanium products was, as far as these parties were concerned, interdicted and could proceed only by the grace of their mutual consent.

This agreement, of course, is exactly the type of scheme that is anathema to the goals of the American antitrust laws as they apply to foreign commerce. Blocking the access of the American company to markets outside of the Western Hemisphere resulted in a limitation of American exports abroad. Precluding the Norwegian company from selling its titanium products in the United States limited the access of American consumers to foreign imports. Even if the effect of the cartel arrangement was to reduce prices, increase sales, and improve product quality, the court in *National Lead* eloquently observed that:

> the major premise of the Sherman Act is that the suppression of competition in international trade is in and of itself a public injury; or at any rate, that such suppression is a greater price than we want to pay for the benefits it sometimes secures. Nor does it necessarily follow that the advance of the art, the rise in production and the decline of prices are attributable to the effects of the combination. Post hoc, propter hoc, is an invalid argument whether used by the plaintiff or the defendant. Anyone is free to speculate whether, in the absence of the arrangement, the stimulus of competition might not have produced far greater strides in these beneficial directions. The economic theory underlying the Sherman Act is that, in the long run, competition is a more effective prod to production and a more trustworthy regulator of prices than even an enlightened combination.

The result is that the courts have no trouble finding this type of arrangement to be a violation of Section 1 of the Sherman Antitrust Act. As was further said by the court in *National Lead*:

> No citation of authority is any longer necessary to support the proposition that a combination of competitors, which by agreement divides the world into exclusive trade areas, and suppresses all competition among the members of the combination, offends the Sherman Act.

Thus, such agreements have been held to be per se violations of the Sherman Act.

A variation of the previously discussed agreement to allocate markets has been for potential competitors to set up jointly owned corporations, commonly called a joint venture, and then to divide the world markets among the various entities. The famous *Timken* antifriction bearings case to which we have previously referred had features of such an arrangement. It is appropriate here to set out the facts of that case, which involved the Timken Roller Bearing Company (American Timken), an American manufacturer of antifriction bearings, in some detail. American Timken joined with Michael B. U. Dewar, an English businessman, to gain control of British Timken, Ltd. (British Timken), a leading British manufacturer of antifriction bearings. A French firm, Société Anonyme Française Timken (French Timken), was then organized by American Timken and Dewar as a joint venture to manufacture antifriction bearings in France. Agreements were entered into by American Timken, British Timken, and French Timken whereby they allocated the world's markets among themselves. British Timken and French Timken continuously kept operative "business agreements" regulating the manufacture and sale of antifriction bearings by the three companies and providing for the use by the British and French corporations of the trademark Timken. Under those agreements the parties (1) allocated trade territories among themselves; (2) fixed prices on products of one sold in the territory of the others; (3) cooperated to protect each other's markets and to eliminate outside competition; and (4) participated in cartels to restrict imports to, and exports from, the United States.

These agreements were attacked by the U.S. Department of Justice as being in violation of the Sherman Act. In defending such agreements before the Supreme Court of the United States, American Timken claimed that the agreements were reasonable and thus not in violation of the Sherman Act. Their claim for reasonableness was founded, in part, on the theory that such agreements were merely ancillary to an allegedly legal joint venture between American Timken and Dewar.

In considering American Timken's argument the Supreme Court observed that in view of the finding of the district court that the dominant purpose of the agreement was to avoid competition among the three companies, it was doubtful that the agreements were merely incidental to an otherwise legitimate joint venture. The Supreme Court went on to hold that, in any event,

> [o]ur prior decisions plainly establish that agreements providing for an aggregation of trade restraints such as those existing in this case are illegal under the [Sherman] Act. . . . The fact that there is common ownership or control of the contracting corporations does not liberate them from the impact of the antitrust laws. . . . Nor do we find any support in reason or authority for the proposition that agreements between legally separate persons and companies to suppress competition among themselves and others can be justified by labeling the project a "joint venture."

As this ruling indicates, and as we shall examine in greater detail in Chapter 8, the key to whether a joint venture between American and foreign firms will run afoul of the U.S. antitrust laws is whether the effect of the undertaking is to suppress, to the detriment of the commerce of the United States, competition that would otherwise exist. A joint venture to market a product in a territory in which neither of the co-venturers was engaged or potentially engaged would, for example, normally withstand challenge.

Another organizational vehicle that has sometimes been used to attempt to allocate world markets is the export association organized pursuant to the Webb-Pomerene Act. As more fully discussed in Chapter 10, that Act provides that the Sherman Act shall not, except in certain enumerated instances, apply to the formation of associations for the purpose of engaging in export trade. In one case in the United States District Court for the Southern District of New York, *United States* v. *United States Alkali Export Ass'n.* (Alkasso), it was claimed by the defendants that the Act permitted such associations to participate in world market allocations that would otherwise be illegal under the Sherman Act. In that 1949 case the defendants, in addition to Alkasso, the principal defendant, were another domestic Webb–Pomerene export association, the California Export Association (Calkex), thirteen corporate members of the associations, Imperial Chemical Industries, Ltd. (I.C.I.) a British corporation, and that corporation's New York subsidiary (I.C.I., New York).

Alkasso and Brunner Mond & Co., the predecessor of Imperial Chemical Industries, Ltd., entered into an agreement whereby the British company agreed to refrain from exporting soda ash and caustic to Cuba. In addition, the agreement imposed restrictions on the amount of alkalis that each party could export to Mexico and South America. Subsequently, Solvay et Cie, a Belgian corporation, joined the cartel under an arrangement whereby the European market was allocated to Solvay; the British Empire (excluding Canada), Egypt, the Levant, Iraq, and Iran were allocated to I.C.I.; and Canada, Mexico, Cuba, Haiti, San Domingo, and the Dutch East Indies were allocated to Alkasso. In addition, certain other markets, including China and Japan, were denominated as joint territories in which each of the members of the cartel could sell alkalis, but only in specifically limited quantities. While this arrangement was in force, a collateral arrangement existed between Solvay, I.C.I., and I.G. Farben-industrie Aktiengesellschaft (I.G. Farben), a German firm, whereby I.G. Farben was alloted Scandinavia as an exclusive territory.

Alkasso and I.C.I. admitted the execution of the agreements relating to the division of world markets and the assignment of international quotas. The individual corporate members of Alkasso admitted knowledge of those arrangements. (There was also price fixing, which will be discussed later.) There remained for determination the question of the legality of such allocations under the Sherman Act, and whether or not, if illegal under the Sherman Act, they were nevertheless exempt because of the provisions of the Webb–Pomerene Act. The court found that in view of the decision in *National Lead,* there was no doubt of the violation of the Sherman Act. The court also had no trouble resolving the issue as to the Webb–Pomerene Act, as posed. It declared:

. . . [T]o hold in this case that defendants, by employing the medium of an export association, may restrain our foreign trade with impunity, uninhibited by the sanctions and proscriptions of the Sherman Act, would be to ignore the plain intent of the statute. To remove cartel agreements, if made by export associations organized under the [Webb–Pomerene] Act, from the comprehensive ban of the Sherman Act, while at the same time condemning similar agreements by others, would be to overlook the fact that it was the evil of restraint on commerce which Congress sought to extirpate, and not the creation of a preferred class which was to be free to continue the evil.

Needless to say, the court held that in light of the import of the Webb–Pomerene Act when read as a whole, and of its legislative history, and "contemporaneous interpretations of the antitrust laws," export associations do not have a license to enter into cartel agreements. Such agreements are not those "agreements in the course of export trade" that the Webb Act places beyond the reach of the Sherman law. The allocations agreed to would foreclose American competitors of those Webb–Pomerene associations from the foreign markets concerned, and "it is unreasonable per se, to foreclose competitors from any substantial market."

In many of the classic agreements to allocate territories the parties attempted to camouflage their design by using the licensing of patents or trademarks as the vehicle for effecting the market allocations. They tried to rely on the fact, discussed more fully in Chapter 9, that in the proper exercise of intellectual property rights, certain restrictive agreements may be permitted. In the previously discussed *National Lead* case, for example, the Titanium Pigment Company, a U.S. subsidiary of National Lead, granted a patent license to Titan A/S (TAS), a Norwegian company, for every one of its existing and future patents related to titanium for use outside of North and South America. TAS granted a similar license to the Titanium Pigment Company for use within North and Central America. The agreement was to continue for sixteen years and be automatically renewed for successive ten-year periods. Each agreed not to question the other's patents. Sublicensees were to be required to abide by these agreements also. In reviewing this aspect of the case the United States District Court for the Southern District of New York succinctly pointed out the lengths to which the parties had gone:

The system of territorial allocation and suppression of trans-Atlantic traffic in titanium compounds and pigments cannot be justified as ancillary to the grant of a license under a patent. True, the network of agreements did involve cross-licensing of patents—but it was not limited thereto. The agreements applied to patents not yet issued and to inventions not yet imagined. They applied to commerce beyond the scope of any patents. They extended to a time beyond the duration of any then-existing patent. . . . They embraced acknowledgement of patent validity with respect to patents not yet issued, nor applied for, and concerning inventions not yet conceived. . . . They extended to countries, such as China, where no system of patent monopolies exists.

The courts have thus been able to perceive and brush aside many guises employed by international cartels in seeking to justify their world allocation of territories among firms who would otherwise be competitors.

Price Fixing

Agreements among competitors to fix prices, because they inherently impair the competitive process, are deemed per se violations of the Sherman Act, assuming that U.S. commerce is affected. Price fixing is often effectuated by direct express or tacit agreements to do so, but it may also be accomplished indirectly by agreements to control production, or to maintain quotas on exports or imports with respect to certain territories.

The quota approach was presented in the *Alkasso* case with reference to foreign markets. As we have seen, the defendants admitted the execution of agreements that among other things, fixed prices in territories other than the United States. Pointing to a lack of any specific reference to the United States in the agreements, the defendants claimed that the United States was not included in the price-fixing scheme. The court did not agree. It found that on the basis of evidence of the "remarkable" stability of the domestic price structure, as well as other evidence, the export association was used by defendants as a means of removing surplus caustic soda from the domestic market in order to maintain the current price. As part of that scheme, in order to neutralize the price-depressing effect that the existing surplus of caustic soda had on the market, defendants stored soda with Alkasso until preferential exports could be made.

Finally, the court waved aside as not necessarily warranted by the evidence defendants' contention that the comparatively small percentage of exports to total production would prove to be an ineffective device for domestic price maintenance. It found that defendants' conduct nevertheless materially interfered with free interchange. It cited *Socony Vacuum* and *Alcoa* as authority, stating that the facts came within the rule that declares

> illegal any agreement for the purchase of distress or surplus material amounting to a small percentage of the total product where it is shown that such practice would materially interfere with the free interchange of those competitive forces which ultimately determine the commodity's going price.

Notwithstanding the general per se rule, it is important to remember that when a price-fixing agreement is made internationally there must still be proof of a substantial effect on U.S. trade for application of the U.S. antitrust laws (see Chapter 3). Where price fixing in foreign markets does have such an effect on U.S. commerce, for example, by dampening U.S. exports, then the law is applicable. If, on the other hand, the effect is minimal, or "peripheral," as in *Alfred Bell & Co., Ltd.* v. *Catalda Fine Arts, Inc.,* a 1947 case in the United States District Court for the Southern District of New York (affirmed in 1951 in the United States Court of Appeals for the Second Circuit), the price fixing will not be held illegal. In *Alfred Bell* the price-fixing charge was put forth as an "unclean hands" defense in a U.S. copyright infringement suit. The price-fixing provision was expressly restricted to Great Britain and Ireland and did not cover sales in the United States, nor was there evidence that the provision was imposed with U.S. sales in mind.

Boycotts and Refusals to Deal

Although the capacity to select those persons with whom one wishes to trade is normally considered within the realm of business discretion, refusals to deal may, depending on their setting, involve significant antitrust implications. As the Attorney General's 1955 Report points out,

> [u]nlike the actual terms in a sale of goods, refusals to deal are not expressly governed by any particular antitrust provision. Instead, the validity of any refusal to deal may depend on the Sherman Act's prohibitions on contracts, monopolization and combinations in restraint of trade; the Clayton Act's control on price discriminations and exclusive arrangements; as well as the general ban on "unfair methods of competition" in Section 5 of the Federal Trade Commission Act.

Because refusals to deal necessarily limit the number of parties eligible to participate in the related transactions, they have the inherent characteristic of restraining trade. An agreement of several persons to engage in a concerted refusal to deal—commonly designated as a group boycott—would therefore be tantamount to a "combination . . . or conspiracy in restraint of trade." Such exclusions by joint action have been deemed so pernicious that "group boycotts" are held to constitute per se violations of Section 1 of the Act. Conversely, because a refusal to deal involving only the actions of a single individual is not, by definition, a concerted refusal, it cannot be construed as violating Section 1. However, to establish the existence of a concerted refusal, it is not necessary that an *express* agreement be shown. The court may find the existence of an agreement as *implied* from the conduct and actions of the parties. For example, a supplier's decision to discontinue sales to a discount dealer after he has received complaints about the latter from several other customers would probably be construed as not a truly "unilateral" decision, but as a manifestation of an unlawful, albeit tacit, agreement to boycott the discounter.

Moreover, even an individual refusal to deal is not necessarily immune from antitrust scrutiny. If such individual action can, by reason of the market power of the firm concerned and the other attendant facts, be characterized as an attempt to create a monopoly, it will be deemed a violation of Section 2 of the Sherman Act. A refusal to accord nondiscriminatory pricing or promotional benefits can be a violation of Section 2 of the Robinson–Patman Act.. In addition, as we shall see in the next chapter, an insistence on dealing only on a prescribed basis, such as an exclusive arrangement or tie-in sales, may raise problems under Section 3 of the Clayton Act and Section 5 of the Federal Trade Commission Act.

As noted, a concerted refusal to deal constitutes a per se violation of Section 1 of the Sherman Act. Accordingly, if there is a concerted refusal to deal, considerations involving the purpose of the group boycott are not relevant. This principle was established in *Fashion Originators' Guild of America, Ltd.* v. *FTC,* a 1941 landmark Supreme Court case involving a concerted refusal to deal undertaken by the Fashion Originators' Guild (the guild), an association of manufacturers of original-design dresses. The members of the guild agreed to refuse to sell such dresses to retailers who also handled dresses copied or "pirated" from these original designs. The Federal Trade Commission refused to hear evidence on the injurious effects of "style piracy," on the ground that the combination was per se illegal under the Sherman Act. Both the court of appeals and the United States Supreme Court upheld the commission's decision. The Supreme Court observed that even if style piracy were an acknowledged wrong, private coercive action was not the appropriate remedy.

Many boycott arrangements result from efforts to "protect" an industry from price-cutting practices or from defaulting customers. Both these considerations, among others, were present in the complex *United States* v. *Watchmakers of Switzerland Information Center* case, other aspects of which we have discussed in earlier chapters. In a series of private agreements several American and Swiss manufacturers and trade associations combined to inhibit the manufacture of watches and watch parts in the United States, to the benefit of the Swiss watch industry. The "Collective Convention," to which these parties adhered, embraced various refusals to deal. Thus, the parties would not deal in products made or sold by firms who were not parties to the Convention and would not aid persons dealing in such competitive products; they would not sell watch parts for manufacturing purposes or certain watchmaking machines to U.S. watch manufacturers. In addition, the parties maintained and circulated "blacklists" in an effort to boycott firms who violated the agreements, firms in the United States who engaged in price cutting of Swiss watches, and customers with a history of financial irresponsibility. The United States District Court for the Southern District of New York held all of these agreements, including the agreement to blacklist, illegal under Section 1 of the Sherman Act, on the authority of *Fashion Originators' Guild* and related cases. The court observed that, "[t]he illegality of defendants' action cannot be cured by a showing that compliance with the blacklist was not always rigidly enforced."

An illegal refusal to deal may be an ingredient of a conspiracy to divide markets. In 1940 two American firms, Bausch & Lomb Optical Company and Carl Zeiss, Inc., as well as Carl Zeiss (a "corporation or association existing under the laws of Germany" and the parent company of Carl Zeiss, Inc.), were indicted for violating Section 1 of the Sherman Act by engaging in a conspiracy to divide the world trade in military optical instruments. One of the counts of the indictment charged that Carl Zeiss, Inc., had refused to sell military optical instruments for use in the United States. The firm protested that this was not an indictable offense inasmuch as it had never manufactured, produced, imported, or traded in such instruments. The court acknowleged that the refusal to sell was not by itself actionable, but that the indictment against Carl Zeiss, Inc., should stand, because the refusal might prove to be an *element* of a conspiracy to divide markets.

Industry "seal-of-approval" programs may be deemed the equivalent of illegal group boycotts, where their effect is arbitrarily to preclude would-be competitors from the market. In the classic case of *Radiant Burners, Inc.* v. *Peoples Gas Light & Coke Co.,* there was challenged a program of the American Gas Association wherein a seal of approval was awarded to gas burners which met the association's tests for safety, utility, and durability. The plaintiff, whose burners had not received the seal, brought an action under Section 1 of the Sherman Act against the association and some of its members, charging that the failure to accord it a seal was arbitrary and capricious, that the utility members of the association refused to provide gas for the plaintiff's burners because these had no seal, and that the pattern of conduct represented a conspiracy to exclude plaintiff from the market. The Supreme Court ruled that the plaintiff had stated a valid claim under the Sherman Act, specifically a "conspiratorial refusal to provide gas for use in plaintiff's Radiant Burners," barring plaintiff from the market.

It should be noted that an element of the plaintiff's claim was that the association's seal program was not based on objective standards. This is one factor that, in a proper case, may distinguish the product approval and standardization cases from the usual per se illegality boycott situation: if there are objective standards for product discrimination established and a genuine public need for such discrimination, the program may pass antitrust muster under a rule-of-reason approach.

An exclusionary program in the international context was successfully challenged recently by the Justice Department in a case involving the American Society of Mechanical Engineers (ASME). Because of the safety hazards presented by boiler and pressure vessel explosions, the ASME promulgated a Boiler and Pressure Vessel Code establishing minimum construction specifications. ASME issued a stamp to manufacturers who were found to be making products in conformity with the code. The presence of the stamp mark on a boiler or pressure vessel became a prerequisite for purchase by many customers and acceptance by many state authorities. The Justice Department brought an action under the Sherman Act, alleging that, inasmuch as safe foreign products could not obtain the ASME stamp, the implementation of the code and stamp programs represented a conspiracy "to discriminate against and exclude from sale in the United States qualified boilers and pressure vessels manufactured outside the United States and Canada. . . . " This arrangement was dissolved by a consent decree directing ASME to put into effect a "fair, reasonable and nondiscriminatory procedure enabling foreign manufacturers who meet the requirements of the ASME to qualify for and receive ASME Certificates of Authorization and Symbol Stamps on an equal basis with domestic manufacturers. . . . " Once again, the thrust of the antitrust challenge was not at the safety program itself, the need for which was not contested, but at the arbitrary and discriminatory way in which it was implemented.

A more subtle illustration of improper association action is provided by the "bottleneck boycott." Such a situation may arise where an association gains control over a facility significant to the industry operation and through its exclusive membership practices precludes access to nonmember competitors. An illustration of a "bottleneck boycott" in the international field—with the target again imported products—was presented in a recent Sherman Act case involving restriction of access to the trade shows conducted by industry associations in the material-handling equipment field. Membership in these associations was limited to firms which domestically manufactured at least 75 per cent of the equipment which they sold in the United States, and association members were barred from exhibiting foreign-manufactured equipment at trade shows. Nonmembers of the association were excluded from displaying in the trade shows, which were important avenues for access to the market place. As in the ASME case, the legality of the arrangement was challenged by the Justice Department in an action that was subsequently settled by a consent decree. The terms of this decree, although allowing some minimum domestic manufacturing as a qualification for association membership, required that any person manufacturing equipment for sale within the United States be allowed to exhibit his products in the associations' trade shows. Moreover, association members are to be permitted to display at the trade shows equipment manufactured abroad.

In sum, any conduct in the nature of a concerted refusal to deal or concerted exclusion runs a serious risk of illegality under the Sherman Act. A naked boycott of particular firms will, however well intentioned, be per se illegal. An industry seal of approval or standardization program will usually be tested under the rule of reason and may pass antitrust muster if it is sound in its purposes, observes due process in its procedures, and is objective in its criteria. Given the severe anticompetitive effects of exclusion, however, and the skepticism with which the enforcement agencies generally regard industry self-regulation, such programs must be prudently evaluated beforehand and, if undertaken, should be implemented only with the greatest care.

Monopolization

We have seen that, expressed in simplified terms, the subject with which Section 1 of the Sherman Act deals is agreements in restraint of trade, and that Section 2, briefly, is concerned with monopolization and attempts to monopolize. Specifically, Section 2 makes it a misdemeanor for a person to commit any one of the following three separate offenses: (1) to monopolize, (2) to attempt to monopolize, and (3) to combine or conspire with any other person to monopolize any part of the trade or commerce among the states, or with foreign nations.

Section 2 is primarily concerned with a situation that Section 1 cannot reach, that in which a single firm achieves or seeks to achieve a position of such size and power that it is capable of restraining trade by its own, unaided efforts. Nonetheless, Sections 1 and 2 are related and sometimes overlap to some extent. There is a relationship in subject matter, in that a monopoly is a species of restraint of trade. Thus, conduct violative of Section 1 when part of an agreement, such as control over price and exclusion of competitors, may constitute essential ingredients of monopolization under Section 2. Moreover, because Section 2 encompasses combinations and conspiracies to monopolize, joint action which severely threatens competition in an industry may violate both Sections 1 and 2. Many of the cases involving international cartel arrangements have, in fact, entailed government charges under both of the sections.

Monopoly, or *monopoly power,* has been defined as the "holding of such dominance within an industry as to command the power to fix or control prices in or exclude competition from the industry." That which is forbidden is not the status of monopoly, but the act or planned or attempted act of monopolization. Therefore, neither mere size of a firm nor the virtual absence of competition within an industry is illegal in and of itself. A monopoly position may, moreover, be lawfully obtained in certain situations. In some instances monopolies or exclusive privileges may be granted by federal, state, or local governments because of the peculiar nature of an industry or the needs of an area. (In such cases the government will usually also impose regulation to preclude the abuse of the monopoly status.) Lawful monopoly may also conceivably be "thrust" upon a firm, because of its unequaled efficiency or product or because, as a practical matter, the market can only support one supplier. Unlawful monopolization, on the other hand, constitutes the attainment of monopoly power by unfair means or the use of that power unfairly to maintain the monopoly and exclude effective competition.

It is usually said that in order to show that monopolization has taken place, it is necessary to establish both that the firm has obtained monopoly power and that it has an intent to monopolize. However, where monopoly power has been attained, specific intent need not be shown and it is generally presumed that intent exists, in the sense that one is presumed to intend the foreseeable effects of his actions. The key thus becomes whether monopoly power exists and, if so, whether it has been unlawfully obtained or exercised.

The degree of market power that must be evidenced to establish the existence of monopoly power has not been definitely established. Where power to control prices or to exclude competitors from the market cannot specifically be shown, the government will seek to have the existence of monopoly power presumed by showing that the firm in question controls a massive percentage of its relevant market. No precise percentage has been established by the courts in this regard because the impact of a firm's commanding a particular percentage share of the market varies with the industry setting. Percentages of less than 50 have been held clearly insufficient to indicate a monopoly position, and percentages of between 60 and 65 have been characterized as doubtful. A percentage over 90 has been deemed clearly sufficient. As a result, if a corporation has the power to fix prices or to exclude competition in the market in which it competes, or if it dominates roughly 75 per cent of the market in which it competes, there is a good chance that a court will hold that it possesses the requisite power for monopolization.

In view of this test for determining market power, ascertaining the scope of the relevant "market" often becomes all-important. The term *relevant market* involves a resolution of two questions. The first is a determination of the *geographic* boundaries of the market. A relevant market may include a portion of the United States, the entire United States, or even areas outside the United States where the nation's foreign commerce is concerned. The geographic bounds of the market are usually determined by an examination of the areas in which the particular firm actually operates or competes. Of course, it is possible for a firm that operates in a broad area, as in world trade, to be charged with monopolizing a narrower and yet distinct portion of that area such as the United States or a part thereof.

In addition to the geographic factor, the term *relevant market* contemplates the definition of the *product (or service)* line in terms of which market power will be measured. Defining the relevant product market strictly along the lines of the accused firm's product is not fair if that product is completely interchangeable in the market place with certain other types of products. Physical characteristics, uses, nature and cost of production, distinctiveness of customers, pricing, and sensitivity to price changes are all factors that go into determining the similarities of two products for relevant product market purposes. Interchangeabilty at the customer level in terms of use and price carries heavy weight in the making of this determination.

The problems involved in determining what constitutes the relevant product market are illustrated by the 1956 Supreme Court's decision in the "Cellophane" case. The government had charged du Pont with violating Section 2 by monopolization of the commerce in cellophane. Du Pont produced almost 75 per cent of the cellophane sold in the United States, but cellophane constituted less than 20 per cent of all sales of flexible packaging materials. The Supreme Court did not question that du Pont had monopoly power over cellophane itself and acknowledged also that cellophane had advantages over other types of flexible packaging materials. But the Court found further that cellophane had to meet competition from other materials in every one of its uses, that a very high degree of "functional interchangeability" existed between the various products, and that high cross-elasticity of demand among the materials existed in that customers would switch from one to another in response to slight price or quality changes. Hence, the Court concluded, cellophane was just a part of the flexible packaging material market and du Pont could not be found to be monopolizing this partial market. The warning should be added that, the *Cellophane* case notwithstanding, the government often succeeds in seeking to keep the relevant product market narrow by pointing out elements of distinctiveness in the product allegedly being monopolized.

As we observed earlier, all monopoly is not illegal. A determination that a firm controls a substantial percentage of a relevant market is not in itself a finding that this firm has transgressed the law. In addition, there must be a finding that the firm obtained this position through unfair or unlawful business practices or, if the position of power was properly obtained, there must be a finding that the firm is seeking to maintain its position by unfair or illegal means. The unfair or illegal methods in question generally include restraints of trade and other practices embraced by the various antitrust laws, such as exclusive dealing, refusals to deal (individual or collective), tie-in sales, discrimination, and corporate acquisitions or mergers. However, a finding of monopolization may occur even without evidence of acts that are predatory or unfair when there is sufficient size coupled with actions that indicate a general intent to monopolize. The best-known characterization of such monopolization is found in the *Alcoa* case, another aspect of which we considered in Chapter 3. The Aluminum Company of America was charged with monopolization of the virgin aluminum ingot field, of which it held 90 per cent. To the defendant's claim that it had done nothing wrongful to achieve this position, the United States Court of Appeals replied that unlawful monopolization had taken place nonetheless because Alcoa was not the "passive beneficiary of a monopoly":

> It was not inevitable that [Alcoa] should always anticipate increases in the demand for ingot and be prepared to supply them. Nothing compelled it to keep doubling and redoubling its capacity before others entered the field. It insists that it never excluded competitors; but we can think of no more effective exclusion. . . .

In addition to monopolization, Section 2 also prohibits attempts and combinations or conspiracies to monopolize. With respect to attempts and conspiracies, there is no requirement that the firm or firms involved actually occupy a dominant position in the relevant market. The firm or firms may fail in their efforts yet be guilty of an attempt or conspiracy, so long as their position is sufficiently strong as to pose a threat of achieving monopoly status. In addition to the dangerous possibility of success, there must be evidence that the firms possess a specific intent to monopolize. This may be inferred from their committing acts or practices that, if performed with success, would result in monopoly.

Monopolization in Foreign Trade

A single firm will seldom be able to monopolize or attempt to monopolize world trade. In many cases, however, a number of firms, dominant in their own countries, have been found guilty of conspiring together to monopolize trade on an international scale. The cartels that we considered earlier in this chapter often involved such conspiracies and, to the extent that they affected the commerce of the United States, incurred charges under both Sections 1 and 2 of the Sherman Act.

In the 1911 Supreme Court case of *United States* v. *American Tobacco Co.,* various American firms and two English corporations engaged in the tobacco trade were charged with monopolization and attempted monopolization under Section 2 of the Sherman Act, as well as a conspiracy in restraint of trade under Section 1. It will be recalled that a division of markets restricting, among other things, sales into and from the United States was involved. The Supreme Court held that the defendants had monopolized interstate and foreign commerce, finding that they had obtained "dominion and control over the tobacco trade." The facts were found to be sufficient to "justify the inference that the intention existed to use the power of the combination as a vantage ground to further monopolize the trade in tobacco . . . either by driving competitors out of business or compelling them to become parties to the combination. . . ."

The *General Electric* incandescent lamp case likewise contained counts filed under both Sections 1 and 2 in an international market-sharing setting. General Electric was found, by reason of its dominant position in the industry, its restrictive agreements with other firms, its use of foreign subsidiaries to eliminate foreign competition, and other activities to have monopolized the U.S. incandescent lamp industry in violation of Section 2. N.V. Philips, a Dutch firm, was also found to have violated Section 2 by aiding General Electric to maintain the latter's monopoly. As we observed earlier, the lack of a specific intent to restrain U.S. trade or to participate in monopolization did not absolve Philips because the necessary general intent could be imputed from the inevitable effects of its activities.

In sum, it is well established that market division and other agreements between American and foreign firms that result in virtual domination of a product market, to the detriment of U.S. commerce, are likely to fall afoul of Section 2 of the Sherman Act, as well as Section 1. There are varied situations involving foreign trade in which it is clear that Section 2 could be invoked. Let us assume, for example, that the Prosperity Company, a U.S. corporation, has attained by proper means an 80 per cent market share of the office furniture sold in the United States. We will assume further that, of the remaining 20 per cent, 15 per cent is shipped in by one Canadian firm. If Prosperity Company were to acquire the Canadian company, or, alternatively, enter into an agreement with the latter providing for restriction of the latter's shipments to the United States, there is little doubt that Prosperity Company would be guilty of violating Section 2. By taking over or curtailing the imports, which are a significant competitive factor in the U.S. market, it would be unlawfully monopolizing the relevant market.

An even more aggravated case involving the seizure of control over imports was presented in the *Sisal* case. As we saw, several American corporations and a Mexican corporation were charged with plotting to become the sole U.S. importers of sisal from Mexico, which was the only significant source of the product. This stranglehold on imports, tantamount to a stranglehold on the market, was labeled by the Supreme Court a "successful plan to destroy competition and to control and monopolize the purchase, importation and sale of sisal," and hence violative of Sections 1 and 2 of the Sherman Act.

Would a conspiracy or individual firm action that controlled or cut off all imports into the United States of a commodity amount to unlawful monopolization if imports represented only a small percentage of the relevant product market in the United States? Arguably, the import trade itself can be the subject of a monopolization charge, even if there is no monopoly established over the interstate trade. As a practical matter, however, the likely situations in which a monopolization case involving imports will be brought are where either (1) the U.S. firm or firms are dominant in the product market and act to cut off imports, with the latter constituting a significant part of the limited competition, or (2) the U.S. market is largely dependent on imports for supply, with action being taken to control that supply, as in *Sisal,* and in other cases including the *International Nickel* decision (Canadian company was primary world producer of nickel), and the *De Beers* case in which foreign defendants produced abroad 95 per cent of the world's diamonds (this case was dismissed on grounds not relevant to this discussion).

A firm or firms may also take action which restricts or controls *exports* from the United States, and this could be the focus or an ingredient of a monopolization charge under Section 2 in a proper case. In the *Minnesota Mining* case, the dominant American producers of coated abrasives were charged with violating both Sections 1 and 2 by establishing joint factories abroad, thus restricting U.S. exports. The court ruled that an unreasonable restraint of trade in violation of Section 1 had been established, but did not reach the issue of whether this also constituted monopolization under Section 2. It would appear, in any event, that the export commerce in a product is sufficiently distinctive and separable to be the subject of a monopolization action, even if domestic commerce is not monopolized or restrained.

Finally, efforts by a single firm or by conspiracy to control transportation facilities of significance to U.S. commerce and firms have been held to be subject to the monopolization proscriptions of Section 2.

In sum, Section 1 of the Sherman Act broadly embraces agreements deemed to restrain unreasonably the interstate or foreign commerce of the United States, whether the challenged activity is undertaken in the U.S. or abroad. Section 2 proscribes efforts by a single firm or by firms in combination to obtain, maintain, or expand a monopoly position in a relevant market, to the detriment of the interstate or foreign commerce of the United States, and also without regard to where the challenged activity is physically undertaken.

chapter **6**

Relations with Suppliers and Customers

The relationship between seller and purchaser, whether formalized by a written agreement or simply reflected in a course of dealing, is at the heart of local, national, and, indeed, international commerce. Although a sales transaction between businessmen may be manifested by only a purchase order and an invoice, where dealings are at all complex or the relationship of the parties a continuing one, there is likely to be an understanding that certain attendant obligations beyond those of the individual sales transaction are entailed.

Some of the obligations contemplated by the parties may affect competition, and these fall within the realm of the antitrust and trade regulation laws. The manufacturer, for example, may want a distributor who, besides buying his product, will commit himself to purchasing from him only, to purchasing the manufacturer's entire range of products, or to reselling in a certain way and at an agreed price. The distributor may, for his part, have expectations that the manufacturer will not sell to other distributors in the area and that the manufacturer will supply him with all of his requirements of the product. Other types of obligations and restraints may be envisioned by the parties as necessary incidents of their relationship and yet raise antitrust questions.

The restraints in question are, in antitrust parlance, referred to as "vertical" inasmuch as they are not entered into between competitors but between links in the chain of distribution that runs from manufacturer or supplier to distributor, retailer, or user. Three basic types of vertical restraints that raise antitrust questions, and that we will examine, are exclusive arrangements, tying agreements, and limitations on price and other conditions of resale. There is little case authority on the application of the antitrust laws to the various vertical arrangements in international trade, so perforce, much of the discussion in this chapter is an extrapolation of principles drawn from interstate commerce cases.

The pertinent laws are Section 1 of the Sherman Act, Section 3 of the Clayton Act, and Section 5 of the the Federal Trade Commission Act. The Sherman and FTC Act provisions are, as we have seen, in the nature of general prohibitions against trade restraints. Section 3 of the Clayton Act was designed specifically to deal with distribution devices and reads as follows:

> It shall be unlawful for any person engaged in commerce, in the course of such commerce, to lease or make a sale or contract for sale of goods, wares, merchandise, machinery, supplies, or other commodities, whether patented or unpatented, for use, consumption, or resale within the United States or any Territory thereof or the District of Columbia or any insular possession or other place under the jurisdiction of the United States, or fix a price charged therefor, or discount from, or rebate upon, such price, on the condition, agreement, or understanding that the lessee or purchaser thereof shall not use or deal in the goods, wares, merchandise, machinery, supplies, or other commodities of a competitor or competitors of the lessor or seller, where the effect of such lease, sale, or contract for sale or such condition, agreement, or understanding may be to substantially lessen competition or tend to create a monopoly in any line of commerce.

Under the phrasing of this provision it is applicable only if the seller or lessor is "engaged in commerce" and makes the transaction "in the course of such commerce." Because *commerce* is defined under the Clayton Act as encompassing "trade or commerce among the several States and with foreign nations," international transactions may be covered. However, the Act's further language limits the statute to sales, contracts of sale, and leases of goods "for use, consumption or resale within the United States" and places under U.S. jurisdiction. This language would seem to exclude sales by American firms abroad (exports), as distinct from sales by foreign firms into the U.S. (imports). A significant portion of United States international trade is thereby beyond the reach of Section 3. Such foreign sales might conceivably, however, be the subject of an action under Section 1 of the Sherman Act or Section 5 of the FTC Act. Of course, none of the three statutes can apply unless the requisite anticompetitive impact on U.S. commerce is established.

Because Section 3 deals only with sales or leases of commodities, such transactions as sales of service, loans of money, and consignment arrangements are also excluded from the statute's coverage. Anticompetitive agreements employing such features may nevertheless be subject to attack under Section 5 of the FTC Act and, in aggravated situations, Section 1 of the Sherman Act.

Section 3 makes a condition, agreement, or understanding that a competitor's goods will not be used or dealt in unlawful only where the transaction or series of transactions are of sufficient magnitude that their effect "may be to substantially lessen competition or tend to create a monopoly in any line of commerce." Only those arrangements that in practice may produce serious anticompetitive effects are forbidden. It is important to note the use of the word *may*. A finding of illegality under Section 3 as well as Section 5 of the FTC Act, unlike Section 1 of the Sherman Act, does not require evidence of actual adverse effects on the competitive structure. It requires only that such effects be *probable* if the particular arrangement is allowed to continue. We turn now to a more specific discussion of the practices in question.

Vertical Restraints on Price

As we have seen, agreements among competitors to fix prices are illegal per se under Section 1 of the Sherman Act. Agreements between seller and purchaser fixing the latter's resale prices, known as resale-price-maintenance agreements, are also illegal per se as price fixing, unless the exemption provided by the Miller–Tydings and McGuire Acts applies. Under this limited exemption provided by Congress, where state law permits, no antitrust liability will attach to a resale-price-maintenance contract involving a trademarked or brand-name product in competition with similar products. This exception is commonly referred to as the "fair trade" exception, and it is based on the rationale that certain resale-price-maintenance contracts should be allowed to protect the manufacturer's good will attached to his trademark or brand name.

The limitations to the exception are important. There must be actual competition existing between the manufacturer's products and those produced by others, and the agreement must be truly vertical in nature, i.e., not between competitors. Moreover, the agreements are legal only in those states that have enacted appropriate fair trade laws. In order to make the fair trade system effective, state laws have traditionally included "nonsigner" provisions, binding to the manufacturer's resale price even retailers who have not agreed to maintain it. Although seventeen states have upheld such provisions, twenty-six states have ruled invalid on state constitutional grounds either that state's fair trade act or the nonsigner provisions in it.

In states that do not have a fair trade law, the manufacturer must avoid any semblance of a resale-price-maintenance agreement with wholesalers or retailers. Technically he still has the legal right, acting unilaterally, to refuse to deal with firms that do not conform to his suggested resale prices. However, the Supreme Court has indicated that the slightest step beyond a mere refusal to sell may result in a finding of an agreement, and hence illegality. Such limited moves toward enforcement of the policy as the collecting of information on nonadherents to the suggested price and the dissemination of expressions of the policy to customers may cross the line of unlawfulness in this area.

The import of the law of resale-price maintenance for international business seems reasonably straightforward. Because price fixing is illegal under the Sherman Act, resale-price maintenance not protected by the state fair trade law exemption will be reached if it restrains either interstate or American foreign commerce. For example, a British manufacturer of high fidelity speakers might wish to enter into price-maintenance agreements with American wholesalers. Such agreements would be illegal if applied to resales by the wholesalers in states without a fair trade law. Furthermore, if the British manufacturer merely set suggested resale prices, and followed up with a program of refusing to deal with any wholesaler who departed from the suggested price, he would have to avoid very carefully any suggestion of an agreement with any other party in carrying out his program. If the manufacturer enlisted the aid of its wholesalers in identifying other wholesalers who were not complying, for example, an illegal combination would be formed.

In the converse situation, wherein an American supplier fixed prices abroad through agreements with foreign distributors, a significant effect on the commerce of the United States would be unlikely. Such an arrangement would therefore not be covered by U.S. antitrust law, although foreign antitrust laws might be applicable.

It should be remembered that price fixing in any guise is impermissible where U.S. commerce is likely to be affected. Even agreements specifying the *maximum* resale price that can be levied have been struck down. The free competitive market is to control the pricing mechanism.

Territorial and Customer Restraints on Resale

As in the case of price fixing, vertical restraints limiting resale in terms of territory or customer may be reached under Section 1 of the Sherman Act or Section 5 of the FTC Act. We have already seen that *horizontal* agreements, those among direct competitors at the same level of distribution, that restrain the sales activities of the parties geographically or by customer categories are per se illegal, so long as U.S. interstate or foreign commerce is involved. Until recently, however, *vertical* agreements of this sort between companies at different levels of distribution had generally not been challenged as being illegal. The most important questions in this context center around the legality of agreements between a manufacturer and its distributors, limiting the resale territories of the latter. The arguments for such restraints have been that they are conducive to an orderly marketing of the product, inducing each distributor to serve his designated area fully while protecting him from forays into his area by the neighboring distributors. Similar arguments have been made to support restrictions as to the types of customers the distributor may serve.

In March 1963, the Supreme Court was faced with territorial and customer restrictions in the *White Motor Company* case. The Court noted that the case was the first one it had considered involving such restrictions in a *vertical* context and concluded that the trial court should explore the facts fully, because too little was known of the actual impact of such restrictions to rule that they constituted per se violations of the Sherman Act. Having been forced to the expense of carrying an appeal to the Supreme Court in order to secure trial on the merits under a rule of reason, however, White Motor ultimately succumbed to the government's attack, accepting a consent decree in 1964 in which White agreed to abandon the challenged territorial and customer restrictions.

The issues of customer and territorial restrictions came before the Supreme Court for the second time in 1967, in the landmark case of *United States* v. *Arnold, Schwinn & Co.* The government had attacked under the Sherman Act Schwinn's requirement that wholesale distributors resell its bicycles only within designated territories and only to franchised Schwinn dealers in those territories. Also challenged were requirements that the franchised dealers not resell to unfranchised dealers, particularly discount retailers. Although Schwinn is one of the oldest and best-known U.S. bicycle producers, its market share had declined from 22.5 per cent in 1951 to 12.8 per cent in 1961, largely as a result of the company's emphasis upon a quality product offered for sale almost exclusively through full-service bicycle shops. Notwithstanding Schwinn's eroding market share, the government's contention was that the various restrictions were clearly anticompetitive in that they prevented "intrabrand" competition.

In its decision, the Court fully examined the extensive evidence adduced at trial and then announced a per se rule with respect to a portion of the Schwinn program. The Court distinguished between the sale-for-resale situation and the sale by consignment or agency and defined an agency arrangement as one "[w]here the manufacturer retains title, dominion, and risk with respect to the product and the position and function of the dealer in question are, in fact, indistinguishable from those of an agent or salesman of the manufacturer. . . ." A consignment is a type of agency arrangement that may take many forms but that is essentially the transfer of a product to a dealer for sale to a third party with title remaining in the transferor until sale is effected. The dealer acts merely as an agent.

The Court declared that in the *sale* to an independent dealer situation it was "unreasonable without more for a manufacturer to seek to restrict and confine areas or persons with which an article may be traded after the manufacturer has parted with dominion over it." The Court declined to enunciate a per se rule in the situation where the manufacturer had consigned the product to an agent and retained title over it until ultimate sale. Such consignment arrangements, rather, were to be evaluated by the rule of reason and might be found acceptable if justified by legitimate business purposes and if the restraint is merely ancillary to those purposes. The presence of price fixing, the Court added, would necessarily doom restraints, even in the context of agency or consignment. (This distinction between independent traders and agents also appears in certain aspects of the rules of competition of the European Economic Community, which are discussed in Chapter 11.)

Furthermore, the Court suggested two possible exceptions to its newly announced per se rule. These, known as the "newcomer in the business" and "failing company" exceptions, may permit territorial or customer limitations by a manufacturer falling within either category.

Because the *Schwinn* case was the first case in which the Supreme Court had reviewed vertically imposed territorial and customer restrictions on their merits, it is difficult to understand the Court's apparent willingness to announce a per se rule based upon examination of only one fact situation. In at least several subsequent Supreme Court decisions, various of the justices have interpreted *Schwinn* as not establishing a broad and inflexible rule of per se illegality for all vertical territorial restrictions. Other U.S. federal courts have also interpreted *Schwinn* as not creating a broad per se rule prohibiting all vertical territorial or customer restraints.

Regardless of the legal confusion that *Schwinn* and its progeny have generated, however, the Department of Justice has made clear its conclusion that any restraint on intrabrand competition is inherently suspect. Given the increased tendency of both the Department of Justice and the Federal Trade Commission to file complaints concerning such activities when they become aware of them, the prudent businessman is well advised to consider the risk that such vertically imposed restrictions will be treated as being per se unlawful, and to seek to accomplish his marketing goals through use of such approaches as assigning areas of primary responsibility and other practices the legality of which is not in issue.

This rule has obvious implications for the foreign supplier, as well as the domestic supplier, who wishes to shape its distribution system in the United States by designating the resale territory or the customers of his own customers. For example, a foreign manufacturer who sells his products to U.S. distributors might want to divide the United States into several exclusive territories and require that each distributor confine his sales to a specified territory. Such an arrangement, unless the application of the newcomer exception or other special circumstances can be invoked, would seem to violate the *Schwinn* stated rule. No case appears to have developed the newcomer justification since *Schwinn* either with respect to a domestic company or in terms of a foreign corporation trying to enter the American market. Prior cases making antitrust allowances for newcomers, however, indicate that, although a small corporation might benefit from the doctrine, it is probable that a large foreign company entering the U.S. market would not find protection as a newcomer. The doctrine seems likely to apply only to small businesses entering a market or struggling to stay in.

Another possibility is that the foreign manufacturer would want to designate the entire United States as the exclusive territory of a particular U.S. distributor, and forbid the distributor to sell outside the country (for example, into Canada) because other distributors have been assigned those markets. There is little question that the manufacturer is entitled to designate one distributor as his exclusive distributor in the United States, that is, the manufacturer may properly commit himself to sell to no other distributors in that area. Moreover, the distributor in question may be told that the United States is his area of primary responsibility, namely, that he is expected to devote his best efforts to covering that territory in seeking to make sales. The objectionable feature of the plan would be the attempt to limit the right of the distributor to deal outside the country. Such a restriction would curtail U.S. exports restraining the foreign commerce of the United States, and thus would probably be illegal per se under the rule of the *Schwinn* case.

Restraints on resale may be vulnerable not only if they inhibit a customer as to where and to whom he can sell, but also as to the form in which he can resell the product. In a decision consistent with the *Schwinn* principles, *United States* v. *Glaxo Group Ltd.,* a Sherman Act challenge was directed against the agreements of some British manufacturers with their American distributors, which included provisions prohibiting the distributors from reselling in bulk form, without the manufacturers' consent, antibiotics purchased from the latter. The court held such restraints on resale to be illegal under the rationale of the *Schwinn* case. In a later opinion on the relief to be fashioned, the court observed that the exclusive distributorship arrangements between the British and American firms were not themselves features of the illegal conduct.

The converse international situation, wherein an American manufacturer attempts to impose resale limitations on foreign distributors, requires application of the same general principles. If the arrangement purports to prevent the distributors from selling in the United States, thus imposing a restraint on American import trade, then the arrangement is likely unlawful. A supplier might, however, restrict the foreign markets of its distributors while not restricting their sales into the United States, without violating the U.S. antitrust laws because, in this context, an adverse effect on U.S. commerce would be unlikely. Such an arrangement would, of course, be subject to the sanctions of any applicable foreign antitrust laws.

Exclusive Distributorships

We have already alluded to the arrangement whereby a supplier desig-
nates a particular distributor or dealer as the "exclusive" one for a particular territory. Such an exclusive arrangement must be carefully differentiated from a vertical territorial resale restriction. In the former, the
supplier is merely binding himself not to deal with other distributors in
the designated territory, and the distributor is left free to sell where and
to whom he pleases. In the latter arrangement, the supplier requires the
distributor not to sell outside the territory. As we saw in the previous
section, such restraints on resale are increasingly being viewed as necessarily anticompetitive and are receiving increasingly harsh antitrust treatment.

Simple exclusive distributorships, in contrast, are normally viewed as
unobjectionable business arrangements. The general leniency of the courts
toward them comes in part because the restraint is viewed as reflecting the
supplier's right to choose with whom he will deal and in part because it is
deemed ancillary to the main purpose of providing the distributor with an
adequate source of supply. Nonetheless, an exclusive distributorship does
restrain the supplier from dealing with other distributors within the
designated territory and therefore forecloses competing distributors within
the territory from access to the supplier's product. Accordingly, it can in
some situations be an improper competitive device, so that its use must be
scrutinized under the rule of reason. The requirements for an exclusive
distributorship to be considered reasonable under the Sherman Act are
that there be other, competing brands of the product readily available on
the market, and that the restraint not extend beyond the confinement of
the supplier's own sales to selected customers.

It is important to note also that it is the substance, and not the form
of an exclusive distributorship that governs. For example, where each of
two competitors appoints the other as its exclusive distributor for a specified
territory, this will be found to be an illegal horizontal agreement to divide
the market. Further, if the establishment of the arrangement does not
represent the independent judgment of the supplier as to his customers,
but rather has been imposed upon him by the distributor, the arrangement
will be suspect. Thus, the unilateral nature of the decision is an important
feature in justifying exclusive distributorships. Finally, even if otherwise
lawful, an exclusive distributorship may be struck down if found to be
part of a general anticompetitive scheme. Thus, in *United States* v. *Imperial
Chemical Industries,* the court found that a British and an American company had conspired to divide the world market and monopolize world
trade. A foreign exclusive distributorship for sporting arms and ammuni-
tion entered into by the American company, and jointly owned by the con-

spirators, was held to be part of and in furtherance of the conspiracy, and was accordingly struck down. The court declined, it should be observed, to alter other distributorships unconnected with the conspiracy, the American manufacturer being held free to designate foreign distributors as its exclusive representatives for their respective countries.

In the context of international business, of course, exclusive distributorships must be examined in terms of their effect on U.S. commerce. In the case of a foreign supplier granting an exclusive distributorship to a domestic distributor, it is American import trade that is subject to restraint because other American distributors within the designated territory cannot buy from the supplier. Because exclusive distributorships are generally permissible, the arrangement is likely to be approved under the rule of reason standard, despite the impact on other U.S. distributors, so long as the latter have access to competitive products and the arrangement reflects a bona fide business decision unhampered by coercion or other restraints. In the converse case of an American supplier and a foreign distributor, it is U.S. export trade that is being limited. Presumably there would be other foreign distributors who would otherwise distribute the American firm's product; the fact that they are unable to order from the American supplier might decrease the supplier's foreign sales, thereby restraining, at least in theory, U.S. export trade. Because this is largely a theoretical restraint, with a highly speculative impact on U.S. commerce, an antitrust challenge would be quite remote, assuming, once again, that the arrangement is not part of a broader conspiracy as was the case in the *ICI* decision.

Other Exclusive Dealing Arrangements

We have thus far considered one limited type of exclusive dealing arrangement, the exclusive distributorship in which a supplier agrees to sell to only one customer within a specified territory. There exist also other types of exclusive dealing relationships, including that in which a customer agrees not to deal in the products of a competitor of his supplier. Agreements of this type commonly are cast into one of two forms. One is the customer's straightforward agreement not to carry a competitor's products; the other, known as a requirements contract, is an agreement by the customer to purchase all of his needs for a product from the particular supplier. Both such forms of agreement may raise antitrust questions because they foreclose competitors of the favored supplier from having access to the customer. Where the customer is a significant factor in the market place, as, for example, a major wholesaler or a chain of retail outlets, the anticompetitive impact of the exclusive arrangement will be obvious.

In domestic antitrust cases, the statute against which such agreements are most often measured is Section 3 of the Clayton Act, which bars those within its coverage where their effect "may be to substantially lessen competition or tend to create a monopoly in any line of commerce." As we earlier observed, in order for Section 3 to apply, the exclusive arrangement must be with respect to a commodity that is used or resold within the United States. Thus, an exclusive dealing contract whereby a foreign distributor, who does not resell into the United States, agrees not to deal in the products of competitors of the American supplier cannot be reached under the Clayton Act. On the other hand, an exclusive dealing contract between a foreign supplier and an American distributor contemplating resale within the United States would be reached by the Clayton Act. Section 1 of the Sherman Act does not have this particular jurisdictional disability in terms of overseas sales, and it can be applied to strike down exclusive dealing arrangements in foreign markets. However, existence of a full-blown trade restraint must normally be shown for invocation of the Sherman Act, as distinct from the "tendency to substantially lessen competition" standard embodied in the Clayton Act.

Section 5 of the Federal Trade Commission Act potentially has the greatest breadth in this area because it may be applied to exclusive dealing without the Clayton Act territorial and subject matter limitations. Moreover, the Supreme Court indicated in *F.T.C.* v. *Brown Shoe Co.* that the competitive effects standard of Section 5 can be even more menacing than that of Section 3, because the "Commission has power under §5 to arrest trade restraints in their incipiency without proof that they amount to an outright violation of §3 of the Clayton Act or other provisions of the antitrust laws." Thus an agreement that for some reason falls short of violating Section 3 may still be held to violate Section 5 if it is anticompetitive in nature and not innocuous in degree.

Neither Section 3 of the Clayton Act nor Section 5 of the FTC Act will apply if the effects or expected effects of the exclusive dealing arrangement are minimal, that is, if the arrangement's tendency is not to "substantially" lessen competition. To evaluate whether any agreement might have the forbidden effects, it is first necessary to determine in what context this evaluation will be made. As interpreted by the courts, this requirement means that the proscribed result must occur in both a product market and a geographic market. The relevant product market may be the subject of argument, with the government seeking to keep it narrow and the corporation wanting to broaden it, but it will often be defined in terms of the commodity covered by the agreement. The relevant geographic market may be a nationwide one or less, and is the "area of effective competition," that to which the supplier under the exclusive arrangement and his competitors normally look for their sales.

In the landmark case of *Tampa Electric Company* v. *Nashville Coal Company,* the Supreme Court explained the test for whether a substantial amount of competition is likely to be foreclosed as follows:

To determine substantiality in a given case, it is necessary to weigh the probable effect of the contract on the relevant area of effective competition, taking into account the relative strength of the parties, the proportionate volume of commerce involved in relation to the total volume of commerce in the relevant market area, and the probable immediate and future effects which pre-emption of that share of the market might have on effective competition therein. It follows that a mere showing that the contract itself involves a substantial number of dollars is ordinarily of little consequence.

Another factor to be taken into consideration in assessing exclusive dealing contracts is the validity of any business considerations offered in justification of the exclusive feature. Where the structural test of substantiality described is inconclusive, the business considerations are more likely to be given weight. Put briefly, if an exclusive dealing arrangement is motivated by a legitimate business goal, and if it goes no further than necessary to achieve that goal, a court will be more inclined to find it legal.

The structural test, however, is a stringent one. Any exclusive dealing scheme foreclosing to competitors more than about 5 per cent of the market, though not necessarily illegal, is immediately suspect. Arrangements affecting a lower percentage of the market may also be attacked, particularly under Section 5. In the *Brown Shoe* case, the Supreme Court sustained, without any reference to the degree of foreclosure, the commission's challenge of contracts between a large manufacturer of shoes and hundreds of independent retail shoe outlets that barred the retailers from carrying competitive shoe lines. The moral is clear: exclusive dealing arrangements that are not insignificant in extent are risky from the antitrust viewpoint.

Let us consider some hypothetical situations in the international context. For example, a Swiss watch manufacturer that markets its products through American distributors and retailers might wish to contract with either or both that they will not carry competitive watches. This agreement would foreclose American competitors, as well as other foreign watch exporters, from getting their goods to market and the U.S. antitrust law, including the Clayton Act, would be fully applicable. Legality would depend in large part on the extent of the foreclosure effectuated which would, in turn, be determined by the market significance of the distributors and/or retailers subject to the contract.

The converse situation might involve an exclusive dealing arrangement between an American agricultural machinery manufacturer and a chain of European distributors. Because Section 3 of the Clayton Act is inapplicable to such arrangements contemplating resale outside the United States, the focus would be under the Sherman or FTC Acts. Legality would turn on the extent to which this agreement would foreclose other U.S. exporters of agricultural machinery from obtaining effective distribution for their products abroad. Here the size and significance of the foreclosed outlets as regards distribution within Europe would be the key factor. Finally, a variation would be presented if the manufacturer who signed up foreign distributors on an exclusive basis were also foreign, rather than American. Although the effect in foreclosing U.S. exports might be no different than in the previous example, a U.S. enforcement action would be unlikely because of the problems of extraterritoriality posed. However, if the foreclosure were very sizeable and the foreign manufacturer had sufficient U.S. "contacts" to permit jurisdiction to be assumed over it, it might be that the Justice Department, under the Sherman Act prohibitions, would step in to protect our exports.

Exclusive and nonexclusive dealing contracts between an American export association and its foreign distributors were upheld in *United States* v. *Minnesota Mining & Mfg. Co.* This case involved an association trading under the Webb–Pomerene Act, and some aspects of the association's activities were held to go beyond the Act's grant of immunity. The distribution contracts, however, were upheld under traditional Sherman Act analysis. Although the European distributors had agreed to limitations on carrying the products of the association's competitors, the court found that there were an ample number of foreign distributors available, so that competition was not substantially affected. It is interesting that in this case the contracts permitted the foreign distributors to handle the products of any American supplier. It would seem that this feature alone would safely immunize the agreement from a charge of restraining American foreign commerce.

Requirements contracts may be treated somewhat differently from other exclusive dealing arrangements, especially where the purchasing party is the user of the product. This is because such a requirements contract will often have a valid business justification. For the buyer, it may assure supply and price, and thus permit long-term planning. For the seller it may offer a reliable market, a known price, and a consistent pattern of doing business. However, requirements contracts are subjected to the same tests for foreclosure as are other exclusive dealing agreements. The courts and agencies simply tend to be more favorably inclined to permit a requirements contract where it has a valid business purpose and does not have a strong foreclosing effect.

An example of a requirements contract involving international trade that was proscribed may be found in a consent decree entered in 1958. The United Fruit Company was enjoined from entering into contracts for the sale of bananas in the United States that required the purchaser to buy all or any specified portion of its requirements from United. Furthermore, United was enjoined from entering into requirements contracts for the sale of bananas abroad when any significant portion of them was destined for resale within the United States. Thus, both domestic and foreign requirements contracts were banned, as long as any significant resale in the United States was involved.

Tying Arrangements

A tie-in sale takes place when a party refuses to sell one item—the tying product—unless the purchaser also agrees to take another distinct item—the tied product. A variant of the classic tie-in is "full-line forcing," conditioning sale of a desired product on the purchaser's taking the seller's full line of products. Tying arrangements have traditionally been treated far more harshly under the antitrust laws than have exclusive dealing arrangements because, as the Supreme Court has stated, the former "serve hardly any purpose beyond the suppression of competition." The seller is using his leverage in one market to block out his competitors in another market.

Tying arrangements are reached directly by Section 3 of the Clayton Act. As noted with respect to exclusive dealing, however, Section 3 applies only to transactions involving commodities and does not apply to all transactions in foreign commerce. As in the exclusive dealing situation, Section 1 of the Sherman Act and Section 5 of the FTC Act may be applied to tie-in sales without these Clayton Act limitations.

Recent judicial decisions have blurred any meaningful distinction in terms of the competitive impact required under the various statutes in regard to tying agreements. The standard of unlawfulness of tying agreements is whether the seller has sufficient economic power in the tying product to induce the buyer to take the tied product, and whether a *not insubstantial* amount of commerce in the tied product is thereby foreclosed. Economic power in the tying product may be gauged by its uniqueness or desirability to consumers.

In the recent *Fortner* case, the Supreme Court considered a situation involving a credit company that was a subsidiary of United States Steel Corp. In order to obtain credit on advantageous terms from the subsidiary, the borrower was required to purchase prefabricated homes from U.S. Steel. The Court held that the terms of the credit, uniquely advantageous in the credit market, were such as to satisfy the requirement for sufficient market power. Thus the arrangement was struck down under the Sherman Act as an illegal tie-in, i.e., conditioning the extension of credit on the purchase of the tied product, the U.S. Steel prefabricated homes. The development of the law in this fashion has created a situation wherein virtually any tie-in sale affecting a not insubstantial amount of commerce in the tied product is likely to be illegal. Courts and commentators, therefore, are today inclined to treat tie-in sales as per se violations of the antitrust laws.

Although business justifications for tying arrangements have been heard, they have seldom been deemed sufficiently persuasive to support the restriction. Arguments to the effect that proper use of the tying product or quality control in its manufacture require concurrent use of the tied product have been accepted in rare instances but more often have been rejected.

"Full-line" arrangements have not been challenged in certain business situations because they appear incidental to genuine business needs. An automobile company, for example, might require as a condition to the grant of a dealership that the dealer carry a full line of its cars and replacement parts for maintenance of the cars. This type of agreement will normally be justifiable as necessary to protect the manufacturer's good will, inasmuch as the public will expect his franchised dealers to be adequately stocked and to be able to handle repairs as the need arises. Lacking such a special situation, which is virtually self-justifying, the prudent course is to avoid full-line forcing.

The application of the law in the international context is much the same for tie-ins as we found it to be for exclusive dealing, except, of course, that the rule of reason test is displaced by something closer to a per se approach. For example, an Italian manufacturer's selling a highly desired line of shoes to an American distributor on the condition that the latter purchase shirts from him also would risk challenge under the Clayton, Sherman, or FTC Acts, assuming that a "not insubstantial" trade in shirts would thereby be diverted. Conversely, if an important American manufacturer conditioned his overseas sales of generators on the purchaser's buying engines from him as well, other American engine producers would be disadvantaged, and the tie-in sale would be vulnerable under the Sherman and FTC Acts.

Summary

As has been seen, there are a number of vertical devices whereby a manufacturer or supplier seeks to impose some restriction on the purchase or sale of products by his distributor. The employment of these devices will often have antitrust implications.

Resale-price maintenance within the United States must be carefully circumscribed to fall under applicable state fair trade laws. Efforts by domestic or foreign suppliers to control U.S. distributors by delimiting their territories of resale or their customers are vulnerable under the antitrust laws. Creation of exclusive distributorships, here or abroad, is normally safe as long as the supplier is simply making a business decision as to whom he will sell. Exclusive dealing arrangements requiring customers not to deal with competitors, however, raise antitrust questions under the rule of reason because they foreclose competition. Finally, tie-in arrangements are so unfavorably regarded that, in the absence of unusual circumstances, they should be entirely avoided.

chapter 7

The Federal Trade Commission
and Robinson-Patman Acts
in International Commerce

Earlier chapters have indicated that the Federal Trade Commission plays
an important part in antitrust enforcement. We have also observed that
Section 5 of the Federal Trade Commission Act gives the commission a
broad mandate for its activity, covering both interstate and foreign commerce. In view of the commission's distinctive and vital role, we will take
a closer look in this chapter at the agency's functions and activities insofar
as they bear on U.S. foreign commerce. The statutory focus of our examination will be the agency's enabling statute, the Federal Trade Commission Act, as well as another important statute enforced by the commission, the Robinson–Patman Act.

The Federal Trade Commission Act

Section 5 of the Federal Trade Commission Act (FTC Act) declares unlawful unfair methods of competition in commerce, and unfair or deceptive
acts or practices in commerce. This is the major statutory provision relating
to the subject matter of the commission's authority. How has this provision been applied in the international sphere? The first step in answering
that question it to consider the FTC's jurisdiction over the various areas of
foreign commerce.

Commerce, as defined in Section 4 of the FTC Act, includes, in addi-

105

tion to interstate commerce, commerce with foreign nations, between any state and any territory or foreign nation, or between the District of Columbia and any state or territory or foreign nation. Section 4 of the Webb–Pomerene Act, or the Export Trade Act of 1918, provides that Section 5 of the FTC Act shall be construed as extending to "unfair methods of competition used in export trade against competitors engaged in export trade, even though the acts constituting such unfair methods are done without the territorial jurisdiction of the United States." This language is not applicable solely to FTC action affecting associations registered under the Webb–Pomerene Act but is a general amendment to the jurisdiction of the Federal Trade Commission. It is also considered to grant the commission "new" jurisdiction.

The question is raised why, when the "commerce" definition of the FTC Act clearly encompasses U.S. foreign commerce, new jurisdictional authority in this regard was deemed a necessary inclusion in the Webb–Pomerene Act. The answer is that the commission was construing its mandate under the FTC Act narrowly insofar as activity abroad was concerned. As stated in the legislative history of the Webb–Pomerene Act:

> [T]he Trade Commission would not have anything to do with unfair competition between two American exporters in China . . . . This act preserves the power of the Trade Commission over the two American exporters, wherever they are in all the world, and if one acts unfairly toward the other in any portion of the world, that one can be brought before the Trade Commission and enjoined.

The term *in commerce,* as used in Section 5 of the FTC Act, is important in determining over what activity the Federal Trade Commission has jurisdiction. The Supreme Court in the 1941 *Bunte Bros.* case determined that the legislative choice of the phrase *in commerce* was an attempt to regulate acts and practices in the flow of interstate or foreign commerce and not purely local intrastate activities, regardless of the effect of the latter on interstate commerce. This interpretation, however, has been considerably eroded by subsequent case law. Interstate commerce was defined to include "[a]ll of those things which stimulate or decrease the flow of commerce, although not directly in its stream," soon after *Bunte Bros.* More recently, it has been held that intrastate activities that are an "integral and indispensable part" of interstate commerce come within the commission's jurisdiction.

The limits of the FTC's "in commerce" jurisdiction are now clear. If the product is destined for interstate or foreign commerce, unfair methods or practices, local in nature, that affect that product are deemed to be in commerce. The existence of minimal interstate or foreign dealings, even only a single unfair act, gives the commission jurisdiction. If a business is engaged in both interstate and intrastate commerce and if its activities are inseparably interwoven, the intrastate activity may be subjected to regulation in aid of the regulation of the interstate phase. It is apparent that the one area that can still escape the regulatory power of the commission is the intrastate sale of goods that have never been and conceivably never will be in interstate commerce and that are sold by a business having an entirely intrastate market. In sum, to an extent, activity that merely *affects* interstate or foreign commerce rather than being *directly wthin it,* is subject to action by the Federal Trade Commission.

Although the Supreme Court has never ruled on the extraterritorial reach of the FTC Act and there have been few significant rulings on this question generally, the statutory mandate described, coupled with the case law authority that does exist, establishes satisfactorily that the FTC Act can be applied broadly with respect to transactions or activities that occur in the course of U.S. foreign commerce.

There has never been any question as to the commission's authority to deal with problems affecting imports into the United States. The cases have therefore dealt with the agency's authority with respect to exports and with respect to activities carried on overseas. An early case concerning jurisdiction over exports arose in 1919, *FTC* v. *Nestle's Food Co.* In that case, a U.S. corporation that produced condensed milk in this country and exported it to Mexico was ordered by the commission to cease using labels on its cans that implied that the product originated in Europe. It was ruled by the commission that such labeling and sales constituted an unfair method of competition in that the respondent gained an undue preference over other American producers by causing purchasers to be misled as to the origin of the milk. The agency concluded that this decision concerning practices in export trade was authorized by Section 5 of the FTC Act, as extended by Section 4 of the Webb–Pomerene Act.

In another early case, *FTC* v. *Caravel Co.,* an American export house sold admittedly inferior California Newtown apples as and at the price of Oregon Newtown Pippins, considered a superior and more expensive apple for export purposes. The commission held that this substitution of goods, which was "to the prejudice of the public and of competitors or respondent," was an unfair method of competition under Section 5 of the FTC Act, as extended by Section 4 of the Webb–Pomerene Act. As both statutes were relied on in the two cases, it may be that the agency did not consider Section 5 of the FTC Act sufficient alone to grant the commission jurisdiction over acts dealing with exports to foreign countries.

The major court case in this area came in 1944 and served to confirm the early administrative rulings, while also shedding light on the extent to which the jurisdiction over foreign commerce under the FTC Act had been affected by the Webb–Pomerene Act addition. In this case, *Branch* v. *FTC,* Branch was charged with engaging in unfair methods of competition and unfair and deceptive acts in commerce. He offered, from his headquarters in Illinois, correspondence courses by advertisements in Latin American countries in thirty-seven different subjects, including architecture, engineering, law, and medicine. Branch represented that he maintained a university, that the courses were approved by the state of Illinois, and that the school was authorized to confer degrees, all of which was untrue. Upon these facts, the commission ordered Branch to cease and desist from making fraudulent representations in the operation of his "diploma mill." This commission action was said to be aimed at compelling Branch to use fair methods in competing with his fellow countrymen, other correspondence schools in the United States, not aimed at protecting his customers in Latin America.

On appeal, Branch argued that the commission had no jurisdiction to issue its order because the acts complained of took place in Latin American countries. The United States Court of Appeals for the Seventh Circuit, however, found this argument of no consequence. It deemed the key factor to be the location of the competitors. As this was the United States, and as Branch himself had directed his acts from the United States, the court saw no problem with the extraterritorial aspects. The court discussed the commission's statutory jurisdiction in this area and concluded that the power granted to the FTC by Congress through Section 5 of the FTC Act was "ample to support the jurisdiction exercised by the Commission in this case." It pointed out: "The United States may protect its commerce from the wrongful acts of its own citizens who remain, as the petitioner did, within the United States and whose wrongful acts are prejudicial to other citizens of the United States who are in competition for that commerce."

The court found Section 4 of the Webb–Pomerene Act to be another and separate source of jurisdiction for the FTC with respect to foreign commerce in general, and export trade in particular. If Section 4 is not to be read as redundant of Section 5, it would appear that the additional power that the courts deem to have been accorded by Webb–Pomerene to the FTC is authority over acts that take place totally outside of the United States, that is, where no aspects of the transaction—or a least no significant parts—take place within the territorial United States. Thus, the commission, under the FTC and Webb–Pomerene Acts, clearly has jurisdiction to prevent unfair methods of competition and unfair or deceptive acts or practices occurring anywhere in the course of U.S. foreign commerce.

Substantive Content of the FTC Act

What are the "unfair methods of competition" and "unfair or deceptive acts or practices" against which the Federal Trade Commission can take action? The Supreme Court has several times made it clear that the FTC has a broad discretion to give these vague phrases specific content. In *FTC*

v. *Motion Picture Advertising Service Co.,* the Supreme Court remarked that, "Congress advisedly left the concept flexible to be defined with particularity by the myriad of cases from the field of business." Very recently, in *FTC* v. *Sperry & Hutchinson Co.,* the Court once again ruled that the commission is not confined to established antitrust violations in determining whether a business practice is "unfair":

> [L]egislative and judicial authorities alike convince us that the Federal Trade Commission does not arrogate excessive power to itself if, in measuring a practice against the elusive, but congressionally mandated standard of fairness, it, like a court of equity, considers public values beyond simply those enshrined in the letter or encompassed in the spirit of the antitrust laws.

Although Section 5 is not limited in scope to the antitrust principles established by other statutes, these are important elements of its sweep. Violations of the Sherman and Clayton Acts, for example, such as price fixing, boycotts, restrictive exclusive dealing, tie-ins, and anticompetitive mergers are also violations of Section 5. Moreover, it is established that Section 5, in reaching these types of practices, is not bound by the limitations of the Sherman and Clayton Acts and therefore can ensnare *incipient* violations of those statutes before a major restraint on trade has been attained. In addition, Section 5 can reach acts or practices that themselves are not precisely of the type proscribed by the other two statutes but that are so closely related that they violate the basic policies of the original statutes. For example, the Robinson–Patman Act prohibits the *granting* of discriminatory advertising allowances by suppliers but has no supplementary provision prohibiting the *inducement* of such allowances by powerful buyers. The commission sought to close this gap by bringing an inducement proceeding under Section 5 against a large chain store and was sustained by the appellate court. The court reasoned that this use of Section 5 went beyond the "technical confines" of the Robinson–Patman Act "but only fully to realize the basic policy of the . . . Act, which was to prevent the abuse of *buying* power."

Prior to 1938, Section 5 dealt only with unfair methods of *competition*. In a deceptive advertising case, for example, this meant that the commission had to prove both that the advertising was deceptive and that it injured competitors. The 1938 Wheeler–Lea amendments to the Federal Trade Commission Act broadened the thrust of the statute to protect the consumer as well. The commission can now proceed against unfair or deceptive acts that injure consumers without reference to any competitive effects.

Among the unfair or deceptive acts or practices against which the commission has moved are deceptive advertising, commercial bribery, product and name simulation, lottery schemes, and shipment of unsolicited goods.

These are only some of the acts that have been held to fall within the scope of Section 5. As new and equally deceptive schemes are devised, the law will no doubt still be found adequate to inhibit them.

Unfair Competition

In considering the early rulings involving application of Section 5 to activities in foreign commerce, we have already noted several cases in which the commission stepped in to protect American businessmen from acts of unfair competition by other American businessmen in overseas markets. The *Nestle, Caravel,* and *Branch* cases all involved misrepresentations directed to foreigners which were deemed to harm American competitors. There have also been FTC cases in the realm of foreign commerce that involved acts in the nature of the traditional trade restraints barred by the Sherman Act.

In *Eastman Kodak Co.* v. *FTC,* Kodak agreed with various movie makers that if they would refrain from purchasing raw film from foreign manufacturers, Kodak would refrain from entering the picture-making field. The commission entered an order against Kodak directing it to cease and desist from maintaining this agreement and Kodak appealed, alleging *inter alia,* that the FTC lacked jurisdiction. The court affirmed the agency's order, reasoning that the commission could promote the interests of foreign raw film makers if it believed that its action was in the public interest. Thus, the commission had jurisdiction over agreements that affected foreign commerce, where the goods had not yet entered the United States and where the primary interest to be protected was allegedly that of foreign manufacturers.

A further example of the delineation of the FTC's authority in the international arena is *Luria Brothers & Co.* v. *FTC.* In that case the commission attacked under Section 5 a series of exclusive supply contracts on the ground that they unlawfully restrained trade and tended to create an incipient monopoly in the scrap metal market, which if undeterred would have violated Sections 1 and 2 of the Sherman Act. An agreement between Office Commun des Consommateurs de Ferraille (OCCF), a central buying office for European steel mills affiliated with the European Coal and Steel Community, and a three-company U.S. scrap broker group, including Luria, provided that the three would supply all metal scrap to be purchased by OCCF over a period of several years. In the early 1950's, Luria controlled about 80 per cent of the scrap metal market in the North Atlantic area. With only 20 per cent of the domestic market available, Luria's competitors were forced to dispose of their scrap abroad. Because OCCF purchased between 66 and 84 per cent of the total scrap exported to Europe in the relevant period, Luria's competitors were effectively foreclosed from both the domestic and foreign scrap markets. On appeal, the commission's conclusion that Luria's practices during the years under investigation showed its intention to monopolize the scrap brokerage business in the foreign market was held to be supported by substantial evidence.

In the area of restraint of trade, in sum, the Federal Trade Commission Act has full reach over agreements and practices that violate antitrust principles or otherwise are acts of "unfair competition." These restraints may be challenged in their incipiency, and they may be challenged even if they involve foreign activity so long as this activity is in the course of the commerce of the United States.

Consumer Protection

Since the passage of the Wheeler–Lea amendments, much of the Federal Trade Commission's activity has been directed against business practices that are deemed to deceive the consumer. This effort has encompassed all manner of product claims and representations. One category of unfair or deceptive practice in this regard is the selling, or offering for sale, of a foreign product in the United States without disclosing the country of its origin. The underlying theory here is that a substantial portion of the purchasing public prefers domestic products and that the purchaser assumes that a product is of domestic origin unless he is apprised to the contrary. Consequently, the purchaser is deceived if not informed of the foreign origin. Certain exceptions, however, have been established or indicated. If the foreign product is of a type that is not produced in the United States, such as cultured pearls, natural pearls, and diamonds, disclosure of the product's foreign origin is not required. Likewise, if it is possible to prove that there is no public preference for a U.S. counterpart of the foreign product, nondisclosure of the product's foreign origin will probably be defensible. Moreover, sellers of foreign products that were lower priced than comparable U.S. products have on rare occasions successfully defended themselves on the ground that there was no proof that the public preferred U.S. products over foreign products when the latter were lower priced. More recently, it has been held that the lack of preference for U.S. goods must be affirmatively proved by the party charged.

If a product manufactured in the United States consists in part of foreign components, the seller of the domestic product may have to disclose the origin of the foreign component. The test usually applied is that if the foreign component retains its essential characteristics of function and appearance then disclosure is required, but if the foreign component has lost its identity in the manufacture of the domestic products, then disclosure is not required.

The concept of labeling the origin of the product has had an interesting ramification. With proliferation in the post-World War II world of divided countries utilizing the same name, including Germany, China, Vietnam, and Korea, there has been a need for labeling that differentiates between the two nations, especially to permit the consumer to distinguish between the products of communist and noncommunist countries. This problem has, for example, been raised with respect to the labeling of wool products under the Wool Products Labeling Act of 1939 as "Chinese." The FTC has ruled that the label must indicate whether the origin is the People's Republic of China or Taiwan.

Analogous to the case of labeling to indicate foreign origin is the problem of domestic products that have trademarks or descriptions tending to create the impression that they are imported. Although the general principle is that Americans prefer domestic products, there is a marked preference by many for particular items that are imported from certain countries, e.g., wine, fashion, or perfume, and therefore the risk exists that American or foreign producers will seek to deceive as to the country of origin. This has been the subject of some enforcement activity by the FTC, which has barred, for example, the use of the word *English* in the designation, advertising, labeling, or description of soap unless it was manufactured in England; has permitted the foreign country of origin for various ingredients to be included on the label if accompanied by a statement that the finished product was made in the United States; and has restrained an importer from using a name that represented to the public that products made in Japan were imported from France.

It is interesting to note that an effort has been initiated to expand further the FTC's role in the area of foreign commerce. The Nixon administration has introduced a bill that would add to Section 6 of the FTC Act commission authority to issue an order excluding imported commodities from entering the country, a function previously implemented by the President. This would be authorized whenever it is found that unfair methods of competition or unfair acts are being employed by importers, where the effect of such conduct is to injure a U.S. industry or substantially impair competition in this country. This proposal demonstrates the likely increasing vitality of the FTC in foreign commerce matters.

The Federal Trade Commission Act, while constituting the primary grant of enforcement jurisdiction to the FTC, does not comprise its sole authority to act with respect to activities in interstate and foreign commerce. Under Secion 11(a) of the Clayton Act, the FTC is given authority to enforce Sections 3, 7, and 8 of that Act, dealing with tying or exclusive dealing agreements, mergers, and interlocking directorates, respectively. The commission also enforces a number of specialized protective statutes including the Wool Products Labeling Act, the Fur Products Labeling Act, and the Textile Fiber Products Identification Act. One further statute under which the commission is granted enforcement authority, and which deserves special attention, is Section 2 of the Clayton Act as amended by the Robinson–Patman Act (commonly referred to as the Robinson–Patman Act) that concerns the discriminatory treatment of purchasers.

The Robinson–Patman Act

In the Depression era, a subject that concerned Congress was the market power wielded by large buying groups, particularly the chain grocery stores. Investigation had shown that the chains were able to secure favored pricing treatment from suppliers by virtue of their large volume purchases. The independent grocery stores were thus placed in an unfavorable competitive position, and there was apprehension for their future. Public support for legislation that would compel suppliers to treat all buyers on a fair and equal basis, in order that the small independents would not be prejudiced by their lack of purchasing power, led to enactment of the Robinson–Patman Act in 1936.

The two primary objectives of the Act are:

1. To prevent unscrupulous suppliers from attempting to gain an unfair avantage over their competitors by discriminating among buyers.
2. To prevent unscrupulous buyers from using their economic power to exact discriminatory prices from suppliers to the disadvantage of less powerful buyers.

Section 2(a) prohibits sellers from discriminating in price between different purchasers of commodities of like grade and quality, where the effect of the discrimination may be substantially to lessen competition. Under that section and Section 2(b), certain limited exceptions and defenses are permitted, including a cost justification of the discriminatory price or a showing that the latter was offered in good faith to meet the equally low price of a competitor.

Section 2(c) is a self-contained section prohibiting the seller from paying any brokerage fee, commission, or an equivalent to a buyer or the buyer's agent. It also prohibits a buyer from accepting any such fee or commission.

Sections 2(d) and 2(e) prohibit a seller from granting discriminatory promotional or merchandising allowances, services, or facilities to a buyer unless such assistance is made available to other competing buyers on proportionally equal terms.

Section 2(f) declares it unlawful for a buyer to knowingly induce or receive a price discrimination forbidden by Section 2(a).

Section 3 of the Robinson–Patman Act, which is not part of the Clayton Act, declares it unlawful for a seller to provide certain secret allowances to the buyer. It also forbids territorial price reductions or sales at unreasonably low prices where the seller's purpose is to destroy competition or to eliminate a competitor. Section 3 is a criminal statute which has been little used, largely because of its vagueness. Moreover, the Supreme Court has held that it is not an "antitrust statute" and therefore does not provide a cause of action for private litigants seeking treble damages.

Competitive Injury

Under Section 2(a), the price discriminations rendered unlawful are only those whose effect may be "[1] substantially to lessen competition or [2] tend to create a monopoly in any line of commerce, or [3] to injure, destroy, or prevent competition with any person who either grants or knowingly receives the benefit of such discrimination, or with customers of either of them. . . . " Competitive injury must therefore be established. This requisite adverse competitive impact is sought by looking for possible injury at any one of several possible levels: (1) the level of the discriminating seller and his competitors, (2) the level of the favored and disfavored purchasers, or (3) a level involving customers still further down the line of distribution who are injured by the unlawful discrimination. Actionable competitive injury may arise at any level in the distribution scheme, the only limitation being the requirement that there be a causal relationship between the unlawful discrimination and the injury suffered.

Section 2(c), relating to illegal brokerage payments, is in the nature of a per se wrong. No competitive injury need be established for a violation. Sections 2(d) and (e), which relate to discriminatory advertising and promotional allowances, services, or facilities, likewise may be violated without a showing of competitive injury. Moreover, the seller has no defense of cost justification. The defense of meeting competition, however, is available to rebut a claim that a seller has violated Section 2(d) or (e).

Robinson–Patman in Foreign Commerce

The prohibition of Section 2(a) is drawn in terms of a seller engaged in interstate or foreign commerce discriminating in price, where either or any of the purchases involved in such discrimination is in interstate or foreign commerce, and where the "commodities are sold for use, consumption, or resale within the United States or any Territory thereof or the District of Columbia or any insular possession or other place under the jurisdiction of the United States. . . . " This quoted language makes it plain that, insofar as international trade is concerned, Section 2(a) extends to discriminatory transactions in import trade, but not to such transactions in export trade. Thus, if a foreign seller discriminates in price between competing American purchasers, the statute will apply. A practical problem may, of course, exist in this situation with respect to obtaining personal jurisdiction over the foreign seller, so as to enforce effectively the law's mandate.

On the other hand, price discrimination by a U.S. seller in foreign commerce is not covered by the Act. Thus, if a seller in the United States discriminates in price between foreign buyers, the transaction cannot be reached by Section 2(a). Under circumstances where price discrimination fits into the pattern of an agreement to restrain trade, or monopolization, it is possible to challenge it in the export situation under the Sherman Act and without reference to the Robinson–Patman Act. In the *Minnesota Mining* case which we discussed earlier, the Webb–Pomerene Export Company set prices 10 to 30 per cent higher for competitive American exporters than for the unit's own foreign distributors. The court, considering this practice in the context of a Sherman Act conspiracy, observed that the price differential was justified only to the extent that the foreign distributors incurred greater costs and obligations than the American exporters. The court stated that, if the defendants were to be permitted to go further in discriminating, "their conduct would be a restraint upon competitive American exporters beyond the sanctions of the Webb–Pomerene Act." A similar position against a scheme of discrimination was taken by the Supreme Court in the 1917 decision, *Thomsen* v. *Cayser*. The defendant steamship lines, which plied between New York and South African ports, adopted uniform freight rates and, for the purpose of constraining shippers to use their ships and avoid others, refunded sums as rebates to shippers who used their lines exclusively. This concerted activity was held by the Court to be a combination in violation of the Sherman Act.

The Sherman Act, however, cannot be used as a simple substitute for the Robinson–Patman Act with respect to export commerce. First, except in the case of monopolization, an agreement or combination is required for a Sherman Act violation, and individual action does not suffice. There may be situations in which it can be argued that the seller and the favored purchaser are, in effect, agreeing to the discrimination against the unfavored purchaser. Of equal importance, though, is that a substantial restraint of trade must be established for a Sherman Act violation, as compared to the "may be substantially to lessen competition" standard of Robinson–Patman. The more likely road to a remedy in this situation is under Section 5 of the Federal Trade Commission, which, as we have seen, can be utilized to fill the "gaps" in the other trade regulation statutes, can halt improper conduct before it amounts to full-fledged restraint, and can be applied to unfair methods of competition in export trade.

In contrast to Section 2(a), the delimitation "within the United States" is not found in subsections (c), (d), and (e), which deal with brokerage payments, promotional allowances, services, and facilities. The courts that have considered this difference in language have done so in the context of subsection 2(c) and have concluded that the omission of the limiting language is significant, permitting the provision to apply to export as well as import trade.

The applicability of Section 2(c) to export commerce was given recognition by the United States District Court for the Western District of Pennsylvania in 1950 in *Baysoy* v. *Jessop Steel Co.* The plaintiff, a Turkish citizen, had sued for breach of an alleged contract whereby the defendant corporation was to sell him ferrochrome, presumably for export. Under the contract, the defendant was to pay the plaintiff-buyer 2 per cent of the purchase price as a commission. Defendant moved to dismiss on the ground that the contract was unenforceable because it was in violation of Section 2(c), which forbids the payment of brokerage by the seller to the buyer or the buyer's agent. The court accepted this contention and dismissed the complaint, rejecting the plaintiff's argument that Section 2(c) does not apply to sales for export. In a later case, *Canadian Ingersoll–Rand Co.* v. *D. Loveman & Sons, Inc.,* decided in 1964 by a federal district court, the applicability of Section 2(c) to sales for export was likewise upheld.

Although subsections (c), (d), and (e) of Section 2 of the Robinson–Patman Act have this theoretical applicability to export commerce, the provisions have seldom been so applied. Their day-to-day relevancy, like that of subsection (a), is in terms of sales of commodities made for resale or use within the United States including domestic and import commerce. As we have noted earlier, foreign corporations selling their products into or in the United States are fully subject to the Robinson–Patman Act prohibitions.

The Robinson–Patman Act does not require that a seller deal with all interested would-be purchasers, of course. It simply tells him that he must treat on a nondiscriminatory basis those purchasers with whom he does deal where competitive injury may result or be presumed. Each provision of the Act has numerous refinements and a rich decisional lore, these being too extensive to discuss here. Some threshold prerequisites to application of the Act deserve emphasis for our purposes, however: there must be one seller and discrimination by him as between two or more purchasers. Given the extent of corporate conglomerations, especially in foreign commerce, difficult questions can arise as to when concurrent sales made by related corporations are, in effect, by a single seller for Robinson–Patman purposes and also as to when transactions between related entities amount to "purchases." Substance, rather than form, is likely to prevail in these situations. For example, a corporation that set up a subsidiary over which it retained complete control could not lawfully utilize the subsidiary to conduct its sales to favored (or unfavored) purchasers on the theory that it and the subsidiary were not a single seller for purposes of the Robinson–Patman Act. Or, let us consider a somewhat different hypothetical situation in which a foreign corporation is selling products to United

States firms at a higher price than it sells to its distributing subsidiary which is also in the United States. It has been held that, where the corporate parent exercises control over the subsidiary's basic policies, the subsidiary is not such a distinct entity as to constitute a favored "purchaser" so as to trigger the application of the statute.

For those planning to market their products in the United States, the implications of the Robinson–Patman Act warrant advance consideration. Although an enforcement proceeding by the Federal Trade Commission is a significant sanction, so also is the private treble-damage suit brought by an aggrieved competitor or customer. In addition, some states have laws that are similar in purpose and content to the Robinson–Patman Act.

chapter 8

Mergers, Acquisitions, and Joint Ventures in Foreign Commerce

As our shrinking world daily brings about closer relationships among people from different nations, so does it enhance international corporate relationships. And from this global corporate contact and the incentive to develop foreign markets there has flourished the international corporate "marriage"—the merger, the acquisition, and the joint venture. Much of the allure is the same as that which may bring two domestic firms together: the advantage of joining complementary product lines, talents, or resources; the desire to diversify; or the wish to obtain ready access to a new geographic market. Indeed, in the international context the last consideration often assumes controlling dimensions. Acquisition of a firm in a foreign country, or entry into a joint venture with such a partner, permits a corporation to vault over national trade barriers into the foreign marketplace and participate in it through a local management, already familiar with the local business, institutions, and language.

International corporate marriages can evoke the usual antitrust concerns. The result may be, for example, a combination that controls a major share of the market, or the snuffing out of invigorating import competition, or the choking off of an important external source of supply on which many competitors are dependent. Clearly, antitrust must apply and does apply in this context. But what are the rules? What concessions, if any, are justified by the fact that a foreign firm is involved and that the conduct in question—given the absence of strong antimerger policy outside of the United States—will generally be regarded as wholly legitimate abroad?

118

There is a further complication in this area that makes misunderstanding even more likely. Investment from abroad is often resisted by governments as a matter of economic policy, as they fearfully confront the specter of their vital industries coming under the control of foreign absentee owners. Vexation and some resistance has been the reaction of European governments as they view the onslaught of American firms making heavy investment inroads in the European countries. In light of these circumstances, it is often difficult to convince both a foreign firm that is acquisition-bound in the United States and the firm's government that our antitrust policy is a nondiscriminatory discipline, rather than an instrument cynically used to block investment efforts in the United States on the part of foreign firms.

It is not surprising, therefore, that diplomatic repercussions may have some relevance in connection with antitrust assessments in this area, particularly where the foreign firm is the one seeking to make the acquisition. The reader should be cautioned in the same breath, however, that reliance on diplomatic considerations will seldom be warranted. As we shall see on review of the cases, there has been no indication of a more lenient view on the part of the antitrust authorities in situations in which foreign firms are involved. Before exploring application of the U.S. antitrust law in particular situations, let us review the statutes that are pertinent.

Relevant Laws

It should be noted at the outset that the antitrust laws applicable to mergers, acquisitions, and joint ventures were, like the antitrust framework generally, devised with primary focus on domestic interstate commerce. The early abuses that led to the legislation did not involve foreign commerce, and the legislative history reveals little about Congress' intentions in this area. Similarly, merger enforcement policy until recently had few opportunities to exert itself in the realm of foreign commerce, and many of the recent cases have been resolved by consent decree, precluding the development of direct judicial precedent. Nonetheless, the scope of the various statutes does extend to international amalgamations, and their application for this purpose now constitutes an articulated and important aspect of antitrust enforcement policy. Moreover, adequate guidance for the lawyer and businessman can be derived by analogizing from the decisions framed in the domestic context.

Sherman Act

Our oldest antitrust law, the Sherman Act, is applicable as an anti-merger law, as well as a proscription against restrictive agreements and practices. Section 1 declares unlawful "[e]very contract, combination . . . or conspiracy, in restraint of trade or commerce among the several States, or with foreign nations. . . . " Section 2 forbids every person to "monopolize, or attempt to monopolize, or combine or conspire . . . to monopolize any part of the trade or commerce among the several States, or with foreign nations. . . ." Explicitly, therefore, the law's ambit extends to combinations and monopolizations affecting our foreign commerce. Its practical inadequacies as an enforcement tool in the merger area have, however, rendered it of limited use in either the domestic or the foreign commerce area, as compared to the Clayton Act.

Although the Clayton Act is clearly designed so as to bar merger transactions that "may . . . substantially . . . lessen competition," the Sherman Act has traditionally been viewed as imposing more stringent standards in terms of existing restraints on trade or efforts to monopolize. Cases brought in the first quarter of the twentieth century involved amalgamations be- . tween large, dominant competitors and no difficulty was encountered in applying the Sherman Act in such situations. The law saw little development until 1948, when the Supreme Court, in the *Columbia Steel Co.* case, upheld a merger between two competing steel companies on the ground that, in light of prevailing conditions in the steel industry, the combination was not an unreasonable restraint of trade and hence not violative of the Sherman Act.

Doubt as to the applicable standard was heightened by the Supreme Court's 1964 decision in *United States* v. *First National Bank & Trust Co. of Lexington* striking down a bank merger with little discussion of the market picture, on the narrow rationale that the two banks were significant competitors in a single county area. Mr. Justice Harlan, in dissent, urged that the government had not sustained the traditional, narrower, Sherman Act standards and that the effect of the Court's holding was to create a "Clayton Act case masquerading in the garb of the Sherman Act." The resulting confusion over the proper standards for application of the Sherman Act has been eclipsed by the pre-eminence that the Clayton Act has clearly assumed in recent years as the primary instrument for antimerger enforcement.

Clayton Act

The nation's second antitrust law, the Clayton Act, was enacted in 1914, with Section 7 of the Act designed to cope with the increased degree of economic concentration that the Sherman Act had failed to stem. According to its legislative history, the Clayton Act sought "to prohibit and make unlawful certain trade practices, which . . . [were] not covered by the [Sherman Act] . . . and thus, by making these practices illegal, to arrest the creation of trusts, conspiracies, and monopolies in their incipiency and before consummation."

Section 7, as originally enacted, was fashioned essentially to halt concentration in its early stages by precluding corporations from merging through the acquisition of the stock of their competitors. Some vital weaknesses were soon perceived in this legislation. First, Section 7 was applied only to acquisitions effected through the purchase of stock, permitting acquisitions through the purchase of assets to go untouched. Second, the Federal Trade Commission and the Antitrust Division of the Justice Department, which have concurrent jurisdiction over violations of Section 7, considered that it could be applied only to acquisitions of competitors and not to other types of anticompetitive acquisitions. Third, the Supreme Court applied the more permissive Sherman Act standards in evaluating anticipated anticompetitive effects. Then, the Court enunciated a further loophole by ruling that the Federal Trade Commission was deprived of jurisdiction to enforce Section 7 if the acquiring corporation exchanged the stock for the assets of the acquired corporation at any time before the issuance of an order.

Despite these loopholes, and largely because of shifts in the public attitude toward concentration, the weaknesses in the law were not remedied until 1950, when the Celler–Kefauver Amendment to Section 7 was adopted. Section 7 was amended to read as follows:

> [N]o corporation engaged in commerce shall acquire, directly or indirectly, the whole or any part of the stock or . . . the whole or any part of the assets of another corporation engaged also in commerce, where in any line of commerce in any section of the country, the effect of such acquisition may be substantially to lessen competition, or to tend to create a monopoly.

The provision was thus broadened so as to reach asset, as well as stock, acquisitions. It was also made clearly applicable to all types of mergers and acquisitions which tend to have the proscribed anticompetitive effects. And an acquisition of stock or assets became illegal where "in any line of commerce in any section of the country, the effect of such acquisition may be substantially to lessen competition, or to tend to create a monopoly." Under this standard, it need not be shown that a merger actually substantially lessens competition or creates a monopoly at the time of challenge. It is sufficient for the government or private plaintiff to establish that there is a reasonable probability that the merger will produce one of those effects in the future. The phrase *any line of commerce* means that an anticipated lessening of competition with respect to *any* product line or service may be the focus of attack, whether a large or a small industry is involved. Moreover, the geographic area for measuring effects on competition may be "any section of the country," as well as the United States as a whole.

The preceding are the substantive standards of the present Section 7 of the Clayton Act. In terms of jurisdictional prerequisites the first is that both the acquiring and acquired firms must be corporations. (A corporation cannot, however, avoid the proscriptions of Section 7 by use of a noncorporate dummy. As in other fields of the law, courts and commissions have looked through form to substance.) Second, Section 7 requires as a condition of its applicability that both corporations be engaged in "commerce." Because that word is defined in Section 1 of the Act to mean "trade or commerce among the several States and with foreign nations . . . , " it is presumably sufficient to establish that each of the two corporations is involved in either interstate commerce (e.g., domestic sales activity) or in the foreign commerce of the United States (e.g., imports or exports), or both.

The Act only applies if the merger or acquisition's anticipated effects will be within the United States, that is, in "any section of the country." Does this mean that the statute cannot apply where a merger reduces competition only in foreign markets, and not in the U.S. domestic market? The precedents offer no help here. However, it is arguable that, even though such a merger would not affect American consumers, it could conceivably affect American competitors adversely in their export trade so as to lessen competition in a "section of the country." This question, while intriguing, appears to be of little practical significance and we will not dwell on it here. First, such a situation will seldom be presented and, as we shall see, antimerger enforcement policy and law have usually focused on transactions that are expected to affect the U.S. home market. Second, the Federal Trade Commission Act or the Sherman Act could presumably be applied in a proper case, were the Clayton Act deemed to be deficient in scope to protect important U.S. antitrust concerns.

Federal Trade Commission Act

Section 5 of the Federal Trade Commission Act is another powerful instrument available for application against mergers and acquisitions. Unlike the Clayton Act, the FTC Act does not require that both the acquiring and acquired corporations be "engaged in commerce" to trigger its jurisdiction. The commission can act against unfair methods of competition and deceptive acts and practices so long as they are "in commerce," this defined to include both interstate and foreign commerce. Moreover, the FTC Act reaches acts by "persons," such as individuals and partnerships, and not solely the "corporations" covered by the Clayton Act. In addition, it is well settled that a violation of Section 5 of the FTC Act can be predicated on activity that falls short of either a Sherman Act or a Clayton Act violation. The statute is considered to apply to mergers and acquisitions under an "incipiency" test, rather than the more stringent test that has been applied under the Sherman Act.

Despite its potential scope, however, Section 5 has seen relatively little use and development in the merger area generally, and less still with respect to mergers in international commerce. The provision's application to mergers was narrowly construed early in its history, and complaint counsel learned to rely on Section 7 of the Clayton Act. Since around 1960 the movement to involve Section 5 in merger control has been steadily gaining momentum. It can be expected that the statute, which has been likened to a "slumbering giant," will see greater development in the merger area in the future.

The Sherman Act, the Clayton Act, and the Federal Trade Commission Act thus comprise an imposing arsenal for the government authorities to utilize against offending mergers, acquisitions, and joint ventures that affect or are likely to affect adversely the commerce of the United States. Such transactions may be prevented by injunction and, if the transaction has already been consummated, the remedies may include divestiture of the stock or assets acquired, the restoration of the acquired company as a going concern, and injunctions against future mergers. Private parties may also seek to enjoin unlawful mergers or acquisitions under the Sherman Act and the Clayton Act and, although there are few precedents, can arguably also seek divestiture and money damages in a proper case.

Mergers: Types and Doctrines

In enforcing the various antitrust laws, governmental authorities assess a corporate merger or acquisition in the light of its functional impact on competition. The governmental purpose is to preserve and protect competition. Thus, the legality of a particular merger or acquisition is determined within the context of the market structure of the relevant industry. This structure will be framed in terms of a relevant product market and of a relevant geographic market. Because the legality of the transaction may well turn on how these two threshold issues are resolved, they are often a cause for substantial dispute between the government lawyers and the company lawyers. For example, where Company X is the largest manufacturer of metallic widgets and wishes to acquire Company Y, also a maker of metallic widgets, the government may argue that plastic widgets are not truly competitive with the metallic items, thus urging a narrow product market consisting just of metal widgets and a considerable potential impact to be anticipated within that market. The company's lawyers may argue, on the other hand, that metal and plastic widgets are similar in function, durability, and price, and that in this broader product market denominated simply "widgets," Companies X and Y are not major factors.

The actual determination of the relevant product market will be determined by the "reasonable interchangeability of use or the cross-elasticity of demand between the product itself and substitutes for it." Often, narrow, well-defined *submarkets* that in themselves constitute relevant product markets for antitrust purposes may exist within a broad market. Judicial rulings have tended to sustain the narrower market definitions urged by the government.

As we shall see, once the relevant product and geographic markets have been defined, the market shares of the companies concerned and the concentration within the market are key issues in determining the lawfulness of the amalgamation. Among the other factors that may be urged as pertinent to this determination are the ease of entry into the relevant market, the purpose of the merger, a history of acquisitions, and the likelihood of additional mergers in the industry. Defensive arguments may be raised where applicable, including the failing-company doctrine. The rationale of this defense that has achieved limited success is as follows: because a failing company is in any event destined, as a result of its financial condition, to cease to be a competitive factor in the relevant market, its merger with another firm cannot be regarded as likely to impair competition.

Those factors that should be given the most weight may vary, depending on what type of merger is contemplated. Traditionally, for purposes of analysis, mergers are classified into three broad categories: horizontal, vertical, and conglomerate.

A *horizontal* merger is one in which one company acquires all or part of the stock or assets of another company that is a direct competitor in the same product line and in the same geographic area. A simple example of an international horizontal merger would be this: two watch manufacturers—one a Massachusetts corporation and the other a Swiss firm—that compete for sales in the eastern United States agree to merge their assets under the control of one of the companies. The lawfulness of the merger will depend largely on what share of the market for watches in the eastern United States each firm held and the number and size of other firms supplying that market.

The market share a company possesses is measured by the company's dollar amount of sales or unit volume of sales divided by the total in the market. The higher the combined market shares of the merging companies and the fewer the remaining competitors, the more vulnerable the merger will be. In the landmark 1963 Supreme Court decision in *United States* v. *Philadelphia National Bank,* the Court held the merger of two large banks in Philadelphia illegal where the combined bank would have had a 30 per cent market share. The magnitude of the market shares did not create a per se finding of illegality, the Court reasoned, but shifted the burden to the proponents of the merger. As the decisions have tended to place more emphasis on market share data, so also have smaller and smaller combined market shares been deemed sufficient to presume anticompetitive effects. In *United States* v. *Von's Grocery Co.,* the Supreme Court, noting an increase in concentration of grocery store chains in Los Angeles, held unlawful a merger of two chains that would have resulted in a combined share of only 7.5 per cent of the market. And in *United States* v. *Aluminum Co. of America,* the Supreme Court found illegal a merger between the largest aluminum cable producer and one of the smallest producers, although Alcoa's percentage of the market was raised from 27.8 to only 29.1 per cent. On the other hand, in the 1974 *General Dynamics* decision the Court chose to play down the importance of market share data, stressing that, "[e]vidence of past production does not, as a matter of logic, necessarily give a proper picture of a company's future ability to compete."

A merger or acquisition is *vertical* when the participating companies are in a supplier–customer relationship. Generally, vertical mergers are subdivided into two types: (1) a "backward vertical integration" merger, which is an acquisition of a supplier (e.g., a domestic cosmetic distributor's acquisition of a French perfume company), or (2) a "forward vertical integration" merger, which is the acquisition of a customer (e.g., a Japanese electronics company's acquisition of a domestic chain of retail hi-fi and stereo shops).

Chief Justice Earl Warren, writing in *Brown Shoe Co.* v. *United States,* described the feared effects of a vertical merger as follows:

> The primary vice of a vertical merger or other arrangement tying a customer to a supplier is that, by foreclosing the competitors of either party from a segment of the market otherwise open to them, the arrangement may act as a "clog on competition" . . . which deprive[s] . . . rivals of a fair opportunity to compete.

In our preceding examples, the concern might be, assuming that all the firms involved were significant factors in the U.S. market, that other perfume or electronics manufacturers, American or foreign, might henceforth be impeded in their efforts to find adequate distribution for their products in the United States. Another concern here might be that other U.S. sales outlets would be disadvantaged by no longer having equal access to the products of the French supplier or the Japanese firm, respectively.

In the context of vertical amalgamations, therefore, the extent of potential market foreclosure, at the supplier level, at the purchaser level, or at both, is likely to be the controlling consideration. The Justice Department, in the Merger Guidelines that it has issued, applies a market-share analysis to both the supplying and the purchasing firms' markets to shape its standard of legality for vertical mergers. If the supplying firm has 10 per cent or more of the sales in its market and the purchasing firm accounts for 6 per cent or more of the total purchases in that market, the government ordinarily will challenge the merger.

Besides market foreclosure, other factors bearing on the likely impact of a vertical merger may be important, such as the creation of an imbalance of financial resources. In the *Reynolds Metals* case the court struck down a merger under Section 7 wherein Reynolds, the largest producer of aluminum foil, had acquired a major aluminum converter which transformed the aluminum foil into decorative foil for the florist trade. The court noted that the integrated operation would foreclose Reynold's competitors from selling to the acquired firm and emphasized that the "power of the 'deep pocket' or 'rich parent' for one of the florist foil suppliers in a competitive group where previously no company was very large and all were relatively small opened the possibility and power to sell at prices approximating cost or below and thus to undercut and ravage the less affluent competition."

During the 1960's the *conglomerate* mergers became the glamour phenomena. Conceptually, the conglomerate merger may be one of three basic types: (1) market-extension, (2) product-extension, or (3) "pure" conglomerate merger.

A market-extension merger results if the two merging companies manufacture or distribute the same products, but do so in different geographic areas. For example, if International Oil, Ltd., a worldwide company selling gasoline in a five-state southeastern sector of the United States, acquired Quad-State Oil Co., a domestic oil company that markets its products in a contiguous four-state southern region, the resulting combination would be described as a market-extension merger. Note that because these companies sell in different areas, this amalgamation would not eliminate any *direct* competition; it would, however, eliminate the potential competition that each posed for the other—that is, it would always be possible that either company might expand internally by extending its marketing into the contiguous area, thereby becoming a direct competitor of the other.

A *product-extension* merger exists upon the merger of two companies that manufacture or distribute products that are functionally related to each other. To illustrate, suppose a New York diversified office equipment company that distributes its products throughout the United States acquires a Canadian manufacturer of dictating equipment that sells in the United States. Although the American firm does not make dictating equipment, its products are so closely related that it might reasonably have been expected to enter that specific product line. Consequently, the combination of these companies eliminated a potential competitor in the dictating equipment market. Whether the merger could nevertheless pass muster would depend on the market shares of the two firms, the concentration in the market, and other industry factors.

The elimination of potential competition by a market-extension or product-extension merger may thus be as actionable as the elimination of actual competition. As the Justice Department's Merger Guidelines enunciate, "potential competition (i.e., the threat of entry, either through internal expansion or through acquisition and expansion of a small firm, by firms not already or only marginally in the market) may often be the most significant competitive limitation on the exercise of market power by leading firms, as well as the most likely source of additional actual competition. . . ." The Supreme Court's 1973 decision in the *Falstaff* case indicates the extensive boundaries of the potential-competition doctrine today. The Justice Department had challenged under Section 7 the acquisition by Falstaff Brewing Corp. of Narragansett Brewing Co. Falstaff was the fourth largest producer of beer in the United States, but did not sell beer in New England, where Narragansett was the largest seller. The evidence showed that although Falstaff desired to sell beer in New England, its management had decided against entry into that market other than by acquisition of a substantial brewery already in that market. The district court concluded that, on these facts, Falstaff was not a potential competitor in New England and the merger was not anticompetitive. The Supreme Court, reviewing under the Expediting Act, reversed and remanded the case for further proceedings. The Court reasoned that the key question was not what Falstaff's internal management decisions were with respect to entering the market but rather that "if it would appear to rational beer merchants in New England that Falstaff might well build a new brewery to supply the northeastern market then its entry by merger becomes suspect under §7." Under *Falstaff* and other pertinent cases, a company's assertions that it has decided against internal expansion into a new geographic market or product market will carry little weight where on an objective basis the company appears to be a natural entrant.

If the products of the two merging firms are totally unrelated, the merger is termed a *pure conglomerate* merger. Although these are generally the safest from the antitrust standpoint, such a merger may nevertheless be open to challenge where the resulting combination is such as to entrench the market power of an already leading firm or to create barriers to entry in an industry. The "deep-pocket" theory may be applied on the rationale, noted earlier with respect to the *Reynolds* case, that a giant firm may use its financial resources to wreak competitive injury in a previously well-balanced industry.

The threat of anticompetitive reciprocal buying is another factor that may be relied on by the government in opposing a conglomerate or other type of merger. Such a threat might be posed if, for example, a large American distributor of wearing apparel acquired a Canadian manufacturer of fabric for suits. The American firm would, in effect, be able to say to apparel manufacturers: "I'll buy your suits if you will purchase my fabric." This would foreclose other fabric suppliers.

Finally, in categorizing merger transactions, it should be noted that the antimerger laws may be applied to strike down *joint ventures*. In *United States* v. *Penn–Olin Chemical Co.,* Pennsalt Chemicals Corporation and Olin Mathieson Chemical Corporation launched a joint-venture corporation to produce and sell sodium chlorate in the southeastern United States. Neither of these two companies were in the sodium chlorate market prior to the joint venture. The Supreme Court ruled that Section 7 applies to joint ventures in general and that this venture was unlawful inasmuch as it created barriers to entry by other companies and foreclosed the likely possibility that the two parent companies would enter the same market.

The preceding discussion has been a short exposition of the basic types of merger transactions and of the considerations pertinent to their review from the antitrust standpoint. As we have seen, the Sherman, Clayton, and Federal Trade Commission Acts each, by their terms, can be applied to merger transactions in which the foreign commerce of the United States is involved. In setting enforcement policy the Antitrust Division and Federal Trade Commission have emphasized that the preservation of competition within the United States entails the challenging of merger transactions that would wipe out invigorating competition from foreign firms in this country. The focus of the cases brought, therefore, has generally been in terms of the impact of the proposed merger on the U.S. home market and on American purchasers, rather than with respect to overseas markets.

Let us turn now to review the different types of situations in which an international merger, acquisition, or joint venture has been subjected to U.S. antitrust scrutiny. We will see that the same law applicable to domestic mergers is applied and that, despite the seemingly exotic setting in which they sometimes appear, the same economic factors tend to be controlling in evaluating the competitive consequences of the transaction in question.

Domestic Company Acquiring a Foreign Firm

Most of the antimerger cases involving international amalgamations have been in the context of an American firm acquiring a foreign firm that is an actual or potential competitor in the U.S. market. Here, the impact on the U.S. market is clear, personal jurisdiction over the acquiring party is easy, and problems of extraterritoriality are minimized. Within this category the situation obviously akin to the domestic merger setting is that in which a domestic corporation acquires a foreign corporation that already has American production facilities. Economically, the effects of this acquisition are not different from the effects of a purely domestic acquisition. This is the case whether the foreign corporation is operating its own production facilities in the United States or is doing so through a wholly owned subsidiary. In either event the economic implications are indistinguishable from the purely domestic case, and the same legal evaluation should therefore follow.

This type of setting was presented in the case of *United States* v. *Jos.*

Schlitz Brewing Co. Schlitz, a Wisconsin corporation, had acquired 39.3 per cent (a controlling interest) of John Labatt Ltd., a Canadian corporation, which in turn controlled a majority interest in the General Brewing Company, a California corporation. The government filed suit against Schlitz and General Brewing, alleging that the Schlitz–Labatt transaction, when coupled with Schlitz' earlier acquisition of another brewing company, Burgermeister, threatened competition in the production and sale of beer in the United States, in the west, and in the state of California in violation of Section 7 of the Clayton Act.

The district court first made the jurisdictional findings requisite under Section 7, namely, that Schlitz and General Brewing were both "engaged in commerce" within the meaning of the Act, and that Labatt was also so engaged inasmuch as the "continuous flow of Labatt beer from Canada to Labatt's distributors in the United States constitutes an engagement in foreign and interstate commerce. . . ." The court then designated beer as the appropriate product market and the United States as a whole, plus various regions thereof, as the relevant geographic markets. It concluded that the reasonably probable effect of the transaction would be to lessen competition substantially in those U.S. markets. Its basic reasoning was that Schlitz was already one of the nation's largest brewers, that the beer industry was trending toward concentration, and that, absent the merger, "Labatt had the desire, the intention and the resourcefulness to enter the United States markets and to make General Brewing a stronger competitor in those markets."

Thus, although viewing Labatt as a likely source of invigorating competition from outside that should be preserved, the court otherwise evaluated the proposed merger with the same analysis as if a purely domestic merger had been involved. The focus was on the merging corporations' existing and potential activities in the United States and on the industry structure in the United States.

Let us turn now to a somewhat different setting wherein the foreign corporation sought to be acquired by an American competitor does not have an American subsidiary or otherwise operate physical facilities on U.S. soil. However, it has substantial exports to the United States, through sales to independent importers, and these products compete with those of the American firm. Therefore the same economic effect is to be feared from the merger—elimination of a substantial competitor—and the antitrust analysis is conducted in much the same fashion. It is possible that the conditions under which the foreign corporation is operating, because of U.S. tariffs and perhaps import quotas, and perhaps because of other factors, such as shipping costs, may limit its effectiveness as a competitor within the United States and, if so, this factor will be taken into consideration. But the mere fact that the foreign corporation is operating from abroad does not immunize the merger or even change the nature of the

antitrust scrutiny. If the requisite anticompetitive impact can be anticipated, the transaction will be vulnerable.

In a recent case somewhat of this genre, the Federal Trade Commission
attacked under Section 7 of the Clayton Act the acquisition by Litton
Industries, Inc., of a number of German corporations, including Triumph–
Werke Nurnberg, A.G. and Adler–Werke, A.G. known together as
"Triumph–Adler." Litton, a large U.S. conglomerate, manufactured and
sold office and portable typewriters, both manual and electric, and ranked
second in U.S. typewriter sales. Triumph–Adler produced electric and
manual typewriters in Germany and sold them throughout the world, including in the United States, where they were successfully marketed
through an independent dealer network. The FTC administrative law judge
ordered the complaint dismissed, finding that the merger did not have any
probability of lessening competition. He found that Litton's sales were
declining and that Triumph–Adler's potential in the United States was
limited. The administrative law judge concluded that because the established
marketing and distribution patterns of the two companies complemented
each other, the merger created a pro-competitive situation.

However, on appeal, the commission reversed the ruling of its trial
judge, finding the merger anticompetitive. The appropriate geographic
market was agreed to be the United States as a whole, and the commission
posited the following relevant product markets and submarkets: (1) the
office typewriter market, including (a) the office electric typewriter submarket and (b) the office manual typewriter submarket; (2) the portable
typewriter market; and (3) the typewriter industry as a whole. In these
five relevant product markets and submarkets, the commission found that
Litton had the largest market share in the office manual submarket and
was a strong second in the others. Triumph–Adler maintained positions of
fifth, sixth, seventh, or eighth in the pertinent markets or submarkets. The
commission further found, "[t]hat the typewriter industry as a whole as
well as the various submarkets within the overall market are highly concentrated is beyond dispute."

In its legal analysis of the acquisition, the commission started with
the observation that it "was a classic horizontal merger between two direct
competitors." It then noted existing merger principles holding that concentrated markets have inherently anticompetitive tendencies. It also recognized, quoting from the *Philadelphia National Bank* case, that in a highly
concentrated industry the "importance of preventing even slight increases
in concentration and so preserving the possibility of eventual deconcentration is correspondingly great." The commission thus concluded:

> Instead of maintaining and improving its market position through internal
> expansion, which would have been consistent with the merger law, Litton
> again chose the acquisition route as the most economical, expeditious and
> less risky alternative to internal expansion. Through its 1969 acquisition of

Triumph–Adler, Litton not only eliminated a significant competitor in the highly concentrated markets, but also exacerbated the concentration and entrenched its leading position in the various markets. This is proscribed by Section 7 of the Clayton Act. The typewriter industry is clearly in need of new competition, and the absorption of a significant competitor by any one of the leading firms is a clear violation of Section 7. The mere fact that IBM has enjoyed the leading position in the office electric typewriter market does not save the acquisition of Triumph–Adler, a dynamic and growing competitor, by a firm with Litton's market position.

It is significant for our purposes to note that in this opinion, as in most previous opinions involving acquisitions of foreign-based corporations, there was no mention of any ramifications or special factors resulting from the international features of the transaction. This case was decided strictly on the basis of domestic merger law.

Potential competition from abroad will also be the subject of protection under the antimerger laws. For example, the Justice Department challenged the acquisition by the Gillette Company, the leading American manufacturer of safety razors, of Braun Aktiengesellschaft, a large German manufacturer of electrical appliances, including electric razors. Pursuant to a pre-existing patent-licensing and distribution agreement that it had with the Ronson Corp., Braun was precluded from selling electric razors in the United States until 1976. The apparent theory of the government in this case, which is still pending, is that upon the expiration of the license agreement Braun will be a potential entrant into the American shaving market. Hence, the suit is seeking to preserve the potential competition of the German-made electric razors to the Gillette safety razors. The government's theory in this case is debatable on a number of grounds but, in any event, the challenge represents another effort to apply established antimerger principles in an international setting.

What if an American company acquires a foreign corporation that is in the same business but sells its products only in foreign markets and, unlike Braun, has neither the intent nor the resources to sell in the United States? Because such a transaction is not expected to affect U.S. commerce, particularly our home market, it is unlikely that it would be attacked. Similarly, it is not likely that the government would challenge a U.S. firm's acquisition of a foreign corporation that sells a few competitive products in the United States but does not have the resources or capacity to become a meaningful competitive factor here.

What of vertical mergers? An instance in which an American corporation's acquisition of a foreign company occurred in the context of a vertical merger was the *Dresser* case before the Federal Trade Commission. Dresser, a Delaware corporation, through its wholly owned subsidiary Magnet Cove Barium Corp., an Arkansas corporation, had acquired all the assets of Canadian Industrial Minerals, Ltd. (CIM), a Canadian corporation. The relevant product market and geographic market was the sale of ground barite to end users for oil well drilling purposes in the Gulf Coast area. Prior to the acquisition, Magnet Cove was the chief purchaser of crude barite from CIM. The second major purchaser was Milwhite, a competitor of Magnet Cove. The hearing examiner dismissed the complaint for lack of evidence establishing that the acquisition tended to lessen competition. The evidence revealed that after the acquisition, Milwhite had found other adequate sources of crude barite and continued to compete as before, even garnering a substantial increase in its share of the relevant market. Without adopting the hearing examiner's opinion, the commission affirmed the dismissal but included with it a stern caveat aimed at future acquisitions in this highly concentrated industry. In sum, despite the international nature of the transaction, the usual evaluation applicable to vertical mergers, an assessment of the threat of foreclosure, was made.

Let us take another example. Suppose Onyx Metals & Jewelry Co., a major American producer of ring settings, acquires Rare Metals, Ltd., a foreign corporation and the leading supplier of special metals to the American ring setting industry. Prior to the acquisition, Onyx was purchasing most of its metal needs from American suppliers. The antimerger laws would clearly be applicable here. Definite entry barriers have been erected to impede other firms from entering the U.S. ring setting market because Onyx now has exclusive control over a major industry supplier. Further, American suppliers of the special metals have been foreclosed from competing for Onyx's business. With this extensive foreclosure at both levels of competition, the merger will be struck down. The fact that Rare Metals, Ltd., is a foreign firm will not affect the result.

The result would probably not be different if the suppliers foreclosed from competing for Onyx's business were foreign instead of domestic. By acquiring a leading supplier, Onyx has still impeded its American competitors and erected barriers to entry into the ring setting industry. Moreover, the court may reason that the foreclosure of the other foreign suppliers from competing for Onyx's business has weakened import competition into the United States, thus further impairing U.S. competition and commerce.

Let us postulate still another vertical merger, wherein an American supplier acquires a foreign customer. If previous to the acquisition other American corporations had been competing for the foreign corporation's business, then obviously the effect of the acquisition has been to foreclose those American corporations from competition. Whether the antimerger laws have been violated will turn largely on whether foreclosure or other detrimental effects resulting from the integration seriously threaten other American firms. If the foreign customer is so significant that the position of other would-be American suppliers is indeed weakened or if the American supplier's integration threatens the vigor of American firms competing at the customer level, then the merger could be challenged. More usually, however, this type of vertical merger would not seem to pose substantial anti-competitive concerns.

We have already discussed product-extension mergers and geographic market-extension mergers in the context of the standards applicable to horizontal mergers. Although these transactions are often called conglomerate mergers, the existence of the potential-competition issue makes them in general a hybrid of the pure conglomerate merger and the horizontal merger, and they are amenable to treatment in either context. Remaining to be considered, therefore, is only the "pure" conglomerate merger, one in which the products of the acquiring and acquired corporations are unrelated.

As previously explained, in the domestic context enforcement agencies and the courts have condemned those mergers where they entrench a company's market position or provide incentives and opportunities for business reciprocity. There is no theoretical bar to the application of these principles to a pure conglomerate merger between an American and a foreign firm, providing the requisite effect on U.S. commerce is anticipated. For example, a merger might be conceived wherein American firms could be coerced into buying Product A from a foreign acquired company because of their desire to sell Product B to the U.S. acquiring corporation. There would be a feared foreclosure of other U.S. suppliers of Product A and a possible basis for challenge, depending on such factors as the extent of the acquiring company's buying power and the structure of the industries involved. A situation might also arise wherein a powerful American corporation acquired a foreign firm exporting to the United States and, because of the small comparative size of the domestic competitors of the foreign firm, threatened to use its resources to give the latter a dominant position in its industry. Although there has not been enforcement activity in this area, such would certainly be conceivable in a proper case.

Foreign Company Acquiring a Domestic Firm

Most of the cases brought to date have involved the acquisition of a foreign firm by an American corporation, rather than the converse. This is not symptomatic of any differences in the antitrust principles involved, because there are none. Both from the jurisdictional point of view and on the merits, the assessment turns on the effects of the transaction upon U.S. commerce, regardless of which corporation is doing the acquiring. The disparity in the cases brought seems to reflect primarily that American firms until recently were acquiring foreign firms more frequently, at least in an economically significant context, than the reverse. Perhaps the balance will shift as foreign investment in the United States increases.

Although the antitrust doctrine itself therefore does not vary, some additional problems may be encountered by the enforcement agencies in the situation where the acquisition is to be by the foreign firm and the merger has not as yet been consummated. Because adjudication and enforcement will prove awkward if the acquiring corporation is not made a party to the lawsuit attacking the merger, the foreign company should be included in the action, and yet in some cases the latter may not have agents or a "presence" within the United States so as to enable personal jurisdiction over it. In addition, where the foreign firm is seeking to do the acquiring, action by the government antitrust authorities is far more likely to be misconceived by the acquiring firm's own government as U.S. economic protectionism, rather than the exercise of nondiscriminatory national legislation. The need to observe the principles of comity may lead the antitrust authorities in these situations to conduct the matter more gingerly, albeit perhaps not differently in substance.

A merger challenge falling generally into this category occurred in 1969–1970 involving Standard Oil Company of Ohio (Sohio) and the British Petroleum Company, Ltd. (BP). BP, a British corporation, alleged by the government to be the second largest foreign industrial company and the world's third largest crude oil producer, had previously begun integrated oil operations in the United States as a result of an acquisition of assets from Atlantic Richfield Company. Sohio was allegedly ranked seventeenth among domestic petroleum companies in terms of total assets. When BP and Sohio reached an agreement whereby BP was eventually to obtain 54 per cent of Sohio's stock, the Antitrust Division challenged the transaction under Section 7, relying on both actual-competition and potential-competition theories. According to the government, Sohio and BP were direct competitors in the sale of gasoline in western Pennsylvania, with sales accounting for 10.3 per cent and 3.5 per cent market shares, respectively. In addition, BP was alleged to be a potential entrant into the highly concentrated Ohio market, which was contiguous to BP's existing marketing territory and in which Sohio accounted for over 30 per cent of total gasoline sales. A consent decree was agreed upon, settling the case. To safeguard competition, Sohio was required to divest itself of a large number of its Ohio retail outlets, with either BP or Sohio being required to divest itself of all its retail outlets in western Pennsylvania, the area of actual competitive overlap.

The Justice Department challenge prompted a strong adverse reaction in Britain and Europe, where the action was regarded by many as an unwarranted American effort to inhibit foreign investment here, despite years of takeovers abroad by American multinationals. From the antitrust standpoint, however, the government's move was not novel or different. As in a case involving two domestic corporations or the acquisition by an American firm of a foreign firm, the issues were the elimination of actual and potential competition within the United States.

Whether the category of merger is horizontal, vertical, product-extension, market-extension, or "pure" conglomerate, the market analysis outlined above will apply, regardless of which corporation is the acquiring party in the merger transaction.

Foreign Company Acquiring Other Foreign Company

In a situation in which the merger is of two foreign corporations once again the basic antitrust (i.e., economic) analysis is the same. The key substantive issues are the anticipated effects on U.S. commerce, as delineated by the industry involved and the economic stature of the merger participants. However, in this context, problems of extraterritoriality, comity, and other jurisdictional problems may well be severe, often sufficiently so to prompt an enforcement decision not to attack the transaction.

Let us picture, for example, a situation in which a German firm and a French firm, each supplying 40 per cent of the world market for widgets, agree to merge. Both firms export heavily into the U.S. market, but have no subsidiaries, agents, or physical facilities here. The merger will obviously substantially affect purchasers of the product within the United States. Yet an effort in the U.S. courts by the antitrust authorities to block this merger or achieve divestiture after consummation would encounter jurisdictional difficulties of every dimension, including a likely inability to enforce any decree. From the international viewpoint, such action by the United States would be likely to provoke vexation in Europe as an extraterritorial intrusion into their affairs. In this situation the United States authorities might well limit their effort to an expression of deep concern to the EEC competition authorities.

By changing the facts somewhat, we can postulate quite a different result. In 1969–1970 two large, diversified Swiss chemical companies, CIBA Ltd. and J. R. Geigy, S.A., agreed to merge their worldwide operations. CIBA and Geigy each maintained subsidiaries in the United States that competed with each other in the manufacture and sale of various products, including dyestuffs and optical brightening agents. The Justice Department brought suit under Section 7 against the parent corporations and their subsidiaries, alleging that a merger of the parents would unlawfully eliminate actual competition in the United States between the two subsidiaries. The government's prayer for relief made it clear that it was the coming into joint control of the *subsidiaries* that it was seeking to enjoin.

Asserting that they were voluntarily submitting to the U.S. district court's jurisdiction, the two Swiss corporations entered into a consent setlement of the case. Under the agreement the companies were required to establish a new corporation that was to be sold by them within two years, and that was to be the recipient of the dyestuffs and optical brightening agents business of CIBA's U.S. subsidiary. Other provisions were also included to bring about divestiture with respect to the competing product lines—including necessary patents, trademarks, ingredients, know-how, and customer lists.

As regards the "voluntary" submittal of the two Swiss corporations to the U.S. court, it was undoubtedly in the interest of those corporations because their U.S. subsidiaries were, in any event, hostages to a successful resolution of the matter. The key to the quick success of the antitrust action here was, in fact, the existence of the two U.S. subsidiaries, because this permitted the Justice Department to avoid any problems as to obtaining personal jurisdiction, as to "extraterritorial" application of U.S. law, and as to having a mechanism for shaping relief and enforcing it.

It is interesting to observe that in this instance, as in the BP–Sohio case, the government was very careful to structure a settlement that excised the threat to competition in the United States, but did not block the merger itself. This approach would seem to have been motivated, at least in part, by a desire to obviate unnecessary international friction over the application of our antitrust laws.

International Joint Ventures

Joint ventures are becoming an increasingly popular business format, both in domestic commerce and, even more so, in international trade. A joint venture is an entity organized and conducted as a separate business by two or more corporations. The utility and versatility of this business form in the international market can be readily appreciated. A corporation that wants to expand its activities to overseas markets can benefit from enlisting a foreign co-venturer who will share in the investment and risk, while contributing valuable knowledge of the local market and economy. In addition, in a political sense, the use of the joint-venture form may be very suitable in countries that either require or look favorably upon businesses that are, at least in part, locally owned and managed.

We have previously noted the application of the U.S. antimerger laws to joint ventures as enunciated in the *Penn–Olin* case. Where an international joint venture is involved, the same antitrust principles that we have been discussing come into play. Briefly stated, this will necessitate an examination of such factors as the existence of competition or potential competition between the co-venturers, the trend toward concentration in the industry, the barriers raised to entry by potential competitors, and, of course, the likely impact of the venture on U.S. commerce.

Obviously, if the device is used to achieve an unlawful objective, such as allocation of markets between competitors, the participants will be vulnerable. In *United States* v. *Imperial Chemical Industries, Ltd.* (ICI), the court held joint ventures between British ICI and a U.S. competitor, du Pont, unlawful under the Sherman Act, reasoning that:

The history of each of these [joint venture] companies demonstrates the unlawful purpose with which they were organized, and demonstrates that they were used as instruments by which territories and countries were divided and assigned for trade and commerce. It also reveals that these companies were intended to and did effect a restraint of American foreign trade and regulation and suppression of competition between ICI, duPont and other American concerns in the nonexclusive territories.

International joint ventures will seldom fall into this category of the hard-core cartel, and will normally have a valid business purpose. Nonetheless, like a merger which has valid business objectives, a well-intentioned joint venture may be unlawful if it threatens competitive injury to U.S. commerce. For example, an international joint venture, like an international merger, may eliminate a competitor or potential competitor, or foreclose access to a supplier or customer, thus making it more difficult for American firms to compete. If such a threat exists, U.S. antitrust law may be applied.

Whether an antitrust challenge will be brought will turn largely, as in the case of mergers, on the extent to which U.S. commerce is likely to be affected and the bases for asserting jurisdiction over one or more of the parties in the U.S. courts. If the joint venturers are all foreigners having no physical operations or agents in the United States, the procedural obstacles and considerations of comity will likely dictate against a U.S. antitrust challenge. On the other hand, there should be no jurisprudential or procedural obstacle to the suit where at least one of the co-venturers is American or has an American base of operations.

In one such case the Justice Department brought suit under Section 1 of the Sherman Act and Section 7 of the Clayton Act to break up a joint venture entered into between a U.S. firm, Monsanto, and a German company, Farbenfabriken Bayer A.G. The two firms, both giant chemical companies on the world scene, had formed Mobay Chemical Co., a Delaware corporation with offices in Pittsburgh, to produce and sell flexible urethane foam. The government reasoned that, because the two parents were competitors in the production of a related product in the United States and the world, the formation of the joint venture eliminated the potential entry of each parent into the urethane foam market. The court entered a decree requiring Monsanto to sell to Bayer all its interest in Mobay.

With the U.S. market directly involved here through the formation of a U.S. joint firm, the resolution of the case appears to be a pure and simple application of the *Penn–Olin* principles. But what of the situation in which a domestic firm and a foreign firm form a *foreign-based* joint venture company? The key once again is whether an adverse impact on U.S. commerce can be anticipated. If the joint-venture company can reasonably be expected to compete solely in foreign markets, and any competitive activities by the two parents in the U.S. market are not affected, an antitrust case will be difficult to mount. On the other hand, if the joint company sells into the U.S. market from abroad and the two parents do not sell in this market, the reasoning of the *Mobay* decision could easily come into play, namely, that the joint effort has dissuaded the two parents from each entering the U.S. market and meeting in competition.

The same type of assessment as to the economic impact on the U.S. market and U.S. competitors applies when the joint venture is formed abroad by two or more domestic corporations. Where the arrangement is deemed to affect competition adversely in the U.S. home market or even U.S. export competition, an antitrust problem exists. As to the protection of export competition, the *Minnesota Mining & Manufacturing Co.* case, brought under Sections 1 and 2 of the Sherman Act, is instructive. In that case four fifths of the American abrasive manufacturers combined, ostensibly in a Webb–Pomerene export association, and established and financed factories in foreign countries. Ruling that the Webb–Pomerene exemption was no defense to the export of *capital* to a foreign company, Judge Wyzanski found a violation of the Sherman Act because the foreign joint venture restrained the co-venturers from competing with each other in the export of products from the United States and also restrained their American competitors from receiving business they might otherwise have received from the markets served by the jointly owned factories. Because almost the entire industry was involved and there was found to be a clear restraint on foreign commerce, the court did not need to reach the separate issue of whether "[j]oint foreign factories like joint domestic price-fixing [are] invalid *per se*" because such cooperation between competitors may "inevitably reduce their zeal for competition *inter sese* in the American market." It would appear that, under existing law, joint production or manufacture abroad by U.S. competitors is not per se illegal. Where it is unaccompanied by joint marketing activities affecting U.S. commerce, and particularly where it seems justified by high capital and risk factors, the arrangement may pass antitrust muster. In view of the types of suspicions expressed in *Minnesota Mining,* however, such joint undertakings are hazardous.

It is to be expected that as the international joint-venture form of entity comes of age, we will see a further development of the antitrust law in this area, as indeed in the entire area of international mergers and consolidations.

chapter 9

The Transfer of Technology and Trademarks

As we have already seen, many businessmen today operate in an international market. This is a situation that the owners of "intellectual property"—patents, unpatented technology, trademarks, and copyrights—have helped to create, primarily through international licensing arrangements. The commerce in these intangibles is formed by a network of agreements, pacts, and understandings that criss-cross the globe and are valued in the billions of dollars.

As the pace of this international exchange has accelerated, the U.S. antitrust laws that bear on the transfer of intellectual property have been applied with ever-increasing sophistication and stringency. Before turning to the application of these antitrust principles, however, let us take a brief look at the concepts of intellectual property that are involved and at the legal framework in which they normally operate. Our focus will be on the areas of technology, patented and unpatented, and of trademarks.

Subject Matter of Intellectual Property Transactions

Among the various types of intellectual property, by far the most important in terms of economic significance is that of technology—patented inventions, trade secrets, and industrial know-how. Pursuant to an express constitutional mandate, the United States Patent Act provides that a patent may be obtained by "[w]hoever invents or discovers any new and useful process, machine, manufacture or composition of matter, or any new and useful improvement thereof. . . . " Conditions for patentability, such as novelty and nonobviousness of the invention, are also set forth in the

139

statute. The patent, when granted, gives the patentee the right, for a period of seventeen years, "to exclude others from making, using, or selling the invention throughout the United States. . . ." This right to exclude others from using the invention gives the patentee a right in the nature of a lawful monopoly.

Under the Patent Act, patents are designated as having the "attributes of personal property" and hence they can be transferred by the patentee either completely by assignment or partially by license. A license may be nonexclusive, which simply permits the licensee to practice the invention free from suit by the patentee, or it may be exclusive, which precludes others from having similar licenses. A provision of the Patent Act specifically authorizes the patentee to grant exclusive rights under his patent "to the whole or any specified part of the United States." As U.S. patents do not operate abroad, and foreign patents likewise do not operate outside of their respective countries, an inventor must seek patents in the individual countries for protection in each instance.

There are, of course, many techniques, processes, formulas, devices, and compilations of data that constitute valuable business know-how and yet are not patented, either because they fail to meet the statutory requirements for a patent or because the owner chooses not to seek patent protection. Where this information is maintained in secrecy it may be recognized as a "trade secret" and protected by applicable judge-made law. Absolute novelty and nonobviousness are not prerequisite to trade secret status, as they are to patentability. On the other hand, there is no statutory reward (such as the patent grant) for the holder of a trade secret. Thus, the value of a trade secret may be lost if the secret is independently discovered by a third party. However, in virtually every state and in most countries, possession of a trade secret is considered a right warranting legal protection, and that protection includes the right to injunctive relief to prevent parties, receiving the information in confidence, from unauthorized use or disclosure of the trade secret. Although some federal decisions had questioned whether the recognition of a property right in trade secrets was inconsistent with the federal patent system, a 1974 Supreme Court ruling settled that the state trade secret laws are enforceable.

Trademarks and servicemarks constitute a rapidly growing factor in intellectual property law. Moreover, when combined with a concept and licensed as part of a complete system, the trademark or servicemark may become the heart of an international franchise operation and affect a large amount of foreign commerce. Motel chains, fast-food houses, and service station operations are but a few of the kinds of franchise systems employing trademarks and servicemarks that have attained prominence on an international basis.

The trademark or servicemark (collectively referred to as trademarks) can consist of any word, symbol, device, or the like capable of identifying a businessman's goods or services and distinguishing them from goods or services of another. Rights in trademarks arise from adoption and actual use of the mark, and they consist of the exclusive right to use the name or symbol in connection with the owner's products or services in the trading area of use. This exclusive right is founded on the judge-made law of unfair competition. Early decisions emphasized the interest of the owner of the trademark in preventing a competitor from passing off his goods as those of the owner. Later courts redefined the legal interest involved to embrace the need for consumer confidence in receiving the actual product sought. These rationales eventually merged and expanded into a general policy of creating a fair plane of competition by forbidding one businessman from poaching upon "the commercial magnetism" of another's trademark.

Trademarks have become an essential instrument in mass advertising. The concomitant increase in the value of trademark rights spurred efforts to create a scheme of federal trademark legislation, which resulted in various federal statutes culminating in 1946 with the Lanham Act. The approach of the Act is to provide for federal registration of a mark, after it has been initially adopted and used in interstate commerce. The effect of registration under the statute is to give constructive notice of the registrant's claim of ownership of the mark, thereby precluding a subsequent user of the mark from claiming that he was using the mark in good faith.

The Act recognizes that marks may be assigned as a part of the transfer of the good will of the business in which the mark is used, or they may be licensed, so long as the licensor controls the nature and quality of the goods or services in connection with which the mark is used. However, because the Lanham Act does not normally operate outside the United States, the businessman must look to foreign trademark laws to seek protection abroad. (A limited exception to this prohibition on extraterritorial application of United States trademark laws exists when the alleged infringer is a U.S. citizen and he participates in the United States in some of the acts that are necessary to effect infringement of the U.S. trademark registration in the foreign country. For example, if a U.S. citizen prepares infringing labels in the U.S. and ships those labels to a foreign country for affixation to goods manufactured and sold in the foreign country, the U.S. trademark owner probably could secure injunctive relief from U.S. courts prohibiting the defendant from continued use of the mark in the foreign country.)

Antitrust and Intellectual Property: The Basic Relationship

The antitrust point of reference for agreements concerning intellectual property rights is usually Sections 1 and 2 of the Sherman Act, which, as we have seen, prohibit contracts in unreasonable restraint of trade and monopolization where either the interstate or the foreign commerce of the United States is involved. Aside from the question of whether a particular transaction affects the foreign commerce of the United States, the problems that the Sherman Act raises for the intellectual property owner are much the same whether the transaction in question is classified as domestic or international. These problems initially arise from the fact that rights in each type of intellectual property permit the owner to exclude others from using the property. Therefore, in a sense, each intellectual property owner is the possessor of a legal, albeit limited, monopoly. However, the boundaries of these legal monopolies may be difficult to ascertain, and when those boundaries are overstepped, the antitrust laws may cause loss of the property rights and even treble-damage awards against the property owner in favor of those injured by the unlawful extension of the monopoly.

When the intellectual property owner simply uses the property in his own business (i.e., by manufacturing and distributing his patented product, by using his patented or trade secret process to manufacture a commercial item, or by using his trademark to identify the product he makes and sells), he is not likely to run into antitrust problems. This is because the only provision of the Sherman Act that can be violated by a person acting singly is the prohibition against monopolization in Section 2, and the "limited monopoly" allowed to intellectual property owners is not in and of itself a violation of that section. This is not to say that a patent holder cannot be guilty of illegal monopolization or attempted monopolization as where, for example, he tries to enforce a fraudulently obtained patent. But such situations are not commonplace.

Contrasted with the situation where the intellectual property owner uses his rights "in-house," a great deal of difficulty can be encountered once he decides to transfer to others the authority to exploit his property rights. The uninitiated owner of intellectual property might react to this suggestion with the rejoinder that because he has the exclusive right to use his property, and by licensing others to use it he is promoting competition, he should be able to attach any conditions to the license that he may choose. This is not the law, however, because the policy of free and open competition embodied in the Sherman Act is strong, and the courts will find that once the intellectual property owner decides to exploit the property by other than "in-house" use, he must satisfy essentially the same antitrust standards as are applicable to normal transactions and agreements.

In addition to the limitations created by the antitrust laws, certain patent-licensing activities in the United States may run afoul of the equitable prohibitions generally referred to as "patent misuse." The patent misuse doctrine has been generally stated as prohibiting a patent owner from illegally expanding the scope of the patent monopoly. The effect of a finding of patent misuse is to cause the patent to be unenforceable until the misuse is purged. Misuse does not, however, necessarily expose the patent owner to liability and treble-damage claims under the antitrust laws, even though many of the licensing activities considered to be misuse are similar in their substantive aspects to activities that may create antitrust exposure. Thus, for example, conditioning a patent license on the licensee's agreement to pay royalties on sales of products not covered by the patent is patent misuse, but it may or may not be an antitrust violation, depending on other factors.

Finally, although not an antitrust law as such, the Tariff Act of 1930 deserves brief consideration at this point, because one of its provisions, Section 337, is relevant to international transactions involving products and processes covered by United States patents. Section 337 states that:

> Unfair methods of competition and unfair acts in the importation of articles into the United States, . . . the effect or tendency of which is to destroy or substantially injure an industry, efficiently and economically operated, in the United States, . . . or to restrain or monopolize trade and commerce in the United States, are declared unlawful . . . [19 U.S.C. § 1337 (1970)].

This statute has been broadly interpreted by the U.S. Court of Customs and Patent Appeals. In the patent area, the court has held that importation of products covered by a United States patent is an unfair method of competition. By virtue of Section 337(a) the importation of unpatented products manufactured abroad by a process covered by a valid U.S. patent is treated in the same way. The Tariff Commission, which has primary jurisdiction to determine what constitutes unfair methods of competition, is not empowered to rule on the validity of the patents which constitute the basis for excluding the importation of goods. Thus, as a result of the Act, goods may be excluded from importation without the United States patentee having to defend the validity of his patent before the commission. Because of this procedural quirk, the party attempting to import goods found to infringe a U.S. patent may be forced to delay importation until he is able to prove in another forum that the infringed patent is invalid.

Although the issue has not been squarely presented to the courts, it seems that, in general, exclusion of products by resort to Section 337 is not inconsistent with the U.S. antitrust laws. For example, in *In re Northern Pigment Co.,* the court rejected the defense by the importer that the imports should be permitted because "importation . . . would tend to destroy a monopoly, protect the public, and thus produce a healthy condition." On the other hand, a firm's resort to Section 337 might be viewed as one of several actions establishing an antitrust violation on its part.

With this background, let us look at some of the important antitrust questions that may be raised when one firm enables another, by license, to use the former's intellectual property rights. Our premise, because we will be focusing on international licensing arrangements, will be that one of the parties is a U.S. firm and that the other is foreign.

Restraints of Trade in International Licenses

Territorial Restrictions

A major concern of both parties in the negotiation of an international licensing agreement is often the territorial scope to be given the license. The licensor, whether the United States or the foreign party, may be willing and anxious to license use of his technology or trademark abroad but may be reluctant to create a new competitor for himself in his home market. He may even have a desire to retain certain established foreign markets for himself, while opening up only the new ones to the licensee. The licensee's objectives, on the other hand, may be to obtain a broad definition of the licensed territory for himself, in addition to a commitment precluding the licensor from using the technology or marketing the trademarked item in competition with the licensee in the latter's home market and other vital territories.

These natural commercial desires cannot be given free rein but must be tested in light of antitrust considerations. For one thing, as we saw in Chapter 5, agreements among competitors to divide world markets and thereby refrain from competition, to the detriment of United States foreign commerce, have generally been held illegal per se under the Sherman Act. This has been the result even though the cartel was achieved through the licensing of patent, know-how, and trademark rights. Obviously, then, licenses under intellectual property rights cannot be used as devices for dominant firms in an industry to carve up markets and choke off competition that would otherwise exist among them.

However, everyday bona-fide commercial licensing ventures do not fall into this clear-cut cartel type of pattern, making the antitrust inquiry more difficult. There is, for one thing, the argument that the normal rule against market divisions should not preclude territorial limitations in a *technology* license agreement where it is the license *itself* that is enabling the licensee to get into the business and become a potential competitor of the licensor. Although the courts have not spoken authoritatively on the subject, commentators and officials of the Antitrust Division of the Justice Department have generally expressed the view that territorial restrictions in international technology licenses are indeed not automatically violative of the antitrust laws, but, rather, should be evaluated on the basis of an inquiry into their reasonableness. That is, the purpose and effect of the limitation in the context of the agreement as a whole between the parties will be examined. The alleged business justifications for the restriction will be examined, and its likely competitive effect in the market place will be explored. Pertinent to this evaluation will be such factors as the size of the licensor and licensee, the extent to which they are established in the various markets, the scope and dollar value of the licensed products, the structure of the industry, the duration of the agreement, whether cross-licensing is involved, and the impact—the "flavor"—of the arrangement over-all. From these facts, a conclusion will be drawn as to whether the territorial limitation is a reasonable and hence permissible one.

It should be recalled that, in the domestic arena, territorial limitations in patent licenses are sanctioned by the express language of the Patent Code, which allows patentees to "grant and convey an exclusive right . . . to the whole or any specified part of the United States." Where an international licensing agreement involves patents alone, a comparable result can be attained on an international basis by the licensing of some countries' patents and not those of others. Normally this is not objectionable from the antitrust viewpoint. Although the Antitrust Division's pending Sherman Act complaint against the arrangement between Westinghouse Electric and the Mitsubishi complex of Japan strikes out at the fact that neither party had licensed the other under the licensor's home country patents, it is plain that these restrictions are viewed as objectionable only as part of a long-term and extensive conspiratorial arrangement to avoid competition.

Territorial restrictions in a license of trade secrets ("know-how") are generally more vulnerable to the antitrust prohibitions than such restrictions in a patent license, because trade secrets are not protected as are patents through statutory schemes of national scope. However, the rule of reason is usually applicable with respect to territorial restrictions in the trade secret context also. Although there is no definitive case law in this area, it is noteworthy that the Department of Justice, in a published memorandum, has taken the following position:

> Where know-how and patents are both involved and are closely related it is usually possible to impose the same restriction on the know-how as those permitted for the accompanying patents.
> Where know-how alone is involved the rule is somewhat more restrictive. . . .

The memorandum goes on to say that international territorial restrictions with respect to know-how alone can be upheld "if the know-how being transferred is of substantial value, the territorial restrictions are limited to a reasonable period and the agreement is not part of a larger plan to divide markets between dominant firms." It is also generally considered that imposition of such territorial restraints on a licensee of know-how can be justified only for a period of time approximating that which the licensee would have needed to break into the market on his own by use of available public information, reverse engineering, and other similar aids.

Let us evaluate some hypothetical situations, so that we can see the practical impact of this application of the law to technology agreements:

1. *Couteau Cie, a French company, holder of patents on an industrial cutting device in various countries, grants Slicer Corp., a U.S. firm, an exclusive license to make, use, and sell the device under its U.S. patent, but grants no rights under its patents in other nations. Slicer is thus not able to export the patented devices to those foreign countries, including France, in which Couteau has its other patent rights.*

The U.S. antitrust laws are pertinent to this transaction because the arrangement, in a sense, limits exports from the United States. However, assuming there are no further anticompetitive considerations that would complicate the situation, this agreement is quite proper. The licensee is merely obliged to observe the licensor's foreign patent rights, duly conferred by foreign law. No new obstacles are being created to impede U.S. export trade.

2. *Same parties and same basic arrangement as (1), but Slicer further agrees not to export the patented devices to countries in which the licensor has no patent protection.*

Once again, the U.S. antitrust laws would reach this transaction. This is a more difficult case to evaluate and one that is not free from doubt under the authorities. Some decisions, like that of the Ninth Circuit in *Brownell* v. *Ketcham Wire & Manufacturing Co.,* have reasoned that the licensor, because he is entitled to grant a license under his U.S. patent only, may require the licensee to observe the territorial limits of the United States. Other decisions and commentators take the view that this understanding is in restraint of trade because it is justified neither by foreign patent rights (which do not exist in the countries in question) nor by U.S. patent rights, because these relate only to the making, using, and selling of patented devices within the United States. The increasing tendency of the courts and the enforcement agencies to construe patent rights narrowly where they are raised in defense of a restriction on trade suggests that the latter view is likely to prevail.

3. *Same parties and some basic arrangement as (1) except that the cutting device is not patented in any country and the license is of secret "know-how," i.e., unpatented technology, relative to the making of the device.*

As we have observed, the courts have not spoken authoritatively on the question of when a license of valuable and secret unpatented technology can validly include, as an "ancillary restraint," a territorial limitation. In some cases, the courts have failed to reach the question, concluding that the know-how involved did not amount to a valuable trade secret or else that the territorial restrictions went too far to be reasonably related to the license.

In the *Cellophane* case, a French firm, eminent in the cellophane field, granted to du Pont, which was in the early stages of developing its cellophane business, the exclusive right to manufacture cellophane in North and Central America under the French secret process. The French company agreed not to compete in du Pont's territory. On a challenge by the government under the Sherman Act, the district court rejected the former's argument that a "territorially limited license under a trade secret process is *per se* illegal." It held the territorial limitation in question to be a reasonable ancillary restraint to the license agreement "since the participants were not in fact competitors" and since the beneficial result of the agreement was the "creation of the American cellophane industry."

Although such a territorial limitation in a license between two sizeable industrial concerns who are active in the same business might not receive the same lenient treatment under the present state of antitrust development, the reasonableness inquiry would appear still valid in evaluating the transaction. The arrangement in our preceding example should pass muster if it met the Justice Department's criteria earlier outlined. Of course, a "license" of know-how will not normally justify a territorial restriction unless there is the prerequisite valid subject matter for a license, that is, a secret and valuable quantum of technology.

4. *Whirlo, an American firm, holder of U.S. and European patents on a patented machine, licenses Vertex, a British firm, under its British patent but not under its U.S. patent.*

As with example 1, this practice will normally be valid. Although a theoretical restraint on U.S. imports may be involved, Whirlo is entitled under the U.S. patent laws to prohibit others from infringing its device within the United States. On the other hand, if Whirlo had no U.S. patent rights, a requirement that Vertex not export the machine into the United States could arguably be struck down as an unjustifiable bar to U.S. imports.

As we have seen, there is much surmise but little authoritative law in this area of territorial restrictions when it comes to anything other than the narrowest case, making the conduct of the reasonableness inquiry particularly difficult in this context. In sum, it must be kept in mind in designing technology agreements that contain territorial restraints that there is an increasing antitrust hostility to such restraints and that the Antitrust Division is of the view that, to be defensible, such restraints must be minimal and justified. Furthermore, none of the permissible licensing restrictions that we have been discussing extend to a restriction on the territory of *resale* of the licensed product. Territorial limitations on resale, if they affect U.S. commerce, are barred, absent special circumstances, by the rationale of the *Schwinn* case. (See Chapter 6.)

Let us look now at the territorial aspects of trademark licenses. It should be noted, in general, that antitrust issues can arise in many facets of international trademark use, yet there have been few cases that have directly addressed these issues. This is partly because trademark uses are often intermingled with other rights or business practices, such as patent and know-how exploitation, making it difficult to distill an independent trademark doctrine out of the general antitrust law.

A leading case in this area is the familiar *Timken Roller Bearing Co.* v. *United States,* where the Supreme Court found that American Timken had combined with its two foreign subsidiaries to create an international cartel for the purpose of dividing markets, fixing prices, and restricting imports to and exports from the United States. The Court rejected all attempts by American Timken to justify such restraints, branding them per se illegal. The government's complaint had suggested that American Timken's plan to dominate the world market for its product had been furthered by requirements that its foreign licensees not manufacture or sell antifriction bearings except under the Timken mark. American Timken responded that its alleged violations were mere steps taken to implement a valid trademark-licensing system. In other words, American Timken sought to categorize the trademark provisions as the centerpiece of its restrictive agreements, thereby immunizing all acts ancillary to that central purpose. The Court did not directly decide whether such a sweeping exemption from the antitrust laws could be sustained, because it concurred with the lower court in the finding that the "trademark provisions [in the agreements] were subsidiary and secondary to the central purpose of allocating trade territories."

The same result, on the reasoning that trademark assignments could not justify a division of world markets, was reached in the 1955 *Bayer* case. Bayer had entered into agreements with I.G. Farbenindustrie that provided for a worldwide territorial division of the pharmaceutical market. Unlike the *Timken* litigation, the trademark issue was in the forefront of the *Bayer* litigation. First, the need to settle various disputes between Bayer and I.G. Farben over rights to the trademarks *Bayer, Bayer Cross,* and *Aspirin* served as the catalyst for the market division agreements. Second, the market divisions were facilitated by cross-assignments of trademark rights between the two firms. Finally, the contracts contemplated assignment of all future trademarks in certain areas to the party in whose favor the area was reserved. The case grew out of an attempt by General Aniline & Film Corp., as assignee of I.G. Farben's rights under the latter's agreements with Bayer, to enforce a provision by which Bayer had agreed to pay royalties to I.G. Farben derived from profits on Bayer's exclusive use in Cuba of the disputed trademarks. Earlier, the government had obtained a consent decree that enjoined Bayer from carrying out the illegal agreements or from paying any money due thereunder. General Aniline, not being a party to the consent proceeding, commenced an action in the Supreme Court of the State of New York to recover I.G. Farben's share of the Cuban profits. The government, in the present case, sought to enjoin General Aniline from prosecuting the New York action and taking any other steps inconsistent with the consent decree.

The court held that the market division agreements were so pervasive as to constitute a per se violation of the Sherman Act. It further found that the transfer of trademark rights was "intended to secure the more effective enforcement of the division of territories and their exploitation." Yet the court ordered no trademark relief, beyond voiding the ongoing agreements. In effect, each party retained its rights to its existing trademarks and, presumably, the ability to prevent infringement by the other. This interpretation was confirmed in *Farbenfabriken Bayer, A.G.* v. *Sterling Drug, Inc.* where a successor to I.G. Farben sought to have Bayer's exercise of its right to exclude infringing goods from U.S. commerce declared in restraint of trade. The Third Circuit rejected the argument that mere exercise of exclusive trademark rights could constitute a basis for action under the antitrust laws, and affirmed summary judgment for Sterling Drug. This decision highlighted the limited effectiveness of the consent and court decrees in the original actions, because all parties were seemingly left free to adhere to market divisions by enforcing their valid trademark rights.

Nonetheless, as we have seen, courts have been hostile in both the domestic and the international setting to territorial restraints among competitors or potential competitors, and they have been cool to the argument that trademark licenses may legitimize such restraints. In *United States* v. *Sealy, Inc.* the defendant licensed manufacturers to make and sell bedding products under the Sealy trademark. Each licensee was allotted an exclusive territory and was thereby insulated from competition from other licensees. The Supreme Court found these arrangements per se illegal. It first held that the agreements not to compete were among competitors, finding that the Sealy company was a mere instrumentality of the licensees, established for the purpose of facilitating territorial allocation. The Court then further held that the market divisions had been inextricably connected with a scheme of unlawful price fixing, and could not, therefore, be upheld as "mere incidents of a lawful program of trademark licensing." The Court thereby left open the possibility that territorial restraints in trademark licenses, even among firms who would otherwise compete, might be upheld when clearly incidental to some valid trademark purpose. Indeed, the Court expressly reserved the hypothetical situation of a group of small grocers combining under a single trademark and a single program of merchandising in order to compete better with large grocery chains. A division of markets in such a compelling business situation, the Court suggested, might not come under the per se rule.

The reasonableness inquiry that the *Sealy* Court had promised in certain cases of horizontal trademark arrangements was, however, rejected in *United States* v. *Topco Associates, Inc.,* in the very situation that *Sealy* had reserved for such greater scrutiny. A group of small and medium-sized grocery chains had combined for the purpose of purchasing their own private-label merchandise in order to compete more effectively with the larger firms that were individually able to order and exploit privately branded goods. As part of its merchandising program, Topco assigned exclusive territories to its members and limited their right to sell to retailers. The case presented a different situation than the one often associated with combinations to divide markets, because the arrangements at issue did not allow for price fixing. On the contrary, their intended effect was to restore price competition to an oligopolistic grocery market dominated by large regional and national firms. Although the Court did not dispute the possible pro-competitive effects of the agreements, it held, nevertheless, that such arrangements between firms that would otherwise compete constituted per se violations of the Sherman Act. Such horizontal territorial limitations are naked restraints of competition and hence unlawful per se, the Court said, regardless of pro-competitive intentions, the absence of price fixing, or anything else.

These precedents indicate that where the effect is to restrain competition in U.S. commerce, trademark-licensing agreements that provide for territorial exclusivity are not likely to pass antitrust muster. Moreover, under the *Schwinn* rationale, the government will normally challenge agreements involving the sale of a trademarked article on conditions which restrict the resale territory of the purchaser. This is not to say, however, that in strictly vertical arrangements it is impermissible to have some understanding regarding a franchisee's territorial rights and responsibility. For example, after the Supreme Court decision in *Topco,* the trial court permitted Topco to establish a geographical area of primary responsibility for each of its franchisees, and this action was affirmed by the Supreme Court. Other cases have permitted similar restrictions on franchisees, such as location clauses, which establish the specific location where the franchisee can conduct his business.

Whereas *agreements* on the subject of territorial divisions are vulnerable, the trademark systems and laws of the various nations, including the United States, set up certain de facto and lawful territorial barriers on national lines. In this connection, it is worthwhile to note that there are U.S. statutory provisions that give the owner of a registered trademark the right to have imported goods bearing his trademark excluded from U.S. commerce, if he records his mark with the Bureau of Customs and meets the requirements outlined in Bureau regulations. These statutory provisions are found in Section 526 of the Tariff Act and Section 42 of the Lanham Act, and they reach the attempted importation of genuine trademarked articles as well as counterfeit ones. Thus, in certain situations, a company could prevent the importation into the United States of not only counterfeit items bearing its trademark, but also the genuine product with the mark correctly identified.

The regulations of the Bureau of Customs do, however, limit the scope of the exclusionary right. For instance, imported goods will not be excluded when both the foreign and the U.S. trademark or trade name are owned by the same person or entity, or when the relationship between the U.S. registrant and the alleged foreign infringer is one of parent–subsidiary or otherwise one of common ownership or control. These regulations will preclude the use of the exclusionary provisions where there is a license or similar relationship between the parties, but not where the foreign and U.S. marks are owned by separate and unrelated entities.

Restrictions Affecting Price

We earlier observed that, absent either a defense under the state laws applicable to fair trade or some other special exemption, the fixing of prices within the United States generally constitutes a per se violation of the antitrust laws. Moreover, it can be expected that agreements by American companies to fix prices in foreign markets will usually receive per se treatment if and when the requisite effect upon U.S. commerce is present. However, to some extent, price fixing has received special antitrust treatment in the context of technology. In 1926, in a landmark decision, the Supreme Court held that a manufacturing patentee *could* properly fix the price at which his manufacturing licensee might sell. In this decision, which involved General Electric's licensing of Westinghouse to manufacture and sell patented lamps at the price set by G.E. for its own sales, the Court reasoned that this was a legitimate restriction because it was necessary to protect the profits G.E. envisioned in retaining for itself a right to make and sell. This doctrine has been attacked by many critics on the premise that it reflects an improper extension of the patent monopoly and violates the usual rule against price fixing. Attempts by the Justice Department in the *Line Material* and *Huck Manufacturing Co.* cases to have the *General Electric* doctrine overruled resulted in divided and inconclusive decisions on the point. Thus, although the doctrine still stands, it does not have much, if any, vitality and cannot be regarded as a sanctuary from antitrust attack. The Third Circuit has, for example, limited the applicability of the *General Electric* rule by holding that where price restrictions are attached to *multiple* manufacturing licenses, Section 1 of the Sherman Act is violated.

Other types of price fixing in the realm of licensing have been established as impermissible. For instance, it is clear that once a patented item has been sold the patentee can claim no right to fix the resale price. In short, apart from the very tenuous shelter of the *General Electric* case, price restrictions affecting U.S. commerce should be approached with the same trepidation in the licensing context as in the usual business situation. If anything, this warning has greater force with respect to know-how licensing. Restrictions on products made from unpatented technology have been analogized to restraints on unpatented products made from patented processes, and in that latter situation the application of the *General Electric* doctrine has been almost uniformly rejected. Moreover, the disfavor in which the doctrine is held makes its extension to the know-how area unlikely.

Where trademarks are concerned, it is not helpful to distinguish between price restrictions on purchasers and price control over licensees who manufacture and sell the trademarked products or do business under the mark. Price maintenance would be per se illegal in both cases, so long as the United States' domestic or foreign commerce is affected. There is one exception to the principle just stated. The Miller–Tydings Act and the McGuire Act permit a trademark owner to set resale prices on his products so long as the transactions come within a fair trade statute in the state of resale and the contracts of resale-price maintenance are between parties at different market levels. Although the Supreme Court has not ruled on the question, this federal fair trade exemption should apply equally to sales by foreign manufacturers within the United States. On the other hand, foreign concerns should be aware that attempts to fix the prices on sales by their trademark licensees or distributors within the United States are per se illegal in nonfair trade states.

Field-of-Use Restrictions

A field-of-use restriction is one whereby the licensor of proprietary technology limits the licensee with respect to the scope or field in which the latter may employ the technology or licensed patent. It was ruled by the Supreme Court in the *General Talking Pictures* case that such a restriction in a patent license may be valid as a permissible benefit of the patent right. The provision considered in that case involved Western Electric's licensing the manufacture and sale of patented vacuum tube amplifiers only as to amplifiers made for noncommercial use. A majority of the Court upheld the restriction, holding that a licensee's manufacture and sale of amplifiers for commercial use constituted infringement of the patent. This decision, like the *General Electric* case, has been the target of much criticism by commentators.

Thus, despite the precedent of *General Talking Pictures,* field-of-use restrictions affecting sales within the United States or our import or export trade must be viewed with caution from the antitrust viewpoint. Top officials of the Antitrust Division have expressed the view that field-of-use restrictions on manufacturing licensees will be carefully scrutinized: where they appear a truly necessary and logical feature of a bona-fide agreement they will pass muster, whereas field or other license restrictions will be challenged when they appear to be used to allocate or divide markets. An example offered of an objectionable arrangement is that of one between two dominant electrical firms whereby one licenses the other in the field of motors over one horsepower and reserves to itself the field of motors under one horsepower.

Although there is thus a "gray" area as to the validity of field-of-use limitations on *manufacturing licensees,* it is clear that the Antitrust Division will give no such leeway where the restriction is sought to be imposed on *purchasers* of the patented product. A former head of the division declared that "there appears to be no justification" for the sale of a patented product with a restriction that it be used or resold only in a particular manner. This position is consistent with the Antitrust Division's general views against customer restraints, which received additional impetus from the ruling in *United States* v. *Arnold, Schwinn and Co.* In the patent context, the government reasons that because the first authorized sale of a patented article exhausts the patent monopoly, further restrictions may not be imposed upon the purchaser by the patentee-seller.

The government has manifested its views on such resale restrictions in a number of recent cases which, interestingly, have often involved international firms, although the principles do not vary. In one such recent case, *United States* v. *Glaxo Group, Ltd.,* the two defendants, Imperial Chemical Industries, Ltd. (ICI) and Glaxo, were British drug companies engaged in the manufacture and sale of an antibiotic compound. Although the compound itself was unpatentable, the two firms owned various patents on the dosage form of the drug and on processes for manufacturing the drug in bulk form, which patents the two formally pooled. ICI and Glaxo sublicensed various American firms, selling them the unpatented drug in bulk form but prohibiting the latter from reselling it in bulk without consent. The United States brought a civil antitrust suit against the two, alleging that these restraints (and the agreement between the defendants that brought them about) were in violation of Section 1 of the Sherman Act. The district court agreed, holding, in reliance on the *Schwinn* decision, that such restraints on alienation were per se violations of Section 1. The Supreme Court later reversed the district court in this case, but only on the ground that it had taken an unduly narrow view concerning the appropriate remedy.

In sum, as is the case in the patent-antitrust area generally, early precedents that upheld some restrictions as permissible incidents of the patent monopoly are today of uncertain permanence insofar as field-of-use restrictions are concerned, with the Justice Department chipping away at their foundations. Such restrictions would appear to be comparably shaky in the context of know-how license arrangements, where the support of the statutory patent monopoly cannot be invoked. Thus, where field-of-use restrictions appear in licenses to U.S. manufacturers, they may create substantial antitrust exposure, depending on the particular facts. Similar restrictions in licenses to manufacturers in foreign countries may not have the requisite effect on U.S. commerce, but if that effect can be shown, similar exposure will exist.

Tying Arrangements

As we saw in Chapter 6, "tying arrangements" may be challenged under a number of the antitrust laws where domestic, import, or export competition is restrained. Because there may be a strong temptation to exploit the patent monopoly by conditioning a license on the purchase by the licensee of unpatented articles, it is not surprising that the legality of tie-in arrangements was early examined in the context of patent rights. In *International Salt Co.* v. *United States,* the Supreme Court invalidated leases that required lessees of patented salt machines to purchase from the patentee-lessor the unpatented salt tablets used in the machines.

The rule against tie-in clauses, as described by the Supreme Court in *Northern Pacific Railway Co.* v. *United States,* a nonpatent case brought under the Sherman Act, is that they "are unreasonable in and of themselves whenever a party has sufficient economic power with respect to the tying product to appreciably restrain free competition in the market for the tied product and a 'not insubstantial' amount of interstate commerce is affected." At least the first part of this test of illegality is readily established where the tying product is patented because the Supreme Court has further declared in *United States* v. *Loew's, Inc.* that "[t]he requisite economic power is presumed when the tying product is patented . . . on the theory that the existence of a valid patent on the tying product, without more, establishes a distinctiveness sufficient to conclude that any tying arrangement involving the patented product would have anticompetitive consequences." Moreover, even where there is no purchase of a patented product involved, there is precedent for regarding the technology license itself as the "tying product" over which the licensor has controlling economic power. It follows that tie-ins in the technology context are also highly susceptible to antitrust challenge.

The Supreme Court did note in the *Loew's* case that "[t]here may be rare circumstances" where attaching a tie-in condition to obtaining a patented product are justified. One such case was *Dehydrating Process Co.* v. *A. O. Smith Corp.,* involving the insistence by the manufacturer of a patented silo unloader that it be sold only for installation in the manufacturer's patented silos. The First Circuit upheld the practice because the evidence showed that purchasers of the unloader had experienced considerable difficulty in using the unloader with silos made by others. In the "rare circumstance" where such a real need for a tie-in exists or where the licensee is taking the additional products of his free volition—i.e., where no leverage is being used by the licensor to foist unwanted products on the licensee—the agreement will pass muster.

Even where tie-ins are practiced in *foreign* patent licenses, they may be subject to review under the Sherman Act, because U.S. competitors in the "tied" product may, as a consequence of the restriction, be limited in their ability to compete for business in foreign markets, thus limiting U.S. exports.

Issues relating to tie-ins have become of great importance in the trademark context. The Lanham Act, as noted earlier, permits trademark licensing where the licensee is controlled "in respect to the nature and quality of the goods or services in connection with which the mark is used." In *Dawn Donut Co. v. Hart's Food Stores, Inc.* the Second Circuit interpreted this provision as placing an "affirmative duty upon a licensor of a registered trademark to take reasonable measures to detect and prevent misleading uses of his mark by his licensees or suffer cancellation of his federal registration." Because a trademark owner will often discharge this affirmative duty by drafting quality and other control provisions in the trademark license, a collision with antitrust doctrine may occur. Indeed, courts have recently extended the law relating to tie-ins to embrace arrangements whereby franchisors control the nature and quality of franchised products or services by, among other things, requiring franchisees to purchase supplies solely from the franchisor or a designated supplier or limiting the nature of the products handled or services dispensed at the franchise location.

In *Susser v. Carvel Corp.*, a majority of the Second Circuit held that contracts obligating franchisees to purchase from Carvel or Carvel-designated sources all ingredients of the end product sold to consumers were reasonable, because the tying trademark lacked the prominence necessary to establish market dominance and the tied products were both necessary to protect goodwill and not susceptible of advance objective specification without imposing an "impractical and unreasonable burden" on the franchisor. Seven years later, however, the Ninth Circuit, in *Siegel v. Chicken Delight, Inc.* built on the language of *Carvel* to affirm a contrary result on a similar set of facts. This change of outcome was partly explained by the intervening decision of the Supreme Court in *Fortner Enterprises, Inc. v. United States Steel Corp.*, holding that market dominance was not the test to be applied in determining the economic power of the tying product, but rather "whether the seller has the power . . . to impose other burdensome terms such as a tie-in." Such power could be presumed from the uniqueness of the product combined with the existence of legal barriers preventing other sellers from offering a similarly *distinctive* article.

On the strength of *Fortner*, the *Chicken Delight* court held that contracts requiring franchisees to purchase "essential cooking equipment, dry-mix food items, and trade-mark bearing packaging exclusively" from defendant, in order to obtain defendant's trademark license, constituted per se violations of the Sherman Act. The tying product in this arrangement was the license to use the Chicken Delight name, trademark, and method of preparation, an item separate and distinct from the tied mixes, packaging, and equipment. The court reasoned that the Chicken Delight trademark was distinctive and had public acceptance, and that it conferred economic power sufficient to bring about a tie-in situation because the registered trademark presented a legal barrier against competition, preventing competitors from offering the distinctive product themselves. Chicken Delight sought to justify the tie-in, *inter alia,* on the ground of its affirmative duty to guarantee the uniformity and quality of its product. The court concurred in recognizing an affirmative duty which devolved on the trademark licensor "to assure that in the hands of his licensee the trademark continues to represent that which it purports to represent." Nevertheless, it rejected the defense, holding that, "to recognize that such a duty exists is not to say that every means of meeting it is justified. Restraint of trade can be justified only in the absence of less restrictive alternatives." Here, the court found, the device of specification of the type and quality of the product to be used was available. Although Chicken Delight had contended that the needed dip, spice mixes, and cooking machinery were not susceptible to specification, the court affirmed a jury finding against Chicken Delight on this factual issue. The court did suggest parenthetically, however, that in cases where product specification would require divulging a trade secret, a tie-in might be acceptable.

Although the rationale of the *Chicken Delight* decision applies presumably with equal force to foreign firms doing business in this country as to U.S. firms, the effect of the doctrine on business carried on abroad is less certain. If the franchisor were an American concern and the franchisees subjected to the tie-in were foreign, a theoretical restriction on U.S. commerce would be posited if it were assumed that the franchisees, free of purchasing restrictions, would direct their business to U.S. companies. It would have to be shown for illegality, however, that a "not insubstantial" amount of commerce in U.S. trade was thereby being affected. Moreover, the initial premise that a trademark and franchise license are sufficiently distinctive and economically significant to be a "tying product" may be unwarranted in foreign markets where the trademark is unknown. Finally, under the circumstances of foreign commerce, a defense based on quality control might meet with greater acceptance. For example, special difficulties in translating specifications and product standards adequately into many different languages and otherwise in instructing foreign franchisees to conduct the necessary quality control might be cited.

Package Licensing

"Package licensing," the licensing of several of the licensor's patents (or, the licensing of patents together with unpatented proprietary data) in one agreement, is often found in international technology transfers. The licensing of a broad array of rights as an undivided grant for a set remuneration has great practical appeal, for it avoids problems such as determining which sales are covered by which license rights, the need for differentiated royalty rates, extensive bookkeeping, and similar administrative irritants. Nonetheless, package licensing may constitute an antitrust violation where the "package" is coercively imposed by the licensor on the licensee, rather than freely embraced by both parties for purposes of convenience. The rationale is the one applicable in "tying" situations generally. As the Supreme Court pointed out in *Ethyl Gasoline Corp.* v. *United States,* "[t]he patent monopoly of one invention may no more be enlarged for the exploitation of a monopoly of another, . . . than for the exploitation of an unpatented article, . . . or for the exploitation or promotion of a business not embraced within the patent."

The key question thus is the difficult and often subjective one of determining whether in a particular case the licensee sought only some of the rights conferred and was coerced into accepting the entire package or whether the licensee voluntarily contracted for all of the rights conferred. Where the licensor can document that he was willing, at the time of contract, to license each of the rights individually on a reasonable basis, he will be able to defend himself against a later charge of coercion. However, the heart of many license negotiations is verbal discussions between the parties, and insufficient documentary "history" remains for the future. Moreover, coercion can be a subtle process that is not easily reconstructed in a court of law.

The safest way for a licensor of various rights to preclude a later charge of package coercion is to make it clear that each of the rights is available to the licensee on an individual basis or in a less than total package and that the terms offered are fairly commensurate with the more limited license rights in question. The Seventh Circuit in the *Hazeltine* case, for example, ruled that it would be proper for Hazeltine henceforth to license "individual patents at rates the sum of which is greater than the package rate so long as the rates for individual patents are not so disproportionate to the package rate as to amount to economic coercion to force the taking of the package. . . . "

These principles apply fully to licensing under U.S. patents. They might also be deemed applicable where a U.S. company was being coerced into accepting an undesired license under foreign patents, the antitrust theory being that the forcing of an improper royalty obligation on the firm could limit its competitive effectiveness abroad and thus affect U.S. foreign commerce. On the other hand, coercing a foreign-based manufacturer to accept a package license under a group of foreign patents might not have the requisite adverse effect on U.S. commerce.

Improper Royalty Formulas

The improper formulation or imposition of royalties in a license agreement is one ground for application of the patent-misuse doctrine and a possible ingredient of an antitrust violation. The reasoning, once again, is that a patent (or other intellectual property right) cannot be used to exercise leverage on a licensee so as to extract compensation from him in areas outside of the licensed subject matter. Royalty questions can arise in a number of contexts.

In *Brulotte* v. *Thys Co.,* a license agreement covering a patented machine provided for the payment of royalties on use of the machine both before and after the expiration date of the patent. The Supreme Court held the imposition of a royalty obligation for postexpiration use of the machine to be an unlawful effort by the patentee to extend the term of his monopoly beyond that granted by the law. It is clear from the decision that the Court would not have objected to the postexpiration payments had they been deferred payments of royalties accruing during the life of the patent. The royalties were improper only by reason of the fact that they were based on postexpiration use of the invention.

It is well settled, as an aspect of the tie-in doctrine, that the patent monopoly cannot be used for leverage on the licensee insofar as unpatented products are concerned, but some difficulty has been encountered in applying this general principle to the subject of royalty formulation. In *Automatic Radio Manufacturing Co.* v. *Hazeltine Research, Inc.,* Automatic Radio claimed patent misuse on the part of its licensor, Hazeltine, on the ground that the license agreement obliged Automatic Radio to pay a percentage royalty based on the selling price of its radio receivers, whether or not any of the licensed patents were used with respect to these receivers. The Supreme Court reasoned that such a provision is not improper per se and concluded that the payment of royalties according to an agreed percentage of the licensee's sales was here reasonable, because "[s]ound business judgment could indicate that such payment represents the most convenient method of fixing the business value of the privileges granted by the licensing agreement."

The import of this decision was considered by the Supreme Court in *Zenith Radio Corp.* v. *Hazeltine Research, Inc.* The Seventh Circuit had concluded, relying on the *Automatic Radio* case, that the receipt by Hazeltine of royalties on the entire production of its licensees, whether or not the license patents were employed, was permissible. The Supreme Court reversed this ruling, holding that "conditioning the grant of a patent license upon payment of royalties on products which do not use the teaching of the patent does amount to patent misuse." The Court went to great pains to distinguish the *Automatic Radio* case on the ground that there the royalty formula had served "as a convenient method designed by the parties to avoid determining whether each radio receiver embodied an HRI patent," whereas here the district court determined that Hazeltine had *conditioned* the grant of patent licenses on adoption by the licensee of the percent of total sales formula. The test, according to the Court, is whether "convenience of the parties rather than patent power dictates the total-sales royalty provision. . . ."

Mr. Justice Harlan dissented from this reasoning, suggesting that the Court was in reality overruling *Automatic Radio* "without offering more than a shadow of a reason in law or economics for departing from that earlier ruling." He suggested that the majority's test of validity is as a practical matter unworkable because "it often will be very hard to tell whether a license provision was included at the instance of both parties or only at the will of the licensor." Thus, uncertainty in license relationships and in litigation would follow in the wake of the Court's postulated standard for illegality. Although the theoretical soundness of the Court's distinction between "convenience" and "conditioning" is defensible, Justice Harlan's prediction as to its doubtful practicability has proved correct. Consequently, a royalty measured by a percentage of the licensee's total sales, where the products making up those sales are not limited to products covered by the licensed technology, invites antitrust exposure on the part of the licensor. The absence of a patent-misuse doctrine in most foreign countries may limit this problem when a license involves only foreign patents.

Although the licensor normally is free to set any rate of royalty that he wishes, including differing royalties for different licensees, there can be situations in which setting differing royalties is improper. Royalty discrimination cannot be practiced so as to cripple certain competitors or exclude new entrants. Nor are royalty differentials permissible where they are used as a device to achieve an unlawful allocation of markets among potential competitors. Let us postulate, for example, a situation in which a major American firm in a concentrated industry licenses a major foreign company in the same industry under the American firm's technology. Let us assume further, recalling our earlier discussion of territorial restrictions, that it would be improper in light of all the attendant economic facts for the American firm to secure the agreement of the foreign firm that it will not sell the licensed products into the United States. It would appear to be equally illegal for the American firm to seek to attain this objective by imposing, instead of an outright territorial limitation, a reasonable rate of royalty for overseas sales by the licensee but a prohibitive rate of royalty for U.S. sales, in effect precluding access by the licensee to the U.S. market.

Grantback Provisions

A "grantback" provision in a technology agreement is a clause that binds the licensee to give to the licensor exclusive rights to use improvements, variations, or other new technology developed by the licensee in the course of using the subject matter of the license. It is understandable for the licensor to want access to improvements in the art that are made possible by reason of the license arrangement. However, the grantback, like other restrictions on the licensee, may sometimes be regarded as an abuse of the licensor's position and thus a misuse or a violation of the antitrust laws. In the *Transparent Wrap* case, in the context of an agreement to assign improvements back to a patent licensor, the Supreme Court enunciated the view that grantbacks are not illegal per se, and hence must be individually evaluated under the rule of reason. This view is still the law and has resulted in many grantbacks being upheld as reasonable, including the one in *Sperry Products, Inc.* v. *Aluminum Co. of America,* which bound the foreign licensees under foreign patents to assign the U.S. patent rights on improvements back to the licensor.

However, where the grantback is part of an overall monopolistic scheme or otherwise has the effect of restraining trade, it will be held a violation of the Sherman Act. Although each clause of this nature must be examined in the light of its own peculiar industry situation, whether or not it is vulnerable as a restraint of trade or patent misuse may well turn on whether it is an exclusive grantback, on the one hand, or merely a nonexclusive license-back, on the other. Where the grantback is to be an assignment or exclusive license, it is more likely to be viewed as an improper effort by the licensor to secure or maintain a stranglehold on a portion of the market place, especially if the period of the agreement is lengthy and the scope of the technology considerable. Reservation of a right to a nonexclusive license under improvements, on the other hand, is usually sufficient to accommodate a licensor's justifiable desire to share in the future development of the technology.

These principles obviously apply to an American or a foreign firm's demanding a grantback of U.S. patent rights. The application of these U.S. antitrust rules to an American or foreign company's demanding grantbacks of foreign patent rights would also appear to be proper, because the accumulation of foreign patents under the control of one firm could impede the efforts of U.S. firms to sell abroad.

Multiple Licenses, Cross Licenses, and Pooling

A licensor's conferring of licenses on a number of competing licensees is by itself not objectionable from the antitrust viewpoint. As long as the terms of each license agreement are fixed between the licensor and each individual licensee, with no collusive agreement or conduct among licensees concerning prices, territory, or the like, the multiple aspect of the licensing program should be unassailable. Of course, it is quite proper and common for one licensee to insist in his negotiations with the licensor that a "most-favored-nation" clause be included in his agreement, entitling the licensee to receive from the licensor terms no less favorable than those offered by the latter to other, comparable licensees.

Cross-license agreements—i.e., agreements between two or more parties wherein there are reciprocal licenses—are also permissible, provided that they are not designed to serve an anticompetitive conspiracy or otherwise effect a restraint of trade, in which case they will result in antitrust exposure. Nonetheless, patent "pools" or "patent interchanges," involving extensive arrangements, have often figured in antitrust cases. An interesting situation concerning foreign trade was presented in *United States* v. *Singer Manufacturing Co.* Singer, a U.S. manufacturer of sewing machines and two competitors, Gegauf of Switzerland and Vigorelli of Italy, had entered into cross-licensing agreements. Although an intention of the parties was to avoid possible patent infringement of each other, they had also discussed the question of Japanese competition in the United States, and Gegauf thereafter assigned to Singer its U.S. patent rights. Singer subsequently filed patent infringement and Tariff Commission proceedings directed against imports of Japanese sewing machines. The government brought suit under Section 1 of the Sherman Act, alleging that this course of action, including the cross licensing and assignment of Gegauf's U.S. patent, was an illegal conspiracy designed to exclude competitive Japanese sewing machines from the United States. The Supreme Court sustained the government's basic position, finding concerted action among the three to restrain trade, particularly insofar as the Gegauf patent had been placed in Singer's hands to enable it to take the desired action against the Japanese imports.

Patent pooling was also involved in the *Hazeltine* and *Zenith* litigation. Zenith's counterclaim for damages and injunctive relief charged that Hazeltine engaged in conspiratorial activities with foreign cartels or patent pools in England, Canada, and Australia that impaired Zenith's export sales to those countries. The important electronics companies in each of these countries had set up a patent pool into which they funneled many of the patents owned or controlled by the pool members (including the Hazeltine patents). The pools' trustees had exclusive rights to license the patents of their member companies, and granted only package licenses, restricted to local manufacture, that inhibited Zenith and others—who feared infringement suits—from shipping into those countries from the United States. The Supreme Court concluded that the "clear purpose [of the Canadian pool] was to exclude concerns like Zenith from the Canadian market unless willing to manufacture there" and that this purpose had been effectuated, resulting in damages to Zenith. As to the English and Australian markets, the Court reasoned from the record that factors other than the activities of the pool had led to Zenith's failure to enter the market.

The Court also made it clear that the fact that these were foreign patent pools did not lessen Hazeltine's antitrust liability, because Hazeltine was a co-conspirator and the requisite effect on U.S. trade was present. "Once Zenith demonstrated that its exports from the United States had been restrained by pool activities, the treble-damage liability of the domestic company participating in the conspiracy was beyond question."

Remedial Decrees Where Licensing Agreements Violate the Antitrust Laws

Technology

An antitrust decree is designed to remedy all aspects of the subject violation and hence may govern patent and know-how rights where these are intertwined in the misconduct. It is well settled that where necessary to restore competition, the antitrust remedy fashioned by a court may include compulsory licensing of a patent at reasonable rates. Compulsory licensing of know-how as a part of an antitrust remedy may also take place, presumably with attendant safeguards to protect the confidential status of this unpatented technology. The fixing of a "reasonable" royalty may pose practical problems, but this form of remedy is quite common in the antitrust context.

Compulsory royaltyfree licensing or dedication of the patent to the public have been much more controversial forms of remedy on the ground that they are so harsh as to amount to penal rather than remedial action. The Supreme Court has several times indicated a lack of enthusiasm for royaltyfree licensing, suggesting that it may be confiscatory, but such provisions have been included in a number of decrees. Of very recent interest is the proceeding filed in January 1973 by the Federal Trade Commission alleging that Xerox Corporation has monopolized the office copier field in violation of Section 5 of the Federal Trade Commission Act. The relief contemplated by the commission, which contends that Xerox has unlawfully used its patents to maintain its dominance, includes "[m]andatory royaltyfree unrestricted licensing of all existing patents pertinent to office copiers (including rights resulting from pending patent applications), mandatory unrestricted licensing of patents pertinent to office copiers obtained during the 20 years following the date of the Order, and disclosure to licensees of knowhow related to practice of licensed patents."

One interesting and important question, where an international agreement involving a license of foreign technology has run afoul of the U.S.

antitrust laws, is whether the court will try to extend the remedial order to regulate use of the foreign-origin intellectual property rights. As we saw in Chapter 4, in one case against Imperial Chemical Industries, the court's decree directed ICI to grant immunity under its British patents that corresponded to the U.S. patents of its co-conspirator, du Pont, with ICI entitled to receive a reasonable royalty upon imports into Great Britain of products manufactured under the patents. District Court Judge Ryan pointed out that his court had jurisdiction in personam over ICI and that the British patents had been used to restrain trade between the two countries; he concluded that "[i]t does not seem presumptuous for this court to make a direction to a foreign defendant corporation over which it has jurisdiction to take steps to remedy and correct a situation, which is unlawful both here and in the foreign jurisdiction in which it is domiciled." Subsequently, another British corporation, British Nylon Spinners, Ltd. (BNS), which had exclusive license right under some of the ICI patents, brought suit in the British courts to enjoin ICI from complying with those parts of the U.S. judgment that allegedly interfered with BNS's contract rights. The British courts eventually ruled that although the U.S. courts might as a general matter properly issue orders against ICI, upon whom they had *in personam* jurisdiction, ICI was obliged under English law to honor its contract with BNS, because the latter had not been before the U.S. court and there was no evidence of wrongdoing on its part.

Trademarks

Aside from problems of comity and jurisdiction similar to those already discussed, the fashioning of trademark relief actually affecting the trademark involved in antitrust litigation is beset by practical difficulties. This is evidenced by the fact that such relief has rarely been forthcoming, even in blatant cartel situations. The *Bayer* case, for instance, illustrates the type of situation where the failure to grant any trademark relief operates to permit trademark owners to re-establish some market divisions through reliance on exclusionary rights derived from Section 526 of the Tariff Act and Section 42 of the Lanham Act. This hesitancy on the part of courts to interfere with trademark ownership may be explained in part by their perception of the functional differences between trademarks and patents. Because trademarks operate to identify origin and give assurances as to a standard of quality, remedies in the nature of compulsory licensing can only serve to confuse consumers by allowing the trademark to represent goods of varying quality and origin.

Intermediate remedies, however, have been developed, forcing trademark owners to surrender some of their rights of ownership or to curtail activities incidental to trademark use. Among these limited types of relief are restrictions on the amount of goods bearing a trademark and requirements that an exporting company adopt an additional trademark in order to pry open foreign markets theretofore closed to its goods.

The usefulness of this latter remedy is demonstrated in cartel-type situations where foreign assignees of trademark rights can continue to exclude American exports by reliance on the law of their native jurisdiction. In such cases the Justice Department is faced with the prospect that a judgment obtained against an American cartel partner will be of limited effect by reason of the rights abroad of the foreign partners. However, the compulsory adoption of an additional trademark in such situations by the United States corporation will at least allow U.S. products to enter the pertinent foreign market. For instance, in *United States* v. *Permutit Co.,* a consent judgment was entered against a domestic manufacturer enjoining it from, among other things, allocating territories or limiting its exports to foreign markets. In order to effectuate the judgment, the defendant was directed to adopt a trademark for use in the export trade that would be "separate and distinct from the mark 'Permutit' or other marks or names owned or controlled" by foreign concerns. The U.S. firm was further required to register the newly adopted mark or otherwise secure the right to its use so as to ensure ingress of the corporation's product in those areas where use of the Permutit name by other than the respective registrant "would bar or hinder ingress . . . or would subject defendant-Permutit . . . . to judicial or administrative proceedings based upon confusion, deception, infringement or any other proceeding based upon a form of unfair competition."

Another noteworthy point involving remedies in trademark cases involves Section 33(b)(7) of the Lanham Act. That section provides that any use of a mark to violate the antitrust laws will constitute a defense to the incontestability status assigned to a mark by the Act after five years of continuous use and registration. Some courts view this provision as merely precluding an assertion by the registrant that his right to use the mark in commerce is conclusively proved by registration and use and is therefore incontestable. Other courts have expanded the role of 33(b)(7) beyond that of merely depriving an alleged misuser of an evidentiary advantage, holding that its invocation may constitute a complete defense to a charge of infringement and, further, may allow for cancellation of the mark as an antitrust remedy. Courts have not, however, either in an antitrust suit or an infringement action, ordered as part of an antitrust remedy a mark's cancellation or dedication to the public. Furthermore, the majority of courts insist that the mark be the actual instrumentality required and used to accomplish the antitrust violation before the alleged misuse can constitute a defense to infringement.

A fascinating and involved case that illustrates one court's application of the misuse defense is *Carl Zeiss Stiftung* v. *V.E.B. Carl Zeiss, Jena,* where defendants offered a defense of antitrust misuse to a charge of trademark infringement. The District Court for the Southern District of

New York first rejected an expansive reading of 33(b)(7), finding that the provision was meant only to deprive the registrant's mark of the presumption of incontestability. Nevertheless, the court held the defense was cognizable under its general equity powers. It went on, however, to find that the evidence was insufficient to establish the defense, because there was no proof that the "mark itself has been the basic and fundamental vehicle" of the violation. Moreover, the court found that the American subsidiaries of the German plaintiff-foundation were entirely responsible for the alleged antitrust violations, and that they retained the necessary degree of independence to require the court to honor their separate corporate status. Because the marks at issue were registered in the name of the foreign plaintiff, and the latter's American subsidiaries had no legal title in the trademarks, infringement could not be excused on the basis of the subsidiaries' alleged acts. Whether the court is likely to pierce the corporate veil is thus another factor that may bear on the international use of trademarks.

Conclusion

We began this chapter by noting the interdependence of owners of intellectual property. We end it by prophesying that they may soon share not only common interests, but common liabilities. The request of the U.S. government in its *Westinghouse–Mitsubishi* complaint for relief which would require Westinghouse and Mitsubishi to license each other nonrestrictively in the United States *and* Japan, as to both present and future U.S. *and* Japanese patents, raises the specter of decrees that will be truly international in scope.

This trend toward a stricter, more embracing antitrust law is required in order to cope with the modern uses of monopoly power. Thus, an invocation of intellectual property rights can no longer ensure special antitrust treatment, nor can a plea of comity or of jurisdictional limitations guarantee a sympathetic hearing by the tribunals of nations that must cope with the era of the multinational enterprise. And yet the need to facilitate the exchange of the products of inventive genius is perhaps greater today than ever before. For instance, only the sharing of advanced technology can effectively narrow the gap between the developed and underdeveloped nations. Solutions to the problems of ecology, health, and safety must also come from an international effort in exchanging and developing new processes, products, and methods of manufacture. Moreover, the international licensing of trademarks can aid efforts directed toward expanding markets and breaking down the barriers of nationalistic buying.

This realization of the importance of intellectual property to world trade and development is reflected in the recent completion of international patent and trademark treaties, which present the hopeful picture of international legal systems sensitive to aiding as well as controlling the efforts of the licensor of intellectual property. For it is beyond dispute that the great majority of businessmen who seek to enter foreign markets and exploit their technological or creative products in an international arena are motivated by bona-fide aspirations, guided by prudent counsel, and performing a vital role in permitting the world's technology to be shared and advanced. As the antitrust laws of the United States and, for that matter, those of the rest of the developed world become more sophisticated in coping with cartels and multinational corporations, it is to be hoped that they will continue to refine the doctrines that seek to distinguish between the bona-fide entrepreneur serving vital economic and social needs and the monopolist.

chapter 10

Antitrust Exemptions Pertinent to International Trade and Commerce

Most businesses engaging in U.S. interstate and international trade and commerce are subject to the federal antitrust laws. However, some businesses qualify for special exemption from the antitrust laws. This chapter is concerned with the subject of antitrust exemptions, in particular those pertinent to international trade and commerce.

Generally speaking, antitrust exemptions offer limited, rather than absolute, protection against liability. For example, an exemption may apply to international trade and commerce but not to interstate commerce; it may cover a part, but not all, of interstate commerce; or it may extend only to interstate commerce. Exemptions are usually restricted to particular types of business activities. Some exemptions are only available to certain kinds of business organizations. And even where qualified business organizations engage in protected activities, exemptions are sometimes forfeited if nonqualified businesses join with the former in the activities. Finally, some exemptions are limited in that they do not come into play until after the activity to be exempted is first approved by a governmental body.

The limited scope given to exemptions is explained by the strong national policy behind the antitrust laws. This policy is amply reflected in the legislative histories of the antitrust laws, the broad language used by Congress in writing the statutes, and the provisions awarding threefold damages, costs, and attorneys' fees to private plaintiffs who succeed in proving antitrust violations. Moreover, the courts have expressly acknowl-

167

edged the existence of this strong national policy and, accordingly, have given broad application to the antitrust laws, while construing exemptions narrowly.

Most antitrust exemptions are embodied in congressional enactments. However, the Supreme Court has created a few exemptions, most notably the one covering professional baseball and the one applying to activities approved or required by governmental bodies. The courts also play a creative role with respect to the statutory exemptions by interpreting and applying them in particular cases. The executive branch of the federal government has sought upon occasion to confer antitrust exemptions. However, its right to do so, absent specific authorization from Congress, has been successfully challenged in court. In a recent case, *Consumers Union of U.S., Inc.* v. *Rogers,* a federal district court decided that the president and the secretary of state could not exempt certain businesses from the antitrust laws. The president had asked a group of Japanese, British, and Western European steel producers to agree upon a reduction of steel imports into the United States and had given them assurances that such an agreement would not violate federal antitrust laws. Congress had not authorized the executive branch to exempt these foreign companies from the antitrust laws. The court concluded that:

> The President clearly has no authority to give binding assurances that a particular course of conduct, even if encouraged by his representatives, does not violate the Sherman Act or other related congressional enactments any more than he can grant immunity under such laws. A flat agreement among private foreign producers mutually to limit a substantial amount of goods to be sold in the United States is a violation of the Sherman Act and to the extent participants are subject to the jurisdiction of our courts criminal penalties may be imposed and civil actions for damage or equitable relief may be pressed.

There are many different reasons why exemptions have been created. Some are designed to compensate for imbalances in the economic strength of different groups; the Capper–Volstead Act exempts agricultural co-operatives to enhance their bargaining power against large food processors, and the Clayton Act exempts labor organizations to bolster their position vis-à-vis employers. National defense objectives have led to exemption of certain defense supplier activities, as provided in the Defense Production Act of 1950. Particular industries, including banking, insurance, communications, and several others, have been granted exemptions because their business activities are subject to close government regulation and supervision. And a number of exemptions have resulted from deliberate congressional efforts to improve the competitiveness of certain sectors of American business in international trade and commerce.

The balance of this chapter is devoted to specific antitrust exemptions which affect international trade and commerce. Several such exemptions do not deserve extended discussion for our purposes either because they primarily affect interstate commerce, applying only to a narrow or insignificant sector of international commerce, or because they simply do not raise important questions of interpretation or application. These minor exemptions include: the Merchant Marine Act of 1920, which exempts associations of marine insurance companies operating in the United States and foreign countries; the Fishermen's Collective Marketing Act of 1934, which exempts cooperative associations of fishermen for the purpose of collective marketing, so long as prices of aquatic produce in the United States are not unduly enhanced; the Wool Products Labeling Act of 1939 and the Textile Fiber Products Identification Act, which provide that certain activities with respect to wool and textile fibers are unlawful under the Federal Trade Commission Act, but exempt manufacturing, transporting, delivering, and selling the products in course of exportation to foreign countries; Public Law 89–175 (designed to protect the U.S. balance-of-payments position), which exempts certain agreements among financial institutions to curtail the flow of capital to foreign countries; and the Small Business Act, which exempts certain organizations and activities of small businesses operating in international, as well as domestic, trade.

The three major antitrust exemptions affecting international trade and commerce are those granted to the ocean shipping industry by the Shipping Act of 1916; to associations of exporters by the Webb–Pomerene Act; and to the aviation industry by the Federal Aviation Act. Each of these exemptions is examined below in terms of its historical development, statutory provisions, and interpretation and application by the courts.

Ocean Shipping

The first of these major exemptions was created in response to a crisis that plagued the ocean shipping industry at the turn of the nineteenth century. Beginning in the late 1880's, available capacity on ships exceeded the needs of shippers. Excess capacity, coupled with the fact that most operating costs are fixed, led to severe rate wars by shipowners. Shipowners were forced to cut rates below levels needed to cover total costs in order to attract enough cargo to pay for the relatively small handling and carrying costs and some portion of fixed costs. The alternative to rate cutting was worse, namely, to keep one's ships idle and earn no offset against fixed costs. Exacerbating the problem was the relative ease of entry in the shipping industry and the absence of governmental control over ocean freight rates.

To alleviate these unstable market conditions, operators of ocean carriers that traversed competitive routes started banding together into conferences. Through the conference medium, member carriers cooperated to fix rates and handle other matters of joint concern, such as allocation of cargo and division of revenues. To be most effective, each conference had to control shipping in its trade route and minimize competition from non-member carriers. This first objective was obtained by having as many competing carriers as possible join the conference; the second was achieved by tying shippers to the conference and by using the "deep pocket" of the conference to drive nonmember lines from the trade.

The early conferences used a number of tactics to tie shippers to member carriers. Deferred rebates, the most popular tactic, were granted to shippers who agreed to utilize only conference ships. The rebate was contingent upon the shipper's loyalty to the conference, and payment was deferred until the shipper entered into a new contract with the conference. If the shipper chose to use a nonconference ship, his refund would be lost. Another tying tactic often used was a simple refusal by conference members to offer their services to shippers who used nonconference vessels. To combat nonmember carriers, the conference used selective price-cutting practices. Member lines would take turns quoting nonprofitable rates so as to minimize the detriment to any one member. Another weapon used against the independent was the so-called fighting ship, which was a conference vessel that followed an independent from port to port and set its rate below that of the independent.

The price-fixing activities of conferences as well as their anticompetitive practices against nonmember carriers eventually drew the attention of the Department of Justice. Several antitrust suits were brought by the United States against conferences, but were dismissed by the Supreme Court with the advent of World War I, which rendered the cases moot. At about the same time, a congressional committee began an investigation of the ocean shipping industry. The investigation was prompted by a precipitous decline in the U.S. share of ocean cargo carriage. In 1914 the committee issued a report that, among other things, examined the role of conferences in the ocean shipping industry and considered whether conferences should be made subject to the federal antitrust laws. The Alexander Report, as the committee's report was called, concluded that the conferences were a mixed blessing. On the positive side, conferences stabilized rates and provided regular sailings. On the negative side, there was evidence that conferences fixed excessive rates, discriminated between shippers in rates and cargo space, and stifled competition with nonmember carriers through devices such as deferred rebates and fighting ships.

The committee believed that some change in the situation had to be made. The alternatives were either to apply the antitrust laws to break up the conferences or to exempt the conferences from antitrust attack while, at the same time, regulating them so as to eliminate some of their more egregious anticompetitive practices. Exemption with regulation was the alternative advocated by the Alexander Report. It was feared that the other alternative—forced dissolution of conferences—would rekindle rate wars that, in turn, would result in increased industry concentration through mergers and elimination of the weak. Moreover, Congress had no power to dissolve conferences operating outside the jurisdictional bounds of American antitrust laws. Consequently, dissolving only those conferences subject to U.S. law would put American exporters at a disadvantage in competing with foreign exporters who would still be able to ship with conferences.

Congress adopted the committee's recommendations of a regulated existence for conferences, coupled with an antitrust exemption. Two years after the Alexander Report was first issued, Congress passed the Shipping Act of 1916. Essentially, the approach taken in the Shipping Act is to require approval by a regulatory agency of certain types of ocean shipping agreements between certain persons and to exempt from the antitrust laws those agreements that are so approved.

The Act specifically prohibits certain anticompetitive practices that were criticized in the Alexander Report, namely, fighting ships, deferred rebates, and the boycotting of shippers who use other lines. Certain discriminatory practices and rates are also forbidden. The Federal Maritime Commission (FMC) is the agency constituted by Congress to regulate shipping conferences and carriers under the Act. Tariff rates and certain periodic reports must be filed by carriers with the FMC. Various civil and criminal penalties are prescribed for violations of the Act. Provisions are also made for FMC investigations and enforcement of FMC orders.

The heart of the Act in regard to the antitrust exemption is Section 15. It requires that certain agreements, as well as modifications and cancellations of such agreements, between "common carriers by water," between "other persons subject to this chapter," or between the two categories of entities be filed with the FMC. The Act defines the term *common carrier by water* to include carriers, except ferryboats running on regular routes, engaged in the transportation by water of passengers or property between the United States or any of its districts, territories, or possessions and a foreign country, whether in the import or export trade. The term also covers common carriers in interstate commerce operating on the high seas and Great Lakes. Further, the Act defines *other person subject to this chapter* to include persons in the business of forwarding or furnishing wharfage, dock, warehouse, or other terminal facilities in connection with a common carrier by water. *Persons,* as used in the Act, means corporations, partnerships, and associations existing under the laws of the United States or of any foreign country.

The specific types of agreements that must be filed with the FMC are those

1. Fixing or regulating transportation rates or fares.
2. Giving or receiving special rates, accommodations, or other special privileges or advantages.
3. Controlling, regulating, preventing, or destroying competition.
4. Pooling or apportioning earnings, losses, or traffic.
5. Allotting ports or restricting or otherwise regulating the number and character of sailings between ports.
6. Limiting or regulating in any way the volume or character of freight or passenger traffic to be carried.
7. In any manner providing for an exclusive, preferential, or cooperative working arrangement.

Section 15 requires the FMC to "disapprove, cancel, or modify" any such agreement that it finds to be unjustly discriminatory or unfair, to operate to the detriment of the U.S. commerce, to be contrary to the "public interest," or to be in violation of the Act. In addition, no approval shall be given to an agreement between carriers or conferences unless each carrier or conference retains the right of independent action; and no approval shall be given to conference agreements that lack fair and reasonable terms for membership admission and withdrawal. Finally, the FMC is directed to disapprove any agreement that does not have adequate policing procedures or procedures for handling shippers' complaints.

The FMC must approve all agreements that it does not disapprove, cancel, or modify. Only approved agreements are lawful, and only lawful agreements are exempted from the antitrust laws. If the exemption applies, participants in the agreement can be assured that neither governmental nor private litigants can successfully challenge the agreement's legality under the antitrust laws.

From the foregoing, it is apparent that whether or not an agreement is exempted from the antitrust laws depends on the answers to four separate questions. First, are the parties to the agreement of the kind that qualify? Second, is the agreement itself of the type that must be filed under Section 15? Third, is the agreement one that should be approved? Fourth and finally, has the FMC approved the agreement? In each case, the answers to all four questions must be affirmative for the exemption to attach. The key to understanding the exemption lies in these questions, and, in this regard, it is instructive to consider how the courts have answered them in actual cases arising under the Shipping Act.

With respect to the kinds of parties whose agreements may qualify for the antitrust exemption, the courts have determined that the definition of *person* in the Act, although technically restricted to corporations, partnerships, or associations, nevertheless extends to a state or municipal government that operates waterfront piers and terminals. In another case, it was decided that railroads, although not common carriers by water, are nevertheless subject to the Act as parties "furnishing wharfage" where they collect monies from truckers for use of their piers in transporting cargo to and from seagoing vessels. The courts have interpreted *common carrier* to mean one who hires out to the public generally to transport goods or passengers. To be a common carrier one need not solicit business, travel regular or predetermined routes, or abstain from contract carriage. The courts have described an "ocean tramp," a type of cargo vessel that is expressly excluded from the statute's definition of *common carrier,* as a free-lance ship that shuns regular schedules and routes in favor of ports where the most profitable cargo is. Court decisions also manifest that a party may be subject to the Act even if his activities are also regulated by other federal laws; for example, a grain elevator operator could not escape the Act despite being also regulated by the secretary of agriculture under the Warehouse Act of 1916.

The courts have added considerable gloss to the statute's provisions dealing with the types of agreements that must be filed with the FMC. It has been held that agreements by foreign carriers, entered into in foreign countries, must nevertheless be filed as long as the agreements are at least partially effectuated or performed in the United States and have a material effect on the foreign commerce of the United States. On the other hand, a conference agreement, involving American shipping lines, need not be filed where it governs transshipment of passengers or goods between foreign ports exclusively. The fact that an agreement is embodied in public, rather than private, documents does not save it from the filing requirement; thus, courts have held that municipal ordinances and charter provisions governing the operation of public wharves must be filed. Nor can filing be avoided by failing to reduce to writing an agreement that otherwise would be covered by the Act. Agreements between ocean carrier conferences covering overland freight rates must be filed, where the rates apply to cargo also shipped by water to or from a U.S. port. An agreement that settles an antitrust lawsuit between competitive shipping lines is not of the type that must be filed with the FMC. In addition, the courts have held that a lease agreement between a port commission and a grain elevator operator falls within the filing requirements if it regulates elevator rates and grants preferential treatment to the operator and that an agreement limiting competition in stevedoring services must be filed with the FMC.

A few years ago, in *Volkswagenwerk Aktiengesellschaft* v. *FMC,* the Supreme Court decided that an agreement between ocean carriers, stevedoring contractors, and marine terminal operators was such as required filing with the FMC. The agreement provided for creation of a multimillion-dollar fund for indemnifying employees against loss of work from technological improvement. In reaching its decision, the Court rejected the view of the FMC and lower court that only agreements that "affect competition" need be filed. However, the Court found that the agreement did affect competition because although the agreement itself did not specify how the money was to be raised, in fact it developed that shippers contributed by paying increased stevedoring and terminal charges. Finally, the Court acknowledged that Congress had, by amendment to the Act in 1961, vested power in the FMC to exempt certain routine agreements from the filing requirement, provided exemption would not hamper effective regulation, be unjustly discriminatory, or be detrimental to commerce. However, the Court found that the agreement in question was not of such a routine nature as to permit exemption from filing.

More recently, a unanimous Supreme Court decision may have resolved an important conflict between the lower courts as to whether merger agreements affecting the ocean shipping industry are of the type that require filing with the FMC. The Ninth Circuit Court of Appeals had held that such agreements must be filed; in separate cases, the federal district court in New Jersey and the District of Columbia Circuit Court of Appeals ruled that such agreements were not covered by the Act and, hence, did not have to be filed. In affirming the decision of the D.C. Circuit in *FMC v. Seatrain Lines Inc.,* the Supreme Court agreed with the latter view, namely, that merger agreements did not have to be filed with the FMC and were not intended by Congress to be eligible for antitrust exemption. Based on a reading of the Act's legislative history and the strong policy of construing antitrust exemptions narrowly, the Court concluded:

> that in enacting §15 [of the Shipping Act], Congress did not intend to invest the Commission with the power to shield from antitrust liability merger or acquisition of assets agreements which impose no on-going responsibilities. Rather, Congress intended to invest the Commission with jurisdiction over only those agreements, or those portions of agreements, which created on-going rights and responsibilities and which, therefore, necessitated continuous Commission supervision.

The Court reached its decision notwithstanding language in Section 7 of the Clayton Act, the antitrust law specifically aimed at unlawful mergers, that "[n]othing contained in this section shall apply to transactions duly consummated pursuant to authority given by the . . . [Federal] Maritime Commission . . . under any statutory provision vesting such power in such Commission. . . ." In the Court's view, this language does not reflect congressional intent to have the FMC approve mergers, because it leaves open the question of whether "such power" over merger agreements has been vested in FMC. This view is supported by the Senate Report to the 1950 amendment to Section 7 of the Clayton Act, which states that Congress did not intend to grant to the FMC "any authority or powers which it does not already possess."

A cogent argument can be made that there are still some types of merger agreements that must be filed with the FMC. In *Seatrain,* the

Supreme Court drew a careful distinction between simple agreements to merge and those involving continuous, on-going obligations. The Court held that only the latter need be filed with the FMC, and the merger agreement at issue was deemed to be of the former type. But what about, for example, a merger agreement between carriers that contains provisions prohibiting or limiting the selling company from re-entering business in competition with the acquiring carrier? Arguably, such an agreement, either in whole or in part, should be filed with the FMC because of its continuing effect in "controlling, regulating, preventing, or destroying competition." Future court decisions may resolve whether such merger agreements must be filed and therefore can qualify for antitrust exemption.

The next question relevant to the antitrust exemption is what kinds of agreements the FMC must approve. The answer as to each agreement lies in whether it meets the statutory standards for approval. The courts have held that the FMC has an obligation to weigh antitrust considerations in deciding whether an agreement meets the "public interest" standard. In so doing, the FMC has developed a rule of practice that works as follows: Where an agreement is found to interfere with antitrust policies, the parties must show that the agreement is required to serve a serious transportation need, public benefit, or valid regulatory purpose before approval will be granted. In effect, the FMC shifts the burden of proof to the parties. This rule of practice has been upheld by the Supreme Court.

In the landmark decision *FMB* v. *Isbrandtsen Co.,* the Supreme Court decided that certain "dual rate" contracts could not properly be approved by the FMC (then called the Federal Maritime Board). A "dual rate" contract is one whereby a shipper agrees to transport his goods exclusively on conference vessels in return for a reduction from standard shipping rates. The Court held that dual rate contracts that were designed to destroy competition with independent carriers were illegal, could not be approved, and therefore were open to antitrust attack. Justice Frankfurter dissented, criticizing the majority decision for creating what he feared would be a per se rule against all dual rate contracts. Frankfurter believed that dual rate contracts were, by nature, designed to tie shippers to conferences and thus to destroy competition with independent carriers. However, he believed that prohibiting dual rate contracts altogether would result in a rekindling of rate wars and other practices inimical to a healthy shipping industry.

The shipping industry shared Frankfurter's alarm. Immediately following the *Isbrandtsen* decision, the conferences petitioned Congress for relief. The dual rate system was supported in testimony before Congress by shippers as well as carriers. Only Isbrandtsen and the American Farm Bureau Federation came before Congress to oppose a moratorium on the enforcement of the *Isbrandtsen* decision. Congress did enact such a moratorium. During this moratorium, studies were made by congressional committees of the shipping industry, the conference systems, and dual rate contract agreements. Reports were issued by these committees.

In 1961 the Shipping Act was amended in several respects by the Bonner Act. The amendments reflect the main conclusions of the investigating committees: conferences are still necessary for regular service and stable uniform rates, the dual rate contract system is necessary for strong conferences, and regulation of the shipping industry is essential. The key provisions of the Bonner Act are an amendment to Section 14 of the Shipping Act that legalizes dual rate contracts meeting certain specifications; an amendment to Section 15 that permits disapproval of any agreement contrary to the "public interest" and requires free admission to conferences, adequate self-policing, and proper consideration of shipper requests and complaints; and an amendment to Section 18 that requires filing and observation of tariffs, thirty days notice of tariff increases, and disapproval of rates so unreasonable as to be detrimental to U.S. commerce.

In addition to its condemnation of dual rate contracts in *Isbrandtsen,* the Supreme Court has found other types of agreements undeserving of FMC approval. In *FMC* v. *Aktiebolaget Svenska Amerika Linien,* the Court struck down two such agreements, which it found to be against the "public interest," "detrimental to the commerce of the United States," and "unjustly discriminatory as between conference and nonconference carriers." The first agreement was that conference members unanimously approve increases in fees paid to travel agents, the result being that fee increases were impeded, thereby making ocean passenger liners less competitive with air carriers. The other agreement was one that required travel agents, who booked passengers on conference ships, to refrain from booking passengers on nonconference ships. The effect of this agreement was to limit the choice of passengers in travel agents, restrict the services of travel agents, and deny nonconference vessels access to a large percentage of passenger traffic.

Once it has been determined that the parties qualify and that their agreement is of the type that should be filed and approved, it is still necessary to show that the FMC has given proper approval before the antitrust exemption applies. Any performance of an agreement of the type that must be approved, prior to its approval, is unlawful. Indeed, the courts have held that the FMC lacks authority to ratify preapproval conduct. The FMC does have authority to withdraw approval previously conferred, and, of course, it may condition approval on modifications that eliminate objectionable features of an agreement. Approval of a basic agreement does not extend to regulations or subagreements thereunder, unless the basic agreement clearly delineates the actions to be taken pursuant to the regulations or subagreements. Finally, the courts have held that approval by the FMC is invalid if not preceded by a fact-finding hearing.

There remains one important question, not previously discussed, that relates to the antitrust exemption under the Shipping Act. That question is under what circumstances must the courts defer to the FMC when an agreement is attacked as violative of the antitrust laws. The answer lies in a trilogy of Supreme Court decisions concerning the doctrine of primary jurisdiction, the principle by which certain claims must be presented to a regulatory agency before seeking judicial relief. As will be seen later on, the doctrine of primary jurisdiction is important with respect to each of the major antitrust exemptions affecting international trade and commerce.

In a 1932 case, *United States Navigation Co.* v. *Cunard S.S. Co.,* a dual rate contract agreement was attacked as unlawful under the antitrust laws. The agreement covered carriers of 95 per cent of all commerce between U.S. Atlantic ports and Great Britain and Ireland. It had been neither approved by nor filed with the FMC. The Supreme Court refused to enjoin implementation of the agreement, stating that the plaintiff's remedy was to be found in the Shipping Act, not through the antitrust laws. Some twenty years later, in *Far East Conference* v. *United States,* the Court affirmed its earlier holding that a party must resort first to the FMC before challenging an agreement in court as unlawful under the antitrust laws. Although the Court dismissed the government's complaint, it recognized that, under certain circumstances, it might be more appropriate to stay judicial proceedings, pending action by the FMC. Most recently, in *Carnation Co.* v. *Pacific Westbound Conference,* the Supreme Court found circumstances that required a stay by the court, rather than dismissal. Under the federal antitrust laws, plaintiffs must file claims within four years of when they accrue. The Court reasoned that dismissal would prejudice the plaintiff's opportunity to refile his claim if the FMC eventually ruled more than four years after the plaintiff's claim arose that the agreement was not entitled to antitrust exemption. The Court also held that a claimant has a choice of remedies for an unlawful agreement: reparations from the FMC under the Shipping Act or treble damages from the courts under the antitrust laws.

The antitrust exemption is an integral part of the Shipping Act, and the protection it affords is a very important factor in helping the United States compete in the ocean shipping industry. For the individual businessman who wants to know if the exemption applies to a particular agreement, the important thing to remember is that the answer will turn upon whether the agreement is between qualified parties and has been properly filed with and approved by the Federal Maritime Commission.

Export Trade

The second major antitrust exemption affecting international trade and commerce is provided for in the Webb–Pomerene Act: "An Act to Promote Export Trade." Passed a scant two years after the Shipping Act, the statutory exemption was created to give American export traders a shot in the arm in their struggle with foreign competitors.

Prior to World War I, American export trade was quite small, as compared to domestic trade or to the export trade of other nations, such as England and Germany. However, with the disruption of the European markets occasioned by the Great War, American export trade increased significantly. Concern that this newly acquired trade might be lost upon termination of the war prompted an investigation by the newly created Federal Trade Commission. The investigation focused on the factors that had given European countries an export trade advantage and the steps that might be taken to enhance American export trade.

The FTC's investigation culminated in a two-volume report, published in 1916. The report cited the cartelization of foreign industries as the main obstacle to U.S. export trade. These cartels were often sponsored or subsidized by foreign governments. With their large buying and selling power, they made it difficult for individual U.S. firms to compete, especially the smaller firms. Because the Sherman Antitrust Act applies to contracts, combinations, and conspiracies in unreasonable restraint of foreign, as well as domestic trade, American firms were effectively deterred from cooperating in their export efforts. The FTC recommended legislation that would encourage cooperative marketing by American exporters. In the FTC's opinion, such legislation would not be inconsistent with the national antitrust policy because, while providing benefits to U.S. export trade, it would not be detrimental to domestic commerce.

In Congress there was heated debate over the proposed legislation. Several congressmen doubted whether companies combining their export activities could, at the same time, keep their domestic activities separate. They seriously challenged the FTC's statement that the domestic market would not be adversely affected by combinations in the foreign market. Nevertheless, with the support of President Wilson, the secretary of commerce, and the FTC, the Webb–Pomerene Act became law on April 10, 1918.

The statute is relatively brief compared to the Shipping Act. A definitional section draws a sharp distinction between "export trade" and "trade within the United States." Export trade refers solely to trade or commerce in goods, wares or merchandise exported from the United States or its territories to a foreign country; it expressly excludes the production, manufacture, or sale for consumption or resale of such items within the United States or its territories. Trade within the United States refers to trade or commerce among the states, territories, and District of Columbia.

The key provisions are Sections 2 and 3. Section 2 provides that associations of export traders and any agreements or acts done by such associations in the course of export trade are exempt from the Sherman Antitrust Act. However, there are three express qualifications to this exemption. First, the associations, agreements, or acts may not be "in restraint of trade within the United States." Second, the export trade of domestic competitors of the associations may not be restrained. Finally, export associations may not act to "artificially or intentionally" affect *domestic* prices of their commodities or substantially lessen competition in domestic trade. Section 3 provides that mergers or acquisitions of corporations "organized solely for the purpose of engaging in export trade, and actually engaged solely in such export trade" are not subject to attack under the antimerger provisions of the Clayton Act. The only such mergers or acquisitions that fail to qualify for this exemption are those that have the effect of restraining trade or substantially lessening competition in the United States. Other provisions of the Act make unlawful under the Federal Trade Commission Act unfair methods of competition in export trade, even though occurring outside the territorial jurisdiction of the United States; require periodic reports by export trade associations to the Federal Trade Commission, failure to file resulting in both civil penalties and loss of the antitrust exemption; and, finally, empower the FTC to investigate possible violations of the Act, to recommend that violators cease their unlawful conduct, and, if the agency's recommendations are not heeded, to refer the matter to the U.S. attorney general.

The FTC has played a significant, albeit problematic, role in interpreting the Webb–Pomerene Act. In 1924, the FTC issued the "Silver Letter," an advisory opinion rendered to a group of silver producers contemplating the creation of an export trade association. In the letter, the commission took the view that Webb–Pomerene allowed an export trade association to enter into agreements with foreign corporations for the sole purpose of operating in foreign markets, the "only test of legality [for such agreements being] the effect upon domestic conditions within the United States." This interpretation of Webb–Pomerene appears overly broad. By definition, the term *export trade* does not extend to joint business activities in foreign countries between export trade associations and foreign corporations. Indeed, two commissioners dissented to the Silver Letter, and a federal district court in 1949 rejected the interpretation as clearly erroneous. Nevertheless, it remained the basis for FTC policy making until 1955.

The next significant action by the FTC occurred in 1940, when it ruled that a Webb association's refusal to sell to competitors was not authorized by the Webb–Pomerene Act. The competitors were American exporters who did not belong to the association. Subsequently, however, this ruling has not been enforced by the FTC. A commentator has suggested that the practice of refusing to sell to competitors is an "indispensable adjunct to the effectiveness of the association."

There were, in fact, eight FTC proceedings in the 1940's that were taken in conjunction with litigation initiated by the Department of Justice against certain Webb associations. Among the practices determined by the FTC in these proceedings to be improper are the following: an association cannot obtain an agreement from nonmembers committing them to export according to association rules; an association cannot enter into an agreement with foreign buyers authorizing them to deduct from the association's assigned quotas the exports of domestic nonmember competitors; an association cannot obtain an agreement from nonmembers that authorizes the association to fix the nonmembers' prices; and an association cannot endeavor to buy out foreign competitors in an attempt to seal off domestic markets.

In 1963 the FTC created the division of Export Trade in the Office of General Counsel. Today the functions of this office are being handled by the Bureau of Competition. Investigations of association activities and the study of annual questionnaires submitted by each export association are some of the activities being conducted. This machinery makes effective regulation of Webb associations by the FTC more feasible. For example, the commission has reviewed the annual questionnaires for evidence of improper activities and, in those instances where improper activities have been discovered, has generally succeeded in obtaining from the offending associations assurances of voluntary discontinuance.

The FTC recently stated its opinion that membership in Webb associations can include United States corporations owned or controlled by foreign interests. However, left unanswered by the FTC is the question of whether foreign corporations can qualify for membership. It would seem that any corporation, whether existing under the laws of the United States or under those of a foreign country and whether owned or controlled by foreign interests, by domestic interests, or by multinational interests, should be able to qualify for membership in a Webb association. This view finds support in the language of the Act. In particular, Section 1 defines a Webb association to include "any corporation or combination, by contract or otherwise, of two or more persons, partnerships, or corporations." The definition is without limitation as to nationality, ownership, or control of association members.

There has been relatively little litigation involving the Webb-Pomerene Act. However, one important question that has been answered by the courts is whether the FTC has primary jurisdiction over alleged antitrust violations by export associations. The answer is no. In a 1945 case, *United States Alkali Export Association* v. *United States,* the Supreme Court held that the Department of Justice could proceed to sue export associations for alleged antitrust violations without first waiting for the FTC to investigate and make recommendations, the association to refuse compliance, and the FTC to refer its recommendations to the attorney general. The Court reached its decision largely on the basis of the limited authority granted to the FTC under the Act; its only function "is to investigate, recommend, and report. It can give no remedy. It can make no controlling finding of law or fact. Its recommendation need not be followed by any court or administrative or executive officer." As we saw in the maritime context, the courts have found that the Federal Maritime Commission possesses primary jurisdiction over activities arguably entitled by the Shipping Act to exemption from the antitrust laws. The explanation for the different answers to the question of primary jurisdiction lies in the stark contrast between the limited role of the FTC under Webb–Pomerene and the very strong role of the FMC under the Shipping Act. Finally, although the *Alkali* case involved the Department of Justice as a plaintiff, there is nothing in the Court's opinion to suggest a different conclusion would have been reached had a private litigant been suing the export association for antitrust violations.

Following the Supreme Court's decision, the *Alkali* case was remanded for trial. The trial court ultimately decided that the defendants—two Webb–Pomerene export associations, individual members of the associations, and a British alkali exporter and its American subsidiary—violated the Sherman Act by collectively acting to restrain both international and domestic trade in alkalis. The court considered and rejected the argument that Webb–Pomerene exempted defendants' conduct from the antitrust laws. The defendants' agreements allocating exclusive territories, assigning quotas, fixing prices, and selling through joint agents were designed to give defendants control over the worldwide market for alkalis and, as such, went beyond mere "agreements in the course of export trade" under Webb–Pomerene. Moreover, the court concluded that, even if defendants' agreements were covered by the Act, no exemption applied because they had restrained trade within the United States, had attempted to eliminate all of their domestic competition in exporting, and had "artificially or intentionally" stabilized domestic prices in alkali by withholding product from the market.

Whereas the *Alkali* case provides guidance as to what Webb associations may not do, another case, decided only a year later, discusses activities that may properly qualify for the antitrust exemption. In *United States* v. *Minnesota Mining & Manufacturing Co.,* the court opined that it may be proper, absent special circumstances revealing unfairness or oppressiveness, for an export association to act as the exclusive foreign outlet for its members; to refuse to handle the exports of American competitors; to determine quotas and price levels for its members; to fix resale prices for the association's foreign distributors; and to limit foreign distributors to handling association goods exclusively. Notwithstanding the court's discussion of possible exempt activities, as we saw in Chapter 5, the defendants were found to have violated the antitrust laws in several ways. First, the defendants, who collectively accounted for four fifths of total U.S. export volume in coated abrasives, had, in effect, unlawfully agreed to reduce exports to foreign markets, so that these markets might be served instead by defendants' jointly owned factories in England, Canada, and Germany. The court also found that an agreement not to withdraw from the export association for nearly twenty years was too restrictive. Accordingly, the court required the time period for withdrawal to be shortened to one or two years. Finally, the court found that defendants had unlawfully discriminated in price by charging competing domestic exporters more than defendants charged their own foreign distributors. Only price differentials that reflect greater services performed by distributors were deemed proper.

The most recent Supreme Court case involving the Webb–Pomerene Act is *United States* v. *Concentrated Phosphate Export Ass'n.* At issue was whether sales by an export association to Korea through the Agency for International Development (AID) were "in export trade" and hence exempted from the antitrust laws by the Webb–Pomerene Act. The export association in this case was composed of five of the largest American producers of concentrated phosphate. The association had set prices and submitted single bids on 300,000 tons of fertilizer destined for Korea under the AID program. AID had selected the commodities, determined the amounts to be procured, controlled the contract procedure, and paid the contract prices. Although these transactions might appear to have been in "export trade" and thus covered by the Act, the Supreme Court decided otherwise. The basis for the Court's decision was its view that the phosphates were purchased in fact, if not in form, by American taxpayers through AID, rather than by the Korean government. Therefore, the sales were made in domestic, not "export trade," and the antitrust exemption afforded by Webb–Pomerene was inapplicable.

From its enactment until the present, the Webb–Pomerene Act has been under a constant barrage of critical fire. Numerous authorities contend that the Act does not perform the functions for which it was created; that the objectives for which it was created are no longer valid; and that it may produce more harm than good. For example, they argue that the Act has not significantly increased exports by American firms unable to match the power of foreign cartels. They question whether American export firms should be using the Act to increase their profits at the expense of foreign consumers. They express concern that price fixing in foreign markets by Webb associations may carry over into domestic markets and injure American consumers. These critics would repeal or amend the Act in order to eliminate or narrow the scope of the antitrust exemption.

On the other hand, the president's conference on export expansion in 1963, the U.S. Chamber of Commerce, the National Association of Manufacturers, the National Constructors Association, and other groups have sought an expansion of the antitrust exemption created by Webb–Pomerene. They express concern that the American businessman is placed in an unequal competitive position by U.S. antitrust laws because other developed nations impose little or no antitrust sanctions on their nationals; encourage and many times initiate the formation of national and international cartels for the purposes of doing business abroad; and give special encouragement to their export cartel associations, including special rediscount rates, guarantees of currency convertibility, and protection against credit and political risks. They point out that the Webb associations formed in the United States are few in number when compared to the export cartels operating in international trade from such industrialized nations as the United Kingdom, Japan, and West Germany.

Recently, the movement for expanding the antitrust exemption accorded export trade associations has gained momentum because of the rising U.S. balance-of-trade deficit and the weakening position of the United States in the sphere of international trade. Several bills have been introduced in Congress that, if passed, would achieve that objective, partly by expanding the meaning of "export trade" to include data, good will, insurance, technological know-how, services, facilities, or similar properties or services. No new legislation has yet resulted, but, regardless of whether the Webb–Pomerene Act is amended, repealed, or left unchanged, there is no denying that to date only a small percentage of American exporters have marketed their products through the medium of a Webb association and the antitrust exemption has not stimulated American export trade to the extent hoped for by Congress.

International Aviation

The final major exemption to be considered is one that applies in the field of international, as well as domestic, aviation. In general terms, this exemption removes from operation of the antitrust laws certain types of government-approved activities and agreements between air carriers and other persons. These include consolidations, mergers, and acquisitions; interlocking directorships and officerships; and cooperative working arrangements, such as agreements on fares and schedules. The exemption first came into existence in 1938 as part of the Civil Aeronautics Act (C.A.A.). Twenty years later, Congress repealed this statute with passage of the Federal Aviation Act (F.A.A.); however, those provisions of the prior legislation pertaining to the antitrust exemption were re-enacted in the new legislation without substantial change.

Unlike the exemptions relative to the ocean shipping and export trade industries, the exemption here was not primarily motivated by concern over the American industry's ability to compete in foreign markets. In fact, at the time the C.A.A. was passed into law, the American aviation industry was perhaps the strongest and largest in the world. On the other hand, congressional concern about extreme cutthroat competition in the domestic aviation market was an important reason for the exemption. American air carriers engaged in severe rate wars among themselves, especially in competing for postal contracts. The result of these rate wars was decreasing profitability that, in turn, stemmed the inflow of investment funds so necessary to a capital-intensive industry. What Congress hoped to do was to foster an American aviation industry that, in war and peace, would provide the fullest, safest, and most efficient use of navigable airways possible, both here and abroad. The federal regulatory scheme for achieving these objectives is immensely complex and pervades areas that are outside the scope of this chapter. Suffice it to say that the antitrust exemption is but one small, albeit important, part of that scheme.

The antitrust exemption derives from Title IV, Section 414 of the F.A.A. That provision states that:

> Any person affected by any order made under [three specifically enumerated provisions of Title IV] shall be, and is hereby, relieved from the operations of the "antitrust laws," . . . insofar as may be necessary to enable such person to do anything authorized, approved, or required by such order.

Person is broadly defined by the Act to mean "any individual, firm, copartnership, corporation, company, association, joint stock association, or political entity as well as any trustee, receiver, assignee, or similar representative of the foregoing." *Order* refers to action by the Civil Aeronautics Board (CAB), the federal agency entrusted by the Act to regulate the aviation industry.

The antitrust exemption only protects conduct that is authorized, approved, or required by a CAB order under three specific provisions of the Act. The first such provision is Section 408. It declares that certain mergers, consolidations, property transactions, and acquisitions of control shall be unlawful unless first approved by order of the board. The provision is limited to such transactions as involve air carriers, foreign air carriers, other common carriers, and other persons engaged in any other phase of aeronautics. These and many other terms are defined with particularity elsewhere in the Act. It is sufficient for purposes here to note that *aeronautics* means the "science and art of flight"; that *air carrier* means a "U.S. citizen engaged in interstate, overseas, and foreign air transportation of persons, property and mail as a common carrier"; and that *foreign air carrier* means a "foreign citizen engaged in air transportation anywhere in the world, including the United States."

The specific part of Section 408 that bears directly on international aviation is that which requires CAB approval for any foreign air carrier to acquire control of any American aeronautics business. Board approval must be given unless the transaction in question is found to be against the "public interest," or would result in monopolization restraining competition with other air carriers. The public interest includes, among other things, promoting the U.S. foreign and domestic commerce; mail service; national defense; safety; adequate, economical, and efficient air service; and competition consonant with the preceding objectives. Specifically, as to competition, the public interest requires avoidance of unjust discrimination, undue preference or advantages, and unfair or destructive competitive practices.

The second provision under which a CAB order triggers an exemption is Section 409. This provision requires that, to be lawful, the board must approve, as being in the public interest, certain interlocking relationships between officers, directors, members, and shareholders of air carriers and other common carriers or other persons engaged in another phase of aeronautics. Foreign air carriers do not appear to be subject to the terms of this provision, at least insofar as the statutory language is concerned; the courts have not yet addressed the question.

The third and final provision of the Act authorizing board orders to which the antitrust exemption may apply is Section 412. This provision is remarkably similar to the antitrust exemption provision of the Shipping Act, Section 15, in that it requires certain contracts or agreements of a working nature to be filed with and approved by the regulatory agency. These are restricted to contracts or agreements between an air carrier and any other air carrier, foreign air carrier, or other common carrier. Specifically, they include those:

1. Pooling or apportioning earnings, losses, traffic, service, or equipment.
2. Relating to the establishment of transportation rates, fares, charges, or classifications.
3. For preserving and improving safety, economy, and efficiency of operation.
4. For controlling, regulating, preventing, or otherwise eliminating destructive, oppressive, or wasteful competition.
5. For regulating stops, schedules, and character of service.
6. For other cooperative working arrangements.

The CAB is required to approve by order all such contracts or agreements that are filed and that are not injurious to the public interest or violative of the Act. Significantly, Section 412 does not govern those cooperative working arrangements that are solely between foreign air carriers. Thus, to the extent such arrangements affect American foreign commerce, they may be nonexempt and subject to the federal antitrust laws.

The foregoing sets forth the statutory framework of the antitrust exemption applicable to international aviation. However, as with the Shipping

Act and Webb–Pomerene exemptions, a full understanding of the scope and import of the instant exemption requires a look at judicial decisions that have interpreted and applied the law in actual business contexts. Judicial activity in this area has not been great, but there have been some important decisions, especially with respect to questions of the CAB's primary and exclusive jurisdiction over alleged antitrust violations.

Prior to 1963 the lower federal courts dealt with the question of primary jurisdiction in three separate cases. In an action by an air carrier against competing air carriers and their trade associations, the plaintiff alleged a broad conspiracy to restrain trade in the sale of airline tickets and other practices. The appellate court held that the trial court should retain jurisdiction over the antitrust claim pending application by the plaintiff to the CAB for a cease and desist order. The agency is empowered under Section 411 of the Act to issue cease and desist orders against unfair or deceptive practices and unfair methods of competition in air transportation. If the CAB were to determine that any of the defendants' acts were outside its jurisdiction, then such acts would be subject to the antitrust laws. If the CAB were to issue a cease and desist order against any of the defendants' acts, then the court could not issue an injunction, but might still award treble damages if such acts were found to violate the antitrust laws. Finally, if the CAB were to find that any of the defendants' acts were authorized or permissible, then such acts could not be enjoined or form the basis for antitrust damages.

In the second case on primary jurisdiction the same approach was taken by a federal district court, which stayed, pending CAB proceedings, an antitrust claim by a ticket agency alleging a conspiracy to destroy its business by foreign and domestic air carriers and others. A different approach was adopted in the third case. There the plaintiff, an air carrier, alleged an antitrust conspiracy between competitive carriers and other persons to destroy its business through predatory rate policies and other practices. The plaintiff sought injunctive relief and treble damages. The CAB had given some consideration to the alleged predatory rates, but other acts by defendants had not been subject to agency review. Nevertheless, the court held that primary jurisdiction did not lie because, in its opinion, a conspiracy to destroy plaintiff's business could not conceivably be approved by the CAB. In allowing the antitrust case to proceed, the court noted that the Civil Aeronautics Act had no reparation provision. Thus, an award of treble damages under the antitrust laws would not duplicate any relief offered by the CAB, because it lacks remedial power. This situation is distinguished from that under the Shipping Act pursuant to which the FMC can order damages paid to complainants.

In 1963 the Supreme Court first looked at the question of the CAB's exclusive jurisdiction over alleged antitrust violations. The court took an expansive view. The case—*Pan American World Airways, Inc.* v. *United*

States—involved a government antitrust complaint against Pan American, a common carrier named W. R. Grace, and Panagra, an air carrier jointly owned by the first two defendants. The government sought injunctive relief against: a division of South American markets by Pan American and Panagra; monopolization by Pan American and Grace of air commerce between the east coast of the United States and west coast of South America and Buenos Aires; and Pan American's use of its control over Panagra to block the latter's efforts to extend its route from the Canal Zone to the United States. The trial court found for defendants on the issues of market division and monopolization, but held Pan American guilty of violating the antitrust laws in preventing Panagra from expanding. Both Pan American and the government appealed to the Supreme Court. The Court, with some dissent, concluded broadly that "all questions of injunctive relief against the division of territories or the allocation of routes or against combinations between common carriers and air carriers" are entrusted exclusively to the CAB. Accordingly, the Court ordered the complaint dismissed in its entirety. It should be kept in mind that this decision, although giving wide application to the antitrust exemption, may only apply to cases wherein injunctive relief is sought. A different decision might have been reached had the lawsuit been just for damages. Because the CAB lacks authority to make damage awards, in such a case judicial relief would not be interfering with or superseding the agency's jurisdiction. Thus, rather than dismiss the complaint the court might decide to stay proceedings until the CAB had been given a chance to rule on the legality of defendants' actions.

More recently, in *TWA* v. *Hughes,* lower courts decided that Hughes Tool Co. (Toolco) had violated the antitrust laws by controlling the acquisition, financing, and delivery of aviation equipment for TWA. The Supreme Court reversed the decision on the ground that Toolco's conduct was protected by the antitrust exemption. Through a series of orders under Section 408 of the Act, the CAB had approved gradual acquisition of control of TWA by Toolco. The acts complained of were committed by Toolco in exercising its control over TWA. Thus, although these acts were not directly approved by the CAB, the antitrust exemption nevertheless was held to apply because, by approving Toolco's acquisition of TWA, the CAB realized that it "would inevitably result in [Toolco's] exercising authority over the day-to-day affairs of TWA" and because the CAB had the power under the Act to investigate and alter the manner in which Toolco exercised such authority over TWA. The Court recognized that monopoly and competition are key considerations in the CAB's regulatory decisions. As previously mentioned, Section 408 of the Act prohibits CAB approval of acquisitions that would result in creating a monopoly or monopolies, or in adversely affecting the public interest. Further, the Court believed that the CAB had an obligation to continue monitoring Toolco's control over TWA to make certain that it remained in the public interest. The Court concluded that the CAB's jurisdiction in these circumstances "preempts the antitrust field." The result of the Court's decision was reversal of a $145 million antitrust judgment against Toolco.

The Supreme Court's decisions in *Pan American World Airways* and *Hughes* have been interpreted and applied by a federal court of appeals in an antitrust treble-damage case between two competing airline companies. In *Aloha Airlines, Inc.* v. *Hawaiian Airlines, Inc.,* the plaintiff alleged that the defendant violated the Sherman Act by attempting to monopolize the market for air transportation between the Hawaiian islands. The defendant was accused of trying to drive the plaintiff out of business by a number of practices, including the scheduling of excessive flights and below-cost servicing to interstate air carriers between stops. None of the defendant's practices under attack had been approved or authorized by order of the CAB. However, the agency had, upon the application of the plaintiff, granted a subsidy to cover "uneconomical competition" from the defendant. The plaintiff had also petitioned the CAB to take action against the defendant under Section 411 of the F.A.A., which authorizes the agency to enjoin "unfair methods of competition" in air transportation. The defendant argued that the CAB had exclusive jurisdiction over the issues in the antitrust case because of the agency's authority under Section 411. The appellate court rejected this argument on the grounds that, as indicated in the *Pan American* case, prospective relief is no substitute for an award of treble damages and that, under the *Hughes* case, exclusive jurisdiction is confined to practices covered by CAB orders, a circumstance clearly lacking in this case. The court also rejected the argument that the antitrust issues were previously litigated in the CAB subsidy proceedings, which covered a narrower time period than the antitrust claims and involved different standards of law. Finally, the defendant argued that, even if exclusive jurisdiction were lacking, the CAB nevertheless had primary jurisdiction. Again the court disagreed. The CAB had already made its findings in the subsidy proceedings and hearing on the petition for relief under Section 411. Beyond finding facts, the agency had no authority to determine whether the elements exist for a valid antitrust claim. Therefore, nothing remained for the CAB to decide that would justify a stay of court proceedings. Moreover, the court concluded that, under no circumstances, could the agency ever authorize or approve practices of the predatory sort alleged to have been committed by the defendant. In sum, the court of appeals held that the CAB had neither exclusive nor primary jurisdiction over the antitrust claims, thereby permitting the trial court to proceed with the antitrust case.

Conclusion

In the broad area of international trade and commerce, antitrust exemptions may not play a very large role. Their availability and attractiveness to businessmen are limited in respects. Exemptions tend to have specialized applications, to require fulfillment of certain preconditions, and to exist, for the most part, only as adjuncts to regulation by federal agencies. Yet for those who do business in the pertinent areas of international trade and commerce, such as ocean shipping, exporting through associations, and aviation, and who take the necessary steps to invoke the applicable exemptions, including submission to government regulations, the end reward is substantial protection against liability under the federal antitrust laws.

chapter 11

Some Important Foreign Antitrust Laws

As we mentioned in Chapter 1, the United States is not the only country that has an antitrust law. In this chapter we will briefly examine the antitrust laws of the European Communities, the United Kingdom, Canada, and Japan. We have selected these four for several reasons. Two thirds of American foreign investment is located in the member states of the European Communities and in Canada. Therefore, these are the laws most likely to be encountered by Americans. The United Kingdom provides an excellent example of the workings of the concurrent Common Market and national antitrust laws as well as an example of an approach to competition problems considerably different from that of the United States. Japan is an acknowledged major factor in multinational business and its system provides an interesting comparison with U.S. antitrust law and practice. We have not attempted to provide an exhaustive or critical analysis of these foreign antitrust laws. Rather we have attempted to describe their major features and to point out significant contrasts to U.S. laws. To assist those who desire more information about the antitrust laws discussed in this chapter, we have provided an extensive bibliography of English language source material in the bibliography section of this book. This chapter also provides background for the next, in which we will discuss the prospects for a truly international antitrust law in the light of the differing approaches and standards exemplified by the various antitrust laws now in existence.

European Common Market

The European Common Market is the result of the post-World War II efforts of Jean Monnet, Robert Schuman, Winston Churchill, and others to revitalize the 100-year-old dream of a "United States of Europe." These men hoped that if the European countries could agree on the goal of political and economic integration, another war in Western Europe would be prevented and recovery from the devastation of World War II would be facilitated. The United States encouraged this idea through the Marshall Plan for the same reasons. The first major step toward this goal was the creation, by Belgium, France, the Federal Republic of Germany, Italy, Luxembourg, and The Netherlands, of the European Coal and Steel Community (ECSC) in 1951. Each member state agreed to eliminate duties, discrimination, quotas, and restrictive practices relating to coal and steel. Thus, a common market in those products was created and placed under supranational control. The ECSC was so successful that the six member states decided to expand the idea to include a common market for nearly all goods and services. Thus, the European Economic Community (EEC) and the European Atomic Energy Community (Euratom) were created in 1957. The separate EEC, ECSC, and Euratom administrations were merged into a single European Council of Ministers and a single European Commission in 1965. In 1973 Denmark, Great Britain, and Ireland joined the European Communities.

The institutions of the European Communities that play a major role in competition law are the commission, the council, and the Court of Justice. Many of the functions performed by the commission are similar to those of independent federal regulatory agencies in the United States, such as the Federal Trade Commission. It issues regulations and directives, investigates, proposes legislation and conducts hearings on and imposes fines for violations of the law and oversees enforcement of the Communities' laws. The council is responsible for achieving the objectives set by the treaties of the Communities in competition policy and other areas and for enacting regulations, directives, and decisions, usually after a proposal from the commission. The Court of Justice interprets the treaties and related laws and settles disputes among Common Market institutions, as well as disputes between those institutions and member states or individuals.

The principal objectives of the Common Market treaties are a harmonious development of economic activities, a continuous and balanced expansion, an increase in stability, and an accelerated raising of the standard of living. These objectives are to be attained through the establishment of a "common market"—free movement of goods and services between the member states, a uniform tariff, and a common commercial policy concerning the exchange of goods with third countries. According to the EEC Treaty one of the tasks involved in establishing such a "common market" is the "establishment of a system ensuring that competition in the common market is not distorted." The treaties contain guidelines for establishing such a system to protect competition, including "Rules on Competition" that deal with anticompetitive practices, dumping, governmental aids to industry, and so on. Several of these areas are outside the scope of this book and, therefore, will not be discussed. These areas include the competition rules pertaining to coal and steel contained in the ECSC Treaty, dumping, and governmental aids. The focus of our attention will be Articles 85 and 86 of the EEC Treaty which govern anticompetitive practices with respect to everything except coal, steel, and atomic energy.

At the outset it is important to understand that there is a two-tiered system of antitrust law in the Common Market. Most member states have their own national system of antitrust law, and these vary considerably in coverage and stringency. Some of these differences are facetiously summarized in the following aphorism used by a distinguished English solicitor: "In Germany everything is forbidden which is not expressly permitted. In England, everything is permitted which is not expressly forbidden. In France, everything is forbidden but nearly anything can be arranged." These national laws co-exist with the EEC's Articles 85 and 86, which are also considered part of the national law of each member state and which may be enforced in the courts of each member state. For example, the fact that a contract violates Article 85 could be used as a defense to a suit for breach of contract in a national court. If there is any conflict between the national law and the law of the Communities, the latter prevails. The discussion of the antitrust law of the United Kingdom that appears later in this chapter will further illustrate this two-tiered system of law within member states.

Even though the national authorities are entitled to apply Articles 85 and 86 in certain circumstances, responsibility for enforcement of the Communities' competition rules rests primarily with the commission.

Enforcement

The commission combines administrative and judicial functions. Each of the thirteen commissioners is assigned an area of responsibility. One commissioner is responsible for competition, as well as some additional areas. That commissioner supervises the Directorate-General for Competition, which has a director-general as its professional chief. The directorate-general is subdivided into a number of directorates for specific subject matters and has a total staff of approximately two hundred forty. The commission may institute administrative proceedings to determine the existence of alleged violations of Articles 85 and 86, either *ex officio* or upon the complaint of a member state or of any "natural or legal persons who claim a legitimate interest." Once the proceedings have commenced, the commission is authorized to conduct broad investigations in order to accumulate economic and legal data pertaining to the existence of the alleged restraint, the degree of the restraint, and the effect on the Common Market. Proceeding through its own agents or through the competent authorities of member states, the commission may examine or make copies of all books and records of enterprises, obtain verbal explanations from officers and employees of enterprises, and have access to all premises, land, and vehicles of the enterprise under investigation.

Upon an evaluation of the data gathered, the commission may decide to raise objections to the agreements or practices on the ground that they violate Article 85 or 86. In such cases the commission will issue a letter of complaint to the parties. The parties are then given an opportunity to submit written statements in their defense. Although the entire procedure may be handled through written communication, the parties can and often do make a request to argue their case with counsel before the commission. The commission "shall" grant such a request if the persons requesting the oral hearing "show a sufficient interest or if the Commission proposes to impose on them a fine or periodic penalty payment."

If, after having heard the enterprises argue in their own behalf, the commission determines that there has been a violation of the Rules on Competition, it may invoke the sanctions set out in Regulation 17, which implements Articles 85 and 86. (These articles and Regulation 17 are reprinted in Appendix II of this book.) In addition to declaring void agreements that are in violation of Article 85(1), the commission may impose fines of from 1,000 to 1 million units of account (1 unit of account is equal to, approximately, $1 U.S.) or up to 10 per cent of the total turnover of sales of the enterprises for the preceding year. Moreover, penalties may be applied after the commission has made an initial determination of illegality if the enterprises persist in their unlawful activity. Such penalties range from 50 to 1,000 units of account per day of violation subsequent to the original decision. In Common Market parlance a "fine" is a monetary punishment for an offense and a "penalty" is imposed not as punishment but as a sanction to secure compliance.

Although, unlike the U.S. antitrust laws, the competition rules contain no provision for private treble-damage actions, the commission has issued a statement that consumers injured by violations of Articles 85 and 86 may claim damages under national law if that law so permits. Thus persons injured by the violations may be reimbursed for their injuries by a national court. The commission also stated that such actions for damages could usefully supplement its own enforcement efforts.

The commission has recently proposed a regulation creating rules applying to its power to impose fines. Under the draft regulation the commission could impose fines for violations of Article 85 or 86 only up to five years after the date on which the violation ceased. After expiration of the five-year period no action against the violation could be brought.

In practice the vast majority of cases involving violations of the competition rules are settled without a formal decision. Most agreements and practices are modified upon the request of the commission or abandoned after the denial of applications for a negative clearance. The negative clearance procedure is explained later in this chapter. For example, in 1973 the commission rendered seven decisions under Articles 85 and 86. During the same year 392 matters were settled without formal decision.

Article 85

Article 85 of the EEC Treaty has three major subparts. Part (1) prohibits agreements between enterprises, decisions of associations of enterprises, and concerted practices by enterprises that may affect trade between member states and that have either the purpose or result of preventing, restricting, or distorting competition within the Common Market. Article 85(2) provides that any agreements which violate Article 85(1) are void. Article 85(3) permits the commission to grant exemptions from Article 85(1) under certain circumstances.

Article 85 (1)

ENTERPRISES

In order to establish a violation of Article 85(1) four separate elements must be proven. First, the article is addressed to "enterprises" (officially translated as "undertakings"). This word is not defined in the treaty, but there is general agreement as to its meaning. The word clearly includes the traditional forms of business entity such as the corporation, the limited-liability company, the partnership, and the sole proprietorship. The Court of Justice and the commission have held that the parties to the challenged agreement, decision, or concerted practice must be legally and economically autonomous. Therefore, agreements between a parent company and its wholly owned subsidiary or between wholly owned subsidiaries of the same parent company have been held not to violate Article 85(1) in cases where the subsidiaries had no economic independence and were under the complete control of the parent. In these cases the commission and the Court of Justice reasoned that if the parties are not autonomous they cannot compete with each other; therefore an agreement between them cannot restrict competition. Such agreements are merely a "distribution of tasks within a single economic unit."

The commission has used similar reasoning to distinguish situations where a manufacturer enters into agreements with independent distributors of his products from those where a manufacturer integrates the distribution of his products into his enterprise by appointing commercial agents or representatives. The former situation is subject to Article 85(1) and the latter is not.

If the other party acts independently of the manufacturer and bears the financial risks connected with the agreement, he is an "independent trader" who is capable of agreeing with the manufacturer to restrain competition. On the other hand, if the other party does not bear the financial risks and is not free to decide when, where, how, and with whom business is to be done, he is merely an agent of the manufacturer. The reality of this relationship rather than its legal form is determinative. Thus even though a party is referred to as an "agent," the commission may determine, after examining the economic realities of the relationship, that he is an "independent trader." Factors which may be relevant include whether the distributor is required to maintain a substantial inventory of the pertinent goods, to which he has legal title; whether he is required to furnish or does furnish substantial free service to customers at his own expense; and whether he is free to determine or does determine prices and conditions of sales to customers.

There is no geographical delimitation of "enterprise" in the treaty. Therefore, the Court of Justice has held that the concept is broad enough to cover companies incorporated and having their headquarters outside the Common Market.

As a result of these rulings non-Common Market businessmen should carefully examine the alternate methods of establishing themselves or otherwise doing business in the Common Market. A decision to organize a foreign subsidiary, purchase a minority or controlling interest in a foreign company, enter into a joint venture, establish an exclusive distributorship, appoint a commercial agent, or open a branch office may well have important competition policy consequences.

AGREEMENTS, DECISIONS, AND CONCERTED PRACTICES

The next element of a violation of Article 85(1) is the existence of an agreement, decision, or concerted practice between the independent enterprises in question. *Agreements* refers to legally binding obligations such as contracts, both oral and written. The few cases where the commission has found the existence of a "decision" have involved actions of a trade association made in accordance with the rules of the association and binding upon the members of the association in their capacity as members. Most commentators believe that a recommendation made by an association that is not legally binding on the members is not a "decision." The scope of the words *concerted practice* has not yet been precisely delineated. The leading case interpreting this phrase involved three price increases in the dyestuffs industry that were nearly identical in coverage, amount, and timing and that were preceded by meetings among the ten manufacturers of dyestuffs. The Court of Justice upheld a commission decision that the conduct of the ten manufacturers constituted a concerted practice. According to the commission, the crucial question was whether, "having due regard to the nature of the dyestuffs market, manufacturers acting independently could in fact have taken the risk of introducing a general across-the-board price increase in their products." The commission argued that although parallel behavior alone does not constitute a concerted practice, "it is nevertheless liable to constitute strong circumstantial evidence when it leads to conditions of competition which do not match the normal conditions of the market, having due regard to the nature of the products marketed, the size and number of the enterprises in the industry and the size of the market itself." This occurs, for example, when parallel conduct permits the enterprises to stabilize prices at a level other than that which would have resulted from competition, and to strengthen acquired market positions to the detriment of free movement of products within the Common Market and the consumers' freedom to select their suppliers. According to the Court of Justice the prohibition of "concerted practices" is aimed at a "form of coordination between enterprises that has not yet reached the point where there is a contract in the true sense of the word but which, in practice, consciously substitutes a practical cooperation for the risk of competition." In the commission's words:

> Each manufacturer prices his own products and for this purpose, can take into account the current or foreseeable behavior of competitors. However, the treaty's competition rules do not allow a producer to cooperate with his competitors—in any way whatever—to work out a coordinated price increase policy and to insure the success of the increase by the prior elimination of any uncertainty as to reciprocal behavior concerning essential aspects such as rates, purpose, timing and location.

MAY AFFECT TRADE BETWEEN MEMBER STATES

The third vital element of a violation of Article 85(1) is that the agreement, decision, or concerted practice must be of such a type that it "may affect trade between Member States." The Court of Justice has held that the requisite effect on trade between member states may be either a direct, indirect, actual, or potential effect upon the flow of trade between member states that may hinder the creation of a common market among those states. To determine whether a particular agreement has such an effect, it is necessary to assess the agreement within the whole surrounding economic and legal context. Among the relevant factors are the nature and quantity of the products which are the subject matter of the agreement; the positions of the parties in the market; the number of parties to the agreement; and the existence of relevant industrial property or analogous rights protected by national laws.

On the other hand, if the effect of the agreement, decision, or concerted practice is confined to the boundaries of a single member state or is confined to markets outside the Common Market, there is no violation of Article 85(1). Consequently, agreements relating to exports or to single-nation exclusive distributorships may fall outside Article 85(1) if they are drafted so as to avoid a potential adverse effect on trade between member states.

It should be remembered, however, that the Common Market authorities assert that their jurisdiction extends to conduct by non-Common Market firms located outside the territory of the Communities that affects trade between member states. For example, in the *Dyestuffs* case mentioned earlier, four of the ten manufacturers were located outside the Common Market—three in Switzerland and one in England, which had not yet joined the Communities. Each of the four had one or more wholly owned subsidiaries within the Common Market that had received binding instructions from the parent company to raise prices. Both the commission and the Court of Justice held that because the subsidiaries had no real autonomy from the parent companies, the conduct of the subsidiaries within the Common Market should be imputed to the parent companies. Therefore, fines were imposed on each parent company for participating in concerted practices contravening Article 85(1).

In this case, and in others such as *Continental Can* and *Commercial Solvents,* the factual situations were limited to activities carried on within the Communities. However, the commission has stated that it has the power to make a claim of "extraterritorial" jurisdiction as broad as that made by the U.S. courts in *Alcoa* and other cases discussed in Chapter 3. For example, the commission published a "statement of principle" that arrangements between Japanese enterprises curtailing the quantity of exports of Japanese products to the Common Market are prohibited under Article 85(1) and added that the "fact that several or all the [enterprises] involved have their principal head offices outside the Community is no obstacle to the application of this rule in so far as the agreements, decisions or concerted practices have effects extending to the Common Market." A year later the commission initiated proceedings against five French and four Japanese manufacturers of ball-bearings, charging them with violating Article 85(1) by participating in a "self-limitation" cartel. The Japanese firms allegedly agreed to limit their exports to France by substantially raising their prices for ball-bearings. Such a sweeping assertion of jurisdiction may be used in the future to challenge the activities conducted by other non-Common Market entities outside the territory of the Communities that affect trade between member states.

PURPOSE OR EFFECT OF RESTRICTING COMPETITION
WITHIN THE COMMON MARKET

The last essential element of a violation of Article 85(1) is that the agreements, decisions, or concerted practices must have as their "object or effect the prevention, restriction or distortion of competition within the Common Market. . . ." In the *Grundig–Consten* case the Court of Justice said "[f]or the purpose of applying Article 85(1) it is superfluous to take into account the concrete effects of an agreement once it appears that it has the object of restricting, preventing, or distorting competition." However, the Court has not consistently applied this widely criticized statement. In practice the effects of the agreement have been examined to determine whether it may in fact affect trade between member states. Moreover, the effects of the agreement must be considered in light of the *de minimis* rule announced by the commission, under which conduct that does not "perceptibly" affect trade between member states is exempt from Article 85(1) because of its "minor importance."

Agreements between enterprises engaged in the manufacture or distribution of goods are exempt from Article 85(1) because of their "minor importance" if:

> (1) The products involved, in the part of the Common Market covered by the agreement, account for no more than five percent of the turnover in the same products or products considered to be similar by consumers on the basis of their properties, utility or price, and (2) The total annual turnover of the enterprises that are parties to the agreement does not exceed 15,000,000 units of account or, for agreements between trading enterprises, 20,000,000 units of account.

The total turnover figure includes turnover among subsidiaries and partially owned affiliates of the enterprises concerned. In addition, the commission has stated that agreements which exceed the figures listed for market share and turnover by less than 10 per cent for two consecutive fiscal years also fall outside of Article 85(1).

The word *competition* is not defined in any of the treaties of the European Communities and the Court of Justice has never defined it. It is best interpreted by reference to the Preamble to the EEC Treaty that calls for "fair competition" to achieve the objectives of the treaty. In other words, the type and degree of competition required to be maintained is that which is needed to insure integration of the nine national economies and to prevent private restrictions from replacing the dismantled governmental barriers to free trade among member states.

Employing this interpretation as a guideline, the Court of Justice has held that Article 85(1) applies to all agreements that restrict competition regardless of whether they are between competitors operating on the same level (horizontal) or between noncompetitors operating on different levels (vertical). Moreover, the Court of Justice has ruled that competition can be restrained by agreements that prevent or restrict competition between one of the agreeing parties and third persons, as well as by agreements that limit competition between the agreeing parties. For example, in the important *Grundig–Consten* case Grundig, a German company, entered into an exclusive-distributorship agreement with Consten, a French company, making Consten the sole distributor in France for radios, tape recorders, and so on, manufactured by Grundig and bearing the Grundig trademark. The agreement provided that Consten could not sell Grundig products outside of France and Grundig agreed not to sell to other persons in France. All other Grundig purchasers, German and foreign, were similarly prohibited from selling outside their assigned national territories. The commission and the Court of Justice held that these agreements restricted competition within the Common Market in two ways. First, the agreements denied French retailers the opportunity of buying from any supplier other than Consten. Second, the agreements prohibited Consten from re-exporting Grundig products to other countries within the Common Market. This type of territorial protection hinders the integration of national markets into a single market and precludes the possibility of parallel imports—importation from other member states into the territory protected by the distribution agreement by persons other than the distributor. According to the commission, the possibility of parallel imports:

> should constitute a corrective factor for excessive prices imposed by an exclusive concession holder and should be an element of price harmonization in a unified market having the same features as a single domestic market. The possibility of parallel imports helps to ensure that users will have a fair share of the advantages accruing from exclusive dealing. The contracting parties must not, therefore, be allowed to restrict the freedom of users and intermediaries to obtain the product concerned from other resellers within the Common Market at more favourable conditions than those granted by the exclusive concession holder in his own area.

The only exception to this prohibition of absolute territorial protection is the case of agreements of "minor importance" discussed earlier.

In an attempt to clarify the words *prevention, restriction, or distortion of competition* five examples of unlawful conduct are listed in the text of Article 85(1). Each of these examples will be discussed later in this chapter. It is important to note that this list is illustrative rather than exhaustive. Therefore conduct not encompassed by the examples may be declared unlawful if it meets the four tests discussed previously.

Article 85 (2)

Agreements or decisions that are unlawful under Article 85(1) are rendered "automatically void" by Article 85(2). Concerted practices are not covered by Article 85(2) because there is no legal transaction to which the voidness could apply. The precise legal consequences of such "voidness" are determined by the civil law in the relevant member state. In general, the agreement or decision is treated as a nullity and is unenforceable in the civil courts of the member states. Thus, neither party to the agreement will be permitted to enforce it against the other party or third parties. Moreover, in some member states a party to the agreement may be able to recover money paid under the "void" agreement. In many cases an agreement is sought to be enforced in a national court of a member state and a defense is raised that the agreement is void under Article 85. The national court may rule on the defense or refer the question to the European Court of Justice under Article 177 of the EEC Treaty which will be discussed later, in the United Kingdom portion of this chapter. Only the portions of the agreement that are prohibited under Article 85(1) are automatically void. Portions of the agreement that are not prohibited by Article 85(1) remain valid unless they cannot be separated from the unlawful parts of the agreement, in which case the entire agreement is void. The decision as to which portions of the agreement are severable is a matter of the national law of the relevant member state.

Article 85 (3)

The broad prohibitions contained in Article 85(1) are counterbalanced by a broad possibility that those prohibitions may be declared inapplicable under Article 85(3). The parties to the agreement, decision, or concerted practice may request the commission to declare that their arrangement meets the four tests listed in Article 85(3) and that they are therefore entitled to a declaration that Article 85(1) is inapplicable. Such a declaration (often called an exemption) may be issued when the agreement, decision, or concerted practice is one which

[1] contributes to improving the production or distribution of goods or to promoting technical or economic progress [*and*] [2] allows consumers a fair share of the resulting benefit, *and which does not*

[3] (a) impose on the enterprises concerned restrictions which are not indispensable to the attainment of these objectives; *and*

[4] (b) afford such enterprises the possibility of eliminating competition in respect of a substantial part of the products in question.

All four of these conditions must be met in order for the parties to qualify for an exemption. Other factors in the market situation are unimportant to the commission's decision. The commission's decisions are subject to review only by the Court of Justice. The grant of an exemption is binding on the national authorities and courts of member states.

Regulation 17

NOTIFICATION

The procedures for obtaining an exemption under Article 85(3) and many other important rules are contained in Regulation 17, the first regulation implementing Articles 85 and 86 of the EEC Treaty, which became effective on March 13, 1962. The most important rules relating to the grant of an exemption can be summarized as follows. The party seeking an exemption must request the commission to rule that in the event it determines that the arrangement violates Article 85(1) the agreement, decision, or concerted practice falls within the four criteria listed in Article 85(3) and is therefore exempt. The commission may not grant an exemption in the absence of such a request. The request is in the form of a "notification" filed with the commission giving various details concerning the arrangement and reasons why the party believes that it falls within Article 85(3). Mere filing of the request does not mean that the exemption will be granted. The party applying for an exemption has the right to a hearing before the commission and notice of the commission's intent to render a decision on the application is published so that interested third parties may present their views to the commission within specified time limits. The words *notification, registration,* and *request* are all used to denote this process of applying for an exemption under Article 85(3).

Unless the party wants to obtain an exemption, there is no requirement that agreements, decisions, or concerted practices be notified to the commission and failure to notify does not in itself make the parties liable to any fines or penalties. However, as long as the agreement is unnotified there is no possibility of obtaining an exemption under Article 85(3). Furthermore, parties who implement an unnotified agreement falling within Article 85(1) are liable to be fined for acts committed while the agreement was unnotified because an exemption granted under Article 85(3) protects the agreement retroactively only to the date of notification.

The following illustration will clarify the importance of these rules. Company A enters into a contract with Companies B and C. The initial question raised is whether the contract should be notified to the commission. If the contract is not notified and is later challenged by the commission as a violation of Article 85(1), there is no possibility of an exemption being granted, either retroactively or prospectively, and the companies may be fined if the contract is outlawed. On the other hand, if the contract is notified to the commission before it is implemented, and even if the exemption is denied, fines may not be imposed for the period between notification and the commission's decision on the request for an exemption. If the contract is notified after implementation of the agreement has commenced, the commission may grant an exemption retroactive only to the date of notification. For the period between the initiation of the agreement and its notification the contract is void and the parties may be fined for acts committed while the agreement was unnotified.

It will be remembered that Article 85(2) provides that agreements or decisions prohibited by Article 85(1) are automatically void. Regulation 17 states that the agreements, decisions, and concerted practices outlawed by Article 85(1) shall be prohibited, "no prior decision to this effect being required. . . ." In other words, from the effective date of Regulation 17, March 13, 1962, all agreements and decisions which violate Article 85(1) are void without the necessity of a decision to that effect. But what about the 37,000 agreements that were notified to the commission shortly after the promulgation of Regulation 17 by parties seeking an exemption under Article 85(3)?

The answer to this question depends on the effective date of the agreement. Agreements made before March 13, 1962 ("old" agreements) are "provisionally valid" until the commission rules on a timely filed request for an exemption, some of which are still pending. This means that the national courts cannot declare the agreement void until the commission has decided whether to grant an exemption. Moreover, such an agreement is enforceable in national courts and a defendant may not object to a suit for nonperformance on the ground that the agreement is invalid.

A different situation exists as to "new" agreements, those made on or after March 13, 1962. Registration of these agreements does not give rise to the type of "provisional validity" granted to "old" agreements. Therefore, even if a new agreement has been registered with the commission, national courts may hear challenges to the agreement's validity. If such a challenge is presented, the national court may declare the agreement void if there is "no doubt" of its incompatibility with Article 85(1). Such a case would arise, for example, if an identical agreement had previously been outlawed by the commission. On the other hand, if the national court "finds that the agreement has no appreciable effect on competition or on trade between the Member States . . . ," it can declare the agreement consistent with Article 85(1) and, therefore, valid. In cases of doubt the Court of Justice has indicated that the proceedings in the national court should be suspended so that an opinion can be obtained from the commission.

A different set of rules applies to "accession" agreements, those agreements made before January 1, 1973 (the date of accession of the three new member states), that violate Article 85(1) *solely as a result of accession* because they "affect trade between Member States" and "prevent, restrict or distort competition within the Common Market." For example, an agreement between a French and a British company that only affected trade between those two countries did not violate Article 85(1) before January 1, 1973, because it did not affect trade *"between* Member States." However, after the United Kingdom's accession, such an agreement does affect trade between member states. An agreement between companies in two acceding member states that did not violate Article 85(1) until the two states joined the Communities would also be an "accession" agreement."

In its Third Report on Competition Policy the commission stated that it "feels that the principles applicable to old agreements could also be applied by analogy to agreements which became subject to Article 85 following the

Accession of the new Member States, provided they were already in force before the date of accession (1 January 1973) and were notified before the end of the six-month period following accession."

The test of whether agreements, decisions, or concerted practices violate Article 85(1) is whether they "may affect trade between Member States and . . . have as their object or effect the prevention, restriction or distortion of competition within the Common Market." Therefore, accession agreements do *not* include agreements that affected trade between the original six member states and restricted competition within those six countries before January 1, 1973. Such agreements should have been notified to the commission as soon as they became effective and are not entitled to provisional validity.

This rule also applies to agreements between entities in foreign countries that meet the tests of affecting trade between member states and causing a restriction of competition within the Common Market. For example, an American export association, operating under a Webb–Pomerene exemption and selling to Common Market buyers, might violate Article 85(1) by causing the prohibited effects within the Common Market. If the export association agreement is not notified there would be no chance of an exemption under Article 85(3).

In summary, registration of agreements establishes eligibility for obtaining an exemption under Article 85(3) and provides immunity from fines by the commission. "Old" agreements and accession agreements are provisionally valid until the commission rules on the application for an exemption. However, according to the Court of Justice, "new" agreements made on or after March 13, 1962, or January 1, 1973, which have been notified "can be applied only at the parties' risk and peril. . . ."

EXCUSED FROM NOTIFICATION

Article 4(2) of Regulation 17 provides that certain classes of agreements need not, but may, be notified to the commission in order to obtain an exemption because, according to the Preamble to Regulation 17, a "number of them have special features which may make them less of a threat to the development of the Common Market." This does not mean that these classes of agreements may not violate Article 85(1). It merely means that they are eligible to be considered for the grant of an exemption under Article 85(3) on review of the agreement even if a notification has not been filed. The categories of agreements, decisions, and concerted practices which need not be notified and yet may be exempted are those (1) that are solely between business enterprises of only one member state and do not involve imports or exports between member states; or (2) in which only two enterprises take part and the sole effect of the agreement is (a) to restrict the freedom of one party to fix resale prices or conditions of sale (vertical resale price maintenance), or (b) to restrict the rights of any person acquiring or using patent, trademark, know-how, or other industrial property rights; or (3) the sole object of which is (a) the development or the uniform application of standards and types, or (b) joint research and development, or (c) specialization in the manufacture of a product, provided that the product does not have more than 15 per cent of the market in a substantial part of the Community and the annual total sales of the cooperating enterprises are not over 200 million units of account.

It is possible for an agreement to fall within several of these categories simultaneously. For example, a license agreement may be exempt under subparagraph (2)(b) and under the exception for single-nation agreements not involving imports or exports contained in subparagraph (1)(a). None of the listed categories has precedence over the others. Therefore, so long as the agreement falls under one exception, it need not be notified.

Block Exemptions

EXCLUSIVE-DISTRIBUTION AGREEMENTS

In addition to the categories of agreements that need not be notified under Article 4(2) of Regulation 17, to be exempted, the Council has authorized the commission to issue "block" exemptions for certain types of agreements. The first of these, Regulation 67/67, exempts certain bilateral exclusive-distribution arrangements if the parties respect certain conditions and do not attempt to provide absolute territorial protection for the sole distributor. This block exemption is unavailable if manufacturers of competing products grant each other exclusive distributorships for their products or if the contracting parties make it difficult for middlemen and consumers to obtain the products covered by the contract from other dealers in the Common Market. This exemption is also not available if both parties to the arrangement are located in the same member state and the agreement concerns the resale of products within that state because, in the commission's view "since it is only in exceptional cases that exclusive dealing agreements concluded within a Member State affect trade between Member States, there is no need to include them in this Regulation." This Regulation 67/67 block exemption for bilateral exclusive-distribution arrangements is available until December 31, 1982.

SPECIALIZATION AGREEMENTS

A second block exemption has been granted to certain types of specialization agreements by Regulation 2779/72. A "specialization" agreement is one in which two or more enterprises agree that one will specialize in the production or sale of one line of products and the other will specialize in another line of products. Promises not to compete with one another's "specialities," prohibitions against entering similar agreements with other enterprises, and reciprocal-supply clauses between the parties are often included in these agreements. The commission issued the block exemption because

> Agreements on the specialization of production in general help to improve the production or distribution of goods, because the enterprises can concentrate on the production of certain products, and thus operate on a more rational basis and offer such products at more favorable prices. Where there is effective competition, it can be expected that users will share proportionately in the resulting benefit.

Of the conditions which must be met before a specialization agreement can be exempted the most important are that the total combined annual turnovers of the parties not exceed 150 million units of account and the products concerned do not represent, in any member state, more than 10 per cent of the total Common Market sales in the same products or in products that the user considers to be equivalent. This block exemption is available until December 31, 1977.

It is possible that a specialization agreement that is ineligible for a block exemption may be exempt under Article 85(3). For example, a German manufacturer of sewing machine needles entered into an agreement with a Belgian company engaged in the same business. The firms agreed to concentrate their production in a single factory. The German factory was closed and its equipment was transferred to the Belgian factory. The German company acquired 25 per cent of the Belgian firm's capital and a guarantee that it would be able to obtain all its requirements of needles from the Belgian factory. Before they consolidated their production in a single factory, the Belgian firm produced 6 per cent of the world output of sewing machine needles and the German company produced 3 per cent. This specialization agreement was not eligible for a block exemption because there was no reciprocal commitment by each of the parties to refrain, for the duration of the agreement, from manufacturing certain products in order to entrust it to its partner. The only commitment was a unilateral one by the German company to cease its production of needles and transfer production to the Belgian company. Despite ineligibility for a block exemption the commission found that the agreement was exempt under Article 85(3) because the concentration of manufacturing agreed on

> has from the point of view of the improvement of production, favorable effects analogous to those of specialization; it causes an increase of at least 50 per cent in the quantity of needles to be manufactured in the Eupen factory, which makes it possible to make more intensive use of the existing plant and to introduce production-line manufacture.
> This rationalization of production has made it possible to reduce the large proportion of labor costs in the producer's cost price. . . . The introduction of mechanized production-line manufacture with increased pro-

ductive capacity also makes it possible to manufacture articles of a more even quality. . . .

[Finally], the agreement does not afford the parties the possibility of eliminating competition in a substantial part of the products in question.

ADDITIONAL AUTHORIZED EXEMPTIONS

The council has authorized the commission to grant additional block exemptions for other types of agreements. The list includes agreements on the application of standards and on the limitation of production to certain types, sizes, and qualities, on joint research and development, and on certain types of industrial property-licensing agreements. To date the commission has not issued regulations pursuant to these authorizations.

Exemptions and the Per Se Rule

The Common Market Rules on Competition, particularly Articles 85 and 86, appear to differ substantially from U.S. antitrust law in that they contain no per se offenses. As we discussed in previous chapters, the concept of per se unreasonableness means that once courts have had sufficient experience with certain types of conduct, they will conclusively presume that such conduct is unreasonable and therefore illegal. The per se rule has been applied in the United States to conduct such as price-fixing agreements, group boycotts, and market-sharing arrangements. In contrast, any restraint of trade falling under Article 85(1) may be permitted to continue if it is eligible for and does meet the four criteria for an Article 85(3) exemption. Thus Article 85(3) has been compared to the American "rule of reason." Nevertheless, the commission has announced in its First Report on Competition Policy that the decisions issued by the commission should provide some general guidelines as to what is impermissible conduct. It pointed out that certain types of arrangements have always been denied exemptions and implied that such arrangements have little chance of ever obtaining an exemption. The commission listed agreements that fix prices; allocate markets, customers, or quotas; or result in the protection of markets within each member state, for example,

> collective reciprocal-dealing agreements for purchases and sales within a member state, . . . agreements for aggregated rebates without the inclusion of purchases from other member states, and . . . national cartels fixing resale prices for imported products or fixing selling prices for exported products.

Of course, these types of agreements can be exempt if they are of "minor importance," do not affect trade between member states, or fall within one of the block exemptions. Therefore, it is accurate to say that there are no per se violations of Article 85 even though the commission's guidelines reveal an approach similar to per se unreasonableness. Although Article 85(3) may resemble the "rule of reason," it is considerably different in both its procedural aspects and in the fact that exemptions may be granted for a specified period of time and may be subject to conditions imposed by the commission.

Official Notices

From time to time the commission issues "official notices" that are intended to give enterprises some indication of the considerations that will guide the commission in its interpretation of Article 85(1). Such clarifications are not exemptions, but are designed to inform enterprises of the types of agreements that the commission believes do not violate Article 85(1), thus obviating the necessity of notifying each agreement. Such a notice is merely a guideline or advisory opinion by the commission that the described agreements do not violate Article 85(1). Such notices are not binding on the Court of Justice, nor on national courts.

To date the commission has issued four of these "official notices." The first two were issued on December 24, 1962, and have thus become known as the Christmas Messages. One of these Christmas Messages dealt with patent-licensing agreements. It has been substantially modified by subsequent case law and will be discussed with the relevant cases later in this chapter. The other Christmas Message concerned exclusive agency contracts with commercial agents. This message was discussed earlier in this chapter in the section concerning enterprises. Essentially the notice states that contracts under which commercial agents agree to negotiate business transactions for the account of the principal and under which the agent does not bear the economic risks of the sales he makes cannot fall under the prohibition of Article 85(1) because such agreements are not deemed to be made "between enterprises" as required by Article 85(1). The third notice related to cooperation among enterprises. In the commission's opinion certain types of cooperation between enterprises, especially small- and medium-sized enterprises, do not restrict competition within the meaning of Article 85(1). Eight groups of cooperation agreements are covered. They include, among others, agreements having as their *sole* object joint procurement of market information, cooperation in accounting, credit information and debt collecting, joint research and development, joint use of production facilities, or joint advertising. The approval of each group of agreements contains the *sole object* qualification, indicating that any additional purposes may cause the agreement to fall under the prohibitions of Article 85(1). The last notice concerned activity of "minor importance," which was explained earlier in this chapter.

Negative Clearance

An enterprise that is in doubt as to the legality of a proposed or existing agreement or practice under Article 85(1) or Article 86 may request the commission to issue a ruling that, based on the information supplied to it, the commission will not challenge the agreement under Article 85(1) or Article 86. Such a ruling is provided for under Article 2 of Regulation 17 and is called a *negative clearance.* This procedure should not be confused with procedures for obtaining an exemption under Article 85(3). The negative clearance provides a method of obtaining an advisory opinion from the commission as to whether the particular agreement falls within Article 85 (1), generally before the contemplated activity is actually engaged in. The grant of a negative clearance means that Article 85 (1) does not apply to the agreement at all. The grant of an exemption under Article 85 (3), on the other hand, means that Article 85 (1) does apply to the agreement, but because of its beneficial aspects the agreement will be permitted to begin or to continue operating.

If the application for a negative clearance is filed before the agreement is implemented and the commission finds that the proposed activity would violate Article 85(1), no violation would yet have occurred and thus there is no liability to fines. In practice, applications for a negative clearance are often accompanied by requests for an exemption so that if the commission finds a violation of Article 85(1), it can immediately determine whether the prohibition is inapplicable because of entitlement to an exemption. Before granting a negative clearance, the commission must publish the essential content of the application and invite interested third parties to submit their comments. The decision to grant a negative clearance means that based on the information supplied to it the commission will not challenge the agreement or practice and is therefore similar to the "railroad release" letters and the Business Review Procedure of the United States Department of Justice. Therefore the enterprise can proceed without fear of challenge by the commission. Because the clearance applies only to the facts of which the commission has been notified, failure to disclose all pertinent facts or a subsequent change in the factual situation may result in cancellation of the negative clearance. The commission may impose fines of 100 to 5,000 units of account for willfully or negligently supplying false or misleading information in a request for a negative clearance. An applicant for a negative clearance may appeal a denial of the application by the commission to the Court of Justice.

Prohibited Agreements and Practices

PRICE FIXING

The first of the five categories of prohibited agreements or practices specifically enumerated in Article 85(1) are those that "directly or indirectly fix purchase or selling prices or any other trading conditions." As we explained earlier, there are no per se violations of Article 85(1), at least as long as the possibility of an exemption under Article 85(3) exists. Thus cases involving price fixing must be examined as all others to determine whether the four elements of a violation of Article 85(1) are present and, if so, whether an exemption under Article 85(3) is warranted. This first illustration covers both horizontal and vertical restraints, including fixing prices, elements used in the calculation of prices, terms of payment, warranties, and the tying together of prices and terms. The *Dyestuffs* case mentioned earlier was a classic example of concerted practices to fix the selling price of various dyestuffs marketed in the Common Market. In other decisions the commission has condemned a decision by a Belgian toiletries and perfume trade association composed of manufacturers, general representatives, and sole distributors of trademarked perfumery products and toiletries, which required members to honor fixed prices to the consumer and under which retailers were supplied only if they sold at the fixed resale prices; a system adopted by an association of Belgian cement producers providing for uniform prices and conditions of sale tied to sales quotas and equalization of receipts; and an obligation imposed on members of a Dutch paint manufacturers' association to respect minimum selling prices and other conditions of sale and delivery for exports within the Common Market. One of the most important cases in this area involved a series of agreements and decisions concerning the sale of cement in Holland. An association of Dutch cement dealers (VCH) that had 408 members whose activity in 1972 covered 67.5 per cent of the cement market in Holland, adopted regulations requiring mandatory resale prices for deliveries of less than 100 tons and a system of recommended prices for deliveries of 100 tons or more. The commission ruled that both the fixed-price and the recommended-price systems violated Article 85(1). The Court of Justice upheld the commission's decision after VCH appealed. The Court noted that what competition existed was in areas of product quality and customer service rather than price. However, the Court stated that Article 85(1) expressly condemns direct and indirect price fixing and added:

> While a system of "fixed prices" is clearly contrary to that provision, the "recommended price" system is equally so. It could not be supposed that the clauses of the agreement relating to the determination of "recommended prices" are devoid of all useful effect. Indeed the fixing of a price even simply recommended affects competition by the fact that it permits all the participants to foresee with a reasonable degree of certainty what the price policy of the competitors will be. That foresight is all the more certain in that to the "recommended prices" provisions is attached the obligation to make a demonstrable profit in all cases and these provisions must in addition be considered in the context of the whole of the internal regulations of the applicant association which are characterised by a rigorous discipline supported by inspections and sanctions.

VCH contended that despite this reasoning Article 85(1) did not apply because the agreement was among enterprises in only one member state and applied only to prices within that member state. Therefore, it fell outside the requirement that the agreement "may affect trade between Member States." Both the commission and the Court of Justice rejected this contention. The Court of Justice held:

> An agreement which extends to the whole of the territory of a Member-State has, by its very nature, the effect of consolidating a national partitioning, thus hindering the economic interpenetration to which the Treaty is directed and ensuring a protection for the national production. More particularly, the restrictive provisions by which the members of the applicant association are bound as well as the exclusion by the association of all sales to re-sellers who are not authorized by it make more difficult the activity or the penetration on the Dutch market of producers or sellers from the other Member-States. It therefore appears that the objection based on the fact that the trade between Member-States is not liable to be affected by the decisions of the applicant association should be dismissed.

In discussing this aspect of the VCH case in its First Report on Competition Policy, the commission stated that because collective action among enterprises of one member state such as the fixing of recommended prices is likely to hinder the establishment of a single Common Market, "[t]here is little chance that such agreements can be exempted from the prohibition of cartels as there is nothing to show, except in very special cases, that the elimination of competition between traders would be more likely to ensure regular supplies to the market on more favourable conditions than competition itself."

LIMITATION OR CONTROL OF PRODUCTION, MARKETS,
TECHNICAL DEVELOPMENT, OR INVESTMENT

This enumeration of violative practices contained in Article 85(1) is very broad. It would include agreements designed to divide product lines, to unify research or development, to form joint purchase or sales organizations, and to apply joint product standards or types. The potential wide range of agreements falling within this illustration has been substantially limited by the block exemptions for specialization and cooperation agreements discussed earlier. Moreover, the commission exempted in certain cases because of their beneficial effects under Article 85(3) several such arrangements that were ineligible for the block exemptions. For example, in the *Henkel–Colgate* case two of the largest manufacturers in the oligopolistic European soap industry created a joint, equally owned subsidiary in Switzerland to conduct research into soap products. The commission found that the agreement eliminated competition in research and therefore violated Article 85(1). However, an exemption was granted under Article 85(3) because the commission believed that such joint research would promote economic and technical progress and because the agreement did not include any restriction at the production or distribution levels for the products manufactured as the result of the joint research. The exemption was subject to two conditions, that the companies inform the commission of all license agreements emanating from the results of the joint research and that they keep the commission informed of all transactions, such as acquisition of share holdings or the establishment of personnel links, that would create a closer relationship between the two enterprises or their affiliates.

In another case, the commission exempted an agreement between two enterprises for technical cooperation, joint research, and development in their work on a new type of electrically powered bus. The agreement contained provisions prohibiting cooperation with third parties within the field covered by the agreement and an obligation to supply only to the other party complementary products needed for the manufacture of the finished product resulting from the joint development. The commission found that these restrictions were justified because they were indispensable if the firms were to earn a reasonable profit on their investments. According to the commission, a decisive factor

> was the fact that the concentration of the manufacture of the new products to a limited number of producers (apart from the fact that these would compete with the manufacturers of buses provided with mechanical propulsion) would not be likely completely to prevent competition between them, as their respective possibilities for selling on all markets of the Community were in no way restricted.

SHARING MARKETS OR SOURCES OF SUPPLY

The commission and the Court of Justice have taken strong positions against market-sharing agreements, especially agreements designed to protect against competition the national markets of each member state. It is therefore not surprising that exclusive-distributorship agreements that contain territorial limitations on resale—agreements under which a distributor agrees to buy only from the manufacturer and not to sell outside his territory—have been the subject of particular attention by Common Market authorities.

We discussed the distinction between a distributor and an agent, based upon responsibility for financial risk, earlier in this chapter. We have also discussed the fact that many distribution agreements that would fall within the prohibition of Article 85(1) have been exempted by a block exemption. It will be recalled from these earlier discussions that Article 85(1) applies to exclusive distributorships but not to agencies, and that bilateral exclusive distributorships without provisions for absolute territorial protection are generally exempt under the Regulation 67/67 block exemption. Exclusive contracts that provide for absolute territorial protection were also dealt with in the previously mentioned *Grundig–Consten* case. As will be recalled, Grundig entered into an exclusive-distributorship agreement with Consten, a French company, making Consten the sole distributor in France for radios, tape recorders, and so on, manufactured by Grundig. The agreement provided that Consten could not sell Grundig products outside of France and Grundig agreed not to sell to other persons in France. All Grundig purchasers, German and foreign, were prohibited from selling outside of their assigned territories. Grundig registered the trademark *GINT* (Grundig International) in Germany and affixed it to Grundig products manufactured in Germany. In each of the other Common Market countries the exclusive distributor, with Grundig's consent, had registered the trademark locally. Both the distribution and trademark provisions were designed to prevent persons other than Consten from importing Grundig equipment covered by the Grundig–Consten agreement into France.

The commission and the Court of Justice held that these agreements restricted competition within the Common Market by prohibiting "parallel" imports into France in two ways. First, as we discussed earlier in this chapter, the agreements themselves prohibited such imports from other Common Market nations. Second, Consten's registration in France of the GINT trademark, which Grundig affixed to all products, was designed to protect against parallel imports into France, by using the national trademark law. The commission argued before the Court of Justice when the decision was appealed that this is not the true function of a manufacturer's trademark—that function is to protect its holders by indicating that the goods come from a specified enterprise, and thereby assure the uniform quality of the product. That function was already performed by the registered Grundig trademark (as distinguished from the registered GINT trademark) that was also affixed to all Grundig products sold by Consten.

The Court pointed out that because the contract between Grundig and Consten, on the one hand, prevented all enterprises other than Consten from importing Grundig products into France and, on the other hand, prohibited Consten from re-exporting such products to other countries of the Common Market, it unquestionably impaired trade between member states. In addition to such limitations on the freedom of trade, there was the limitation on third parties that might result from Consten's registration in France of the GINT trademark. Third parties would be threatened with infringement suits in France should they import Grundig products (which always bore the GINT trademark) into that country. All these limitations, the court ruled, were sufficient to "affect" trade and distort competition within the meaning of Article 85(1).

Grundig and Consten contended that there was no violation of Article 85(1) because trade had increased rather than decreased under the agreements. The Court rejected this argument on the ground that the crucial factor is whether the agreement directly or indirectly, actually or potentially, is capable of "jeopardizing the freedom of trade between Member States in such a manner as to prejudice realization of the objectives of a single market between States. Thus the fact that an agreement helps to bring about a considerable increase in the volume of trade between Member States is not sufficient to preclude the possibility that such agreement can 'affect' trade within the meaning stated above." To "affect trade adversely" there must be more than a change in the normal course of trade. The change brought about by an agreement must also be apt to endanger free internation trade in a way that might prejudice the achievement of a single common market.

The Court of Justice's decision in *Grundig–Consten* also provides an ironic footnote to the development of international antitrust law. The decision came in 1966, four years after enforcement of Article 85 was begun by the commission. Over a year later, in the 1967 case of *United States* v. *Arnold, Schwinn & Co.*, the United States Supreme Court ruled for the first time that such a vertical allocation of exclusive resale territories by a manufacturer to its distributors violated the seventy-seven-year-old Sherman Act.

The *Grundig–Consten* decision explains why the Regulation 67/67 block exemption for exclusive distributorships, which was issued one year after the decision, does not apply if the parties create an impediment which prevents dealers and consumers from obtaining the products in question from other Common Market sources. This usually occurs when the contracting parties, as in *Grundig–Consten*, exercise intellectual property rights to prevent dealers or consumers from obtaining in other areas of the Common Market supplies of the products properly marked and marketed, or to prevent others from selling the products in the contract territory.

However, it is important to remember that Regulation 67/67 does permit "relative" as opposed to "absolute" territorial protection. In other words, the agreement must not prevent the possibility of parallel imports but it may prohibit the exclusive distributor from advertising the products outside the contract territory and from establishing a branch or distribution warehouse outside the contract territory.

The commission's efforts to eliminate "absolute" territorial protection can be seen in the *Kodak* case, where the commission granted a negative clearance only after the companies modified their uniform sales conditions. Each Kodak subsidiary in different member states had identical conditions of sale for Kodak products, including conditions that prohibited customers from exporting or reselling the supplied products for export. The commission believed that these conditions isolated the market of each member state and protected the prices charged in each of the markets from competition from one or more member states, and therefore violated Article 85(1).

A recent development in this field is the exemption of certain "selective-distribution" systems under which the producer restricts distribution of his products to a limited number of dealers. For example, Omega, a Swiss watch producer, limited grants of distributorships to those who satisfied certain requirements of expert knowledge and possession of sophisticated equipment. These requirements were not deemed to restrict competition. However, Omega refused to establish more than a fixed number of authorized retailers in each territory based on the expected level of sales in that area. This policy, which was contained in the distribution agreements, was considered to be a restriction on trade because it excluded a large number of qualified retailers. Nevertheless, an exemption under Article 85(3) was granted after the agreements were altered to provide that appointed retailers could in future obtain supplies from any of Omega's exclusive importers in the Common Market and that the appointed retailers were free to export to other Common Market countries by selling to other appointed retailers or to consumers at freely determined prices. Under these conditions the commission stated that an Article 85(3) exemption may be granted

> if the products concerned [are] highly technical and relatively highly priced, and for which after sales service and guarantee are of particular importance. In this case, the Commission considered that, in order to avoid any deterioration in the distribution of the products concerned, it was essential to provide the appointed retailers, with a turnover high enough to encourage them to make a genuine effort in sales promotion and service. Admission to the ranks of appointed retailers for all those retailers who, within the Common Market, have the necessary knowledge and equipment demanded by Omega to sell Omega watches would have reduced the sales of each of them to only a few units per annum.

The narrowness of the exemption for "selective-distribution" systems such as the one in *Omega* was demonstrated in the commission's October 1973 decision against Deutsche Philips. Philips entered into a series of written agreements with German wholesalers and retailers concerning large domestic appliances, electric shavers, and television sets. The agreements provided that wholesalers were to supply only to specialized retailers, that other wholesalers were not to be supplied unless Philips gave prior written consent in each particular case, and that retailers were to sell only to consumers. The commission held that these provisions violated Article 85(1) because they "prevented wholesalers and retailers in Germany from supplying dealers in other Member States at the same trading stage. Such bans on horizontal supplies can have the same effect on cross-frontier trade as export bans" (which were condemned in the *Grundig–Consten* case).

INTELLECTUAL PROPERTY

Intellectual property rights—patents, know-how, trademarks, and copyrights—are regulated by the national laws of each member state of the Common Market. These laws have not yet been harmonized and consequently each law applies only to the territory of the respective member state. This situation raises a problem of reconciling the exercise of property rights granted by a member state and the Communities' goal of integrating the nine national markets into a single market. There are no specific references to property rights in Articles 85 and 86. However, two other Articles of the EEC Treaty, Articles 36 and 222, do mention property rights. Article 36 provides that other articles in the EEC Treaty that prohibit quantitative restrictions on trade between member states "shall not preclude prohibitions or restrictions on imports, exports or goods in transit justified on grounds of . . . the protection of industrial and commercial property. . . ." Article 222 of the EEC Treaty states, "This Treaty shall in no way prejudice the rules in Member States governing the system of property ownership."

In a series of cases the Court of Justice has developed the doctrine that although the *existence* of property rights is not affected by the EEC Treaty, the *exercise* of these rights may fall within the scope of Articles 85 and 86. The Court reasons that Articles 36 and 222 permit restrictions on the free movement of goods, which in the absence of these articles would violate Article 85(1), because they are necessary to protect property rights. Article 36 also provides that, "[s]uch prohibitions or restrictions [on the free movement of goods] shall not, however, constitute a means of arbitrary discrimination or a disguised restriction on trade between Member States." Therefore, the exercise of property rights can only be permitted insofar as the exercise is necessary to preserve the specific reasons for the existence of such property rights—adequate remuneration for invention and safe transfers of technology.

The major area of dispute involves the principle of "territoriality," which enables the holder of exclusive national intellectual property rights to prohibit the importation of identical products from another member state, thereby preventing parallel imports and preserving fragmented markets within the Communities. As we saw in *Grundig–Consten,* the commission strongly opposes such obstacles to the free movement of goods and to the achievement of a unified market. For example, one article of Regulation 67/67, governing block exemptions for distributorship agreements, provides that the exemption does not apply "where the contracting parties exercise industrial property rights in order to prevent dealers or consumers in other parts of the Common Market from obtaining supplies of the contract products properly marked and offered for sale, or from selling such products in the contract territory." The Preamble to the Regulation adds that "industrial property rights and other rights may not . . . be exercised in an abusive way so as to create absolute territorial protection."

Trademarks

As we have discussed earlier, the Court of Justice held in the *Grundig–Consten* case that a series of bilateral exclusive-distributorship agreements providing for enforcing national trademark rights violate Article 85(1) if they result in absolute territorial protection. The Court of Justice stated that registration in France by Consten, the French corporation, of the GINT trademark that Grundig, the German corporation, affixed to all of its products, was designed to fortify the agreement's built-in protection against parallel imports and was therefore a disguised restriction on trade between member states. No third party could import Grundig products from other member states for resale in France without incurring the possibility of an infringement suit.

Sirena, a later trademark case, extended the *Grundig–Consten* holding to situations where assignments between the trademark owner and his assignees are used to prevent the importation into one member state of lawfully marked goods from other member states. Sirena, an Italian company, had an exclusive right for Italy to use a trademark of an American firm on jars of medicated cosmetic cream. The product had also been trademarked under parallel rights granted in Germany. Sirena sought to prevent the importation into Italy of goods that were lawfully marked in Germany with the same trademark. The Court of Justice ruled that the exercise of a trademark right may come within the prohibitions of Article 85(1), when it appears to be the subject, the means, or the result of an agreement which appreciably affects trade between member states. The Court of Justice overcame the difficulty that there was no agreement among the enterprises, as required by Article 85(1), by pointing out that both the Italian and German firms had acquired their respective rights to use the trademark under agreements with the same *third* party, the American manufacturer. Therefore Article 85(1) may be used to stop the maintenance of exclusive national territories by preventing imports from other member states of articles bearing the same trademark.

Copyrights

A similar basic approach underlies the landmark *Deutsche Grammophon* decision of June 1971. A German record manufacturer sold records to its French subsidiary, from whom they were purchased, taken to Switzerland, reimported into Germany, and offered for sale at a price below the legal resale price authorized by the German manufacturer. In an attempt to bar the reimportation into Germany of records it had sold into France where resale price maintenance is illegal, the German manufacturer invoked a German law, similar to copyright, that grants recording manufacturers exclusive rights of sale in Germany for records made in that country. The Court of Justice stated that Article 36 of the EEC Treaty, which permits exceptions to the general free movement of goods, applies only to the extent that such exceptions are justified in order to safeguard rights that are the specific object of such property. In this case there was no legal basis for protecting the German manufacturer's exclusive rights of sale because the records had been put into circulation in a foreign market (France) by him or with his consent. Prohibiting reimportation would be contrary to the fundamental goal of integrating national markets into a single market.

Patents

The law in regard to patents is still unsettled. *Parke–Davis,* the only major case to be decided by the Court of Justice to date, concerned an attempt by Parke–Davis, an American company that held Dutch patents protecting certain processes for making drugs, to prevent imports into the Netherlands of antibiotics from Italy where patents could not be granted for such processes. The Court of Justice ruled that Parke–Davis could bar the imports from Italy because if the imported drugs made by the unpatented process circulated freely, the purpose of the patent would have been frustrated because there would be no remuneration for the invention. The commission believes that this was a very special case and when understood correctly is not inconsistent with the later *Deutsche Grammophon* and *Sirena* decisions. The key factors in *Parke–Davis* were the absence of patent protection in the exporting country (Italy) and the fact that therefore the Dutch patentee did not receive any financial benefit from the Italian exporter. Thus, the commission contended in its argument to the Court of Justice that the Court's decision should be different if the patent holder were able to benefit directly or indirectly from his patent in the area where the goods were lawfully put into circulation. In such a case the national patent in the importing state should not be permitted to bar the importation of a product which was put into circulation in one of the member states either by the patent holder himself or with his consent.

Earlier in this chapter we mentioned the 1962 Christmas Message of the commission pertaining to patent-licensing agreements. Several of the sections in that message have subsequently been overruled by commission decisions. The first formal decisions on licensing agreements came in December 1971. The two cases, *Burroughs–Geha* and *Burroughs–Delplanque,* involved requests for negative clearances for manufacturing licenses for a new carbon black paper under Burroughs' French and German patents. Both licensees, Delplanque in France and Geha in Germany, received nonexclusive-production licenses under some patents and exclusive-production licenses under others. These cases, two later decisions, *Davidson Rubber* and *Raymond–Nagoya,* and various statements by the commission may be synthesized to provide the following guidelines. According to the commission, the following obligations, at least in a nonexclusive patent or know-how license, will not be treated as restraints:

1. The obligation to grant no sublicenses except to wholly dependent companies of the licensee.

2. The obligation to keep know-how secret. In the *Burroughs* cases the commission upheld obligations to keep know-how secret for ten years after the expiration of the license and requiring the return of all designs, models, etc., within ninety days of termination of the contract.
3. The obligation to produce the licensed products in sufficient quantities to satisfy demand.
4. Obligations to follow standards of quality and technical instructions of the licensor.
5. Obligations to mark the products with the patentee's trademark or patent information and to indicate on the product that they were made under license.
6. The obligation to settle disputes by arbitration.
7. The obligation not to grant sublicenses.
8. The obligation to pay a minimum royalty.
9. Nonexclusive grant-back obligations. In *Raymond–Nagoya* the commission disapproved a provision that any improvement made by Nagoya to the Raymond technique would become the property of Raymond. Under the approved version Nagoya is required to grant to Raymond a nonexclusive license on the patents which it would obtain if patentable improvements or changes were to be made to the Raymond technique.

On the other hand, the commission has clearly condemned clauses prohibiting the licensee from contesting the validity of the patents of the licensor.

An analysis of the preceding cases and statements by the commission leads to the following conclusions. Under *Deutsche Grammophon* the first marketing of goods protected by concurrent property rights in several member states by a common holder or holders acting in agreement will exhaust the protection. This means that the owners or licensees of such property rights in other member states cannot prohibit the import of the goods concerned by invoking their existing national property right. To date the Court of Justice has only ruled on this principle as to copyright. However, the commission has made it clear in its Reports on Competition Policy that it believes that the principle applies to patent and trademark rights. *Parke–Davis* indicates that the abolition of the concept of territorial protection for property rights does not extend to those situations where there is no concurrent protection. In general, the Court of Justice and the commission will invoke Articles 36 and 85(1) to prevent national property rights from partitioning the Common Market.

Many of the problems created by the conflict between the national property laws and the goal of market unification may be solved by the proposed European Community Patent Convention that would establish standardized rules for the validity and use of patents within the member states.

There would be a Community Patent that would have the same effect throughout each member state of the Community and would co-exist with national patent rights during a transition period. This convention will supplement the proposed European Patent Grant System under which twenty-one European countries, including the nine Common Market countries, will have a centralized patent examination and grant procedure. These new patent systems are presently expected to become operational in 1976 or 1977.

Know-how and Trade Secrets

The commission's position on know-how and trade-secret agreements has not been fully developed. The only guidance issued to date other than that in the cases synthesized earlier is the following passage from the commission's First Report on Competition Policy.

> In order to enable *know-how* to be marketed, the Commission decided that it would not consider a restriction on competition the obligation—often included in know-how contracts—not to divulge the know-how and not to use the latter after the termination of the agreement. Secrecy is the essence of technical know-how relating to industrial processes which are not protected by the laws on industrial property. Secrecy is, in fact, a necessary condition for enabling the owner to pass such know-how on to other enterprises for the purpose of full exploitation prior to it becoming public property.

Article 86

Article 86 of the EEC Treaty provides that "any abuse by one or more [enterprises] of a dominant position within the Common Market or in a substantial part of it shall be prohibited as incompatible with the Common Market insofar as it may affect trade between Member States." Four examples of such abuse are listed in the text of the article. On its face, Article 86 differs in two important respects from Article 85. First, although Article 85 requires an agreement, decision, or concerted practice between two independent enterprises, one enterprise acting alone may violate Article 86 by abusing its dominant position. Nonetheless, Article 86 may also apply to abuses by more than one enterprise. Second, unlike Article 85, Article 86 contains no provision for an exemption. However, an enterprise may apply for a negative clearance from Article 86 as well as from Article 85.

Four elements must be present for Article 86 to apply. There must be a (1) "dominant position," (2) within the Common Market or a substantial part thereof, (3) abuse of that position, and (4) a potential effect on trade between member states.

Dominant Position

Article 86 does not define *dominant position*. However, the commission has stated that it believes

> that a dominant position is characterized by the fact that those in such a position are able to take decision without taking their competitors, buyers or suppliers into account. The domination of a market is not solely defined by the share of the market held by enterprises, but by their share of the market combined with the availability of technical knowledge, raw material or capital.

As in monopoly cases under U.S. antitrust law, the first step in determining whether a dominant position exists is to identify the relevant product and geographic markets. Because enforcement of Article 86 did not begin until 1971 there are very few cases and rulings from which guidelines may be ascertained.

The relevant geographic market may be the Common Market as a whole or a substantial part of it. The commission has contended that the territory of either one of the larger member states (France, Germany, Great Britain, Italy) or the territories of the Benelux countries together with Northern Germany are a "substantial" part of the Market. Therefore, a dominant position in one member state may fall within Article 86 if it potentially affects trade between member states.

The Court of Justice has held that the holding of a copyright, patent, or trademark does not in itself constitute a dominant position and that a larger product market must be examined. The relevant products were defined in the *Continental Can* case as those "which are especially suited for satisfying a continuing demand and appear to be interchangeable with other products only to a small degree." In the same case the Court rejected the commission's classification of three separate product markets—light containers for canned meats, light containers for canned fish, and metal closures for the canning industry—because the commission had not precisely identified the traits that distinguish these three markets from each other and from the general market for light metal containers. The Court then gave the following guidelines:

> It can be assumed that these products have a separate market only if they are distinguishable from others not just by the mere fact that they are used for packaging certain products, but also because of special production features that make them specifically suited for that purpose. On this basis, a dominant position [in] the market for light metal containers for canned meats and fish is not shown so long as it has not been proved that competitors in other areas of the market for light metal containers cannot, by making a simple adjustment, step into that market with sufficient strength to provide a serious counterbalance.

Thus, in any one case the definition of a dominant position depends on several factors, including the market share of the relevant markets, the possession of intellectual or industrial property rights, the ability of new enterprises to enter the market, and the financial capacity of the enterprise in question.

Abuse

Until the Court of Justice's *Continental Can* decision of 1973 there had been a dispute as to whether Article 86 was limited to cases of market behavior or whether it also covered structural changes in the market. As early as 1966 the commission contended that in certain circumstances a merger or takeover (the commission uses the word *concentration* to describe what Americans term a *merger*) could violate Article 86 by elimination of actual or potential competition. The *Continental Can* case was a carefully selected test case for the commission's theory.

In 1969 Continental Can, an American manufacturer of metal containers, brought to 85 per cent its interest in a German container manufacturer (SLW), which was the largest producer of certain types of light metal containers in Continental Europe. Continental Can invited an English company, Metal Box, a Dutch firm, TDV, and a French company, Carnaud, to participate in a plan to form a holding company to operate in the European container market. Carnaud declined to participate, but the other three agreed that Continental Can would establish a Delaware corporation, Europemballage, to which Continental would transfer its interests in SLW. After Europemballage was established, it offered to purchase the shares of TDV. Shortly after publication of the Europemballage tender offer the commission notified the parties that it objected to the plan as a violation of Article 86. Metal Box postponed its participation in the plan, but the tender offer was completed and Europemballage acquired 80 per cent of the stock of TDV, giving Continental a total holding of 91 per cent. The next day the commission instituted a proceeding against Continental Can and Europemballage on the ground that the acquisition of a majority of the TDV stock eliminated competition in the market for certain types of metal containers. The commission ruled that Continental Can had abused the dominant position that it held through SLW by taking over TDV, one of its principal competitors. The acquisition was viewed as enabling Continental Can to strengthen its own dominant position in such a manner as practically to eliminate its existing competition.

On appeal to the Court of Justice, Continental Can contended that Article 86 was not intended to prohibit mergers or other structural methods of combining that increase an enterprise's share of the market nor to prohibit the mere establishment or growth of a dominant position. Rather, it was argued to apply only to "abusive exploitation of a dominant position" through practices employed in the marketplace. A key passage in Continental Can's pleadings read:

> Nothing in Article 86 indicates that combinations of enterprises, mergers, the acquisition of the majority of or all shares in other enterprises should be prohibited, also when an already dominant enterprise acquires another and thereby monopolizes the already partially monopolized market further. Though the examples of "misuse" in Article 86 are not exhaustive, examples in a statute are however indicative of what the legislator meant and what he did not mean. It is a characteristic of the practices quoted that they either take place directly *in the* market—examples a), c) and d)—or that they at least *in fact and provably* damage those who are supplied, in particular the consumer, and not only *may* lead to such damage.

The Court of Justice rejected this contention and held that Articles 85 and 86 are to be interpreted in the light of the principles laid down in Article 2 (harmonious development of economic life within the EEC) and Article 3(f) (the "institution of a system ensuring that competition in the common market is not distorted") of the EEC Treaty. The Court reasoned that because Article 3(f) of the EEC Treaty requires the establishment of a system ensuring that competition within the Common Market is not distorted, it requires *a fortiori* that competition not be eliminated. If enterprises could impair competition through mergers, the objectives of Article 85 would be subverted and there would be a major loophole in the system intended to ensure free competition. Therefore, the Court agreed with the commission that

> abusive conduct could be present where an enterprise in a dominant position strengthens that position to the point where the degree of domination achieved substantially hampers competition, so that only enterprises which in their market conduct are dependent on the dominant enterprise would remain on the market.
> . . . the strengthening of the position held by one enterprise can be an abuse and prohibited under Article 86 of the Treaty regardless of the methods or means used to attain it, provided it has the effects described above.

The Court went on to accept the commission's view that an "abuse" occurs "where an enterprise in a dominant position so strengthens its position through a merger that actual or potential competition in the relevant products would be virtually eliminated in a substantial part of the Common Market." Moreover,

> It can . . . be considered an abuse if one enterprise acquires a dominant position to the point that the objectives of the Treaty are circumvented through a substantial alteration of the supply situation, so that the consumer's freedom of action on the market is seriously jeopardized; this is necessarily the case where virtually all competition is eliminated. While

such a limiting condition as the elimination of all competition need not be present in all cases, the Commission must, when it bases its decision on such elimination of competition, furnish grounds that are legally sufficient for this purpose, or *at least prove that competition was so substantially affected that any remaining competitors can no longer provide a sufficient counterbalance.*

The Court reversed the decision of the commission because it had failed to demonstrate, in accordance with the previously quoted test, that competition was affected to the point where the producers of other types of light metal containers could no longer provide a counterbalance to the merged enterprise by slightly adjusting their production procedures to pro- duce the subject products. Moreover, the commission had failed to justify its delineation of product submarkets with respect to the various types of light metal containers.

The Court's three-to-two decision interpreting Article 86 has been criticized by some European lawyers for allegedly ignoring the clear word- ing of Article 86 limiting its application to abusive exploitation of a domi- nant position and relying instead on the general principles of the EEC Treaty. Therefore, it is possible that the Court of Justice, which has three new member judges as a result of the accession of the United Kingdom, Ireland, and Denmark, may in a future case reverse its interpretation of Article 86.

Despite the reversal of the commission's decision, its interpretation of Article 86 was upheld by the Court. Consequently, *The Economist* accu- rately titled its story on the case "Battle Lost, War Won." However, the Court's decision was deemed by the commission to be too narrow on two points. First, it did not consider the commission authorized to act until after the merger had taken place. Second, the decision seemed to be applicable only to mergers where one of the enterprises is already in a dominant position, and not to mergers which result in the attainment of a dominant position. To remedy these deficiencies the commission submitted to the council a draft regulation on the control of mergers which would go beyond the *Continental Can* decision. Under the draft regulation, mergers involving enterprises at least one of which is established in the Common Market, whose joint sales are over 1 billion units of account, would be re- quired to notify the commission of an intended merger and wait three months before implementing it. In addition, mergers that would have the direct or indirect effect of acquiring or enhancing the power to hinder effective competition (a dominant position) would be subject to such prior notification. According to the draft regulation:

> The power to hinder effective competition shall be appraised by ref- erence in particular to the extent to which suppliers and consumers have a possibility of choice, to the economic and financial power of the under- takings concerned, to the structure of the markets affected, and to supply and demand trends for the relevant goods or services.

Enterprises that intentionally or negligently fail to notify would be subject to fines of from 1,000 to 1 million units of account. The commission's decisions under the draft regulation would be reviewable by the Court of Justice. Mergers involving enterprises with an aggregate turnover of less than 200 million units of account and having less than 25 per cent of the market in the relevant goods or services would be exempt from the draft regulation. The commission hopes that the council will put this new regulation into operation sometime in 1975.

The merger situation is not the only abuse covered by Article 86. The article itself contains four examples. They are (1) the imposition of unfair buying or selling prices or other unfair trading conditions, (2) the limitation of production, markets, or technical development to the prejudice of consumers, (3) discriminations in commercial transactions, and (4) tying arrangements. Case law has made additions to this list, including a decision by a de facto monopolist to discontinue supplies to a firm so as to eliminate it as a competitor; conditioning the sale of a product to wholesalers on their agreeing to resell only to certain customers and for certain uses; and charging high prices that are not the product of independent objective economic circumstances. In a case involving the practices of a clearinghouse for all copyrights of musical productions and compositions in Germany (GEMA), the commission listed six abuses by GEMA of its dominant position:

1. Discriminating against nationals of other member states.
2. Subjecting its members to unnecessary obligations.
3. Preventing the establishment of a single market for the services offered by music publishers.
4. Extending the copyright monopoly to unprotected works.
5. Favoring record manufacturers and discriminating against independent importers of records.
6. Discriminating against importers.

Implementation of Article 86 is still in a very early stage of development and the precise course of its future development is unclear. However, it is expected to become increasingly more important in Common Market competition law.

Comparison with U.S. Law

There are a number of differences, in both substance and procedure, between the antitrust laws of the United States and the competition law of the European Communities. As we discussed earlier in this chapter, there is no per se rule of unreasonableness in the Common Market, and exemptions granted under Article 85(3) are only partly analogous to the rule of reason in U.S. law. In practice, the commission takes a very pragmatic and flexible approach to restrictive practices. For example, Common Market officials are encouraging the development of larger "Community-sized" companies in order to reduce national barriers to trade and to develop locally controlled firms capable of competing effectively with American and Japanese multinational enterprises. So far there has been no attempt comparable to U.S. law under section 7 of the Clayton Act to arrest in their incipiency concentrations of economic power through mergers that, if allowed to develop, would constitute unreasonable restraints of trade.

On the other hand, the potential penalties that can be imposed are more severe than those under U.S. law. For example, the maximum penalty for violating Section 1 of the Sherman Act is $50,000, whereas firms that violate Article 85 could be fined 10 per cent of their total turnover (sales) for the preceding business year for all products, not just those products that were the subject of the complaint. Although the commission has imposed heavy fines in a few cases, these maximum penalties have not yet been invoked. However, the fines that have been imposed have been gradually increasing in amount. In addition, the Court of Justice held in December 1972 that the members of a quinine cartel who had been fined by U.S. courts could not offset the fines paid in the United States against the fine imposed by the commission for activities by the cartel that violated Article 85(1). The cartel members contended that a general legal principle prohibits a duplication of penalties for the same act and that the conduct condemned by the U.S. courts and by the commission was identical. The Court of Justice did not deem it necessary to decide this issue because it held that, "Even though the facts on which the fines were imposed in both cases stem from the same set of agreements, they are basically different both in their subject matter and in their geographic location."

Perhaps the most significant difference between Common Market and U.S. antitrust is not in the antitrust laws themselves, but in the setting in which they operate. The European Communities are, to an extent, striving to weave their nine member states into a federal system akin to that which has existed in the United States for nearly 200 years. Thus, they face many of the problems relating to dismantling national barriers to the free flow of goods that the U.S. federal government faced with the newly independent English colonies. Many of the differences between Common Market competition policy and U.S. antitrust laws can be explained by the fact that these two federal systems are at very different stages of development. The European Communities have a distance to travel before they reach the goal of a common market. Nevertheless, to date they have dealt with the many obstacles blocking attainment of their goals with remarkable success.

United Kingdom

As we mentioned at the beginning of this chapter, most of the member states of the European Communities have their own national antitrust laws, in addition to being subject to the EEC Rules on Competition. Now that we have examined the operation of the EEC Rules, we will examine the national antitrust law of one of the member states, the United Kingdom, to illustrate the operation of a national antitrust law within the Communities that is considerably different from either U.S. law or the EEC Rules. The United Kingdom of Great Britain (England, Scotland, and Wales) and Northern Ireland joined the European Communities on January 1, 1973.

Interplay of Supranational and National Antitrust Laws in the EEC

Before passing to the applicable British law, let us briefly review the role it will play in the context of the EEC. The Communities' Rules on Competition and their implementing regulations are binding within each member state. Nonetheless, they do not supersede existing legislation in each member state, but supplement it. Articles 85 and 86 of the EEC Treaty are applicable only insofar as agreements or practices may perceptibly affect trade between member states. Existing national legislation continues to apply where there is no effect on trade between member states.

Article 9(3) of Regulation 17 implementing Articles 85 and 86 provides that "as long as the Commission has not initiated any procedure under Articles 2 [negative clearance], 3 [termination of infringements], or 6 [decisions pursuant to Article 85(3)], the authorities of the Member States shall remain competent to apply Article 85(1) and Article 86. . . ." In January 1974 the European Court of Justice interpreted the words "authorities of the Member States," as used in this Article of Regulation 17, to mean national antitrust authorities but not national courts. Therefore a national court may continue to apply the rules on competition contained in the Treaty of Rome after the commission has initiated proceedings against the same parties. In practice, the commission informs the national antitrust authorities concerned when it initiates proceedings. It should be noted that national courts have no power to grant exemptions under Article 85(3); this power lies exclusively with the European Commission.

Because Community law takes precedence over national law, any conflict between the two co-existing legal systems will be resolved in favor of the Community law. Therefore, an agreement can and should be declared invalid under Articles 85 and 86 by a national court, in a proper case, even though the agreement would be valid under national law.

National courts have increasingly been requested by litigants to apply the prohibitions of Articles 85 and 86, most frequently in cases where one party is attempting to enforce an agreement that the other contends is unenforceable because it violates the EEC Rules on Competition. The drafters of the EEC Treaty recognized that such proceedings in national courts might result in varying interpretations of the treaty and decisions of the Court of Justice. Therefore, in an attempt to insure uniform interpretation of Community law, there was included a provision, Article 177, in the EEC Treaty for national courts to request the Court of Justice for a preliminary ruling interpreting the treaty, its implementing statutes, and acts of the institutions of the Community. National courts from which there is no possibility of appeal under national law *must* request such a preliminary ruling if the question of interpretation is necessary to enable the court to give judgment. Other national courts *may* request such a preliminary ruling by the Court of Justice. However, national courts may refuse to seek such a preliminary ruling, even if requested to do so by the parties, if they believe that an answer to the question is not necessary to enable the court to render judgment or that the meaning of the provision in question is obvious. The use of this theory of *acte clair* originated in French law and has been criticized by many commentators. However, because the Court of Justice can only hear cases under Article 177 upon the request of a national court, if such a request is not made the Court of Justice cannot intervene.

Relevant Legislation in the United Kingdom

The national antitrust law of the United Kingdom is contained in six statutes, with the later ones amending or expanding on their predecessors. These statutes are usually referred to by the dates of their enactment, which are 1948, 1956, 1964, 1965, 1968, and 1973. Taken as a whole, these laws created a two-pronged system for dealing with restrictive practices and monopolies. Concerted activity and agreements among competitors in restraint of trade, similar to the type of activity proscribed by Section 1 of the Sherman Act, are under the jurisdiction of a Director General of Fair Trading and a Restrictive Practices Court. Monopolization and mergers are dealt with by the Department of Prices and Consumer Protection (DPCP) and the Monopolies and Mergers Commission, acting with the assistance of the director-general.

Restrictive Agreements and Their Registration

Certain types of agreements must be submitted to the director-general, who is required to compile and maintain a public register of these agreements and to refer certain of them to the Restrictive Practices Court, which must decide whether the restrictions are contrary to the public interest. The Court's decisions on matters of law may be appealed to the

Court of Appeal and then to the House of Lords. There is no appeal from decisions of the Restrictive Practices Court on matters of fact.

The director-general is appointed by the secretary of state for prices and consumer protection for a term not exceeding five years. In addition to the duties formerly performed by the registrar of restrictive trading agreements, whose office was abolished in 1973, the director-general has very broad duties, which the 1973 Act describes thus:

(1) (a)   to keep under review the carrying on of commercial activities in the United Kingdom which relate to goods supplied to consumers in the United Kingdom or produced with a view to their being so supplied, or which relate to services supplied for consumers in the United Kingdom, and to collect information with respect to such activities, and the persons by whom they are carried on, with a view to his becoming aware of, and ascertaining the circumstances relating to, practices which may adversely affect the economic interests of consumers in the United Kingdom, and

(b)   to receive and collate evidence becoming available to him with respect to such activities as are mentioned in the preceding paragraph and which appears to him to be evidence of practices which may adversely affect the interests (whether they are economic interests or interests with respect to health, safety or other matters) of consumers in the United Kingdom.

(2)   It shall also be the duty of the Director, so far as appears to him to be practicable from time to time, to keep under review the carrying on of commercial activities in the United Kingdom, and to collect information with respect to those activities, and the persons by whom they are carried on, with a view to his becoming aware of, and ascertaining the circumstances relating to, monopoly situations or uncompetitive practices.

In order to carry out these greatly enlarged responsibilities the staff of the director-general will number about 175, as compared to the staff of seventy the registrar maintained.

One of the director-general's primary duties is to refer certain registrable agreements to the Restrictive Practices Court. Section 6(1) of the 1956 Act enumerates two criteria that make an agreement registrable. First, the agreement must be "between two or more persons carrying on business within the United Kingdom in the production or supply of goods [*or services* was added by the 1973 Act] or in the application to goods of any process of manufacture. . . ." Because there must be *two* persons carrying on business within the United Kingdom, an agreement between a party in the United Kingdom and a foreign company which does not operate in the U.K. is not registrable. Moreover, a company is not deemed to carry on business within the United Kingdom if it is merely represented by an agent within the United Kingdom who is required to refer all transactions to his principal. Similarly, if a foreign supplier sells goods to purchasers in the United Kingdom c.i.f. (price covers cost of goods, insurance, and freight) British port or c.i.f. purchaser's factory, it is generally not held to carry on business in the United Kingdom. Finally, it should be remembered that the business must be in the production, supply, or processing of goods or services.

The second criterion of a registrable agreement is that it must be an agreement:

> under which restrictions are accepted by two or more parties in respect of the following matters, that is to say:
> (a) the prices to be charged, quoted or paid for goods supplied, offered or acquired, or for the application of any process of manufacture to goods;
> (b) the terms or conditions on or subject to which goods are to be supplied or acquired or any such process is to be applied to goods;
> (c) the quantities or descriptions of goods to be produced, supplied or acquired;
> (d) the processes of manufacture to be applied to any goods, or the quantities or descriptions of goods to which any such process is to be applied; or
> (e) the persons or classes of persons to, for or from whom, or the areas or places in or from which goods are to be supplied or acquired, or any such process applied.

Restrictions as to the relevant matters must be accepted by at least *two* parties. Thus, for example, if Gargantua Oil Company refuses to supply a filling station with gasoline unless the station owner agrees not to sell any other brand, the agreement is not registrable because only the station owner accepts a restriction. Gargantua accepts no restriction, it merely refuses to supply the station owner unless he accepts a restriction. The two or more parties who accept restrictions need not themselves necessarily carry on business within the United Kingdom, provided that there are at least two parties to the agreement who do carry on business in the United Kingdom. For example, an agreement among an American manufacturer exporting to the United Kingdom, an English manufacturer exporting to the United States, and an English merchant under which the manufacturers each agree not to export to the other's home market would be registrable because the two English firms satisfy the condition about carrying on business in the supply of goods in the United Kingdom and at least two parties have accepted a relevant restriction.

The word *restriction* is not defined except that it must be in respect of one of the matters listed in subparts (a) to (e) and, under another section of the 1956 Act, the word is said to include "any negative obligation, whether express or implied and whether absolute or not." An example of an implicit restriction is contained in the *British Basic Slag* case. Several steel manufacturers set up a jointly owned company, Basic, to which each manufacturer sold its entire output of slag, a by-product of steel making that can be used as a fertilizer. Each separate contract between Basic and a manufacturer provided that the manufacturer would sell its slag only to

Basic and Basic would use its best efforts to dispose of the slag in fair and equitable proportions. These separate contracts were held to be registrable because both the manufacturers and Basic had accepted restrictions. The manufacturers agreed not to sell to anyone else and Basic agreed not to buy from manufacturers other than the particular vendor such quantities of slag as would prevent it from disposing of the vendor's fair proportion of Basic's total purchases.

The word *restriction* does not include a limitation in an agreement that goes no further than an existing law. For example, a provision in a contract for the sale of waste paper that the paper must be free of certain impurities was held not to be a restriction because a sales statute forbade the sale of such impure products.

In addition to agreements meeting these two criteria of registrability, certain types of "information agreements"—agreements to exchange information made by two or more persons carrying on business in the production, supply, or processing of goods within the United Kingdom—are also registrable. The secretary of state for prices and consumer protection, who is the head of the DPCP, has the power to issue orders requiring that information agreements relating to prices, terms, quantities, costs, manufacturing processes, persons to or from whom goods are supplied, and places of supply be registered and, if necessary, examined by the Restrictive Practices Court. To date the secretary has issued only one order and it makes information agreements relating to prices, terms, and conditions of sale of goods registrable. This order exempts certain types of agreements from registration, including agreements involving the supply of information to a government department and the exchange of information that had already been published in such a manner that it was readily available to customers. An agreement between buyers to exchange information that relates solely to the prices charged or quoted to them is also exempted by the order.

Until 1973 restrictive agreements relating to services were not registrable. The 1973 Act empowers the secretary of state to issue orders that certain classes of services and information agreements relating to services be registrable. The definition of *services* does not include

> the application to goods of any process of manufacture or any services rendered to an employer under a contract of employment, but, with those exceptions, includes engagements (whether professional or other) which for gain or reward are undertaken and performed for any matter other than the production or supply of goods, and any reference to the supply of services or to supplying, obtaining or offering services or to making services available shall be construed accordingly.

The 1973 Act also makes registrable agreements under which restrictions are accepted as to: "the prices to be recommended or suggested as the

prices to be charged or quoted in respect of the resale of goods supplied."
Thus, an agreement between producers, suppliers, manufacturers or wholesalers of goods setting the price to be recommended to retailers or other
dealers which the latter are to charge on the resale of the goods to their
customers is now registrable. Trade association recommendations as to
recommended resale prices for their members' customers are also now subject to registration. Recommendations made by trade associations to their
members in respect of prices which the members of the association are to
charge were already subject to registration.

The word *agreement* includes contracts, whether or not they are intended to be legally enforceable, recommendations by trade associations
whether express or implied, and arrangements. *Arrangement* was defined in
the *British Basic Slag* case by means of the following example,

> it is sufficient to constitute an "arrangement" between A and B if (i) A
> makes a representation as to his future conduct with the expectation and
> intention that such conduct on his part will operate as an inducement to B
> to act in a particular way, (ii) such representation is communicated to B,
> who has knowledge that A so expected and intended, and (iii) such repre-
> sentation or A's conduct in fulfillment of it operates as an inducement,
> whether among other inducements or not, to B to act in a particular way.

Details of agreements which contain restrictions regarding any of the
matters mentioned previously must be furnished to the director-general
before the relevant restrictions take effect and, in any event, within three
months after the day on which the agreement is made. This time limit
may be extended by the director-general, but only upon application for an
extension made within the prescribed time. If the agreement is not registered within the proper time, all the proscribed restrictions contained in
the agreement are void and any party to the agreement who carries on
business within the United Kingdom commits a breach of statutory duty
by enforcing or complying with the restrictions, for which he is civilly
liable in damages to anyone affected by the agreement. Failure to register
is not itself a criminal offense. However, knowingly or recklessly furnishing
materially false information and willfully altering, suppressing, or destroying any document required to be furnished are offenses for which directors
and officers may be criminally liable.

Once the particulars of the agreement have been filed, the director-
general may represent to the secretary of state that the relevant restrictions
"are not of such significance as to call for investigation by the Restrictive
Practices Court." After such a representation by the director-general, the
secretary of state may give directions discharging the director-general from
referring the agreement to the Restrictive Practices Court. Such directions
may be withdrawn if there is a subsequent material change of circumstances.

The Restrictive Practices Court

The Restrictive Practices Court was created by the 1956 Act and is composed of both High Court judges and lay members, who are "qualified by virtue of [their] knowledge of or experience in industry, commerce or public affairs." Each case is heard by a panel of at least three members, one of whom must be a judge. The criterion by which the practices are examined is the public interest. Although *public interest* is not defined, restrictive practices under review are presumed contrary to the public interest unless the industry or trade association supporting them can prove that one or more of seven specified escape clauses or *gateways* is applicable. These gateways include such things as protecting the public against injury, helping exports, reducing unemployment, helping small businessmen meet the restrictive measures or dominant power of other firms, and conferring "specific and substantial" benefits on the public. The 1968 Act added an eighth gateway to the 1956 Act, through which the parties to an agreement will pass if they can satisfy the court, "That the restriction does not directly or indirectly restrict or discourage competition to any material degree in any relevant trade or industry and is not likely to do so." It is likely that this gateway will be used mostly for information agreements, because when dealing with other types of agreements, counsel usually admit that there is a material restriction, thereby foreclosing reliance on this new gateway, and argue that the restriction is beneficial under one of the other gateways.

If the respondents can prove by the balance of probabilities that one or more of the eight types of circumstances enumerated in the gateways exist, a clause in the 1956 Act known as the *tailpiece* requires the court to balance the advantages of allowing the practice to continue against the harm to the public in general created by the existence of the practice. Only if the benefits outweigh this harm can the practice be permitted to continue.

In striking this balance between benefits and detriments, the parties to the agreement can rely on only the "circumstances" falling within the "gateways" that they have already proven to exist. On the other hand, the director-general is not so limited and may draw the court's attention to any detriment

> to the public or to persons not parties to the agreement (being purchasers, consumers or users of goods produced or sold by such parties, or persons engaged or seeking to become engaged in the trade or business of selling such goods or of producing or selling similar goods) resulting or likely to result from the operation of the restriction.

For example, in the *Yarn Spinners* case a group of Lancashire spinners of cotton yarn agreed on a formula for fixing the minimum prices they would charge weavers. The spinners contended, among other things, that removal of the restrictions would be likely to have a serious adverse effect on unemployment in certain geographic areas. The Court concluded that the restrictions did qualify under the unemployment gateway. However, the detriments to the public from the operation of the restrictions, in particular the waste of natural resources through the preservation of excess capacity in the industry, were held such that, on balance, it would be unreasonable to permit continuation of the restriction.

In summary, in order to justify a restrictive agreement, the proponents must be able to establish the existence of a gateway situation and also to establish that the benefits arising from the restriction outweigh any detriment to the public "resulting or likely to result from the operation of the restriction."

All agreements, except those for the collective *enforcement* of conditions as to resale prices, which are prohibited by the 1956 Act, may be permitted if they satisfy the gateways and tailpieces. Thus, for all but the statutorily prohibited agreements, there are no per se rules of unreasonableness as there are in U.S. antitrust law.

The Restrictive Practices Court took a surprisingly tough attitude in its first two fully litigated decisions, invalidating major agreements in the drug and textile fields. Consequently, the great majority of restrictive agreements registered were not defended when they were referred to the Court, and the Court proceeded to enjoin their enforcement. By 1973 twenty-five agreements had been declared contrary to the public interest after full trials and several hundred had been enjoined without any defense. Very few agreements have been upheld. Those that have been upheld include agreements whereby publishers set resale prices for books, which were saved on the ground that without these "net book" contracts there would be fewer books and book-sellers available to the reading public; a price-fixing arrangement among manufacturers of water-tube boilers saved on the ground that the arrangement helped exports; and a price-fixing agreement among manufacturers of cement, very similar to the agreement condemned by the United States Supreme Court in the 1948 case of *Federal Trade Commission v. Cement Institute,* saved on the ground that the agreement kept prices low.

If the restrictions contained in the agreement are declared by the Restrictive Practices Court to be contrary to the public interest the Court may, upon application made by the director-general, issue an order enjoining enforcement of the relevant restrictions. There is no provision for imposing fines for violations of the Restrictive Trade Practices Act. However, violation of such an injunction subjects the violator to penalties for contempt of court. If the parties to the agreement give the Court an undertaking that they will take or refrain from taking certain actions and later fail to abide by such undertaking they are liable to fines.

The 1973 Act extended the powers of the Restrictive Practices Court to include, for the first time, the issuance of orders against trade associations as such (as opposed to individual members) and the issuance of interim orders upon application by the director-general against agreements that contain prohibited restrictions if the Court is satisfied that the restrictions "could not reasonably be expected to be shown to fall within any of [the gateways] and that

> the operation of the restrictions, during the period likely to elapse before an order can be made in respect of them under section 20(3) of [the 1956] Act, is likely to cause material detriment to the public or a section of the public generally, or to a particular person who is not a party to the agreement. . . .

The director-general also has the power to bring proceedings in the Restrictive Practices Court against a person who engages in a persistent course of conduct detrimental to the economic, health, safety, or other interests of consumers. Such a course of conduct would include a contravention of a statute which imposes duties, prohibitions or restrictions enforceable by criminal proceedings, and breach of a contractual or other duty owed to any person by virtue of a law enforceable by civil proceedings.

Exemption from Registration

The secretary of state for prices and consumer protection has the power to exempt from registration an agreement "of importance to the national economy" if it satisfies each of five conditions listed in the 1968 Act. These conditions are

> (a)   that the agreement is calculated to promote the carrying out of an industrial or commercial project or scheme of substantial importance to the national economy;
> (b)   that its object or main object is to promote efficiency in a trade or industry or to create or improve productive capacity in an industry;
> (c)   that the object cannot be achieved or achieved within a reasonable time except by means of the agreement or of an agreement for similar purposes;
> (d)   that no relevant restrictions are accepted under the agreement other than such as are reasonably necessary to achieve that object; and
> (e)   that the agreement is on balance expedient in the national interests; and in considering the national interest for the purposes of paragraph (e) of this subsection the [secretary] shall take into account any effects which an agreement is likely to have on persons not parties thereto as purchasers, consumers or users of any relevant goods.

The parties to a proposed agreement inform the secretary of state of their plans and provide him with a copy of the proposed agreement. If he believes that the proposed agreement complies with the five conditions just quoted, he may issue an order *before* or *on the date of* the conclusion of the agreement. Copies of the order and of the pertinent agreement are laid before each house of Parliament and a copy of the agreement is made available for public inspection.

An order issued under this provision is for a specified time, which may be extended by a subsequent order, and it may be revoked at any time if the secretary becomes aware of circumstances by reason of which, if known at the material time, the agreement would not have been exempted. The order may also be revoked at any time after one year from the date of its issuance if the object of the agreement has not been or is not likely to be achieved or if the agreement is used for purposes other than those for which it was approved.

There are numerous other exemptions from registration. The most important are the following.

RESTRICTIONS RELATING TO THE GOODS SUPPLIED

In an agreement for the supply of goods or for the application of any process of manufacture to goods "no account shall be taken of any term which relates exclusively to the goods supplied, or to which the process is applied. . . ." If, therefore, there are only two parties to an agreement for the supply of goods and the restrictions accepted by one of the parties relate exclusively to the goods supplied in pursuance of the agreement, the agreement is not registrable. For example, the following agreement is not registrable: Acme Widget Company agrees to sell and Fred's Retail Store agrees to buy 120,000 widgets over the next twelve months; Acme agrees not to sell widgets to any other retailer in a certain territory and Fred's agrees not to sell widgets outside its territory. Because the restriction accepted by Fred's relates exclusively to the goods supplied in pursuance of the agreement no account is to be taken of it. Therefore, only Acme has accepted a registrable restriction under the agreement and the agreement is, therefore, not registrable.

EXCLUSIVE DEALING

Agreements for the supply of goods between two, and only two, persons, neither of whom is a trade association, are exempt from registration if the only prohibited restrictions that are incorporated are

(a) by the party supplying the goods, in respect of the supply of goods of the same description to other persons; *or*
(b) by the party acquiring the goods, in respect of the sale, or acquisition for sale, of other goods of the same description.

This exemption was intended to apply to requirements contracts and sole-agency agreements between a single buyer and a single seller, in which the former agrees not to handle competing products and the latter agrees not to appoint other agents in the buyer's territory. No restrictions other than those in the preceding list are permissible if the agreement is to be exempt from registration. If restrictions are accepted as to goods not "of the same description" by either party, such as tie-in sales, the whole agreement loses its exemption and becomes registrable.

PATENT LICENSES

Licenses granted by the owner or any licensees of a patent or a registered design, or by an inventor who has applied for a patent or for the registration of a design, are exempt from registration if restrictions are accepted only as to the invention or design, or articles made by use of the invention or to which the design is applied. Thus, an agreement between a licensor and a licensee on prices at which either or both will sell the patented article is not registrable if there are only *two* parties to the agreement. For example, if Company A grants Company B a license under which they agree that A shall sell only in England goods made by use of the patented invention at not less than $10 per unit and that Company B shall sell only in Scotland at the same price, the agreement is *not* registrable. This exemption does not apply to patent and design pooling agreements and licenses granted in pursuance (directly or indirectly) of such agreements. The definition of "patent or design pooling agreement" is complex, one of the key elements of the definition being, however, that there must be at least *three* parties to the agreement. Thus, patent cross-licensing arrangements between *two,* but not *three* or more, parties and patent licenses under which the licensor and licensee agree to grant each other licenses under improvement patents are exempt from registration provided the restrictions in the agreement relate solely to things made under the patent or design.

KNOW-HOW AGREEMENTS

A much narrower exemption than that for patent licenses is available for know-how agreements. There must be only *two* parties to the agreement, neither of which is a trade association, and the parties must *exchange* information, that is, both must supply information. The information exchanged must be "relat[ed] to the operation of process of manufacture (whether patented or not)," and the only restrictions accepted must relate to the "descriptions of goods to be produced by those processes or to which those processes are to be applied." Therefore, the exchanged information cannot relate to trading or selling methods, pricing, or installation techniques. Moreover, the restrictions accepted cannot be of the type referred to in Sections 6 (1) (a), (b), (d), or (e) of the 1956 Act, which we earlier enumerated, nor can the restrictions be related to the quantities of goods produced.

EXPORT AGREEMENTS

If all the prohibited restrictions relate *exclusively* to exports from the United Kingdom, or to the production of goods abroad, or to the acquisition of goods to be delivered outside the United Kingdom (rather than imported into the United Kingdom), the agreement is not registrable, but it must be notified to the director-general, who can refer the agreement to the Monopolies and Mergers Commission (but has never done so).

OTHER EXEMPTIONS

Other exemptions from registration are provided for agreements or terms of an agreement that are made at the request of various government agencies and that relate exclusively to limiting price increases or to price reductions. Agreements covered by any authorization given for the purposes of any provision of the European Coal and Steel Community Treaty relating to restrictive trade practices are also exempt from registration.

Impact of Accession on Restrictive Agreements

As a result of the United Kingdom's accession to the European Communities, it is possible that the same companies could be subject to two proceedings for the same conduct, one before the Community authorities under Articles 85 and 86 and the other before national authorities under national law. The Court of Justice has approved this "double-barrier" theory that national authorities may act against a cartel under internal law, even if the cartel is being examined by the commission under Community law. However, because of the supremacy of Community law, the Court of Justice has held that both sets of laws can apply only in so far as the "application of the national law does not prejudice the full and uniform application of Community law or the effect of the measures taken to implement it." The Court of Justice has also stated that the possibility of fines imposed for the same activity by both Community and national authorities is not a sufficient reason to prohibit parallel proceedings, provided that the first fine is taken into account in the computation of the second fine.

In practice, the Court of Justice's decision means that, in the case of concurrent proceedings, if a commission decision precedes one by national authorities, the latter are bound to comply with the decision and its effects. In order to minimize potential conflicts the United Kingdom's European Communities Act provides that the director-general may refrain from exercising his statutory duty of taking an agreement that has been registered before the Restrictive Practices Court and the Court may decline or postpone the exercise of its jurisdiction whenever in their discretion it is appropriate to do so, having regard for directly applicable provisions of the Community Law or "to the purpose and effect of any authorisation or exemption granted in relation thereto. . . ." To facilitate the exercise of this discretionary authority by the Court and the director-general, the registrar issued regulations, effective in June 1973, governing the "Registration of Restrictive Trading Agreements (EEC Documents)," which require that the director-general be notified by a party within thirty days of any of the following: an application to the European Commission for negative clearance, the grant of a negative clearance, notification by the commission to the parties to the agreement of their opportunity to be heard in relation to objections raised against them, or a decision of the commission to grant an exemption from Article 85.

The United Kingdom's European Communities Act also specifically provides that the 1956 British Restrictive Trade Practices Act applies regardless of whether the agreement in question is void under Article 85 of the EEC Treaty or is lawful under a Community decision. For example, in some circumstances the grant of a negative clearance by the commission would not prevent the Restrictive Practices Court from prohibiting the agreement in the United Kingdom. Thus, if a negative clearance were granted on the basis that the agreement did not have a perceptible effect on trade between member states, it might nevertheless be prohibited by the Restrictive Practices Court for having a significant adverse effect within the United Kingdom. Similarly, if the commission granted an agreement an exemption under Article 85(3), it would nonetheless be possible for the Restrictive Practices Court to prohibit certain aspects of the agreement that related solely to the United Kingdom. The converse is, however, different. What the commision has condemned, the domestic court cannot approve.

The most important results of the United Kingdom's accession will be in relation to those agreements which are exempt from registration under the Restrictive Trade Practices Acts. For example, the principal type of restrictive agreements permitted under the "goods supplied" exemption are those in which there is a restriction accepted by the distributor not to sell outside his territory. This type of restriction, although exempt from registration under United Kingdom law, may well violate Article 85(1) of the EEC Treaty. The Court of Justice's decision in the *Grundig–Consten* case prohibits absolute territorial protection of a distributor including a ban on a distributor exporting the product outside his contract territory and a ban imposed by the supplier on other distributors exporting into the contract area. Therefore, a restriction on the distributor not to sell outside his territory would violate Article 85(1) if the agreement has a perceptible effect on trade between member states and the distributor is economically autonomous of the supplier. Moreover, if the agreement that contains such a "no poaching" clause is made between parties in the United Kingdom and another member state, the agreement falls outside of the block exemption granted by the European Commission for exclusive dealing agreements.

Resale-Price Maintenance

Collective enforcement of resale-price maintenance was prohibited by the 1956 Act; however, individual enforcement was not covered. The 1961 "net book" decision of the Restrictive Practices Court, which allowed publishers to maintain minimum resale prices for books, led to a call for new, broader legislation and resulted in the Resale Prices Act of 1964, which expanded the jurisdiction of the registrar and of the Restrictive Practices Court to include cases involving resale-price maintenance that is accomplished by direct contract terms or by refusals to supply those who sell below the resale price or by refusals to supply such price cutters except on unfavorable terms. The statute contains a general presumption that resale-price maintenance is contrary to the public interest, but suppliers can apply to the Court for exemptions based on "gateways" where the abolition of resale-price maintenance would be detrimental to consumers. There is also a "tailpiece" that requires the Court to balance this latter detriment against the detriment presumed to result from the resale-price maintenance itself. The 1964 Act required the registrar to compile a list of suppliers who wished to claim an exemption, arrange them into classes, and bring cases before the Restrictive Practices Court. Until the Court made a decision about goods in a particular class, the suppliers of those goods were allowed to continue resale-price maintenance. However, once the decision was rendered in one representative case, it was binding on all goods in the class. Many industries initially claimed an exemption but abandoned the case before a court decision. Of 160 cases only three went to trial and only one of these, relating to ethical and proprietary drugs, resulted in the grant of an exemption. In that case the Court upheld resale-price maintenance by wholesalers on the ground that it encouraged wholesalers to hold stocks of drugs, thereby providing the important service of quick delivery to retailers when needed. The Court thought that without this service, the availability of many essential drugs would decrease, to the injury of the buying public. In 1971 the registrar stated that resale-price maintenance, at least as publicly practiced, had largely disappeared in the United Kingdom except for the exempted areas of drugs and books.

Monopolies and Mergers

The second prong of the United Kingdom's antitrust legislation relates to monopolization and mergers, an area dealt with exclusively by administrative agencies, including the Department of Prices and Consumer Protection (DPCP), the Monopolies and Mergers Commission, and the director-general. The DPCP and also the director-general follow the financial press for information on possible monopoly situations and mergers (there is no requirement that companies report mergers to the department), and, sometimes on advice from the director-general, the DPCP decides which activities to refer to the commission for investigation.

The DPCP has complete discretion as to what practices or mergers it will refer to the commission, except for mergers involving newspaper interests, above a certain size, which must be referred. The director-general, who is independent of the DPCP, may refer monopoly situations to the commission, except for enumerated exclusions, but such a reference can be countermanded by the secretary of state. The commission may be asked by the DPCP or the director-general merely to render a factual report as to whether a monopoly or merger situation as defined in the statute exists or to also determine whether the monopoly or merger operates against the public interest under guidelines listed in relevant statutes and to recommend action to alleviate the problem. The commission may request the director-general for information in his possession and for "any other assistance which the Commission may require, and which it is within his power to give. . . ."

The commission is a purely advisory body of lawyers and laymen most of whom serve on a part-time basis. It has no power to carry out any of its recommendations to the DPCP. The DPCP may issue an order implementing some or all of the commission's recommendations. Such orders are enforceable by civil proceedings brought by the Crown for an injunction or for any other appropriate relief. Very few such orders have been issued. The normal procedure is to negotiate with the companies and try to obtain a voluntary compliance agreement. There is no judicial review of the commission's proceedings, though an order of the DPCP can be challenged in the courts.

Monopolies

As with Section 2 of the Sherman Act, monopolization rather than the mere existence of a monopoly is prohibited. A "monopoly situation" exists whenever one quarter or more of the supply of goods or services in the United Kingdom is controlled by one person or by two or more persons acting together to restrain competition. Except for situations relating to exports of goods from the United Kingdom, the agency (the DPCP or the director-general) making the reference to the Monopolies and Mergers Commission may "if it appears to him or them to be appropriate in the circumstances to do so, determine that consideration shall be limited to a part of the United Kingdom." In other words, the relevant geographic market may be defined as the entire United Kingdom or any part of it. Two of the commission's most recent reports illustrate the type of evaluation that is made and the questions that are raised.

In June 1971 the commission was asked by the DPCP to investigate the supply of ready-cooked breakfast cereals and whether the "determination of the level of prices at which breakfast cereals are supplied is a thing done by the parties concerned [the manufacturers of breakfast cereals], and whether, if this was the case, this was operating against the public interest." The commission found that the Kellogg Company of Great Britain supplied 60 per cent of the cereals sold in the country during the late 1960's. Having established that a "monopoly situation" existed, the commission examined the structure of the industry, and the amounts spent on advertising relative to sales and profits of the cereal companies, and concluded that Kellogg's profits, which were 70 per cent on capital invested in the mid-1960's and 46 per cent in the late 1960's, were "excessive." However, by the time the investigation and report were concluded, Kellogg's profits had fallen to 25 per cent, which the commission was not prepared to call excessive. Therefore, the commission concluded that the present price level did not operate against the public interest. Nevertheless the commission recommended that all future price increases proposed by Kellogg for its breakfast cereals must be submitted to the government for approval to ensure that the company's profits remain at an "acceptable level" and do not return to the excessive levels of the 1960's. The DPCP accepted this recommendation and imposed the price-increase review procedure on Kellogg for an indefinite period of time.

In July 1966 the commission was asked by the DPCP to investigate whether a monopoly situation existed in the beer industry, and if so whether any practices in that industry were against the public interest. The commission's report was issued in 1969 and it found that a monopoly did exist because many brewers sold beer through a system of "tied" houses. Under this system each pub in which beer was sold to the public was "tied" to a brewer, usually as a tenant, with a requirement that he buy beer exclusively from his landlord and sell to the public only its brands or others permitted by the brewer. The commission found this entire "tied-house" system against the public interest as a method of distribution that preserved inefficient brewers and prevented the establishment of independent wholesalers or the entrance into the industry of new brewers. The only competition in the industry was among brewers in acquiring captive retail outlets. Finally, the system eliminated all price competition between the "tied" outlets. The commission found no way to remedy this situation in the context of the usual licensing system for public houses and recommended a relaxation of this system to permit the sale of alcoholic drinks by any retailer who met certain minimum standards. The DPCP entered into negotiations with the brewery companies and government departments, which are still continuing, to determine the best methods of alleviating the defects in the "tied-house" system.

During 1973 the Monopolies and Mergers Commission issued four monopoly reports and five new monopoly cases, involving such items as restrictions upon advertising by accountants, the supply of flour and bread, and the supply of building bricks, were referred to it.

Mergers

All mergers are not covered by the legislation empowering the DPCP to refer a merger to the Monopolies and Mergers Commission. The legislation applies to any completed or prospective merger or take-over either where the result of the merger is to create or strengthen a "monopoly situation"—a position where one quarter or more of the supply of goods or services is controlled by one or more persons—or where the value of the assets taken over or to be taken over exceeds 5 million pounds. Thus, the statute applies to horizontal, vertical, and conglomerate mergers. It should be noted, however, that unlike the monopoly situation, the relevant geographic market for a merger is the "United Kingdom or *substantial part thereof.*" As we have seen, the relevant market in a monopoly case can be any portion of the U.K. that appears "to be appropriate." Therefore it is possible in theory to have a geographic area that is sufficient for a monopoly case but that is not large enough to be a "substantial part" of the United Kingdom and therefore is not sufficiently large for a merger case.

The statutory definitions of *merger* and *common control* are complicated and detailed. A guide to DPCP practice regarding mergers states that the legislation applies

> when two or more enterprises (an enterprise is defined as the activities or part of the activities of a trade or business) have ceased to be separate enterprises within the previous six months or where arrangements are in progress or contemplation which will lead to their ceasing to be separate enterprises. Enterprises cease to be separate when they are brought under common ownership or control or when one of them ceases to be carried on as a result of arrangements to prevent or restrict competition.

The guide to mergers also states that the legislation adopts "a broadly neutral attitude to mergers. . . ." The functions of the DPCP and of the commission are to balance the increased efficiency, technological progress, and ability to compete effectively with large foreign and domestic rivals produced by mergers against the injury to the public interest. The 1973 Act prescribes a list of criteria for evaluating the public interest and the 1965 Act states that the commission should "take into account all matters which appear in the particular circumstances to be relevant and have regard (amongst other things) to any matters to which the [DPCP] may from time to time direct them to have regard. . . ."

Only the secretary of state may refer mergers to the commission and he may issue interim orders after a merger reference has been made while the commission is investigating the merger. Such an order may "prohibit or restrict the doing of things which in his opinion would constitute action [which adversely affects the public interest]," including preventing Company A from acquiring Company B. The secretary of state may also limit the scope of the commission's consideration of a merger to elements specified in the reference. In such a case the commission could only consider whether the specified elements or their possible consequences operate against the public interest. The director-general is required to keep himself apprised of actual or prospective mergers that may qualify for investigation and to give advice to the secretary of state on the action to be taken on the mergers. The secretary of state has power to refer a completed merger at any time if prior notice of material facts about the proposed merger was not given to the secretary of state or to the director-general and the facts concerning the merger were not made public more than six months before the date of the merger. If the commission reports that the merger will damage the public interest and recommends prevention of a proposed merger or dissolution of a completed merger, the DPCP can order such prevention or dissolution.

The DPCP and the commission have taken a lenient approach to mergers as compared to American standards. There is no attempt to stop concentration in its incipiency, as under Section 7 of the Clayton Act, and one expert commentator has stated that the "Commission . . . seems to be loath to say a merger may operate against the public interest. . . ." In practice the vast majority of mergers are screened and cleared by the DPCP within three or four weeks. During 1973 the DPCP examined 120 mergers or proposed mergers and nine were referred to the Monopolies and Mergers Commission. From the passage of the Act in August 1965 until October 1973, nineteen mergers have been referred to the commission, of which seven were declared contrary to the public interest. Among the seven, one involved the proposed merger between the two largest British national banks, Barclay's Bank and Lloyd's Bank; two were horizontal mergers involving, respectively, large deep-sea fishing and retail clothing companies; and one was a conglomerate merger between two diversified companies, the Rank Organisation and the De La Rue Company. Many large mergers are not even referred to the commission. For example, the merger between the British Motor Corporation and Leyland Motors was not referred, although at the time of the merger between them the companies manufactured over half of the trucks and 40 per cent of the cars produced in the country and were the second largest of builders of engines. However, this method of handling mergers has been criticized by businessmen because a reference to the Monopolies and Mergers Commission sometimes results in the abandonment of merger plans before the commission issues a report. Of the nineteen mergers referred to the commission, three were abandoned before the commission issued a report.

The United Kingdon's accession to the European Communities should have little effect on the operation of the DPCP and the Monopolies and Mergers Commission.

The Fair Trading Act 1973

In addition to amending the provisions relating to restrictive practices, monopolies, and mergers the 1973 legislation added several new sections to the existing laws. An entirely new provision permits the secretary of state to refer to the Monopolies and Mergers Commission, at any time, questions involving restrictive labor practices—any practice under which restrictions, other than those relating exclusively to rates of pay, operate in relation to the employment of workers in any commercial activities in the United Kingdom. However, this new clause does not provide for the exercise of any order-making powers under the Act. This provision would apply to activities of trade unions, except that the commission must "disregard anything which appears to them to have been done, or omitted to be done, in contemplation or furtherance of an industrial dispute. . . ."

Another new section establishes a Consumer Protection Advisory Committee of ten to fifteen members, some of whom are to be experienced in the supply of goods to consumers and some of whom are to be experienced in consumer protection activities. The secretary of state, other government ministers, and the director-general may refer to the committee the question of whether a "consumer trade practice" adversely affects the economic interests of consumers in the United Kingdom. *Consumer trade practices* are defined as "specific practices relating to the sale or other supply of goods or services to consumers." The committee is not to consider monopoly situations or practices relating to the supply of specified professional services. It may consider practices in public services, such as electricity, common carriers, or gas, only with the government's consent. The director-general may include in his reference to the committee proposals for remedial action by the secretary of state whenever he believes that the consumer trade practice has the effect, or is likely to have the effect

(a)   of misleading consumers as to, or withholding from them adequate information as to, or an adequate record of, their rights and obligations under relevant consumer transactions, or

(b)   of otherwise misleading or confusing consumers with respect to any matter in connection with relevant consumer transactions, or

(c)   of subjecting consumers to undue pressure to enter into relevant consumer transactions, or

(d)   of causing the terms or conditions, on or subject to which consumers enter into relevant consumer transactions, to be so adverse to them as to be inequitable.

The committee must issue its report and recommendations within three months. The secretary of state may issue such orders as are necessary to remedy the adverse effect on consumers. Violation of such an order is punishable by a fine up to 400 pounds or imprisonment not exceeding two years, or both. Orders are enforced by the local weights and measures authorities, who are given wide powers to make test purchases and to inspect and seize documents. In April 1974 the first references were made to the committee by the director-general. He proposed that shops be prohibited from displaying notices stating "No goods exchanged" or "No cash refunded" and that a manufacturer's guarantee contain a clearly worded statement to the effect that the guarantee has no effect upon the consumer's rights against his supplier (usually the retailer) if the goods prove to be faulty.

A third new section was added to the government's 1973 bill by a parliamentary committee. It deals with "pyramid selling and similar trading schemes." The secretary of state is empowered to issue regulations governing the issue, circulation, and distribution of documents that (1) contain any invitation to persons to become participants in pyramid or similar selling schemes or (2) contain any information calculated to lead directly or indirectly to persons becoming participants in such schemes. The regulations may also prohibit the promoter or any participants in the trading scheme from

(a) supplying any goods to a participant in the trading scheme, or
(b) supplying any training facilities or other services for such a participant, or
(c) providing any goods or services under a transaction effected by such a participant, or
(d) being a party to any arrangements under which goods or services are supplied or provided as mentioned in any of the preceding paragraphs, or
(e) accepting from any such participant any payment, or any undertaking to make a payment, in respect of any goods or services supplied or provided as mentioned in any of paragraphs (a) to (d) of this subsection or in respect of any goods or services to be so supplied or provided.

Persons guilty of an offense under these regulations are liable to a fine or to imprisonment for a term not exceeding two years, or to both.

The Fair Trading Act represents a major expansion of United Kingdom law in the area of consumer protection and a toughening of the former approach to restrictive practices, monopolies, and mergers. The combination of this new law and the direct applicability of the EEC Rules on Competition portend a significant change in the antitrust climate of the United Kingdom.

Canada

As we mentioned at the beginning of this chapter, two thirds of American foreign direct investment is located in Canada and the European Communities. Until 1969 the book value of U.S. investment in Canada exceeded that of U.S. investment in Europe. Thus American businessmen are frequently confronted by problems involving Canadian law.

In order to avoid conflicts between Canada and the United States that might arise because of multinational business activity involving the large amount of U.S. investment in Canada or because of the extraterritorial enforcement of the U.S. antitrust laws the two countries established an informal arrangement on "Antitrust Notification and Consultation Procedure" in 1959. This arrangement was modified in 1969 to conform to the Recommendations on Cooperation of the Organization for Economic Cooperation and Development (OECD) regarding restrictive business practices affecting international trade. The new arrangement is known as the Mitchell–Basford Agreement because it was signed by then U.S. Attorney General John Mitchell and Canadian Minister of Consumer and Corporate Affairs Ron Basford. The agreement provides that each country notify the other prior to the institution of an antitrust suit that involves the interest or citizens of the other country and provides for consultations concerning the contemplated lawsuit. Each country also agrees to provide the other with information in its possession concerning activities or situations affecting international trade that the other needs in order to determine whether there has been a breach of its antitrust laws.

Enforcement of Canadian Antitrust Law

Canadian antitrust legislation originated in 1889, one year before the passage of the Sherman Antitrust Act in the United States. The current version of this legislation is the Combines Investigation Act of 1952, popularly known as the Anti-Combines Law. The basic purpose of this legislation is to preserve the public interest in free competition by prohibiting three classes of anticompetitive practices: (1) agreements or combinations that prevent or lessen unduly competition in the production, purchase, sale, storage, rental, or transportation of commodities or in the price of insurance; (2) mergers or monopolies that are likely to lessen competition to the detriment of the public; (3) unfair trade practices, including price discrimination, predatory pricing, certain promotional allowances, misrepresentation, and resale price maintenance.

Although these practices are similar to those proscribed by American antitrust laws, the impact of the Anti-Combines Law on business is considerably short of the impact of American laws in similar situations. This difference can be explained in several ways. First the Canadian legislation is entirely a criminal law. There are no provisions for the awarding of civil damages, treble or otherwise. Enforcement of the legislation is a matter of determining whether or not there has been a criminal offense. The onus is on the prosecution to prove an offense beyond a reasonable doubt and the accused is entitled to the presumption of innocence. Administrators have no power to regulate industry or to issue cease and desist orders. Secondly, the Anti-Combines Law does not apply to service industries except to the extent that specific services, such as insurance, rental of goods, storage, and transportation, are expressly included in the statute or services are combined with the production or supply of goods. The activities of banks are expressly excluded from the Anti-Combines Law. Finally, publicity, rather than penalties, has historically been seen as the major deterrent to anticompetitive behavior.

Administration of the Anti-Combines Law is vested in the office of the director of investigation and research, which is part of the federal government's Department of Consumer and Corporate Affairs, and in the Restrictive Trade Practices Commission. The director's function is to initiate inquiries into possible violations of the Anti-Combines Law whenever he has reason to believe that an offense has been or is about to be committed; whenever directed to do so by the registrar general of Canada; or upon the application of six or more Canadian citizens. Most inquiries are commenced by the director on his own initiative after receipt of an informal complaint. The director has broad investigatory powers, including the power to search for, inspect, and seize documents, examine witnesses under oath, and compel the production of requested information. Upon completing the investigation the director can conclude that the evidence does not indicate an offense and drop the matter; refer the matter to the attorney general of Canada for consideration of appropriate action, such as prosecution or application for an injunction; or, the most common course of action, refer the matter to the Restrictive Trade Practices Commission for a hearing and issuance of a report.

The commission receives a full statement of the evidence of the alleged offense from the director, conducts an adversary hearing, and writes a report to the minister of justice, who is required to publish the report within thirty days after receiving it. Unlike the American Federal Trade Commission, the Restrictive Trade Practices Commission has no power to determine rights and liabilities or to issue rules governing industry conduct. Rather, its function is to write reports and make recommendations. The attorney general of Canada decides whether the report warrants a prosecution, which is usually brought in the criminal court of the province in which the offense took place or in the Exchequer Court of Canada. Conviction may result in a fine, the limit of which is within the court's discretion, imprisonment for up to two years, or both. In practice, the courts have never imprisoned offenders but have issued fines and orders prohibiting continuation of the offense. The commission may also recommend that other relief be awarded by the court, including injunctive relief, dissolution of an illegal merger or monopoly, patent or trademark impeachment, and tariff action by the governor. Although the Canadian law is entirely criminal law and all violations must be tried in the traditional criminal way, there is a "Program of Compliance" administered by the director of investigation and research that provides a procedure for informal clearance of proposed business activity and is frequently used to avoid litigation.

Restrictive Agreements

Section 32(1) of the Anti-Combines Law prohibits agreements, combinations, and conspiracies that "unduly" prevent, limit, or lessen competition, such as price fixing, market sharing, group boycotts, production control, and profit sharing. Subsection 2 of Section 32 exempts agreements that relate to the exchange of statistics, definition of product standards, exchange of credit information, definition of trade terms, cooperation in research and development, and restriction of advertising so long as the agreements are not likely to lessen competition unduly with respect to prices, quantity, or quality of production, markets, customers, channels, or methods of distribution or market entry or expansion. Agreements relating only to exports are also exempt, provided the agreement does not reduce the volume of exports, prevent entry into the export business, or lessen competition unduly in the domestic market.

The essence of the offense is conspiracy—an express or tacit agreement among the parties to suppress competition. As with the Sherman Act, direct evidence is not necessary to establish the existence of a conspiracy. Such can be inferred from the actions of the persons involved that must be more than merely consciously parallel, and the parties are guilty of violating the law even if the objective of the conspiracy is not achieved. The Anti-Combines Law differs from the Sherman Act in that there are no per se offenses under the Canadi..n law. The conspiracy only violates the law when its objective or effect is to lessen competition unduly. This statutory "rule of reason" has been interpreted to mean that if the conspiracy would materially interfere with competition in a substantial sector of trade it unduly lessens competition. This determination is a question of fact that, as one Canadian judge put it, is based upon a "common sense view as to the direct object of the arrangement complained of." Because there are no per se offenses, factors to be considered in each case include the share of the market occupied by the conspirators and the nature of the competition that remains in the market. In determining whether competition has been limited unduly the Canadian courts do not consider the overall effects of the conspiracy. Once it has been established that the conspiracy has unduly limited competition, injury to the public is conclusively presumed even if specific benefits to the industry and the public can be demonstrated.

Mergers and Monopolies

Section 33 of the Anti-Combines Law proscribes formation and operation of mergers and monopolies. *Merger* is defined as the "acquisition of any control or interest in the business of another that, to the detriment of the public, lessens competition in trade or industry, or among the sources of supply or the outlets for sales of a trade or industry." *Monopoly* is defined as a "situation where one or more persons substantially or completely control throughout Canada or any area thereof the class or species of business in which they are engaged and have operated or are likely to operate that business to the detriment of the public." The definition excludes rights granted under the Patent Act or under other special Canadian legislation. Mergers of banks and other financial institutions are passed upon by the federal Department of Finance. Mergers in service industries are exempt.

This provision covers horizontal, vertical, and conglomerate mergers as well as both forward and backward integration. The test of illegality is whether the merger lessens competition "to the detriment or against the interests of the public." The emphasis is on the degree of competition remaining after the merger, and the courts have required the prosecution to prove limitation of competition amounting to the creation of a virtual monopoly before finding a detriment to the public. This stringent test of illegality and the fact that there is no requirement that the anticombines authorities approve or even be notified of proposed mergers have led to a very low level of governmental activity. The director of investigation and research recently stated that not more than one dozen of the 500 annual mergers in Canada are scrutinized by his office. There have been two court cases involving mergers since 1960 and the first conviction under the merger provision did not come until 1970. There is no attempt to prevent concentration or monopoly in its incipiency as there is under Section 7 of the Clayton Act.

The abuse of monopoly power rather than the mere existence of monopoly is proscribed. The *Eddy Match* case is the only Canadian judicial decision involving a monopoly. Eddy Match acquired all its competitors in the wooden match industry in 1927. In succeeding years each time a new independent match company was established it was either acquired or driven out of business by Eddy Match, which employed such practices as preferred pricing, special discounts, industrial spying, and rebates. The courts found a public detriment to exist because Eddy Match had excluded, for all practical purposes, the possibility of any competition. The court noted that once the type of monopoly control shown here is proved there is a presumption of a detriment to the public that can be rebutted by evidence that such control has resulted in actual benefit to the public.

Unfair Trade Practices

The Anti-Combines Law also contains provisions relating to unfair trade practices, similar to practices covered by the Robinson–Patman Act, including price discrimination, predatory pricing, certain types of discriminatory promotional allowances, and misleading price advertising. Resale-price maintenance is absolutely prohibited and the offense may be committed in two ways: by requiring or inducing (or attempting to) another person to maintain the resale price or by denying supplies to an outlet by reason of the latter refusing to maintain the resale price. In 1960 certain statutory defenses to a charge of resale-price maintenance were enacted. Under these a dealer is entitled to refuse to supply an article if he has reasonable cause to believe that the purchaser is using his products as a "loss-leader"—defined as "not for the purpose of making a profit thereon but for purposes of advertising"—engaging in misleading advertising in respect to the article, failing to provide proper servicing for the article, or disparaging its value. However, there is no "fair trade exception" similar to the Miller–Tydings Act and the McGuire Act.

The Anti-Combines Act has no counterpart to Section 5 of the Federal Trade Commission Act. Thus, proceedings can be initiated only against practices that are specifically enumerated and not against "unfair methods of competition." Because there are no specific provisions relating to such practices as exclusive dealing and tying arrangements, they are legal under the Anti-Combines Law. There has been little litigation involving the enumerated unfair trade practices because the director of investigation and research has chosen to rely on a program of advising businessmen on the legality of proposed trade practices known as the Program of Compliance.

Deceptive Advertising

In 1969, a new provision was added to the Anti-Combines Law that prohibits the publication of an advertisement containing a statement that purports to be a statement of fact but is untrue, deceptive, or misleading and the publication in an advertisement of a statement or a guarantee of the performance, efficacy, or length of life of an item that is not based on an adequate and proper test of that item. In recent years heavy emphasis has been placed on this section by the anti-combines authorities and the vast majority of court decisions under the Anti-Combines Law have involved misleading advertising. The most significant court decision to date involved an advertising campaign conducted by Imperial Tobacco Products, Ltd. concerning the introduction of a new brand of cigarettes, Casino. The advertisement contained the statement that there was "five dollars in every pack of new Casino." The evidence disclosed that there was not $5 in each pack. Rather each pack contained a game that if won by the purchaser would lead to a prize of $5. The odds against a purchaser selecting the winning combination were 400 to 1. The defense argued that no reasonable man would believe that he would receive $5 by purchasing a package of cigarettes. However, the Supreme Court of Alberta held that the provision made no reference to a reasonable man standard and that the section protects the public in general, including the "ignorant, the unthinking, and the credulous." The court further held that a criminal intent is not an essential ingredient of the offense.

Proposed Amendments

In recent years there has been increasing criticism of the Anti-Combines Law. Many Canadians believe that the reliance on criminal penalties and publicity lead to inflexibility and to the very low level of enforcement activity against conspiracies, mergers, monopolies, and unfair trade practices. Others criticize the exemption of the growing service industries from the statute. In response to this criticism the Canadian federal government requested the Economic Council of Canada, an independent advisory body, to make a comprehensive review of Canadian competition policy and to recommend changes in the existing law. Between 1967 and 1971 the Economic Council issued a series of reports on various aspects of competition policy. These reports were supplemented by other government studies devoted to topics such as foreign ownership of Canadian industry and foreign investment in Canada. On the basis of these studies and recommendations the government of Prime Minister Pierre Trudeau introduced, in June 1971, draft legislation that would have replaced the Anti-Combines Law. This proposed Competition Practices Act was intended to initiate public discussion and was allowed to die at the end of the parliamentary session. In November 1973 the government introduced a bill containing a series of amendments to the Anti-Combines Law that, according to the government minister who introduced the bill in the Canadian House of Commons, represents the "first stage of our program to modernize competition laws and also provides for increased consumer protection against undesirable business practices. . . . "

The bill would extend the coverage of the Anti-Combines Law to include services and would provide a civil right of recovery for persons who suffer loss or damage as a result of conduct prohibited by the Anti-Combines Law. The unfair trading prohibitions of the Anti-Combines Law would be broadened to include pyramid selling, double ticketing, referral selling, bait and switch selling, selling above advertised prices, and promotional contests. Another new provision would authorize the Federal Court of Canada or a superior court of criminal jurisdiction to issue an interim injunction against prohibited conduct to avoid irreparable injury. Similarly, for the first time the Restrictive Trade Practices Commission would be empowered to issue orders where there is a refusal to deal that affects the ability of a person to carry on business or a misuse of consignment selling practices or exclusive dealing, market restriction, or tied selling.

The most important proposed change in the existing Canadian Anti-Combines Law for non-Canadians is a new provision that authorizes the Restrictive Trade Practices Commission to order that no action be taken in Canada to implement a "judgment, decree, order or other process given, made or issued by or out of a court or other body in a country other than Canada. . . " if the implementation in whole or in part of the judgment, decree, order or other process in Canada would

> (i) adversely affect competition in Canada,
> (ii) adversely affect the efficiency of trade or industry in Canada without bringing about or increasing in Canada competition that would restore and improve such efficiency,
> (iii) adversely affect the foreign trade of Canada without compensating advantages, *or*
> (iv) otherwise restrain or injure trade or commerce in Canada without compensating advantages.

This provision reflects Canadian objections to American assertions of extraterritorial jurisdiction. Such objections are based on concepts of sovereignty, as well as economics. Canadian subsidiaries of American companies have been compelled by U.S. courts to produce documents and to follow court orders and instructions, and the implementation of U.S. antitrust decrees has been held to adversely affect the Canadian economy. This new provision of the law would make enforcement of foreign judgments and the foreign court orders including discovery much more difficult in Canada. At this writing the prognosis for this provision and for the bill as a whole is unclear.

Japan

At first glance the Japanese antitrust laws appear very similar to U.S. antitrust legislation. This similarity is not coincidental. At the end of World War II the Allied Powers were determined to democratize the Japanese economy and to prevent the rejuvenation of the zaibatsu ("money group")— large conglomerate family holding companies—that had monopolized the Japanese economy before and during the war. Thus, the U.S. occupation authority, General MacArthur, specifically directed the Japanese government to enact a law which would "eliminate and prevent private monopoly and restraint of trade." In response to this directive the Japanese government enacted the "Act Concerning Prohibition of Private Monopoly and Maintenance of Fair Trade" (Antimonopoly Act) in 1947. The law had been drafted jointly by the Japanese government and General MacArthur's staff. It was modeled on the Clayton, Federal Trade Commission, and Sherman Acts, but was more stringent and more detailed than the American legislation. The 1947 Antimonopoly Act has been substantially changed twice, in 1949 and 1953, and has undergone numerous minor alterations. These changes in the original legislation have been designed to weaken or permit circumvention of the 1947 law, which many Japanese businessmen view as unrealistically rigid.

The Act and several related laws are enforced by the Fair Trade Commission (FTC), an independent five-man regulatory commission modeled on the U.S. Federal Trade Commission, and by the courts. In Japan the FTC is the only agency authorized to initiate administrative action against persons or companies violating the Antimonopoly Act. If the existence of unlawful activity is suspected, the commission staff, which numbered 356 in 1972, investigates and determines whether initiation of an administrative action will serve the public interest.

The majority of cases are settled by "recommended decisions"—a procedure under which the commission recommends that an alleged violator cease and desist from specific activities. The decision is issued without an administrative trial on the merits if the alleged violator accepts the recommendation. If the latter rejects the recommendation, an administrative trial is usually initiated. Such trials consist of a formal charge by the investigator and a defense by the respondent in much the manner of a court trial. The commission's decision can be appealed to the Tokyo High Court and then to the Japanese Supreme Court. Between October 1971 and September 1972, twenty-four decisions were issued by the FTC, and, of these, five were rendered after a formal hearing and nineteen were recommended decisions.

There are no specific provisions for private damage suits for violations of the Act. However, a violation of the Antimonopoly Act is regarded as a tort and a claim for damages may be brought in court. In such a case the claimant must show either willful violation of the Act or negligence by the party violating the Act in the sense that the violator should have known that his action would injure the claimant. However, a tort claim may be brought to the Tokyo High Court after the FTC has issued a decision in the case in question. When a decision has been issued it may serve as conclusive evidence of illegality in a subsequent tort claim action. Private monopolization and unreasonable restraint of trade are criminal offenses punishable by a fine or imprisonment or both. Such criminal actions have rarely been brought. In patent cases the relevant patents may be revoked.

The wide breadth and complexity of the Antimonopoly Act are disclosed in Section 1:

> This Act, by prohibiting private monopolization, unreasonable restraint of trade and unfair business practices, by preventing the excessive concentration of economic power and by eliminating unreasonable restraint of production, sale, price, technology, and the like, and all other undue restriction of business activities through combinations, agreements, etc., aims to promote free and fair competition, to stimulate the initiative of entrepreneurs, to encourage business activities of enterprises, to heighten the level of employment and people's real income, and thereby to promote the democratic and wholesome development of the national economy as well as to assure the interests of consumers in general.

The Act has five major substantive provisions:

PRIVATE MONOPOLIZATION

Section 3 of the Antimonopoly Act states "no entrepreneur shall effect private monopolization." An *entrepreneur* is "any natural or juridical person who carries on any commercial, financial or business enterprise." *Private monopolization* occurs when one or more entrepreneurs (1) exclude or make it difficult for other entrepreneurs to compete in any field of commerce, usually by discriminatory pricing, exclusive dealing, or controlling the necessary resources for manufacture or sale; or (2) control the business activities of other entrepreneurs by eliminating their freedom to make business decisions, usually by exclusive dealing, interlocking directorates, mergers, resale-price maintenance, or tying contracts. In either of these two situations there must be a "substantial restraint of competition in any particular field of trade" that is contrary to the public interest. The abuse rather than mere existence of monopoly power is forbidden. The approach taken is very similar to that expressed in the *Alcoa* case in 1945 by Judge Learned Hand. There is no "monopolization" under the Japanese Antimonopoly Act if a dominant firm has monopoly "thrust upon" it by purely technological or other objective factors not controlled by the firm or enjoys its position "by virtue of . . . superior skill, foresight, and industry." However, if the company acts to preserve or exploit its dominance, actions that are not the result of such objective factors, a violation occurs.

Under Japanese law the market monopolized need not be the one in which the company effecting "private monopolization" is primarily engaged. For example, a Japanese bank attempted to gain control of the silk export trade in one prefecture by making loans available to silk mills on the condition that they sell all their finished products to an affiliate of the bank. This attempt to exclude competitors of the affiliate was held to be a prohibited attempt at private monopolization by the bank.

The phrases *substantial restraint of competition in any particular field of trade* and *contrary to the public interest* are repeated in many sections of the Antimonopoly Act and are the two basic standards for applying the Act. The words *in any particular field of trade* refer to the concept of the relevant market within which the anticompetitive effects of the activity are to be judged. Market delineation can concern such factors as geographical trade patterns, product identity, and the level of distribution common to the entrepreneurs involved. The Tokyo High Court has interpreted the words *substantial restraint of competition* to mean the "bringing about of such a situation where competition itself decreases and a particular entrepreneur or a group of entrepreneurs is able to control the market by willfully influencing, to a substantial extent, price, quality, volume of supply or various other business conditions." Market control is not determined merely by the size of the market controlled. Rather it is a case-by-case analysis depending on economic conditions such as capital procurement ability, marketing ability, and the possibility of new entry or countervailing power.

The phrase *contrary to the public interest* was originally viewed in strictly per se terms; that is, any restraint of competition was in itself regarded as contrary to the public interest. However, the trend has been away from this type of inflexibility to a rule-of-reason approach judging each case on its unique facts. Moreover, many of the per se sections of the original Antimonopoly Act have been deleted by subsequent legislation.

UNREASONABLE RESTRAINT OF TRADE

Section 3 of the Antimonopoly Act also provides that no entrepreneur "shall undertake any unreasonable restraint of trade." The statute defines unreasonable restraints to include price fixing and restrictions on customers, facilities, products, production, suppliers, or technology. The Japanese legislature and courts have severely restricted the possible impact of this section by limiting its application to situations where there are (1) substantial restraints, (2) imposed by concerted action, (3) by parties in competition with each other, and (4) mutually applicable to all the competitors involved. Thus Section 3 applies only to horizontal agreements among competitors that suppress competition among themselves and does not proscribe vertical restraints of trade. For example, the Tokyo High Court ruled that an agreement to allocate sales districts made between a group that published newspapers and a group that distributed the papers did not violate the Antimonopoly Act because the two groups were not in competition with one another. As in the United States, consciously parallel action alone is not proof of a conspiracy to suppress competition but is merely evidence relevant in determining whether a conspiracy exists. Cases under this provision have been limited to flagrant abuses, usually price fixing which is considered to be per se contrary to the public interest.

UNFAIR BUSINESS PRACTICES

The Antimonopoly Act provides that the Fair Trade Commission can designate certain types of business practices as "unfair" and such practices are prohibited by Section 19 of the Act. It is also a violation of the act for a trade association to cause entrepreneurs to employ any designated unfair business practices. The FTC has established two groups of unfair business practices, "generally designated" and "specifically designated." The twelve categories of "generally designated" unfair practices, encompassing activity condemned in the United States under the Clayton, Federal Trade Commission, and Robinson–Patman Acts, apply to all industries. These practices include unreasonable refusals to deal, discrimination in price, service, or terms, paying unduly high prices or supplying at an unduly low price (dumping), use of economic advantage and disadvantage to induce or coerce customers of competitors, exclusive dealing, tying arrangements, interference in the affairs of a competitor, and exploitation of a dominant position.

"Specifically designated" unfair practices are announced after investigation and hearings into specific industrial practices. They are additional, not alternative, to the generally designated practices. The activities condemned by these specific designations vary widely and have included the use of gifts and entertainment to procure sales in the soy sauce and paste market and specific practices such as the demand by retailers that wholesalers furnish their employees to work in the retailers' stores. In 1959 a specific designation was issued for shipping conferences which dealt with unreasonable refusals to admit to the conference, undue discrimination by shipping lines, retaliation for shipping on nonconference vessels, and the abuse of exclusive contracts.

The Fair Trade Commission also administers and enforces the Act Against Unjustifiable Premiums and Misleading Representations, which was enacted to strengthen the Antimonopoly Act by curbing specific unfair business practices. The Act limits the offering of gifts to customers upon their purchase of goods or services. For example, in 1968 a Tokyo seller of room coolers who offered a TV set to every person who bought his room cooler was ordered to stop the practice. The same Act also prohibits deceptive or misleading labeling, advertising, or other representations.

RESTRICTIONS ON THE CONCENTRATION OF
ECONOMIC POWER

The Japanese Antimonopoly Act contains several provisions relating to the concentration of enterprises. Originally most of these prohibitions were strict per se rules designed to eliminate the oligopolistic structure that had dominated Japan's industry before and during World War II. All these restrictions, except the absolute prohibition of holding companies, have been modified to incorporate the "substantial restraint" standard. Stockholding, interlocking directorates, mergers, and transfers of business are prohibited where the effect may be substantially to restrain competition in any field of trade. Financial companies, such as investment houses, are forbidden to own more than 10 per cent of the stock of other companies without obtaining prior government approval. It is important to note that the word *company* used in these provisions is defined as including foreign companies as well as Japanese companies.

Mergers are prohibited if the effect of the merger may be substantially to restrain competition or if the acquisition has been effected by unfair business practices. The Fair Trade Commission has held that a merger may substantially restrain competition "when the market structure as compared with that prevailing prior to the merger becomes noncompetitive and where, as a result, a particular entrepreneur may attain a controlling position in the market." Companies wishing to merge must notify the FTC of their intention and wait thirty days before consummating the merger. Companies may also seek informal advance clearances for proposed mergers in a procedure similar to that of the U.S. Federal Trade Commission.

Many Japanese businessmen opposed the merger restrictions on the ground that Japanese business can compete successfully with international competitors only by expanding and consolidating their operations through mergers. The Japanese government, agreeing with these contentions, attempted to give the Ministry of International Trade and Industry (MITI) the power to exempt mergers from the Antimonopoly Act, by introducing a special industries promotion bill. However, the bill failed to pass the Diet and consequently the Act as amended in 1953 remains unchanged. Despite thousands of mergers, mostly horizontal, during the past twenty-five years the FTC has issued only three complaints against proposed mergers. In 1969 the two largest companies in the iron and steel industry, Yawata and Fuji, accounting for 22.1 and 22.4 per cent of the Japanese pig iron market, respectively, asked the FTC whether their plan to merge was legal. After negotiations and a public hearing the commission issued a recommendation to the companies not to merge. The companies refused to accept the recommendation and the FTC initiated a formal trial-type hearing. After a series of hearings the defendant companies asked for a consent decision to eliminate the violation. Thereupon, the FTC approved the merger on the condition that the merging companies transfer certain equipment and securities to rivals, supply rivals with certain products on reasonable terms, and provide rivals with certain technical assistance.

INTERNATIONAL CONTRACTS

Section 6 of the Antimonopoly Act prohibits an entrepreneur from entering into an oral or written international agreement or contract that would contain matters violating the Act's provisions relating to unreasonable restraints of trade or unfair business practices. An entrepreneur who has entered into an international contract must file a report thereof with the FTC within thirty days from the date of the conclusion of the contract. International contracts creating an agency relationship or involving a single transaction that can be completed within a year are exempted from this reporting requirement. This section was intended to protect Japanese entrepreneurs from unfair business practices imposed by foreign entrepreneurs, usually in the area of patent-licensing contracts. This section had only minor importance before 1968 because all international contracts that involved remittance to foreign countries had to be approved by the Japanese Foreign Investment Council. Objectionable clauses under the Antimonopoly Act were usually removed during negotiations under the council's approving process and were, therefore, eliminated before the contract was reported to the FTC. However, in the last few years the council has been less stringent in its surveillance of foreign investment in Japan. Consequently, although Section 6 has been rarely used to date, it is expected to take on growing importance as a device for controlling the activities of foreign investors in Japan. For example, the FTC has issued guidelines for international patent-licensing and import distributorships.

CARTEL ARRANGEMENTS

In February 1974 the FTC, for the first time in its history, filed a request with the procurator-general that a criminal indictment be issued for a violation of the Antimonopoly Act. The FTC alleged that Japanese manufacturers of petroleum products had formed a cartel to fix prices and to restrict production of petroleum products. After a three-month investigation the Tokyo Public Prosecutor's office indicted the Petroleum Association of Japan, twelve oil-refining companies, which account for 85 to 90 per cent of petroleum product sales in Japan; and seventeen industry executives for conspiracy to fix prices and to restrict refinery production. The indictment charged that a "study group" of industry executives conspired to raise oil prices in Japan's domestic market five times during 1973 and had restricted production to reinforce the price increases. A spokesman for the industry stated that the industry's defense in the trial before the Tokyo High Court would focus upon the relationship between the industry's actions and the "administrative guidance" that had been received from the MITI. Officials of the MITI have denied that they encouraged the formation of a cartel in their informal consultations with the industry.

EXEMPTIONS

The Antimonopoly Act provides for exemptions from the Act for natural monopolies such as public utilities, canals, and railways; for activities authorized by special laws, including the copyright, patent, and trademark laws; for many types of cooperatives similar to Capper–Volstead Act exemptions; for resale-price-maintenance agreements relating to specific commodities; for export activities comparable to those exempted by the Webb–Pomerene Export Trading Act; for "rationalization cartels" (cartels to achieve advancement of technology, improvement of quality of goods, reduction of cost, increase in efficiency, and so on); and for "depression cartels" (cartels in a manufacturing field where the price of the items is below the average cost of production and a substantial number of manufacturers are in danger of being forced to discontinue their business).

In addition to exemptions contained in the Antimonopoly Act itself, the Diet has continued to reduce the scope of the Act's application by a series of exemptions written into other laws. It has been estimated that in the aggregate these numerous exemptions have made the Antimonopoly Act wholly or partly inapplicable to more than half of Japan's manufacturing, most of distribution and foreign trade, and significant parts of the service industries.

The history of the Antimonopoly Act, especially after the return of Japanese sovereignty in 1953, has been one of government and business hostility and hence shrinking applicability. Japanese leaders have viewed the Act's emphasis on competition as an impediment to the creation of a strong national economy and the improvement of Japan's foreign-trade position. Consequently amendments to the Act have deleted the stringent per se prohibitions of the original legislation or have replaced per se rules with a test of reasonableness in the circumstances, as viewed from a Japanese perspective. The close cooperation between the Japanese government, business management, and labor has led to a substantial degree of concentration in big business, and of cartelization in small business, and to the re-establishment of gigantic business structures similar to the prewar zaibatsu (Mitsui, Mitsubishi, Sumitomo, and so on). Competition in most major industrial Japanese markets is among oligopolists. Moreover, the government, together with management and labor, marshalls technology, manpower, and capital so that entry into foreign markets will be coordinated. Competition for foreign markets is considered to be inefficient and wasteful of capital. One knowledgeable American businessman has analogized the Japanese situation to one of the U.S. Justice Department encouraging U.S. Steel, General Motors, and du Pont to bid jointly on an international project and then loaning the consortium money through a branch of the Federal Reserve Bank.

It should be remembered, however, that, at least on paper, several of the Japanese antitrust laws, such as the total prohibition of holding companies (defined as a company "whose principal business is to control the business activities of a company or companies in Japan by means of stockholding. . . ."), are more rigorous than their American counterparts, and that many of the amendments to the original Antimonopoly Act have merely changed the drastic original provisions to provisions comparable to the current applications of American antitrust legislation.

chapter 12

Groping for a Truly International Antitrust Law

It is generally recognized that internationally we are in an era of growing economic interdependence, shared economic leadership, and dramatic economic change. World trade now totals $429.2 billion annually, up 24 per cent in 1973. Twenty-five years of postwar economic interaction has resulted in a polycentric world order. America is no longer the sole, dominating economic power. The Common Market, not the United States, is now the world's largest trading unit. Japan and Canada too have seen enormous development and will continue to be more significant factors in the world economy along with many developing nations. In commenting on this global phenomenon in his testimony concerning the proposed Trade Reform Act of 1973, then Secretary of the Treasury Shultz noted:

> [However], along with this diffusion of economic power has gone a reluctance to remove restrictions that are contrary to the principles of an open world economy. At one time those restrictions could have been considered necessary to support weak economies in the face of overwhelming U.S. economic power or as temporary aids to promote political objectives such as regional integration. No longer is this true.

The realignment of economic power centers has in fact been facilitated by years of multilateral trade agreements, such as the General Agreement on Tariffs and Trade (GATT), under which much of the trading world has progressively reduced restrictions on the free flow of trade and capital. Production protected from competition by high national barriers and domestic markets closed to foreign businessmen have been perceived to be inherently inefficient, costly, and inflationary.

260

Along with the economic need for and current trend toward liberalization of international commerce must be a continued effort to curb and control private business practices affecting trade between nations. Private restrictions on trade can be as direct and far-reaching as governmental restrictions (i.e., tariffs and quotas) and equally as detrimental. Indeed, private restraints can defeat the objectives of reduced governmental restrictions by replacing the latter with equally effective barriers. A 1960 GATT resolution warned: "[B]usiness practices which restrict competition in international trade may hamper the expansion of world trade and the economic development in individual countries and thereby frustrate the benefits of tariff reduction and removal of quantitative restrictions or may otherwise interfere with the objectives of the General Agreement on Tariffs and Trade. . . ." The same caveat was again voiced in the preamble to the 1967 *Organization for Economic Co-Operation and Development* (*OECD*) *Recommendation on Restrictive Business Practices* with the added concern: "that the unilateral application of national legislation, in cases where business operations in other countries are involved, raises questions as to the respective spheres of sovereignty of the countries concerned."

The international businessman has been learning to live in a world replete with proliferating and sometimes conflicting antitrust laws. But it is a world in which the signposts are becoming more difficult to read and the perils of a misstep are increasingly severe. The inconsistency in antitrust attitudes and in the application of antitrust laws of the United States, the European Communities, Canada, Japan, and other countries makes it difficult for international businessmen to shape the policies of their enterprises and to frame agreements that meet all legal standards. This chapter will summarize the shortcomings of the existing antitrust regime, which is based on national laws and their extraterritorial application and will review the attainments and limitations of international organizations and schemes designed to cope with the problem of restrictive business practices on an international basis.

In the minds of some, a system based on national laws and their extraterritorial application is inherently inadequate and incapable of controlling restrictive practices internationally. An international structure of supranational law and enforcement is therefore one suggested solution. For others, an international antitrust law is too fraught with impracticality because of the weaknesses inflicted by competing nationalistic interests on all international institutions. From this viewpoint the economic and social realities preclude a supranational law solution. Let us now examine these premises and also try to draw some conclusions of our own. In evaluating the present nation-oriented antitrust regime, our focus will be on U.S. law and policy, which have been elaborated in the earlier portions of this book.

Limitations of National Antitrust Laws and Their Foreign Application in Curbing Restrictive Business Practices

Traditionally, it has been the political role of the nation state to fashion a competitive or noncompetitive situation among its own industries. The traditional approach is, however, flawed in the context of international economic integration. The legal system of any one country appears inadequate to curb restrictive business practices in an international setting both because of the inherent limitations of a system based primarily on protection of one's own national market and industry and because of the increasing number of activities of the multinational enterprise that are either subject to the vagaries of conflicting national laws or else escape effective regulation entirely.

U.S. Legal Nationalism—"Substantial and Material Effect" Limitation

To restate the legal basis and judicial reasoning explored in detail in Chapter 3, the application of the U.S. antitrust laws to activity abroad derives from the constitutional authority of Congress to regulate the trade of the nation in interstate commerce and with foreign nations. Whereas public international law places virtually no restraints on the jurisdiction of a state over its own nationals wherever they may roam, the rule is more open to question where foreign nationals are sought to be held liable by a nation for conduct in their own country. In 1945 Judge Hand in the *Alcoa* case made it clear that the Sherman Act extended to restrictive business practices of non-American firms abroad if these practices were intended to affect, and did affect, the commerce of the United States. Even after *Alcoa,* it has often been argued, unsuccessfully, by defendants in U.S. antitrust cases that the exercise of jurisdiction over acts committed outside the territorial borders of the United States violates public international law. Later cases have limited the reach of *Alcoa* somewhat by insisting that such acts or contracts have a *substantial and material effect* upon our foreign and domestic commerce. Even if this narrowing of the *Alcoa* reach is read as respect for the possibly conflicting policies and interests of another nation, it is still drawn in terms of concern for American competitive interests, the protection of our economy and trade. Yet it is self-evident that anything that affects the external trade and commerce of the United States also affects the trade and commerce of other nations, and may have far greater economic consequences, adverse or beneficial, elsewhere than in the United States. In addition, because the policy of the U.S. antitrust laws is to reach only restrictive business practices having a "substantial effect" on the *American* competitor and consumer, those restrictive practices that are insubstantial and those that affect others go unchecked. The "extraterritorial" approach therefore is one fundamentally limited in vision and in relevance, at least from the international viewpoint.

Invitation to Self-defense—Disregard of Comity Limitation

Another major limitation of the "extraterritorial" application of a nation's antitrust laws is the political misunderstanding likely to result from the disregard of international comity. *Comity* is literally *courtesy,* but is defined in international law as the "recognition which one nation allows within its territory to the legislative, executive, or judicial acts of another nation, having due regard both to international duty and convenience, and to the rights of its own citizens, or of other persons who are under the protection of its laws." Antitrust laws, after all, are not enacted in a vacuum. They have a role within an entire framework of laws designed to promote distinct national policy objectives. One nation may regard cartels as essentially benign, whereas another does not. A developing nation may well have priorities and economic concerns that are more pressing than competition. The fact that different nations have different economic policy objectives not only goes to the heart of the comity problem, but also represents the most difficult obstacle to successful development of international antitrust standards. In addition, "extraterritorial" application of one nation's antitrust law often appears to downgrade the values and economic interests of the other countries concerned. The decision in the *Swiss Watchmakers* case is perceived by some Swiss as a case of American disregard of both Swiss sovereignty and international comity. There, it will be recalled, the U.S. court declared unlawful various restrictive practices permitted by the Swiss government. Although the Department of Justice argued that it was trying to reach only those aspects of the restrictive practices that affected American commerce, the original judgment was seen by many as directed in fact against the very operation of the Swiss watch industry in Switzerland, and drawn without due consideration for Swiss economic and political policies. Even the modified judgment of the original *Swiss Watchmakers* case, as worked out in 1965 by the Swiss government, the Department of State, the Department of Justice, and the court retained many proscriptions affecting the Swiss watch industry.

Such measures may lead to quick retaliation and countermeasures from abroad. An order from a U.S. court for discovery of documents in a foreign country or for compliance with an American decree abroad may meet foreign laws designed to forbid compliance with such American decisions. This type of adversary interplay not only negates the idea of comity among nations, and also serves to defeat U.S. antitrust policy, but in addition presents international businessmen with the dilemma of violating either domestic or foreign laws in carrying out their normal business activities.

Compelling State Law or Act of State— Deference to the Sovereign Limitation

Other limitations to the application of U.S. antitrust laws with respect to conduct abroad stem from the deference accorded a foreign state where it seeks to mandate business activities within its territorial jurisdiction. An otherwise restrictive business practice "compelled" by foreign *state law* or an *act of state* is exempted from the U.S. antitrust laws. This deference to sovereign authority, whether based on public international law or the judicial rules of self-restraint, accords supremacy to national interests, albeit those of another nation, at the possible expense of international control of restrictive business practices.

Moreover, the refined legal distinction between governmental acts and laws that *compel* and those that merely *permit* business activity has left an uncertainty that can make business planning difficult. This lack of predictability contravenes a major function of law, the function of guiding people in their actions. The court in *Swiss Watchmakers* was clear in stating that mere approval of the defendant's activities by the Swiss government did not "convert what is essentially a vulnerable private conspiracy into an unassailable system resulting from foreign governmental mandate." Nonetheless, in the modified judgment the court emphasized that the decision was *not* to be construed as "limit[ing] or circumscrib[ing] the sovereign right and power" of the Swiss government or prohibiting any person from "(1) performing any act in Switzerland which is required of it under the law of Switzerland; [or] (2) refraining from any act in Switzerland which is illegal under the law of Switzerland."

An Anomaly: The Webb–Pomerene Act Limitation

Another noteworthy limitation on the application of U.S. antitrust law to international transactions is the Webb–Pomerene Act, which exempts U.S. export associations from certain antitrust restrictions. The law was enacted with the specific goal of helping small U.S. businesses compete with export cartels sponsored by foreign governments. (For greater detail see Chapter 10.) Perhaps more than any other limitation this exemption dramatizes the nationalistic perspective of the United States, and, in fact, of any national antitrust law. It does not appear to be consistent policy to advance steadfastly the principle of international trade liberalization, maintenance of a competitive domestic market structure, and at the same time the exemptive, anticompetitive provisions of the Webb–Pomerene Act. However, until there is more evidence of the good-faith inclination of other nations to remove substantial trade barriers, the Webb–Pomerene exemption will continue to receive strong support in Congress from many proponents. In a system lacking international economic strictures, individual nations are often compelled to protect their own industry at the expense of international progress toward free trade.

The Multinational Enterprise

The single most important development in international business during the past quarter of a century has been the dramatic growth of the multinational enterprise. As we mentioned in the Preface, between 1945 and 1973 American investment in foreign firms rose from $8 billion to $107.3 billion and foreign investment in American companies from $2.5 billion to $17.7 billion. According to a 1973 study by the U.S. Tariff Commission, private institutions on the international financial scene, the majority of which are multinational enterprises, controlled $268 billion in short-term liquid assets at the end of 1971. This figure is more than twice the total of all international reserves held by all central banks and international monetary institutions in the world on the same date.

For present purposes a multinational enterprise may be defined as an enterprise with the following characteristics: (1) it conducts significant business operations in two or more countries; (2) these are carried on by legally distinct business units, which are related by common nongovernmental ownership; and (3) the operations are, at least to some extent, coordinated and controlled vertically in accordance with a common strategy. The existence of this type of enterprise gives rise to two areas of conflict. First, there is the conflict between the sovereignty of the individual country and the economic liberty and power of the multinational enterprise. Second, conflict may arise from competing claims of power to control the same enterprise made by different states. Because different members of the enterprise are chartered in different countries, there is no single law that governs the whole cluster of legally distinct entities. The recent U.N. Report on the Multinationals concluded that:

> [I]ndeed, no single national jurisdiction can cope adequately with the global phenomenon of the multinational corporation, nor is there an international authority or machinery adequately equipped to alleviate the tensions that stem from the relationship between multinational corporations and nation states.

The antitrust legal mechanism of any single country is unable to cope fully with these economic giants because the regulators—the national legal systems—are still territorially fragmented while the regulated—the business organizations and their economic practices—are transnationally integrated. Jean-Jacques Servan Schreiber has described the threat this way:

> The problem is that this new strength and political power of worldwide industry is so overpowering and the national states are so weakened in the face

of these corporations, that we are creating a new kind of jungle—a world of no law, no human law. It is a world created by the confrontation between economic giants in which the politicians, representing only their fellow citizens, have less and less say.

One practical problem where foreign-based firms are sought to be reached (dealt with in Chapter 4) is obtaining personal jurisdiction for purposes of antitrust enforcement. An alien parent or an alien subsidiary may not be subject to U.S. jurisdiction if it does not have an alter ego or agency relationship with its U.S. subsidiary or U.S. parent and does not have sufficient business contacts with the U.S. to make it *present* within its own right. Jurisdiction over only part of a multinational corporate empire may therefore be attainable. A government that can legally obtain information and enforce decrees with respect to only part of a corporate structure is easily thwarted in its effort to curb restrictive business practices.

Proposals for coping with multinational enterprises are made frequently, and the 1973 U.N. study reiterates several of the most well known. In 1967 George Ball proposed the "Cosmocorp," a denationalized corporation chartered by international law and similar to the draft EEC Company law. There would be a substantive international law with a secretariat and procedures for enforcement. Critics argue that such a law would either cover too little and is therefore not essential, or else too much, in which case nations could not reach agreement on it. Other suggestions frequently offered include a GATT-like agreement for multinational corporations, a registration of multinational corporations under the aegis of the U.N. or the negotiation of a code of behavior for multinational enterprises. All these suggestions would take several years to implement, even if the nations could today agree on one of them. In the meantime the prospect for the foreseeable future is for an increasing awareness among the separate national governments of the need for international cooperation to prevent abusive practices.

Efforts at Attaining a Supranational Antitrust Law

The need for worldwide intergovernmental cooperation in antitrust matters is dramatized by the marked limitations of domestic laws and their extraterritorial reach as detailed earlier in this chapter. It appears imperative in the long run to design international safeguards, especially to encompass the noncommunist industrialized nations where competition is intended to be a critical element of economic development and trade.

Two basic obstacles have impeded the efforts made to date to lay the groundwork for a truly international antitrust law. First, many nations see a binding international regime as inconsistent with concepts of national sovereignty and the freedom to carry out important national policies. Second, common antitrust norms do not emerge easily from widely disparate national attitudes shaped by dissimilar economic, political, and social development. There is still no consensus as to what commercial conduct, apart from the most flagrant activity, constitutes restrictive business practices that should be outlawed. There is also no agreement on the procedures for making the necessary factual and legal determinations and on the enforcement mechanisms needed to carry out decisions. Internationalists have had to cope with these same problems since the International Economic Conference at Geneva in 1927.

Reflection on these basic difficulties might tempt one to conclude that no progress has been made toward curbing restrictive business practices on an international basis. This would be an unduly gloomy conclusion. Review of the efforts made to date indicates that they have drawn the community of nations significantly closer to an understanding of common restrictive business practices and to means of cooperation in acting to curb them. It must be expected that the development of any discipline of international law, by its very nature, is a slow process; international antitrust, because of the diverse nature of world economics, will take a particularly long time.

The Havana Charter of 1948 and Its Parent American Draft

The most ambitious proposals yet devised for curbing international business restraints evolved from the United States' postwar economic philosophy of free trade. Private restrictive business practices were, like governmental tariffs and quotas, viewed as substantial barriers to the expansion of world trade and employment and, as such, were to be eliminated. The comprehensive 1945 proposals of the United States and Great Britain were translated into a draft charter released by the United States that delineated the American feeling toward restrictive business practices: any activities "which restrain competition, limit access to market, or foster monopolistic control in international trade" would have been presumed violations of this international compact. An organization called the International Trade Organization (ITO) was to be vested with the power to coordinate and implement antitrust policy. Private parties, not just member states, were to be empowered to petition the ITO with their complaints. Certain enumerated anticompetitive practices were to be considered per se violations, including price fixing, dividing markets, discriminating against firms, limiting production, suppressing technology, and misusing patent rights.

The participants in the international conference that convened in Havana to consider the American proposal failed to give it their support. What finally emerged from the conference in 1948 was a revision of the

American draft, which became officially known as the Havana Charter. Unable to reconcile differing economic policies and unwilling to relinquish national sovereignty, the participants produced a weak compromise. On the question of cartel policy, the United States, Canada, and the developing countries regarded cartels as per se harmful. A substantial bloc of European countries, with Great Britain generally in agreement, was equally adamant that combinations and cartels were an intelligent means of allocating resources even though they gave rise to abuses in some situations. The latter position was ultimately embraced in the Charter. Not only did the Havana Charter lack a code of per se violations, but its sanction provisions were very weak. The International Trade Organization could only "request each member concerned to take every possible remedial action."

The Havana Charter died in 1950, even after representatives of fifty nations signed it, because the United States failed to ratify it. The United States, the nation that initially had been the most willing to share its sovereignty with a strong investigative and enforcement organization and bind itself to a specific code of international restrictive practices, let the Charter expire in the course of hearings before the U.S. Congress because of protectionist sentiments in the nation. Even though the original American draft was not accepted, it did set an outer parameter for what might be expected from a supranational agency with a supranational code and enforcement mechanism. The Havana Charter and the draft from which it evolved were important but premature efforts.

The GATT—Finally an Agreement

After the 1950 failure of the Havana Charter and the similar fate of the U.N.'s Economic and Social Council draft in 1953, which would have coupled procedures for antitrust implementation with most of the substantive law articles of Chapter V of the Havana Charter, a natural question was whether any international organization would ever be empowered to regulate cartels. The General Agreement on Tariffs and Trade [GATT], formed in 1947, operated principally to reduce tariffs. However, in 1960 the participating governments to the GATT decided to make the "consultation principle" the basis for a new resolution against *private* restrictive business practices. The GATT agreement was simply a mild exhortation that member nations should consult and "accord sympathetic consideration to" requests for consultations on the harmful effects of any private restrictive business practices to which they were a party or their residents were a party "with a view to reaching mutually satisfactory conclusions, and if possible eliminating such harmful effects." Skeptics might question the actual usefulness of this ad hoc consultative mechanism void of any objective way to define restrictive business practices and any investigative means to illuminate the facts. Nevertheless, the resolution represented the first commitment reached among nations to cooperate in curbing the admitted evil of restrictive business practices. Eighty-one nations are now full members of the GATT, and their foreign trade represents 80 per cent of the total volume of world trade. The consultation principle of the GATT, therefore, is one tentative step in the direction of an international antitrust law.

The EEC Experience—A Successful "Regional" Supranational Regime

In spite of the substantial differences not only in the national antitrust laws of the member states, but also in their economic and political traditions, a model for intergovernmental antitrust cooperation is impressively at work in the European Economic Community. The first striking fact, as we have seen, is that the law of the EEC on questions of competition is supreme in the Community, although national antitrust law applies concurrently as long as it does not conflict with Common Market law. Second, the restrictive-practice provisions of the EEC Treaty, Articles 85 and 86, and the ECSC Treaty, Articles 65 and 66, have raised the antitrust standards with respect to most of the member countries. Indeed, Italy still does not have a national antitrust law.

Encouraging, too, in terms of an eventual reconciliation of world antitrust laws, are the points of similarity between the law of the ECC and the law of the United States. These similarities can be explained by the historical fact that the EEC law of competition is partially derived from the early U.N. studies of restrictive practices and partially from the West German law, the strictest of any of the European laws of competition, which was in turn based on the American antitrust law. As we explained in Chapter 11, however, the EEC law differs from U.S. law with respect to such concepts as per se violations and the rule of reason. The EEC also differs from the U.S. law in its policy toward mergers and in its policy that certain restraints of trade may be outweighed by beneficial effects. Thus, a common European–American standard on a number of important points, including merger policy, has by no means been reached yet.

In looking toward the eventual development of an international antitrust law, we must continue to watch developments in the EEC closely for two reasons. First, it is a supranational organization with powers of enforcement that bind private members of the nations within the Community. Its laws, policies, and proposals are the most tangible example of a supranational antitrust law. Second, on the question of attaining a common standard of competitive behavior, consistent norms must be reached by the EEC and the United States if we are to have a global policy.

OECD—The Voluntary Recommendations of the 5th of October, 1967, and OECD Investigation into Restrictive Business Practices

An integral part of international antitrust collaboration must be the exchange of information about the restrictive business practices that have international significance. Such exchanges are useful to the enforcement of national laws. They are also a prerequisite for taking common action. The Organization for Economic Cooperation and Development [OECD], consisting of twenty-three members including the nations of Western Europe, the United States, Canada, Australia, Japan, and Turkey, with New Zealand and Yugoslavia having a special status, has attempted programs of exchange.

In 1967 the OECD devised a procedural mechanism for consultation. It was patterned after the very successful Canadian–American agreement for antitrust notification and consultation known as the Fulton–Rogers Agreement, which has in turn been strengthened by the OECD Recommendation. The OECD Recommendation is more specific than the GATT resolution in setting out the exact nature of its consultation procedure. One of the organization's concerns is the possible political misunderstanding that results from the "extraterritorial" enforcement of national antitrust law (as in the *Swiss Watchmakers* case described in Chapter 3 or the *Dyestuffs* case mentioned in Chapter 11). Through the consultation procedure, countries on the verge of instituting proceedings can give advance warning and facts of the complaints to the authorities in countries where the perpetrators of the alleged antitrust violation are located. Where two or more member countries simultaneously contemplate proceedings against an international trade restraint, the consultation procedure can be used to exchange information and coordinate efforts. It has been reported that cooperation has increased in the last two years and taken on a multilateral form in an increasing number of cases. A recent example of this growing cooperation involved a report issued by the British Monopolies Commission exposing and condemning the pricing practices of a large multinational pharmaceutical firm. Copies of the report were sent to other governments, and the United States, Dutch, and German governments, as well as the Common Market Commission, quickly announced that they would undertake similar investigations.

In addition, the OECD Committee of Experts on Restrictive Business Practices meets twice a year and maintains a Guide to Legislation on Restrictive Business Practices of its member nations, which is constantly being updated with new information. The committee has also published studies and a glossary of terms relating to restrictive practices. This regular contact among the antitrust authorities of member states of the OECD Committee of Experts has helped broaden the pool of common antitrust knowledge. It has also encouraged some to suggest a further step to provide a mechanism for voluntary conciliation of differences through the committee. The committee would then be permitted to conduct a case-by-case examination of the substantive issues involved in the problems submitted for conciliation. This could lead the member countries closer to the attainment of common standards and mechanisms with respect to antitrust.

Some Concluding Observations

In any consideration of the formulation of a "truly international antitrust law," fundamental questions as to the value, nature, and structure of competition, the definition of trade restraints, and the exercise of governmental power must be addressed. These are factors about which there are intranational—not to mention international—differences of opinion. As the texture and complexity of international life develop, with increasingly interdependent national economies and more and more powerful multinational enterprises, so will the demand for international rules to help organize the economic activities and relations of nations and their citizens in the pursuit of common ends. The common end in the antitrust field is freer trade with the by-products of expansion of trade, more efficient use of resources, and economic growth. Freer trade policy facilitates access to markets for entrepreneurs and traders. Freer international trade, which results from this access, benefits the consumer by preserving his right to select in product, quality, and price from among many independent competing sellers from different nations. Furthermore, if only to gain effective control over the activities of multinational enterprises, it may well be necessary to harmonize existing antitrust laws and also to agree on new rules governing multinational activities.

As a result of twenty-five years of experiments in cooperation, some international standards as to what private restrictive practices should be controlled or prohibited, and how to control such practices, appear to be slowly emerging. This conclusion is a tentative and qualified one. For one thing, the distinction between the mere existence of parallel standards governing domestic restrictive practices and the creation of new supranational standards controlling multinational business transactions must be kept in mind. For example, many countries, including the United States, the European Communities, and Japan, exempt export activities from their antitrust laws. In this sense they all have parallel standards governing export activities. This is considerably different from an international agreement on what antitrust standards should govern export trade among nations.

Moreover, to date the various attempts at international cooperation have been centered primarily in the industrialized noncommunist countries. These nations generally recognize that national and international policies that promote competition are in their interest. Even among these nations, however, Japan is one example of a contrasting point of view. Although Japan is industrialized, has democratic institutions comparable to those of Western Europe and America, and thrives on competition internationally, her national economy is highly cartelized. In fact, many Japanese believe that a rigid national policy of competition would weaken them economically. In addition to these differences in attitude as among the democratic industrialized nations, really fundamental differences with respect to the nature and control of competition exist in comparing the former, the communist nations, and most developing nations. In short, the obstacles posed in integrating into an international antitrust scheme countries at different stages of economic development with divergent political and social institutions are sizable.

a substantive international law of antitrust and powers of enforcement is remote at this time. We have historical examples, such as the Havana Charter, and also active proposals, as in the U.N. Study on Multinational Corporations, but the current level of interest in reaching binding commitments and the areas of agreement on standards of competition are not such as to portend a global EEC. The short-term international goals seems more to be further cooperation, consultation, exchange of information and the avoidance of conflicts between national laws. Thus, until a broader international antitrust system can be fashioned, cooperation between national enforcement authorities within international organizations or bilaterally will remain the primary means for international antitrust activity. If the industrial nations of the world choose to remain interested in international competition and do not retreat behind protective national barriers, fresh opportunities for the development of an international antitrust law and mechanism will continue to present themselves.

appendix I

Selected Bibliography

GENERAL WORKS

ABA Antitrust Developments 1955–1968, Supplement to the Report of the Attorney General's National Committee to Study the Antitrust Laws, 1955. (Chicago: ABA, 1968).

Brewster, *Antitrust and American Business Abroad* (New York: McGraw-Hill Book Company, 1958).

Fugate, *Foreign Commerce and the Antitrust Laws* (Boston: Little, Brown & Co., 2d ed. 1973).

Kintner, *An Antitrust Primer* (New York: Macmillan Publishing Co., Inc., 2d ed. 1973).

Report of the Attorney General's National Committee to Study the Antitrust Laws (Washington, D.C.: Government Printing Office, 1955).

chapter 1:
International Antitrust: Overview of Antitrust
Development Around the World

Beach, *A Treatise on the Law of Monopolies and Industrial Trusts as Administered in England and in the United States of America* (St. Louis: Central Law Journal Co., 1898).

Carnegie, *The Empire of Business* (Garden City, N.Y.: Doubleday & Company, Inc., 1902).

Edwards, *Control of Cartels and Monopolies: An International Comparison* (Dobbs Ferry, N.Y.: Oceana Publications, Inc., 1967).

Kaysen and Turner, *Antitrust Policy: An Economic and Legal Analysis* (Cambridge, Mass.: Harvard University Press, 1959).

Neale, *The Antitrust Laws of the U.S.A.* (New York: Cambridge University Press, 2d ed. 1970).

Organization for Economic Cooperation and Development, *Guide to Legislation on Restrictive Business Practices* (Paris: OECD, Looseleaf Updated Quarterly, 3d ed. 1971).

Reynolds, *The Control of Competition in Canada* (Cambridge, Mass.: Harvard University Press, 1940).

Thorelli, *The Federal Antitrust Policy* (Baltimore: The Johns Hopkins Press, 1955).

Van Cise, *The Federal Antitrust Laws* (Washington, D.C.: American Enterprise Institute for Public Policy Research, 2d ed. rev. 1967).

Wilberforce, Campbell, and Elles, *The Law of Restrictive Trade Practices and Monopolies* (London: Sweet & Maxwell, 2d ed. 1966 and Supp. 1973).

chapter 2:
Survey of the Pertinent United States
Antitrust and Trade Regulation Laws

CASES

Corn Products Refining Co. v. *FTC*, 324 U.S. 726 (1945).

FTC v. *Beech-Nut Packing Co.*, 257 U.S. 441 (1922).

FTC v. *Bunte Brothers, Inc.*, 312 U.S. 349 (1941).

FTC v. *Cement Institute*, 333 U.S. 683, *rehearing denied*, 334 U.S. 839 (1948).

FTC v. *Keppel & Brothers, Inc.*, 291 U.S. 304 (1934).

FTC v. *Motion Picture Advertising Service Co.*, 344 U.S. 392 (1953).

FTC v. *Raladam Co.*, 283 U.S. 643 (1931).

Fashion Originators' Guild of America v. *FTC*, 312 U.S. 457 (1941).

Fosburgh v. *California & Hawaiian Sugar Refining Co.*, 291 F. 29 (9th Cir. 1923).

Guziak v. *FTC*, 361 F.2d 700 (8th Cir. 1966), *cert. denied*, 385 U.S. 1007 (1967).

Nash v. *United States*, 229 U.S. 373 (1913).

Northern Pacific Ry. v. *United States,* 356 U.S. 1 (1958).

Shreveport Macaroni Manufacturing Co. v. *FTC,* 321 F.2d 404 (5th Cir. 1963).

Standard Oil Co. of New Jersey v. *United States,* 221 U.S. 1 (1911).

Swift & Company v. *United States,* 196 U.S. 375 (1905).

United States v. *Addyston Pipe & Steel Co.* 85 F. 271 (6th Cir. 1898), *modified & aff'd,* 175 U.S. 211 (1899).

United States v. *General Dyestuff Corp.,* 57 F. Supp. 642 (S.D.N.Y. 1944).

United States v. *General Electric Co.,* 80 F. Supp. 989 (S.D.N.Y. 1948).

United States v. *General Electric Co.,* 82 F. Supp. 753 (D.N.J. 1949).

United States v. *Sisal Sales Corp.,* 274 U.S. 268 (1927).

United States v. *Topco Associates, Inc.,* 405 U.S. 596 (1972).

United States v. *Women's Sportswear Manufacturers Association,* 336 U.S. 460 (1949).

chapter 3
Subject Matter Jurisdiction: When Does U.S.
Antitrust Law Apply?

Beausang, *The Extraterritorial Jurisdiction of the Sherman Act,* 70 Dick. L. Rev. 187 (1966).

Fugate, *Antitrust Aspects of Transatlantic Investment,* 34 L. & Contemp. Prob. 135 (1969).

Maw, *United States Antitrust Law Abroad—The Enduring Problem of Extraterritoriality,* 40 ABA Antitrust L. J. 796 (1971).

Note, *Act of State Doctrine—Antitrust Law,* 12 Va. J. Int'l. L. 413 (1972).

Note, *Antitrust Law—U.S. Foreign Shipping,* 5 Tex. Int'l. L. F. 176 (1969).

Note, *International Law—Extraterritoriality, Antitrust Law—Development of the Defense of Sovereign Compulsion,* 69 Mich. L. Rev. 888 (1971).

Restatement (Second) Foreign Relations Law of the United States (St. Paul, Minn.: American Law Institute Publishers 1965).

Steiner and Vagts, *Transnational Legal Problems* (Mineola, N.Y.: Foundation Press, 1968).

Timberg, *Antitrust and Foreign Trade,* 48 Nw. U. L. Rev. 411 (1953).

Trautman, *A Study of the International Environment: The International Reach of American Regulatory Legislation Other Than The Sherman Act,* in *Antitrust and American Business Abroad,* 309–49 (Brewster, ed. New York: McGraw-Hill Book Co., 1958).

CASES

American Banana Co. v. *United Fruit Co.*, 213 U.S. 347 (1909).

Banco Nacional de Cuba v. *Sabbatino*, 173 F. Supp. 375 (S.D.N.Y. 1961), *aff'd*, 307 F.2d 845 (2d Cir. 1962), *rev'd*, 376 U.S. 398 (1964).

Branch v. *FTC*, 141 F.2d 31 (7th Cir. 1944).

British Nylon Spinners Ltd. v. *Imperial Chemical Industries, Ltd.*, [1952] 2 All E. R. 780 (C.A.).

British Nylon Spinners Ltd. v. *Imperial Chemical Industries, Ltd.*, [1954] 3 All E. R. 88 (Ch.).

Consumers Union of U.S., Inc. v. *Rogers,* 352 F. Supp. 1319 (D. D.C. 1973), appeal pending 73–1095, 73–1113, 73–1135, 73–1138 (D.C. Cir. 1974).

Continental Ore Co. v. *Union Carbide & Carbon Corp.,* 370 U.S. 690 (1962).

Gibbons v. *Ogden,* 9 Wheat. 362, 6 L. Ed. 23 (1824).

Interamerican Refining Corp. v. *Texaco Maracaibo, Inc.,* 307 F. Supp. 1291 (D. Del. 1970).

Joseph Muller Corp. Zurich v. *Société Anonyme de Gerance et d'Armements,* 451 F.2d 727 (2d Cir. 1971), *cert. denied,* 406 U.S. 906 (1972).

Occidental Petroleum Corp. v. *Buttes Gas & Oil Co.,* 331 F. Supp. 92 (C.D. Cal. 1971), *aff'd,* 461 F.2d 1261 (9th Cir. 1972), *cert. denied,* 409 U.S. 950 (1972).

Pacific Seafarers, Inc. v. *Pacific Far East Line, Inc.,* 404 F.2d 804 (D.C. Cir. 1968), *cert. denied,* 393 U.S. 1093 (1969).

Sanib Corp. v. *United Fruit Co.,* 135 F. Supp. 764 (S.D.N.Y. 1955).

Standard Oil Co. of New Jersey v. *United States,* 221 U.S. 1 (1911).

Thomsen v. *Cayser,* 243 U.S. 66 (1917).

United States v. *Aluminum Co. of America,* 148 F.2d 416 (2d Cir. 1945).

United States v. *American Tobacco Co.,* 221 U.S. 106 (1911).

United States v. *General Electric Co.,* 82 F. Supp. 753 (D. N.J. 1949).

United States v. *General Electric Co.,* 115 F. Supp. 835 (D. N.J. 1953).

United States v. *Holophane Co.,* 119 F. Supp. 114 (S.D. Ohio 1954), 1954 Trade Cases ¶67,679 (judgment) (S.D. Ohio 1954), *aff'd per curiam,* 352 U.S. 903 (1956).

United States v. *Imperial Chemical Industries, Ltd.,* 105 F. Supp. 215 (S.D.N.Y. 1952).

United States v. *Learner Co.,* 215 F. Supp. 602 (D. Hawaii 1963).

United States v. *Minnesota Mining & Manufacturing Co.,* 92 F. Supp. 947 (D. Mass. 1950).

United States v. *National Lead Co.*, 63 F. Supp. 513 (S.D.N.Y. 1945), *aff'd*, 332 U.S. 319 (1947).

United States v. *R. P. Oldham Co.*, 152 F. Supp. 818 (N.D. Cal. 1957).

United States v. *Sisal Sales Corp.*, 274 U.S. 268 (1927).

United States v. *Timken Roller Bearing Co.*, 83 F. Supp. 284 (N.D. Ohio 1949), *modified & aff'd*, 341 U.S. 593 (1951).

United States v. *Watchmakers of Switzerland Information Center, Inc.*, 1963 Trade Cas. ¶70,600 (S.D.N.Y. 1962), *order modified*, 1965 Trade Cas. ¶71,352 (S.D.N.Y. 1965).

chapter 4:
Procedural and Related Considerations

Brewster, *Extraterritorial Effects of the U.S. Antitrust Laws*, 11 ABA Antitrust Section 65 (1957).

Comment, *Antitrust Venue: Transacting Business Under the Clayton Act*, 55 Geo. L.J. 1066 (1967).

Comment, *Creditor's Remedies: Foreign Attachment Held to Meet Due Process Requirements*, 57 Minn. L. Rev. 396 (1972).

Comment, *Venue in Private Antitrust Suits*, 37 N.Y.U.L. Rev. 268 (1962).

Davis, *Investigations by the Department of Justice—As Seen by the Potential Defendant*, 29 ABA Antitrust Section 54 (1965).

Foster, *Judicial Economy: Fairness and Convenience of Place of Trial: Long-Arm Jurisdiction in District Courts*, 47 F.R.D. 73 (1969).

Golomb, *Recognition of Foreign Money Judgments: A Goal Oriented Approach*, 43 St. John's L. Rev. 604 (1969).

Jessup, *Transnational Law* (New Haven, Conn.: Yale University Press 1956).

Jones, *International Judicial Assistance: Procedural Chaos and a Program for Reform*, 62 Yale L.J. 515 (1953).

Jurisdiction with Respect to Crime, 29 Am. J. Int. L. Supp. 435 (1935).

Kaplan, *Amendments of the Federal Rules of Civil Procedure, 1961–1963* (pts. 1–2), 77 Harv. L. Rev. 601, 801 (1964).

Kilgore, *Antitrust Judgements and Their Enforcement*, 4 ABA Antitrust Section 102 (1954).

Kintner, *Post-Hearing Procedures and Compliance*, 4 ABA Antitrust Section 196 (1954).

Kintner, *Recent Changes in Federal Trade Commission Discovery Practice*, 37 ABA Antitrust L.J. 238 (1968).

Moore, *Federal Practice* (New York: Matthew Bender & Co., 2d ed. 1953).

Moore, Vestal and Kurland, *Moore's Manual: Federal Practice and Procedure* (New York: Matthew Bender & Co., 1966).

Nadelmann, *French Courts Recognize Foreign Money-Judgments: One Down and More to Go*, 13 Am. J. Comp. L. 72 (1964).

Needham and Pollack, *Collecting Claims and Enforcing Judgments* (New York: Practicing Law Institute 1969).

Note, *Attachment of Subsidiary's Assets in Action Against Parent Corporation*, 12 Stan. L. Rev. 854 (1960).

Note, *Doing Business as a Test of Venue and Jurisdiction Over Foreign Corporations in the Federal Courts,* 56 Colum. L. Rev. 394 (1956).

Note, *Federal Practice: Venue in Actions Against Corporations*, 19 Okla. L. Rev. 197 (1966).

Note, *Legislative Survey: Convention on the Taking of Evidence Abroad in Civil or Commercial Matters*, 5 L. & Pol. Int'l Bus. 837, 906-919 (1973).

Note, *Limitations on the Federal Judicial Power to Compel Acts Violating Foreign Law*, 63 Colum. L. Rev. 1441 (1963).

Note, *Subpoena of Documents Located in Foreign Jurisdictions Where Law of Situs Prohibits Removal*, 37 N.Y.U.L. Rev. 296 (1962).

Onkelinx, *Conflict of International Jurisdiction: Ordering the Production of Documents in Violation of the Law of the Situs*, 64 Nw. U. L. Rev. 487 (1969).

Price, *International Judicial Cooperation and the Practicing Lawyer*, 27 J. Mo. Bar 264 (1971).

Rashid, *New Trends in Antitrust Investigation*, 37 ABA Antitrust L.J. 188 (1967).

Restatement (Second) Foreign Relations Law of the United States (St. Paul, Minn.: American Law Institute Publishers, 1965).

Smit, *International Aspects of Federal Civil Procedure*, 61 Colum. L. Rev. 1031 (1961).

Smit, *International Litigation Under the United States Code*, 65 Colum. L. Rev. 1015 (1965).

Timberg, *International Combines and National Sovereigns: A Study in Conflict of Laws and Mechanisms*, 95 U. Pa. L. Rev. 575 (1947).

2 United Nations, *Laws and Regulations on the Regime of the High Seas: Laws Relating to Jurisdiction over Crimes Committed Abroad or on the High Seas* (New York: United Nations, 1952).

Vestal, *Expanding the Jurisdictional Reach of the Federal Courts: The 1963 Changes in Federal Rule 4*, 38 N.Y.U.L. Rev. 1053 (1963).

Ward, *The Federal Trade Commission and Unfair Methods of Competition in Foreign Commerce*, 40 ABA Antitrust L.J. 806 (1971).

Wengler, *Laws Concerning Unfair Competition and the Conflict of Laws*, 4 Am. J. Comp. L. 167 (1955).

Williams, *Investigations by the Department of Justice*, 29 ABA Antitrust Section 50 (1965).

Wright and Miller, *Federal Practice and Procedure* (St. Paul, Minn.: West Publishing Co., 1973).

CASES

ABC Great States, Inc. v. *Globe Ticket Co.*, 304 F. Supp. 1052 (N.D. Ill. 1969).

Adams Dairy Co. v. *National Dairy Products Corp.*, 293 F. Supp. 1135 (W.D. Mo. 1968).

Adams v. *FTC*, 296 F.2d 861 (8th Cir. 1961).

Advertising Specialty National Association v. *FTC*, 238 F.2d 108 (1st Cir. 1956).

Albert Levine Associates v. *Bertoni & Cotti*, 309 F. Supp. 456 (S.D.N.Y. 1970).

Albert Levine Associates v. *Bertoni & Cotti, S.p.A.*, 314 F. Supp. 169 (S.D.N.Y. 1970).

Ambatielos v. *Foundation Co.*, 203 Misc. 470, 116 N.Y.S. 2d (1952).

American Anthracite and Bituminous Coal Corp. v. *American S. S. Co.*, 131 F. Supp. 244 (E.D. Pa. 1955).

American Industrial Contracting, Inc. v. *Johns-Mansville Corp.*, 326 F. Supp. 879 (W.D. Pa. 1971).

Application of Chase Manhattan Bank, 192 F. Supp. 817 (S.D.N.Y. 1961), *aff'd*, 297 F.2d 611 (2d Cir. 1962).

Ash Grove Cement Co., [1970–1973 Transfer Binder] Trade Reg. Rep. ¶19,349 (FTC 1970).

Banco Nacional de Cuba v. *Sabbatino*, 376 U.S. 398 (1964).

Blackmer v. *United States*, 284 U.S. 421 (1931).

British Nylon Spinners v. *Imperial Chemical Industries, Ltd.*, [1952] 2 All E.R. 780 (C.A.).

British Nylon Spinners v. *Imperial Chemical Industries, Ltd.*, [1954] 3 All E.R. 88 (Ch.).

Brown v. *Beckham*, 137 F.2d 644 (6th Cir. 1943), *cert. denied*, 320 U.S. 803 (1944).

Brunette Machine Works, Ltd. v. *Kockum Industries, Inc.,* 406 U.S. 706 (1972).

California Clippers, Inc. v. *United States Soccer Football Association,* 314 F. Supp. 1057 (N.D. Cal. 1970).

Cannon Manufacturing Co. v. *Cudahy Packing Co.,* 267 U.S. 333 (1925).

Charles Pfizer & Co. v. *Laboratori Pro-Ter Prodotti Therapeutici,* S.p.A., 287 F. Supp. 148 (S.D.N.Y. 1967).

De Beers Consolidated Mines, Ltd. v. *United States,* 325 U.S. 212 (1945).

Det Bergenske Dampskibsselskab v. *Sabre Shipping Corp.,* 341 F.2d 50 (2d Cir. 1965).

Eastman Kodak Co. v. *Southern Photo Materials Co.,* 273 U.S. 359 (1927).

Edward J. Moriarty & Co. v. *General Tire & Rubber Co.,* 289 F. Supp. 381 (S.D. Ohio 1967).

FTC v. *Bowman,* 248 F.2d 456 (7th Cir. 1957).

FTC v. *Browning,* 435 F.2d 96 (D.C. Cir. 1970).

FTC v. *Tuttle,* 244 F.2d 605 (2d Cir. 1957), *cert. denied,* 354 U.S. 925 (1957).

Falsone v. *United States,* 205 F.2d 734 (5th Cir. 1953), *cert. denied,* 346 U.S. 864 (1953).

First National City Bank v. *IRS,* 271 F.2d 616 (2d Cir. 1959), *cert. denied,* 361 U.S. 948 (1960).

Fox-Keller, Inc. v. *Toyota Motor Sales, U.S.A.,* 338 F. Supp. 812 (E.D. Pa. 1972).

Fuentes v. *Shevin,* 407 U.S. 67 (1972).

Gillars v. *United States,* 182 F.2d 962 (D.C. Cir. 1950).

Gulf Oil Corp v. *Gilbert,* 330 U.S. 501 (1947).

Hawkins v. *National Basketball Association,* 288 F. Supp. 614 (W.D. Pa. 1968).

Hilton v. *Guyot,* 159 U.S. 113 (1895).

Hirshhorn v. *Hirshhorn,* 278 App. Div. 1006, 105 N.Y.S.2d 628 (App. Div. 1951).

Hoffman Motors Corp. v. *Alfa Romeo, S. p. A.,* 244 F. Supp. 70 (S.D.N.Y. 1965).

Horwitz v. *United States,* 63 F.2d 706 (5th Cir. 1933), *cert. denied,* 289 U.S. 760 (1932).

Illinois v. *Harper & Row Publishers, Inc.,* 308 F. Supp. 1207 (N.D. Ill. 1969).

Ings v. *Ferguson*, 282 F.2d 149 (2d Cir. 1960).

In re Ampicillin Antitrust Litigation, M.D.L. Dkt. No. 50 (Misc. No. 45–70) (D. D.C., filed Nov. 4, 1970).

In re Grand Jury Investigation of the Shipping Industry, 186 F. Supp. 298 (D. D.C. 1960).

In re Investigation of World Arrangements with Relation to the Production, Transportation, Refining and Distribution of Petroleum, 13 F.R.D. 280 (D. D.C. 1952).

International Shoe Co. v. *Washington,* 326 U.S. 310 (1945).

Japan Gas Lighter Association v. *Ronson Corp.,* 257 F. Supp. 219 (D. N.J. 1966).

Johnston v. *Compagnie General Transatlantique,* 242 N.Y. 381, 152 N.E. 121 (Ct. App. 1926).

Kritzik v. *FTC,* 125 F.2d 351 (7th Cir. 1942).

Kurt M. Jachmann, Co. v. *Hartley, Cooper & Co.,* 16 F.R.D. 565 (S.D.N.Y. 1954).

Lawlor v. *National Screen Service Corp.,* 10 F.R.D. 123 (E.D. Pa. 1950).

Lehigh Portland Cement Co., [1967–1970 Transfer Binder] Trade Reg. Rep.

¶ 18,265 (FTC 1968).

Levin v. *Ruby Trading Corp.,* 248 F. Supp. 537 (S.D.N.Y. 1965).

Levine Associates v. *Bertoni & Cotti,* 314 F. Supp. 167 (S.D.N.Y. 1970).

McCloskey v. *Chase Manhattan Bank,* 11 N.Y.2d 936, 228 N.Y.S.2d 825 (Ct. App. 1962).

McNeil v. *Director,* 407 U.S. 245 (1972).

Montship Lines, Ltd. v. *FMB,* 295 F.2d 147 (D.C. Cir. 1961).

Morton Buildings of Nebraska, Inc. v. *Morton Buildings, Inc.,* 333 F. Supp. 187 (D. Neb. 1971).

National Petroleum Refiners Association v. *FTC,* 482 F.2d 672 (D.C. Cir. 1973).

New York v. *Morton Salt Co.,* 266 F. Supp. 570 (E.D. Pa. 1967), *aff'd,* 385 F.2d 122 (3d Cir. 1967), *cert. denied,* 390 U.S. 995 (1968).

Oklahoma Press Publishing Co. v. *Walling,* 327 U.S. 186 (1945).

O.S.C. Corporation and O.S.C. Corporation of California v. *Toshiba America, Inc. and Tokyo Shibaura Electric Co., Ltd.,* 491 F.2d 1064 (9th Cir. 1974).

Philadelphia Housing Authority v. *American Radiator & Standard Sanitary Corp.*, 291 F. Supp. 252 (E.D. Pa. 1968).

Philadelphia v. *Morton Salt Co.*, 289 F. Supp. 723 (E.D. Pa. 1968).

Pure Oil Co. v. *Suarez*, 384 U.S. 202 (1966).

Quartet Manufacturing Co. v. *Allied Traders Ltd.*, 343 F. Supp. 1302 (N.D. Ill. 1972).

River Plate Corp. v. *Forestal Land, Timber & Ry. Co.*, 185 F. Supp. 832 S.D.N.Y. 1960).

School District v. *Harper & Row Publishers, Inc.*, 267 F. Supp. 1006 (E.D. Pa. 1967).

Scriptomatic, Inc. v. *Agfa-Gevaert, Inc.*, 1973–1 Trade Cas. ¶74,594 (S.D.N.Y. 1973).

SEC v. *Minas de Artemisa, S.A.*, 150 F.2d 215 (9th Cir. 1945).

SEC v. *VTR, Inc.*, 39 F.R.D. 19 (S.D.N.Y. 1966).

Seilon, Inc. v. *Brema, S.p.A.*, 271 F. Supp. 516 (N.D. Ohio, 1967).

Société Internationale pour Participations Industrielles et Commerciales, S.A. v. *McGrath*, 11 F.R.D. 294 (D. D.C. 1951).

Société Internationale pour Participations Industrielles et Commerciales, S.A. v. *Rogers*, 357 U.S. 197 (1958).

Steele v. *Bulova Watch Co.*, 344 U.S. 280 (1952).

Stewart v. *Bus & Car Co.*, 293 F. Supp. 577 (N.D. Ohio 1968).

The J. B. Austin, Jr., 1 F.2d 451 (E.D.N.Y. 1924).

The Case of the S.S. "Lotus," Pub. Permanent Ct. Int'l Justice, Ser. A., No. 10 (The Hague 1927).

Uebersee Finanz - Korporation v. *Brownell*, 121 F. Supp. 420 (D. D.C. 1954).

United States v. *5,898 Cases of Sardines*, Ad. No. 105-37 (S.D.N.Y. 1930), CCH *Federal Antitrust Laws, with Summary of Cases Instituted by the United States*, Case No. 373.

United States v. *383,340 Ounces of Quinine Derivative*, Ad. No. 98–242 (S.D. N.Y. 1928), CCH *Federal Antitrust Laws, with Summary of Cases Instituted by the United States*, Case No. 341.

United States v. *A.B.C. Canning Co.*, Eq. No. 54-93 (S.D.N.Y. 1930), CCH *Federal Antitrust Laws, with Summary of Cases Instituted by the United States*, Case No. 374.

United States v. *Aluminum Co. of America*, 20 F. Supp. 13 (S.D.N.Y. 1937).

United States v. *Aluminum Co. of America*, 148 F.2d 416 (2d Cir. 1945).

United States v. *American Tobacco Co.,* 164 F. 700 (S.D.N.Y. 1908), *rev'd,* 221 U.S. 106 (1911).

United States v. *De Beers Consolidated Mines, Ltd.,* Civ. No. 29–446 (S.D. N.Y. 1948); 1948–1949 Trade Cas. ¶62,248.

United States v. *N.V. Amsterdamsche Chininefabriek,* Eq. No. 44–384 (S.D. N.Y. 1928), CCH *Federal Antitrust Laws, with Summary of Cases Instituted by the United States,* Case No. 3371.

United States v. *One Hundred and Seventy-five Cases of Cigarettes,* Cr. No. 9506-02 (E.D. Va. 1907), CCH *Federal Antitrust Laws, with Summary of Cases Instituted by the United States,* Case No. 52.

United States v. *First National City Bank,* 396 F.2d 897 (2d Cir. 1968).

United States v. *First National City Bank,* 379 U.S. 378 (1965).

United States v. *General Electric Co.,* 115 F. Supp. 835 (D. N.J. 1953).

United States v. *Glaxo Group, Ltd.,* 302 F. Supp. 1 (D. D.C. 1969), *rev'd,* 410 U.S. 52 (1973).

United States v. *Haim,* 218 F. Supp. 922 (S.D.N.Y. 1963).

United States v. *Holophane Co.,* 119 F. Supp. 114 (S.D. Ohio 1954), *aff'd per curiam,* 352 U.S. 903 (1956); decree *reprinted in,* 1954 Trade Cas. ¶67,679.

United States v. *Imperial Chemical Industries, Ltd.,* 105 F. Supp. 215 (S.D. N.Y. 1952).

United States v. *Morton Salt Co.,* 338 U.S. 632 (1950).

United States v. *National Lead Co.,* 63 F. Supp. 513 (S.D.N.Y. 1945), *modified & aff'd,* 332 U.S. 319 (1947).

United States v. *N. V. Nederlandsche Combinatie Voor Chemische Industrie,* Civ. No. 70–2080 (S.D.N.Y., filed May 21, 1970).

United States v. *N. V. Nederlandsche Combinatie Voor Chemische Industrie,* Civ. No. 70–2079 (S.D.N.Y., filed May 21, 1970).

United States v. *N. V. Nederlandsche Combinatie Voor Chemische Industrie,* Crim. No. 68CR870 (S.D.N.Y., filed Oct. 25, 1968).

United States v. *Pink,* 315 U.S. 203 (1942).

United States v. *Proctor & Gamble Co.,* 356 U.S. 677 (1958).

United States v. *Scophony Corp. of America,* 333 U.S. 795 (1948).

United States v. *Standard Oil Co. (N.J.),* 23 F.R.D. 1 (S.D.N.Y. 1958).

United States v. *Timken Roller Bearing Co.,* 83 F. Supp. 284 (N.D. Ohio 1949), *modified & aff'd,* 341 U.S. 593 (1951).

United States v. *Watchmakers of Switzerland Information Center, Inc.*, 133 F. Supp. 40 (S.D.N.Y. 1955), *reargument denied*, 134 F. Supp. 710 (S.D.N.Y. 1955), *dismissed* as to Information Center, 1963 Trade Cas. ¶70,600 (S.D.N.Y. 1962), *order modified*, 1965 Trade Cas. ¶71,362 (S.D.N.Y. 1965).

Uphaus v. *Wyman*, 360 U.S. 72 (1959).

Vanity Fair Mills v. *T. Eaton Co.*, 234 F.2d 633 (2d Cir. 1956), *cert. denied*, 362 U.S. 871 (1956), *rehearing denied*, 352 U.S. 913 (1956).

Weitzel v. *Weitzel*, 27 Ariz. 117, 230 P. 1106 (1924).

chapter 5:
Contracts, Conspiracies, and Monopolization in
Foreign Commerce

Chadwell, *Legal Tests for Violation of Section 2 of the Sherman Act and Section 7 of the Clayton Act in the Light of the Cellophane Opinion*, 2 Antitrust Bull. 499 (1957).

Cox, *Competition and Section 2 of the Sherman Act*, 27 ABA Antitrust Section 72 (1965).

Handler, *Twenty-five Years of Antitrust* (New York: Matthew Bender & Co., 1973).

Kramer, *The Application of the Sherman Act to Foreign Commerce*, 41 Marq. L. Rev. 270 (1957).

McAllister, *Where the Effect May Be to Substantially Lessen Competition or Tend to Create a Monopoly, Proceedings,* 3 ABA Antitrust Section 124 (1953).

CASES

Albrecht v. *Herald Co.*, 390 U.S. 145, *rehearing denied*, 390 U.S. 1018 (1968).

Alfred Bell & Co. v. *Catalda Fine Arts*, 191 F.2d 99 (2d Cir. 1951).

Eastern States Retail Lumber Dealers' Association v. *United States,* 234 U.S. 66 (1914).

FTC v. *Cement Institute*, 333 U.S. 683 (1948).

Fashion Originators' Guild of America, Inc. v. *FTC*, 312 U.S. 457 (1941).

Northern Pacific Ry. Co. v. *United States*, 356 U.S. 1 (1958).

Radiant Burners, Inc: v. *People's Gas Light & Coke Co.*, 364 U.S. 656 (1961).

Standard Oil Co. of New Jersey v. *United States*, 221 U.S. 1 (1911).

Theatre Enterprises, Inc. v. *Paramount Film Distributing Corp.* 346 U.S. 537 (1954).

United States v. *Aluminum Co. of America,* 148 F.2d 416 (2d Cir. 1945).

United States v. *American Society of Mechanical Engineers, Inc., and the National Board of Boiler and Pressure Vessel Inspectors,* 1972 Trade Cas. ¶74,028, ¶74,029 (S.D.N.Y. 1972).

United States v. *American Tobacco Co.,* 221 U.S. 106 (1911).

United States v. *Bausch & Lomb Optical Co.,* 34 F. Supp. 267 (S.D.N.Y. 1940).

United States v. *Container Corp. of America,* 393 U.S. 333 (1969).

United States v. *De Beers Consolidated Mines, Ltd.,* Civ. 29–446 (S.D.N.Y.), unreported opinion, 1944-1945 Trade Cas. ¶57,354 (S.D.N.Y 1945), *rev'd,* 325 U.S. 212 (1945).

United States v. *E. I. DuPont de Nemours & Co.,* 351 U.S. 377 (1956).

United States v. *General Electric Co.,* 115 F. Supp. 835 (D. N.J. 1953).

United States v. *General Electric Co.,* 82 F. Supp. 753 (D. N.J. 1949).

United States v. *Griffith,* 334 U.S. 100 (1948).

United States v. *Grinnell Corp.,* 384 U.S. 563 (1966).

United States v. *International Nickel Co. of Canada, Ltd.,* Civ. 36–31, (S.D. N.Y., filed May 16, 1946), CCH *Fed. Antitrust Laws, with Summary of Cases* (1890–1951), Case No. 849 (1952); consent judgment entered July 2, 1948, 1948–1949 Trade Cas. ¶62,280.

United States v. *Material Handling Institute, Inc.,* 1973–1 Trade Cas. ¶74,362 (W.D. Pa. 1973).

United States v. *Minnesota Mining & Manufacturing Co.,* 92 F. Supp. 947 (D. Mass. 1950).

United States v. *National Lead Co.,* 63 F. Supp. 513 (S.D.N.Y. 1945), *aff'd,* 332 U.S. 319 (1947).

United States v. *Sisal Sales Corp.,* 274 U.S. 268 (1927).

United States v. *Socony Vacuum Oil Co., Inc.,* 310 U.S. 150 (1940).

United States v. *Timken Roller Bearing Co.,* 83 F. Supp. 284 (N.D. Ohio 1949), *modified & aff'd,* 341 U.S. 593 (1951).

United States v. *United States Alkali Export Association,* 86 F. Supp. 59 (S.D. N.Y. 1949).

United States v. *Watchmakers of Switzerland Information Center, Inc.,* 1963 Trade Cas. ¶70,600 (S.D.N.Y. 1962), *order modified,* 1965 Trade Cas. ¶71,352 (S.D.N.Y. 1965).

chapter 6:
Relations with Suppliers and Customers

Fulda, *Individual Refusals to Deal: When Does Single-Firm Conduct Become Vertical Restraint?*, 30 Law & Contemp. Prob. 590 (1965).

Levi, *The Parke, Davis–Colgate Doctrine: The Ban on Resale Price Maintenance*, 1960 Sup. Ct. Rev. 258 (Chicago: University of Chicago Press. The Law School, University of Chicago, 1960).

Turner, *The Definition of Agreement Under the Sherman Act: Conscious Parallelism and Refusals to Deal*, 75 Harv. L. Rev. 655 (1962).

Wheeler, *Some Observations on Tie-Ins, The Single Product Defense, Exclusive Dealing and Regulated Industries*, 60 Calif. L. Rev. 1557 (1972).

CASES

Albrecht v. *Herald Co.*, 390 U.S. 145 (1968).

Alfred Bell & Co. v. *Catalda Fine Arts, Inc.*, 191 F.2d 99 (2d Cir. 1951).

Brown Shoe Co. v. *United States*, 370 U.S. 294 (1962).

Cherokee Laboratories Inc. v. *Rotary Drilling Services, Inc.*, 383 F.2d 97 (5th Cir. 1967).

Dr. Miles Medical Co. v. *John D. Park & Sons*, 220 U.S. 373 (1911).

FTC v. *Beech-Nut Packing Co.*, 257 U.S. 441 (1922).

FTC v. *Brown Shoe Co.*, 384 U.S. 316 (1966).

Fortner Enterprises, Inc. v. *United States Steel Corp.*, 394 U.S. 495 (1969).

Northern Pacific Ry. Co. v. *United States*, 356 U.S. 1 (1958).

Packard Motor Car Co. v. *Webster Motor Car Co.*, 243 F.2d 418 (D.C. Cir. 1957), *cert. denied*, 355 U.S. 822 (1957).

Schwing Motor Co. v. *Hudson Sales Corp.*, 138 F. Supp. 899 (D. Md. 1956), *aff'd per curiam*, 239 F.2d 176 (4th Cir. 1956), *cert. denied*, 355 U.S. 823 (1957).

Siegel v. *Chicken Delight, Inc.*, 311 F. Supp. 847 (N.D. Cal. 1970), *modified*, 448 F.2d 43 (9th Cir. 1971), *cert. denied*, 405 U.S. 955 (1972).

Tampa Electric Co. v. *Nashville Coal Co.*, 365 U.S. 320 (1961).

United States v. *Arnold, Schwinn & Co.*, 388 U.S. 365 (1967).

United States v. *Bausch & Lomb Optical Co.*, 45 F. Supp. 387 (S.D.N.Y. 1942), *aff'd by equally divided ct.*, 321 U.S. 707 (1944).

United States v. *Chicago Tribune—New York News Syndicate, Inc.*, 309 F. Supp. 1301 (S.D.N.Y. 1970).

United States v. *Colgate & Co.*, 250 U.S. 300 (1919).

United States v. *General Dyestuff Corp.*, 57 F. Supp. 642 (S.D.N.Y. 1944).

United States v. *Glaxo Group, Ltd.*, 302 F. Supp. 1 (D. D.C. 1969).

United States v. *Glaxo Group, Ltd.*, 328 F. Supp. 709 (D. D.C. 1970), *rev'd on other grounds*, 410 U.S. 52 (1973).

United States v. *Imperial Chemical Industries, Ltd.*, 105 F. Supp. 215 (S.D. N.Y. 1952).

United States v. *Loew's Inc.*, 371 U.S. 38 (1962).

United States v. *Minnesota Mining & Manufacturing Co.*, 92 F. Supp. 947 (D. Mass. 1950).

United States v. *Parke, Davis & Co.*, 362 U.S. 29 (1960).

United States v. *Timken Roller Bearing Co.*, 83 F. Supp. 284 (N.D. Ohio 1949), *modified & aff'd*, 341 U.S. 593 (1951).

United States v. *United Fruit Co.*, 1958 Trade Cas. ¶68,941 (E.D. La. 1958).

White Motor Co. v. *United States*, 372 U.S. 253 (1963).

chapter 7:
The Federal Trade Commission and Robinson–Patman
Acts in International Commerce

4 Callmann, *The Law of Unfair Competition, Trademarks and Monopolies*, §94.6(b) (Mundelein, Ill.: Callaghan & Co., 3d ed. 1970).

Kintner, *A Robinson-Patman Primer* (New York: Macmillan Publishing Co., Inc., 1970).

Patman, *Complete Guide to the Robinson-Patman Act* (Englewood Cliffs, N.J.: Prentice-Hall, Inc., 1963).

6 von Kalinowski, *Antitrust Laws and Trade Regulation* (New York: Matthew Bender & Co., 1971).

Ward, *The Federal Trade Commission and Unfair Methods of Competition in Foreign Commerce*, 40 ABA Antitrust L. J., 806 (1971).

CASES

Advertising Specialty National Association v. *FTC*, 238 F.2d 108 (1st Cir. 1956).

Asheville Tobacco Board of Trade, Inc. v. *FTC*, 263 F.2d 502 (4th Cir. 1959).

Baldwin Bracelet Corp. v. *FTC*, 325 F.2d 1012 (D.C. Cir. 1963), *cert. denied*, 377 U.S. 923 (1964).

Baysoy v. *Jessop Steel Co.*, 90 F. Supp. 303 (W.D. Pa. 1950).

Branch v. *FTC*, 141 F.2d 31 (7th Cir. 1944).

Canadian Ingersoll-Rand Co., Ltd. v. *D. Loveman & Sons, Inc.*, 227 F. Supp. 829 (N.D. Ohio 1964).

Eastman Kodak Co. v. *FTC*, 7 F.2d 994 (2d Cir. 1925).

Edward P. Paul & Co. v. *FTC*, 169 F.2d 294 (D.C. Cir. 1948).

Etablissements Rigaud Inc. v. *FTC*, 125 F.2d 590 (2d Cir. 1942).

FTC v. *Beech-Nut Packing Co.*, 257 U.S. 441 (1922).

FTC v. *Bradley*, 31 F.2d 569 (2d Cir. 1929).

FTC v. *Brown Shoe Co.*, 384 U.S. 316 (1966).

FTC v. *Bunte Brothers, Inc.*, 312 U.S. 349 (1941).

FTC v. *Caravel Co.*, 6 F.T.C. 198 (1923).

FTC v. *Cement Institute*, 333 U.S. 683 (1948), *rehearing denied*, 334 U.S. 839 (1948).

FTC v. *Motion Picture Advertising Service Co.*, 344 U.S. 392 (1953), *rehearing denied*, 345 U.S. 914 (1953).

FTC v. *Nestle's Food Co.*, 2 F.T.C. 171 (1919).

FTC v. *Simplicity Pattern Co.*, 360 U.S. 55 (1959), *rehearing denied*, 361 U.S. 855 (1959).

FTC v. *Sperry & Hutchinson Co.*, 405 U.S. 233 (1972).

Fashion Originators' Guild of America v. *FTC*, 312 U.S. 457 (1941).

Ford Motor Co. v. *FTC*, 120 F.2d 175 (6th Cir. 1941), *cert. denied*, 314 U.S. 668 (1941).

Grand Union Co. v. *FTC*, 300 F.2d 92 (2d Cir. 1962).

Guziak v. *FTC*, 361 F.2d 700 (8th Cir. 1966), *cert. denied*, 385 U.S. 1007 (1967).

Holland Furnace Co. v. *FTC*, 269 F.2d 203 (7th Cir. 1959), *cert. denied*, 361 U.S. 932 (1960).

Hybern, Inc., 54 F.T.C. 1566 (1958).

L. Heller & Son, Inc., 47 F.T.C. 34 (1950), *aff'd*, 191 F.2d 954 (7th Cir. 1951).

Luria Brothers & Co. v. *FTC*, 389 F.2d 847 (3d Cir. 1968), *cert. denied*, 393 U.S. 829 (1969).

Manco Watch Strap Co., 50 F.T.C. 553 (1953).

Manco Watch Strap Co., 60 F.T.C. 495 (1962).

Nashville Milk Co. v. *Carnation Co.*, 355 U.S. 373 (1958), *rehearing denied*, 355 U.S. 967 (1958).

Reines Distributors, Inc. v. *Admiral Corp.*, 256 F. Supp. 581 (S.D.N.Y. 1966).

Segal v. *FTC*, 142 F.2d 255 (2d Cir. 1944).

Thomsen v. *Cayser*, 243 U.S. 66 (1917).

United States v. *Minnesota Mining & Manufacturing Co.*, 92 F. Supp. 947 (D. Mass. 1950).

Waltham Watch Co. v. *FTC*, 318 F.2d 28 (7th Cir. 1963), *cert. denied*, 375 U.S. 944 (1963), *rehearing denied*, 375 U.S. 998 (1964).

Winslow v. *FTC*, 277 F. 206 (4th Cir. 1921), *cert. denied*, 258 U.S. 618 (1922).

chapter 8:
Mergers, Acquisitions, and Joint Ventures in
Foreign Commerce

Bridges, *Foreign Mergers Under Section 7 of the Clayton Act*, 52 A.B.A.J. 360 (1966).

Comment, *Antitrust Considerations in International Corporate Activity: Technical Assistance Agreements and Foreign Acquisitions*, 12 B. C. Ind. & Com. L. Rev. 453 (1971).

Donovan, *Antitrust Considerations in the Organization and Operation of American Business Abroad*, 9 B. C. Ind. & Com. L. Rev. 239 (1968).

Donovan, *The Legality of Acquisitions and Mergers Involving American and Foreign Corporations Under the United States Antitrust Laws (pts. 1-2)*, 39 So. Cal. L. Rev. 526 (1966) & 40 So. Cal. L. Rev. 38 (1967).

Graham, Hermann, and Marcus, *Section 7 of the Clayton Act and Mergers Involving Foreign Interests*, 23 Stan. L. Rev. 205 (1971).

Joelson, *"International Antitrust": A Look at Recent Developments*, 12 Wm. & Mary L. Rev. 565 (1971).

Sproul, *United States Antitrust Laws and Foreign Joint Ventures*, 54 A.B.A.J. 889 (1968).

CASES

Allis-Chalmers Manufacturing Co. v. *White Consolidated Industries, Inc.*, 414 F.2d 506 (3d Cir. 1969), *cert. denied*, 396 U.S. 1009 (1970).

Brown Shoe Co. v. *United States*, 370 U.S. 294 (1962).

Dresser Industries, Inc., 63 F.T.C. 250 (1963).

FTC v. *British Oxygen Co., Ltd.*, 1974 Trade Cas. ¶75,004 (D. Del 1974).

FTC v. *Procter & Gamble Co.*, 386 U.S. 568 (1967).

Ford Motor Co. v. *United States*, 405 U.S. 562 (1972).

General Foods Corp. v. *FTC*, 386 F.2d 936 (3d Cir. 1969), *cert. denied*, 391 U.S. 919 (1968).

Litton Industries, Inc.,[1970–1973 Transfer Binder] Trade Reg. Rep. ¶20,267 (FTC 1973).

Reynolds Metals Co. v. *FTC*, 309 F.2d 223 (D.C. Cir. 1962).

United States v. *Pabst Brewing Co.*, 384 U.S. 546 (1966).

United States v. *Aluminum Co. of America*, 377 U.S. 271 (1964), *rehearing denied*, 377 U.S. 1010 (1964).

United States v. *CIBA Corp.*, Civil No. 70-3078 (S.D.N.Y. 1970), 1970 Trade Cas. ¶¶73,269, 73,319; 5 Trade Reg. Rep. ¶45,070, Case No. 2118.

United States v. *Columbia Steel Co.*, 334 U.S. 495 (1948).

United States v. *Falstaff Brewing Corp.*, 410 U.S. 526 (1973).

United States v. *First National Bank & Trust Co.*, 376 U.S. 665 (1964).

United States v. *General Dynamics Corp.*, 94 S. Ct. 1186 (1974).

United States v. *Gillette Co.*, Civil No. 68-141 (D. Mass., filed Feb. 14, 1968), [1961–1970 Antitrust Cases Summaries Transfer Binder] Trade Reg. Rep. ¶45,068, Case No. 1988.

United States v. *Imperial Chemical Industries, Ltd.*, 100 F. Supp. 504 (S.D. N.Y. 1951).

United States v. *Jos. Schlitz Brewing Co.*, 253 F. Supp. 129 (N.D. Cal. 1966), *aff'd per curiam*, 385 U.S. 37 (1966), *rehearing denied*, 385 U.S. 1021 (1967).

United States v. *Minnesota Mining & Manufacturing Co.*, 92 F. Supp. 947 (D. Mass. 1950).

United States v. *Monsanto Co.*, Civil No. 64-342 (W.D. Pa. 1967), 1967 Trade Cas. ¶72,001.

United States v. *Pan American World Airways, Inc.*, 193 F. Supp. 18 (S.D.N.Y. 1961), *rev'd on other grounds*, 371 U.S. 296 (1963).

United States v. *Penn-Olin Chemical Co.*, 378 U.S. 158 (1964).

United States v. *Philadelphia National Bank*, 374 U.S. 321 (1963).

United States v. *Standard Oil Co.*, Civil No. 69-954 (N.D. Ohio 1970), 1970 Trade Cas. ¶72,988.

United States v. *Swiss Bank Corp.*, Civil No. 1920 (D. N.J. 1941), 1940–1943 Trade Cas. ¶56,188.

United States v. *Von's Grocery Co.*, 384 U.S. 270 (1966).

United States v. *Wilson Sporting Goods Co.,* 288 F. Supp. 543 (N.D. Ill. 1968).

chapter 9:
The Transfer of Technology and Trademarks

Adelman and Brooks, *Territorial Restraints in International Technology Agreements after Topco,* 17 Antitrust Bull. 763 (1972).

Austin, *The Tying Arrangement: A Critique and Some New Thoughts,* 1967 Wis. L. Rev. 88.

Barton, *Limitations on Territory, Field of Use, Quantity and Price in Know-how Agreements with Foreign Companies,* 28 U. Pitt. L. Rev. 195 (1966).

Baxter, *Legal Restrictions on Exploitation of the Patent Monopoly: An Economic Analysis,* 76 Yale L.J. 267 (1966).

Chevigny, *The Validity of Grant-Back Agreements Under the Antitrust Laws,* 34 Fordham L. Rev. 579 (1966).

Derenberg, *The Impact of the Antitrust Laws on Trade-Marks in Foreign Commerce,* 27 N.Y.U.L. Rev. 414 (1952).

Gibbons, *Field Restrictions in Patent Transactions: Economic Discrimination and Restraint of Competition,* 66 Colum. L. Rev. 423 (1966).

Harmonizing Patent Law and Antitrust Law Objectives, address by Richard H. Stern, Chief, Patent Unit, Antitrust Division, U.S. Department of Justice, Before the Practising Law Institute Conference on Current Developments in Patent Licensing, Oct. 7, 1971 (Department of Justice Mimeograph).

Hollabaugh and Rigler, *Scope of Relief in Government Patent and Know-how Antitrust Cases,* 28 U. Pitt. L. Rev. 249 (1966).

Jones, *Fundamentals of International Licensing Agreements and Their Application in the European Community,* 7 Int'l Law. 78 (1973).

Kestenbaum, *Foreign Trademark Licensing and Antitrust Policy,* 58 Trademark Rep. 325 (1968).

Ladas, *Legal Protection of Know-how,* 7 Idea 397 (1963).

Ladas, *Trademark Licensing and the Antitrust Law,* 63 Trademark Rep. 245 (1973).

MacDonald, *Know-how Licensing and the Antitrust Laws,* 62 Mich. L. Rev. 351 (1964).

McCarthy, *Trademarks and Unfair Competition* (Rochester: The Lawyers Cooperative Publishing Co., 1973).

McLaren, *Patent Licenses and Antitrust Considerations,* 13 Idea 61 (1969) (Conference Number).

Memorandum of the U.S. Department of Justice Concerning Antitrust and Foreign Commerce, 5 Trade Reg. Rep. ¶50,129 (1972).

Milgrim, *Trade Secrets* (New York: Matthew Bender & Co., 1967).

Nimmer, *Nimmer on Copyright* (New York: Matthew Bender & Co., 1972).

Nims, *The Law of Unfair Competition and Trademarks* (New York: Baker, Voorhis & Co., 4th ed. 1947).

Nordhaus and Jurow, *Patent–Antitrust Law* (Chicago: Jural Publishing Co., 1961).

Oppenheim, *The Patent–Antitrust Spectrum of Patent and Know-how License Limitations: Accommodation? Conflict? or Antitrust Supremacy?,* 15 Idea 1 (1971).

Report of the Antitrust Subcommittee B of the American Patent Law Association, *Grant-Back Licensing,* 1966 A.P.L.A. Bull. 387.

Stern, *The Antitrust Status of Territorial Limitations in International Licensing,* 14 Idea 580 (1970).

Steutermann, *Selected Antitrust Aspects of Trademark Franchising,* 60 Ky. L.J. 638 (1972).

Turner, *Antitrust Enforcement Policy,* 29 ABA Antitrust Section 187 (1965).

Turner, *Patents, Antitrust and Innovation,* 28 U. Pitt. L. Rev. 151 (1966).

Turner, *The Validity of Tying Arrangements under the Antitrust Laws,* 72 Harv. L. Rev. 50 (1958).

Wood, *The Validity Under the Antitrust Laws of Cooperative Arrangements Among Patent Owners,* 28 U. Pitt. L. Rev. 221 (1966).

CASES

Automatic Radio Manufacturing Co. v. *Hazeltine Research, Inc.,* 339 U.S. 827 (1950).

Becton, Dickinson & Co. v. *Eisele & Co.,* 86 F.2d 267 (6th Cir. 1936), *cert. denied,* 300 U.S. 667 (1937).

British Nylon Spinners, Ltd. v. *Imperial Chemical Industries, Ltd.,* [1952] 2 All E. R. 780 (C.A.).

British Nylon Spinners, Ltd. v. *Imperial Chemical Industries, Ltd.,* [1954] 3 All E.R. 88 (Ch.).

Brownell v. *Ketcham Wire & Manufacturing Co.,* 211 F.2d. 121 (9th Cir. 1954).

Brulotte v. *Thys Co.,* 379 U.S. 29 (1964), *rehearing denied,* 379 U.S. 985 (1965).

Bulova Watch Co. v. *Steele,* 194 F.2d 567 (5th Cir. 1952), *aff'd,* 344 U.S. 280 (1952).

Carl Zeiss Stiftung v. *V.E.B. Carl Zeiss, Jena,* 298 F. Supp. 1309 (S.D.N.Y. 1969), *modified,* 433 F.2d 686 (2d Cir. 1970), *cert. denied,* 403 U.S. 905 (1971).

Dawn Donut Co. v. *Hart's Food Stores, Inc.,* 267 F.2d 358 (2d Cir. 1959).

Dehydrating Process Co. v. *A. O. Smith Corp.,* 292 F.2d 653 (1st Cir. 1961), *cert. denied,* 368 U.S. 931 (1961).

Dunlop Co. v. *Kelsey-Hayes Co.,* 484 F.2d 407 (6th Cir. 1973), *cert. denied,* 94 S. Ct. 1414 (1974).

Ethyl Gasoline Corp. v. *United States,* 309 U.S. 436 (1940).

Farbenfabriken Bayer, A. G. v. *Sterling Drug, Inc.,* 153 F. Supp. 589 (D. N.J. 1957) & 197 F. Supp. 627 (D. N.J. 1961), *aff'd,* 307 F.2d 210 (3d Cir. 1962), *cert. denied,* 272 U.S. 929 (1963).

FTC v. *Beech-Nut Packing Co.,* 257 U.S. 441 (1922).

Fortner Enterprises, Inc. v. *United States Steel Corp.,* 394 U.S. 495 (1969).

General Talking Pictures Corp. v. *Western Electric Co.,* 305 U.S. 124 (1938).

In re Amtorg Trading Corp., 75 F.2d 826 (C.C.P.A. 1935), *cert. denied,* 296 U.S. 576 (1935).

In re Northern Pigment Co., 71 F.2d 447 (C.C.P.A. 1934).

International Salt Co. v. *United States,* 332 U.S. 392 (1947).

Kewanee Oil Co. v. *Bicron Corp.,* 94 S. Ct. 1879 (1974).

Laitram Corp. v. *King Crab, Inc.,* 244 F. Supp. 9 (D. Alas. 1965), *modified,* 245 F. Supp. 1019 (D. Alas. 1965).

Mishawaka Rubber & Woolen Manufacturing Co. v. *S. S. Kresge Co.,* 316 U.S. 203 (1942).

Northern Pacific Ry. Co. v. *United States,* 356 U.S. 1 (1957).

Siegel v. *Chicken Delight, Inc.,* 448 F.2d 43 (9th Cir. 1971), *cert. denied,* 405 U.S. 955 (1972).

Sperry Products, Inc. v. *Aluminum Co. of America,* 171 F. Supp. 901 (N.D. Ohio 1959), *aff'd in part, rev'd in part,* 285 F.2d 911 (6th Cir. 1960), *cert. denied,* 368 U.S. 890 (1961).

Susser v. *Carvel Corp.,* 332 F.2d 505 (2d Cir. 1964), *cert. dismissed,* 381 U.S. 125 (1965).

Transparent-Wrap Machine Corp. v. *Stokes & Smith Co.,* 329 U.S. 637 (1947).

United States v. *Arnold, Schwinn & Co.,* 388 U.S. 365 (1967).

United States v. *Bayer Co.,* Civil No. 15–364 (S.D.N.Y. 1941), 1940–1943 Trade Cas. ¶56,151.

United States v. *Bayer Co.,* 135 F. Supp. 65 (S.D.N.Y. 1955).

United States v. *E. I. DuPont de Nemours & Co.*, 118 F. Supp. 41 (D. Del. 1953), *aff'd*, 351 U.S. 377 (1956).

United States v. *General Electric Co.*, 272 U.S. 476 (1926).

United States v. *Glaxo Group, Ltd.*, 302 F. Supp. 1 (D. D.C. 1969), *rev'd*, 410 U.S. 52 (1973).

United States v. *Huck Manufacturing Co.*, 227 F. Supp. 791 (E.D. Mich. 1964), *aff'd*, 382 U.S. 197 (1965).

United States v. *Imperial Chemical Industries, Ltd.*, 100 F. Supp. 504 (S.D. N.Y. 1951).

United States v. *Imperial Chemical Industries, Ltd.*, 105 F. Supp. 215 (S.D. N.Y. 1952).

United States v. *Jerrold Electronics Corp.*, 187 F. Supp. 545 (E.D. Pa. 1960), *aff'd per curiam*, 365 U.S. 567 (1961).

United States v. *Line Material Co.*, 333 U.S. 287 (1948).

United States v. *Loew's, Inc.*, 371 U.S. 38 (1962).

United States v. *National Lead Co.*, 63 F. Supp. 513 (S.D.N.Y. 1945), *aff'd*, 332 U.S. 319 (1947).

United States v. *Permutit Co.*, Civil No. 32–394 (S.D.N.Y. 1951); 1950–1951 Trade Cas. ¶62,888.

United States v. *Sealy, Inc.*, 338 U.S. 350 (1967).

United States v. *Singer Manufacturing Co.*, 374 U.S. 174 (1963).

United States v. *Timken Roller Bearing Co.*, 83 F. Supp. 284 (N.D. Ohio 1949), *modified & aff'd*, 341 U.S. 593 (1951).

United States v. *Topco Associates, Inc.*, 405 U.S. 596 (1972).

United States v. *United States Gypsum Co.*, 340 U.S. 76 (1950).

United States v. *Westinghouse Electric Corp.*, Civil No. C 70–852 SAW (N.D. Cal., filed Apr. 22, 1970); [1961–1970 Antitrust Cases Summaries Transfer Binder] Trade Reg. Rep. ¶45,070.

Walker Process Equipment, Inc. v. *Food Machinery & Chemical Corp.*, 382 U.S. 172 (1965).

Wells Fargo & Co. v. *Wells Fargo Express Co.*, 458 F. Supp. 1065 (D. Nev. 1973).

Xerox Corp., FTC Dkt. No. 8909 (issued Jan. 31, 1973), [1970–1973 Transfer Binder] Trade Reg. Rep. ¶¶20,164, 20,207.

Zenith Radio Corp. v. *Hazeltine Research, Inc.*, 239 F. Supp. 51 (N.D. Ill. 1965), *aff'd in part, rev'd in part*, 388 F.2d 25 (7th Cir. 1967), *aff'd in part, rev'd in part*, 395 U.S. 100 (1969).

chapter 10:
Antitrust Exemptions Pertinent to
International Trade and Commerce

Antitrust Exemptions, 33 ABA Antitrust Section 1 (1967).

Civil Aeronautics Board Held to Have Exclusive Jurisdiction to Grant Injunctive Relief Against Acts Allegedly in Violation of Antitrust Laws, 63 Colum. L. Rev. 923 (1963).

Diamond, *The Webb-Pomerene Act and Export Trade Associations,* 44 Colum. L. Rev. 805 (1944).

Gordon, *Shipping Regulation and the Federal Maritime Commission,* 37 U. Chi. L. Rev. 90 (1969).

McGee, *Ocean Freight Rate Conference and the American Merchant Marine,* 27 U. Chi. L. Rev. 191 (1960).

Montague, *The Webb Bill and the Antitrust Laws,* 3 A.B.A.J. 145 (1917).

Note, *An Appraisal of the Webb-Pomerene Act,* 44 N.Y.U.L. Rev. 341 (1969).

Note, *Federal Maritime Board Procedure and the Legality of Dual Rate Shipping Contracts,* 64 Yale L.J. 569 (1955).

Note, *Rate Regulation in Ocean Shipping,* 78 Harv. L. Rev. 635 (1965).

Note, *The American Shipping Industry and The Conference System,* 11 Stan. L. Rev. 136 (1958).

Note, *Maritime Law—Mergers—The Federal Maritime Commission is Without Authority to Approve Mergers of Shipping Lines Under Section 15 of the Shipping Act,* 40 Geo. Wash. L. Rev. 322 (1971).

Note, *The Webb-Pomerene Act: Some New Developments in a Quiescent History,* 37 Geo. Wash. L. Rev. 341 (1968).

Note, *The Twilight Zone of Antitrust Law: Vanishing Exemptions in the Export and Shipping Fields,* 1 L. & Pol. Int'l Bus. 175 (1969).

Ocean Shipping Conferences, 33 ABA Antitrust Section 56 (1967).

CASES

Aloha Airlines, Inc. v. *Hawaiian Airlines, Inc.,* 1973–2 Trade Cas. ¶74,821, 489 F.2d 203 (9th Cir. 1973).

Armement Deppe, S.A. v. *United States,* 399 F.2d 794 (5th Cir. 1968), *cert. denied,* 393 U.S. 1094 (1964).

Baltimore & O. R. Co. v. *United States,* 201 F.2d 795 (3d Cir. 1953).

Board of Commissioners v. *FMC,* 440 F.2d 1312 (5th Cir. 1971).

California v. *United States,* 320 U.S. 577 (1944).

Carnation Co. v. *Pacific Westbound Conference,* 383 U.S. 213 (1966), *modified,* 383 U.S. 932 (1966).

Consumers Union of U.S., Inc. v. *Rogers,* 352 F. Supp. 1319 (D. D.C. 1973).

Far East Conference v. *United States,* 342 U.S. 570 (1952).

FMB v. *Isbrandtsen Co.,* 356 U.S. 481 (1958).

FMC v. *Aktiebolaget Svenska Amerika Linien,* 390 U.S. 238 (1968).

Greater Baton Rouge Port Commission v. *United States,* 287 F.2d 86 (5th Cir. 1961), *rehearing denied,* 293 F.2d 959 (5th Cir. 1961), *cert. denied,* 368 U.S. 985 (1962).

Marine Space Enclosures, Inc. v. *FMC,* 420 F.2d 577 (D.C. Cir. 1969).

National Bank of North America v. *S.S. Oceanic Ondine,* 315 F. Supp. 386 (S.D. Tex. 1970).

Pacific Coast European Conference v. *FMC,* 439 F.2d 514 (D.C. Cir. 1970), *cert. dismissed sub nom., States Marine Lines, Inc.* v. *FMC,* 401 U.S. 967 (1971).

Pacific Seafarers, Inc. v. *Pacific Far East Line, Inc.,* 404 F.2d 804 (D.C. Cir. 1968), *cert. denied,* 393 U.S. 1093 (1969).

Pan American World Airways, Inc. v. *United States,* 371 U.S. 296 (1963).

Sabre Shipping Corp. v. *American President Lines,* 298 F. Supp. 1339 (S.D.N.Y. 1969).

Seatrain Lines, Inc. v. *FMC,* 460 F.2d 932 (D.C. Cir. 1972), *aff'd,* 411 U.S. 726 (1973).

Toolson v. *New York Yankees, Inc.,* 346 U.S. 356 (1953), *rehearing denied,* 346 U.S. 917 (1953).

Trans-Pacific Freight Conference of Japan v. *FMC,* 314 F.2d 928 (9th Cir. 1963).

Trans World Airlines, Inc. v. *Hughes,* 308 F. Supp. 679 (S.D.N.Y. 1969), *aff'd & modified,* 449 F.2d 51 (2d Cir. 1971), *rev'd,* 409 U.S. 363 (1973), *rehearing denied,* 410 U.S. 975 (1973).

United States Alkali Export Association, Inc. v. *United States,* 325 U.S. 196 (1945).

United States v. *Borden Co.,* 308 U.S. 188 (1939).

United States v. *Concentrated Phosphate Export Association, Inc.,* 393 U.S. 199 (1968).

United States v. *Minnesota Mining & Manufacturing Co.,* 92 F. Supp. 947 (D. Mass. 1950).

United States v. *United States Alkali Export Association, Inc.,* 86 F. Supp. 59 (S.D.N.Y. 1949).

United States Navigation Co. v. *Cunard S.S. Co.,* 284 U.S. 474 (1932).

Volkswagenwerk Aktiengesellschaft v. *FMC,* 390 U.S. 261 (1968), *modified,* 392 U.S. 901 (1968), *rev'g & remanding,* 371 F.2d 474 (D.C. Cir. 1966).

chapter 11:
Some Important Foreign Antitrust Laws

EUROPEAN COMMON MARKET

Adler and Belman, *Antimerger Enforcement in Europe—Trends and Prospects,* 8 J. Int'l L. & Eco. 31 (1973).

Antitrust Developments in the European Common Market, Report of the Subcommittee on Antitrust and Monopoly of the Committee on the Judiciary of the U.S. Senate, 88th Cong., 2d Sess. at 9 (Washington, D.C.: U.S. Government Printing Office, 1964).

Alexander, *Market Division Within the European Common Market by Means of Trademarks Belonging to An International Group of Companies,* 61 Trademark Rep. 14 (1971).

Alexander, *The EEC Rules of Competition* (London: Kluwer & Harrap, 1973).

Bellamy and Child, *Common Market Law of Competition* (London: Sweet & Maxwell, 1973).

Commission of the European Communities, *First Report on Competition Policy* (Luxembourg: 1972).

Commission of the European Communities, *Second Report on Competition Policy* (Luxembourg: 1973).

Commission of the European Communities, *Third Report on Competition Policy* (Luxembourg: 1974).

Common Market Law Reports (London: Common Law Reports, Ltd., 1962).

Common Market Reporter (Chicago: Commerce Clearing House, Inc., 1965).

Cunningham, *The Competition Law of the EEC: A Practical Guide* (London: Kogan Page, Ltd., 1973).

Dam, *Exclusive Distributorships in the United States and the European Economic Community,* 16 Antitrust Bull. 111 (1971).

Dashwood, *Exclusive Licenses in the Common Market,* 1973 J. Bus. L. 205.

Deringer, *Future Trends in Common Market Antitrust Enforcement,* 8 J. Int'l L. & Eco. 203 (1973).

Deringer, *The Competition Law of the European Economic Community* (New York: Commerce Clearing House, Inc., 1968).

Deringer, *The Common Market Competition Rules, with Particular Reference to Non-member Countries,* 12 Int'l & Comp. L.Q. 582 (1963).

Devine, *Foreign Establishment and the Antitrust Law: A Study of the Antitrust Consequences of the Principal Forms of Investment by American Corporations in Foreign Markets,* 57 Nw. U. L. Rev. 400 (1962).

Dietz, *Enforcement of Anti-Trust Laws in the EEC,* 6 Int'l Law. 742 (1972).

Ebb, *Common Market Anticartel Law and Trademark and Patent License Agreements,* 16 U.C.L.A. L. Rev. 545 (1969).

Forcione, *Intra-Enterprise Conspiracy Under the Antitrust Regulations of the Common Market,* 25 Bus. Law. 1419 (1970).

Galloway, *Trade Mark and Competition Law in the EEC: The Sirena Case,* 6 J. World Trade L. 550 (1972).

Graham, *Antitrust Problems of Corporate Parents, Subsidiaries, Affiliates and Joint Ventures in Foreign Commerce,* 9 ABA Antitrust Section 32 (1956).

Graupner, *Commission Decision-Making on Competition Questions,* 10 Comm. Mkt. L. Rev. 291 (1973).

Graupner, *An Outline of the Law of Restrictive Practices in the European Economic Community,* 1972 Jurid. Rev. 248.

Graupner, *The Rules of Competition in the European Community* (The Hague, Netherlands: Martinus Nijhoff, 1965).

Hawk, *Antitrust in the EEC—The First Decade,* 41 Fordham L. Rev. 229 (1972).

Hug, *The Applicability of the Provisions of the European Community Treaties Against Restraints of Competition to Restraints of Competition Caused in Non-member States, but Affecting the Common Market,* 2 Cartel & Monopoly in Modern Law 639 (1961).

Joliet, *Resale Price Maintenance Under EEC Antitrust Law,* 16 Antitrust Bull. 589 (1971).

Jones, *A Primer on Production and Dominant Positions Under E.E.C. Competition Law,* 7 Int'l Law. 612 (1973).

Jones, *Practical Aspects of Commercial Agency and Distribution Agreements in the European Community,* 6 Int'l Law. 107 (1972).

Jones, *Fundamentals of International Licensing Agreements and Their Application in the European Community,* 7 Int'l Law. 78 (1973).

Kestenbaum, *Foreign Trademark Licensing and Antitrust Policy,* 58 Trademark Rep. 325 (1968).

Korah, *Concerted Practices,* 36 Mod. L. Rev. 220 (1973).

Ladas, *Assignment of Trademarks and Antitrust Law—The Sirena (Sirena S. r.l. v. Eda GmbH (1971) 10 Comm. Mkt. Rep. 260) Case of the Court of Justice of the European Communities,* 62 Trademark Rep. 566 (1972).

Mann, *Dyestuffs Case (Imperial Chemical Industries Ltd.* v. *Commission of the European Communities,* Case No. *48/69, [1972] CMLR 557) in the Court of Justice of the European Communities,* 22 Int'l & Comp. L.Q. 35 (1973).

Markert, *Antitrust Aspects of Mergers in the EEC,* 5 Texas Int'l L.F. 32 (1969).

Markert, *The Application of German Antitrust Law to International Restraints of Trade,* 7 Va. J. Int'l L. 47 (1967).

Markert, *The Dyestuff Case: A Contribution to the Relationship Between the Antitrust Laws of the European Economic Community and Its Member States,* 14 Antitrust Bull. 869 (1969).

Mestmacker, *Concentration and Competition in the EEC* (pts. 1–2), 6 J. World Trade L. 615 (1972) & 7 J. World Trade L. 36 (1973).

Newburg, *Application of the Antitrust Laws of the European Common Market to International Transactions,* 13 Prac. Law. 83 (Apr. 1967).

Newes, *The EEC Treaty as Applied to Distribution Arrangements and Industrial Property Rights, in ABA Current Legal Aspects of Doing Business in Europe* (Theberge ed., Chicago: ABA, 1971).

Note, *Antitrust—E.E.C. Treaty—Acquisition and Merger of Enterprise by Firm Holding a Dominant Position Within Common Market with Effect of Eliminating Actual or Potential Competition in a Substantial Part of the Community Violates Article 86 of the E.E.C. Treaty,* 5 Vand. J. Transnat'l L. 525 (1972).

Note, *Antitrust: Per Se Doctrine—Tying Arrangements and the Market Power Requirement,* 8 Tulsa L.J. 235 (1972).

Note, *Common Market—Antitrust—Interpretation of Concerted Practices Within the Meaning of Article 85—Extraterritorial Jurisdiction of European Commission,* 14 Harv. Int'l L.J. 621 (1973).

Note, *Common Market Antitrust Law; Jurisdiction: Limitations Imposed by Article 85(1) of the Treaty of Rome,* 6 Cornell Int'l L.J. 163 (1973).

Note, *Developments in Common Market Competition Policy: The Quinine and Dyestuff Cases,* 2 L. & Pol. Int'l Bus. 259 (1970).

Note, *European Economic Community Antitrust Law: The Continental Can [EEC* v. *Continental Can Co., 2 CCH Comm. Mkt. Rpt., ¶9481 (1973)] Decision—Forerunner of a New European Antimerger Policy?,* 47 Tul. L. Rev. 829 (1973).

Note, *Extraterritorial Application of Antitrust Legislation in the Common Market,* 12 Colum. J. Transnat'l. L. 169 (1973).

Oberdorfer, Gleiss, and Hirsch, *Common Market Cartel Law* (Chicago: Commerce Clearing House. 2d ed. 1971).

Quesenberry, *The European Patent Club—Members and Guests,* 32 Fed. Bar. J. 87 (1973).

Rahl, ed., *Common Market and American Antitrust* (New York: McGraw-Hill Book Co., 1970).

Riske, *Antitrust Philosophy of the Common Market—Restraint or Prohibition,* 17 De Paul L. Rev. 144 (1967).

Swann, *Concentration and Competition in the European Community,* 13 Antitrust Bull. 1473 (1968).

Symposium, *Expansion of the Common Market,* 37 L. & Contemp. Prob. 219 (1972).

van den Heuvel, *Civil-Law Consequences of Violation of the Antitrust Provisions of the Rome Treaty,* 12 Am. J. Comp. L. 172 (1963).

Waelbroeck, *Cooperation Agreements and Competition Policy in the E.E.C.,* 1 N.Y.U.J. Int'l L. & Pol. 5 (1968).

Zaphiriou, *Rule of Reason and Double Jeopardy in European Antitrust Law,* 6 Texas Int'l L.F. 1 (1970).

CASES

ACEC - Berliet, Official Journal L201/7, 1968, [1968] 7 C.M.L.R. D35, [1965–1969 Transfer Binder] CCH Comm. Mkt. Rep. ¶9251 (EEC Comm'n 1968).

Association of German Manufacturers of Ceramic Wall and Floor Tile, Official Journal L10/15, 1971, [1971] 10 C.M.L.R. D6 [1970–1972 Transfer Binder] CCH Comm. Mkt. Rep. ¶9409 (EEC Comm'n 1971).

Belgian Toiletries Trade Association (Association Syndicale Belge de la Parfumerie (A.S.P.A.)), Official Journal L148/9, 1970, [1970] 9 C.M.L.R. D25, [1970–1972 Transfer Binder] CCH Comm. Mkt. Rep. ¶9379 (EEC Comm'n 1970).

Boehringer Mannheim GmbH v. *EEC Commission,* Case No. 7/72, [1973] 12 C.M.L.R. 864, 2 CCH Comm. Mkt. Rep. ¶8191 (ECCJ 1971).

S.A. Brasserie de Haecht v. *Wilkin & Janssen,* Case No. 48/72, [1973] 12 C.M.L.R. 287, 2 CCH Comm. Mkt. Rep. ¶8170 (ECCJ 1973).

Brauerei A. Bilger Söhne GmbH v. *Jehle,* Case No. 43/69 [1967–1970 Court Decisions] CCH Comm. Mkt. Rep. ¶8076 (ECCJ 1970).

Burroughs Corp./Geha Werke GmbH & Burroughs Corp./Establissements L. Delplanque et Fils, Official Journal L13/50, 53 1971–2, [1972] 11 C.M.L.R. D67, D72, [1970–1972 Transfer Binder] CCH Comm. Mkt. Rep. ¶9485, ¶9486 (EEC Comm'n 1971).

Christiani Nielsen N/V/Christiani & Nielsen A/S, Official Journal L165/12 1969, [1969] 8 C.M.L.R. D36, [1965–1969 Transfer Binder] CCH Comm. Mkt. Rep. ¶9308 (EEC Comm'n 1969).

La Cimenterie Belge—CIMBEL, S.A., Official Journal L303/52, 1972, [1973] 12 C.M.L.R. D167, 2 CCH Comm. Mkt. Rep. ¶9544 (EEC Comm'n 1972).

Commercial Solvents Corp./ICI/ZOJA, Official Journal L299/51, 1972, [1973] 12 C.M.L.R. D50, 2 CCH Comm. Mkt. Rep. ¶9543 (EEC Comm'n 1972), *aff'd,* 2 CCH Comm. Mkt. Rep. ¶8209 (1974).

Company for Musical Performance and Mechanical Reproduction Rights (Gesellshaft für musikalische Ausführungs und mechanische Vervielfältigungsrechte (GEMA)), Official Journal L134/15, 1971, [1971] 10 C.M.L.R. D35, [1970–1972 Transfer Binder] CCH Comm. Mkt. Rep. ¶9438 (EEC Comm'n 1971); *modified* Official Journal L166/22, 1972 [1972] 11 C.M.L.R. D115, [1970–1972 Transfer Binder] CCH Comm. Mkt. Rep. ¶9521 (EEC Comm'n 1972).

Consten S.A., Etablissements, and Grundig—Verkaufs—GmbH v. *EEC Commission,* Case Nos. 56/64 and 58/64 [1966] 5 C.M.L.R. 418, [1961–1966 Court Decisions] CCH Comm. Mkt. Rep. ¶8046 (ECCJ 1966).

Davidson Rubber Co., Official Journal L143/31, 1972, [1972] 11 C.M.L.R. D52, [1970–1972 Transfer Binder] CCH Comm. Mkt. Rep. ¶9512 (ECC Comm'n 1972).

de Geus v. *Robert Bosch GmbH,* Case No. 13/61, [1962] 1 C.M.L.R. 1, [1961–1966 Court Decisions] CCH Comm. Mkt. Rep. ¶8003 (EECJ 1962).

Deutsche Grammophon GmbH v. *Metro-SB-Grossmärkte GmbH & Co. KG.,* Case No. 78/70, [1971] 10 C.M.L.R. 631, 2 CCH Comm. Mkt. Rep. ¶8106 (ECCJ 1971).

Deutsche Philips GmbH, Official Journal L293/40, 1973, [1973] 12 C.M.L.R. D241, 2 CCH Comm. Mkt. Rep. ¶9606 (EEC Comm'n 1973).

Europemballage Corp. & Continental Can Co. v. *EEC Commission,* Case No. 6/72, [1973] 12 C.M.L.R. 199, 2 CCH Comm. Mkt. Rep. ¶8171 (ECCJ 1973).

Henkel-Colgate-Palmolive, Official Journal L14/14, 1972, [1970–1972 Transfer Binder] CCH Comm. Mkt. Rep. ¶9491 (EEC Comm'n 1971).

Imperial Chemical Industries, Ltd. (ICI) v. *EEC Commission,* Case No. 48/69, [1972] 11 C.M.L.R. 577, 2 CCH Comm. Mkt. Rep. ¶8161 (ECCJ 1972), *aff'g Dyestuffs Manufacturers,* Official Journal L195/11, 1969, [1969] 8 C.M.L.R. D23, [1965–1969 Transfer Binder] CCH Comm. Mkt. Rep. ¶9314 (EEC Comm'n 1969).

Italy v. *EEC Council and EEC Commission,* Case No. 32/65, [1969] 8 C.M.L.R. 39, [1961–1966 Court Decisions] CCH Comm. Mkt. Rep. ¶8048 (ECCJ 1966).

Kodak Subsidiaries, Official Journal L147/24, 1970, [1970] 9 C.M.L.R. D19, [1970–1972 Transfer Binder] CCH Comm. Mkt. Rep. ¶9378 (EEC Comm'n 1970).

Omega, Official Journal L242/22, 1970, [1970] 9 C.M.L.R. D49, [1970–1972 Transfer Binder] CCH Comm. Mkt. Rep. ¶9396 (EEC Comm'n 1970).

Parfums Marcel Rochas Vertriebs—GmbH v. *Bitsch,* Case No. 1/70, [1971] 10 C.M.L.R. 104, 2 CCH Comm. Mkt. Rep. ¶8102. (ECCJ 1970).

Parke, Davis & Co. v. *Probel, Reese, Beintema-Interpharm & Centrafarm Cos.,* Case No. 24/67, [1968] 7 C.M.L.R. 47, [1967–1970 Court Decisions] CCH Comm. Mkt. Rep. ¶8054 (ECCJ 1968).

S.A. Portelange v. *S.A. Smith Corona Marchant International,* Case No. 10/69, [1967–1970 Court Decisions] CCH Comm. Mkt. Rep. ¶8075 (ECCJ 1969).

A. Raymond & Co./Nagoya Rubber Co. Official Journal L143/39, 1972, [1972] 11 C.M.L.R. D45, [1970–1972 Transfer Binder] CCH Comm. Mkt. Rep. ¶9513 (EEC Comm'n 1972).

BRT v. *SABAM & Fonior,* Case No. 127/73, 2 CCH Comm. Mkt. Rep. ¶—— (ECCJ 1974).

Sirena S. r. l. v. *Eda, GmbH,* Case No. 40/70, [1971] 10 C.M.L.R. 260, 2 CCH Comm. Mkt. Rep. ¶8101 (ECCJ 1971).

Vereeniging van Cementhandelaren v. *EEC Commission* (VCH), Case No. 8/72, [1973] 12 C.M.L.R. 7, 2 CCH Comm. Rep. ¶8179 (EECJ 1972).

Vereeniging van Vernis—en Verffabrikanten in Nederland (VVVF), Official Journal L168/22 1969, [1970] 9 C.M.L.R. D1, 1 CCH Comm. Mkt. Rep. ¶2412.91 (EEC Comm'n 1969).

Walt Wilhelm v. *Bundeskartellamt Berlin,* Case No. 14/68, [1969] 8 C.M.L.R. 100, [1967–1970 Court Decisions] CCH Comm. Mkt. Rep. ¶8056 (ECCJ 1969).

William Prym—Werke KG/S.A. Beka, Official Journal L296/24, 1973, [1973] 12 C.M.L.R. D250, 2 CCH Comm. Mkt. Rep. ¶9609 (EEC Comm'n 1973).

UNITED KINGDOM

Allen, *Monopoly and Restrictive Practices* (London: Allen & Unwin, 1968).

Board of Trade, *Mergers: A Guide to Board of Trade Practice* (London: H.M.S.O., 1969).

Board of Trade, *Monopolies, Mergers and Restrictive Practices* (London: H.M.S.O., 1964).

Brock, *The Control of Restrictive Practices from 1956: A Study of the Restrictive Practices Court* (New York: McGraw-Hill Book Company, 1966).

Brown, *Refusals to Deal,* 40 ABA Antitrust L.J. 1029 (1971).

Cyriax and Schaffer, *Monopoly and Competition* (London: Longman Group, Ltd., 2d ed. 1970).

De Richemont, *The Regulation of Resale Price Maintenance Under U.S., French, German, British and EEC Law: A Comparative Analysis,* 5 L. & Pol. Int'l Bus. 440 (1973).

Edwards, *Control of Cartels and Monopolies: An International Comparison* (Dobbs Ferry, N.Y.: Oceana Publications, Inc., 1967).

Edwards, *Trade Regulation Overseas: The National Laws* (Dobbs Ferry, N.Y.: Oceana Publications, Inc., 1966).

Howe, *Rethinking British Merger Policy,* 17 Antitrust Bull. 283 (1972).

Jacobs, *The Application of the EEC Rules on Competition in the United Kingdom after Accession,* 88 L.Q. Rev. 483 (1972).

Korah, *The EEC Dyestuffs Case,* 1972 J. Bus. L. 319.

Korah, *Legal Regulation of Corporate Mergers in the United Kingdom,* 5 Texas Int'l L.F. 71 (1969).

Korah, *Monopolies and Restrictive Practices* (London: Penguin Books, Ltd., 1968).

Lever, *Bipartite Arrangements and the Restrictive Trade Practices Acts 1956 and 1968,* 85 L.Q. Rev. 177 (1969).

Lever, *The Extra-territorial Jurisdiction of the Restrictive Practices Court,* in The British Institute of Int'l. & Comp. Law, *Comparative Aspects of Antitrust Law in the United States, the United Kingdom and the European Economic Community* 117 (London: Eastern Press, Ltd., 1963).

Lever, *The Law of Restrictive Practices and Resale Price Maintenance* (London: Sweet & Maxwell, 1964).

Lever, *Restrictive Trading Agreements,* in 2 Chitty, *Chitty on Contracts* 569 (London: Sweet & Maxwell, 23d ed. 1968).

Mitchell, Kuipers, and Gall, *Constitutional Aspects of the Treaty and Legislation Relating to British Membership,* 9 Comm. Mkt. L. Rev. 134 (1972).

Morse, *Mutual Recognition of Companies in England and the EEC,* 1972 J. Bus. L. 195.

Organization for Economic Cooperation and Development, *United Kingdom,* 2 *Guide to Legislation on Restrictive Business Practices* (Paris: OECD 3d ed. 1971).

Organization for Economic Cooperation and Development, *Annual Reports on Competition Policy in OECD Member Countries* (April 1973).

Pass, *Horizontal Mergers and the Control of Market Power in the U.K.,* 17 Antitrust Bull. 811 (1972).

Raskind, Professor of Law, Ohio State University, Statement on British Antitrust, in *Hearings pursuant to S. Res. 191 on International Aspects of Anti-*

trust before the Subcommittee on Antitrust and Monopoly of the Senate Committee on the Judiciary, 89th Cong., 2d Sess., pt. 1, at 438 (1966).

Report of the Registrar of Restrictive Trading Agreements, United Kingdom, for the Period July 1, 1963–June 30, 1966, partially reprinted in 12 Antitrust Bull. 351 (1967).

Restrictive Trading Agreements in the United Kingdom, Report of the Registrar, July 1, 1966–June 30, 1969, partially reprinted in 15 Antitrust Bull. 563 (1970).

Rhinelander, *British Antitrust Laws,* 40 ABA Antitrust L.J. 827 (1971).

Rhinelander, *The British Resale Prices Act,* 51 Va. L. Rev. 1467 (1965).

Rhinelander, *The British Restrictive Trade Practices Act,* 46 Va. L. Rev. 1 (1960).

Rostow, *British and American Experience with Legislation Against Restraints of Competition,* 23 Modern L. Rev. 477 (1960).

Rowley, *Mergers and Public Policy in Great Britain,* 11 J.L. & Econ. 75 (1968).

Sich, *The British Approach to Antitrust Developments During the Last Fifteen Years,* 40 ABA Antitrust L.J. 908 (1971).

Stevens and Yamey, *The Restrictive Practices Court* (London: Weidenfeld & Nicholson, Ltd., 1965).

Sutherland, *The Monopolies Commission in Action* (London: Cambridge University Press, 1969).

Wasserstein, *British Merger Policy from an American Perspective,* 82 Yale L.J. 656 (1973).

Wilberforce, Campbell, and Elles, *The Law of Restrictive Trade Practice and Monopolies* (London: Sweet & Maxwell, 2d ed. 1966 & 1973 Supp.).

Whiteman, *The New Judicial Approach to the Restrictive Trade Practices Act 1956,* 30 Modern L. Rev. 398 (1967).

Zeydel, Asst. Chief, American-British Law Division, Law Library, Library of Congress, Statement on the United Kingdom, in *Hearings pursuant to S. Res. 40 on Foreign Trade and the Antitrust Laws before the Subcommittee on Antitrust and Monopoly of the Senate Committee on the Judiciary,* 89th Cong., 1st Sess., pt. 2, at 649 (1965).

CANADA

Anisman, *Takeover Bid Legislation in Canada: The Definitions, Exemptions and Substantial Requirements,* 11 West. Ont. L. Rev. 1 (1972).

Arnett, *Canadian Regulation of Foreign Investment: The Legal Parameters,* 50 Can. B. Rev. 213 (1972).

Blair, *Combines: The Continuing Dilemma,* in *Contemporary Problems of Public Law in Canada* 127 (Lang. ed., Toronto: University of Toronto Press, 1968).

Bracher, *Combines and Competition: A Re-appraisal of Canadian Public Policy,* 38 Can. B. Rev. 523 (1960).

Cayne, *Market Power, Efficiencies, and the Public Interest in Canadian Combines Law,* 16 McGill L.J. 488 (1970).

Comment, *The Canadian Foreign Investment Review Act: Red, White and Gray,* 5 L. & Pol. Int'l Bus. 1018 (1973).

Crysler, *Restraint of Trade and Labour* (Toronto: Butterworth & Co., Ltd., 1967).

Economic Council of Canada, *Interim Report on Competition Policy* (1969) (pts. 1–2), *partially reprinted in,* 14 Antitrust Bull. 933 (1969) & 15 Antitrust Bull. 103 (1970).

Fox, *The Canadian Law of Trademarks and Unfair Competition* (Toronto: The Carswell Co., Ltd., 3d ed. 1972).

Goldman, *Canadian Competition Law and Unfair Trade Practices,* 13 B. C. Indus. & Com. L. Rev. 1303 (1972).

Gosse, *The Law on Competition in Canada* (Toronto: The Carswell Co., Ltd., 1962).

Hansard, *The "Antitrust" Laws of Canada,* 17 ABA Antitrust Section 447 (1960).

Henry, *Anti-Monopoly Legislation in Canada,* in *Nationalism and the Multinational Enterprise* (Hahlo, Smith and Wright, eds., Dobbs Ferry, N.Y.: Oceana Publications, Inc., 1973).

Henry, *Current Trends in Canadian Antitrust Enforcement,* 40 ABA Antitrust L.J. 780 (1971).

Henry, *Mergers in Canada Under the Combines Investigation Act,* 5 Texas Int'l L.F. 1 (1969).

Henry, *Canadian Anticombines Legislation,* 1964 N.Y. State Bar Assoc. Antitrust Law Symposium 32.

McDonald, *Canadian Competition Policy: Interim Report of the Economic Council of Canada,* 15 Antitrust Bull. 521 (1970).

Organization for Economic Cooperation and Development, *Canada, 1 Guide to Legislation on Restrictive Business Practices* (Paris: OECD, 3d ed. 1971).

Phillips, *Canadian Combines Policy—The Matter of Mergers,* 42 Can. B. Rev. 78 (1964).

Richardson, *The Control of Monopolies and Restrictive Trade Practices in the United States of America, Canada and the United Kingdom* (pt. 2), 35 Aust. L.J. 363 (1962).

Rosenbluth and Thorburn, *Canadian Anti-combines Administration 1952–1960* (Toronto: Toronto University Press, 1963).

Skeoch, *Merger Issues in Canada*, 16 Antitrust Bull. 131 (1971).

Skeoch, *Restrictive Trade Practices in Canada* (Toronto: McClelland & Stewart, Ltd., 1966).

Stevenson, *"Extraterritoriality" in Canadian–United States Relations*, 63 Dep't State Bull. 425 (1970).

Task Force on the Structure of Canadian Industry, *Report on Foreign Ownership and the Structure of Canadian Industry* (Ottawa: Privy Council Office, 1968).

Torrens, *An Evaluation of the Enforcement of the Combines Investigation Act.,* 3 Osgoode Hall L.J. 1 (1964).

Wang, *Canadian Anti-Combines Legislation—A Review*, 12 Am. J. Comp. L. 236 (1963).

Zeydel, Ass't. Chief, American–British Law Division, Law Library, Library of Congress, Statement on Canada in *Hearings pursuant to S. Res. 40 on Foreign Trade and the Antitrust Laws Before the Subcommittee on Antitrust and Monopoly of the Senate Committee on the Judiciary*, 89th Cong., 1st Sess., pt. 2, at 607 (1965).

JAPAN

Acino, *Experimenting With Antitrust Law in Japan*, 3 Japanese Ann. of Int'l L. 31 (1959).

Ariga, *Antitrust and Trade Regulation Laws and Practice*, in *Current Legal Aspects of Doing Business in the Far East* 33 (Allison ed., Chicago: ABA, 1972).

Ariga, *Merger Regulation in Japan*, 5 Texas Int'l L.F. 112 (1969).

Ariga, *The Anti-monopoly Act*, in *Joint Ventures and Japan* (Ballon, ed., Tokyo: Sophia University 1967).

Ariga and Rieke, *The Anti-monopoly Law of Japan and Its Enforcement*, 39 Wash. L. Rev. 436 (1964).

Douglas, *Legal Aspects of Doing Business in Japan*, 6 Am. Bus. L.J. 679 (1968).

Edwards, *Control of Cartels and Monopolies: An International Comparison* (Dobbs Ferry, N.Y.: Oceana Publications, Inc. 1967).

Edwards, *Control of Cartels and Monopolies: An International Comparison* Oceana Publications, Inc. 1966).

Ehrenzweig, Ikehara and Jensen, *American-Japanese Private International Law* (Dobbs Ferry, N.Y.: Oceana Publications, Inc. 1964).

Hadley, *Antitrust in Japan* (Princeton, N.J.: Princeton University Press, 1969).

Henderson and Henderson, *Will a "Zaibatsu" Control Our Economy?*, 26 Fed. B.J. 187 (1966).

Hildebrand and Matsushita, *Anti-monopoly Law of Japan—Potential Consequences of International Contract Violations Under Article 6*, 6 N.Y.U.J. Int'l L. & Pol. 215 (1973).

Iyori, *Anti-monopoly Legislation in Japan* (New York: Federal Legal Publications, 1969).

Japanese Fair Trade Commission Decision on the Yawata-Fuji Steel Merger, 15 Antitrust Bull. 803 (1970).

Lobb, *"Japan, Inc."—The Total Conglomerate*, 6 Colum. J. World Bus. 39 (Mar. - Apr. 1971).

Matsushita, *The Anti-monopoly Act of Japan and International Transactions*, 14 Japanese Ann. Int'l L. 1 (1970).

Matsushita and Hildebrand, *Anti-monopoly Law of Japan—Relating to International Business Transactions*, 4 Case W. Res. J. Int'l L. 124 (1972).

Ohara, *Legal Aspects of Japan's Foreign Trade*, 1 J. World Trade L. 1 (1967).

Organization for Economic Cooperation and Development, *Japan*, 3 *Guide to Legislation on Restrictive Business Practices* (Paris: OECD, 3d ed. 1971).

Pearl, *Liberalization of Capital in Japan* (pts. 1–2), 13 Harv. Int'l L.J. 59, 245 (1972).

Restrictive Trade Practices Specialists Study Team, *Control of Restrictive Trade Practices in Japan* (Japan Productivity Center 1958).

Rotwein, *Economic Concentration and Monopoly in Japan*, 72 J. of Pol. Econ. 262 (1964).

Sung Yoon Cho, Far Eastern Law Division, Law Library, Library of Congress, Statement on Japan, in *Hearings Pursuant to S. Res. 40 on Foreign Trade and the Antitrust Laws Before the Subcommittee on Antitrust and Monopoly of the Senate Committee on the Judiciary*, 89th Cong., 1st Sess., pt. 2, at 977 (1965).

Trade Bulletin Corporation, *Japan's Anti-monopoly Policy in Legislative and Practical Perspective* (20 Japan Industry Series: Tokyo, 1968).

Tsuji, *Regulation of Resale Price Maintenance in Japan*, 18 N.Y.L.F. 397 (1972).

Tsurumi, *Japanese Multinational Firms*, 7 J. World Trade L. 74 (1973).

Yamumura, *The Development of Anti-monopoly Policy in Japan: The Erosion of Japanese Anti-monopoly Policy 1947–1967,* 2 Studies in L. & Eco. Development 1 (1967) (now the J. of Int'l L. & Eco.).

chapter 12:
Groping for a Truly International Antitrust Law

Ball, *"Cosmocorp:" The Importance of Being Stateless,* 2 Colum J. World Bus. 25 (Nov.–Dec. 1967).

Fine, *The Control of Restrictive Business Practices in International Trade—A Viable Proposal for an International Trade Organization,* 7 Int'l Law. 635 (1973).

Furnish, *A Transnational Approach to Restrictive Business Practices,* 4 Int'l Law. 317 (1970).

Goldberg and Kindleberger, *Toward a GATT for Investment: A Proposal for Supervision of the International Corporation,* 2 L. & Pol. Int'l Bus. 295 (1970).

Joelson, *"International Antitrust": A Look at Recent Developments,* 12 Wm. & Mary L. Rev. 565 (1971).

Maw, *United States Antitrust Law Abroad—The Enduring Problem of Extraterritoriality,* 40 Antitrust L. J. 796 (1971).

Organization for Economic Cooperation and Development, *Guide to Legislation on Restrictive Business Practices* (Paris: OECD, 3d ed., 1971).

Rahl, ed. *Common Market and American Antitrust, Overlap and Conflict* (New York: McGraw-Hill Book Co., 1970).

Rubin, *Multinational Enterprises and National Sovereignty: A Skeptic's Analysis,* 3 L. & Pol. Int'l Bus. 1 (1971).

Servan-Schreiber, *American Capitalism in Europe—A European Point of View,* 40 Antitrust L.J. 962 (1971).

United Nations, *Multinational Corporations in World Development,* U.N. Doc. ST/ECA/190 (1973) (New York: United Nations, 1973).

Vagts, *The Multinational Enterprise: A New Challenge for Transnational Law,* 83 Harv. L. Rev. 739 (1970).

Weiner and Parzych, *Webb–Pomerene Export Trade Act: U.S. Antitrust Exemption,* 6 J. World Trade L. 119 (1972).

CASES

Imperial Chemical Industries Ltd. v. *EEC Commission* 2 CCH Comm. Mkt. Rep. ¶8161 (ECCJ 1972), *aff'g Dyestuffs Manufacturers* [1965–1969 Transfer Binder] Comm. Mkt. Rep. ¶9314 (EEC Comm'n 1969).

United States v. *Aluminum Co. of America*, 148 F.2d 416 (2d Cir. 1945).

United States v. *Watchmakers of Switzerland Information Center*, 1963 Trade Cas. ¶70,600 (S.D.N.Y. 1962), *order modified*, 1965 Trade Cas. ¶71,352 (S.D.N.Y. 1965).

Walt Wilhelm v. *Bundeskartellamt, Berlin* Case No. 14/68, [1967–1970 Court Decisions] CCH Comm. Mkt. Rep. ¶8056 (ECCJ 1969).

Summaries and Texts of the Principal U. S. Antitrust Statutes

SHERMAN ACT[1]

[As amended by Public No. 314, 75th Congress, August 17, 1937; 15 U.S.C. §§ 1-7 (1970)]

An Act to protect trade and commerce against unlawful restraints and monopolies.

Be it enacted by the Senate and House of Representatives of the United States of America in Congress assembled, that

Sec. 1. Every contract, combination in the form of trust or otherwise, or conspiracy, in restraint of trade or commerce among the several States, or with foreign nations, is hereby declared to be illegal: *Provided,* That nothing herein contained shall render illegal, contracts or agreements prescribing minimum prices for the resale of a commodity which bears, or the label or container of which bears, the trade mark, brand, or name of the producer or distributor of such commodity and which is in free and open competition with commodities of the same general class produced or distributed by others, when contracts or agreements of that description are lawful as applied to intrastate transactions, under any statute, law, or public policy now or hereafter in effect in any State, Territory, or the District of Columbia in which such resale is to be made, or to which the commodity is to be transported for such resale, and the making

---

[1] Sections 1, 2 and 3 of this Act were amended to increase criminal penalties from $5,000 to $50,000 by Public Law 135, 84th Cong., H.R. 3659, approved July 7, 1955.

of such contracts or agreements shall not be an unfair method of competition under section 5, as amended and supplemented, of the act entitled "An Act to create a Federal Trade Commission, to define its powers and duties, and for other purposes," approved September 26, 1914: *Provided further*, That the preceding proviso shall not make lawful any contract or agreement, providing for the establishment or maintenance of minimum resale prices on any commodity herein involved, between manufacturers, or between producers, or between wholesalers, or between brokers, or between factors, or between retailers, or betweens persons, firms, or corporations in competition with each other. Every person who shall make any contract or engage in any combination or conspiracy hereby declared to be illegal shall be deemed guilty of a misdemeanor, and, on conviction thereof, shall be punished by fine not exceeding fifty thousand dollars, or by imprisonment not exceeding one year or by both said punisments, in the discretion of the court.

Sec. 2. Every person who shall monopolize, or attempt to monopolize, or combine or conspire with any other person or persons, to monopolize any part of the trade or commerce among the several States, or with foreign nations, shall be deemed guilty of a misdemeanor, and, on conviction thereof, shall be punished by fine not exceeding fifty thousand dollars, or by imprisonment not exceeding one year, or by both said punishments, in the discretion of the court.

Sec. 3. Every contract, combination in form of trust or otherwise, or conspiracy, in restraint of trade or commerce in any Territory of the United States or of the District of Columbia, or in restraint of trade or commerce between any such Territory and another, or between any such Territory or Territories and any State or States or the District of Columbia, or with foreign nations, or between the District of Columbia and any State or States or foreign nations, is hereby declared illegal. Every person who shall make any such contract or engage in any such combination or conspiracy shall be deemed guilty of a misdemeanor and, on conviction thereof, shall be punished by fine not exceeding fifty thousand dollars, or by imprisonment not exceeding one year, or by both said punishments, in the discretion of the court.

Sec. 4. The several district courts of the United States are hereby invested with jurisdiction to prevent and restrain violations of this act; and it shall be the duty of the several United States attorneys, in their respective districts, under the direction of the Attorney General, to institute proceedings in equity to prevent and restrain such violations. Such proceedings may be by way of petition setting forth the case and praying that such violation shall be enjoined or otherwise prohibited. When the parties complained of shall have been duly notified of such petition the court shall proceed, as soon as may be, to the hearing and determination of the case; and pending such petition and before final decree, the court may at any time make such temporary restraining order or prohibition as shall be deemed just in the premises.

Sec. 5. Whenever it shall appear to the court before which any proceeding under section four of this act may be pending, that the ends of justice require that other parties should be brought before the court, the court may cause them to be summoned, whether they reside in the district in which the court is held or not; and subpoenas to that end may be served in any district by the marshall thereof.

Sec. 6. Any property owned under any contract or by any combination, or pursuant to any conspiracy (and being the subject thereof) mentioned in section one of this act, and being in the course of transportation from one State to another, or to a foreign country, shall be forfeited to the United States, and may be seized and condemned by like proceedings as those provided by law for the forfeiture, seizure, and condemnation of property imported into the United States contrary to law.

Sec. 7. The word "person," or "persons," wherever used in this act shall be deemed to include corporations and associations existing under or authorized by the laws of either the United States, the laws of any of the Territories, the laws of any State, or the laws of any foreign country.

Approved July 2, 1890.

Amended August 17, 1937.

WILSON TARIFF ACT

[28 Stat. 570—53d Congress, as amended by Public No. 475—61st Congress, as amended by Public No. 370—62d Congress, as amended by Public No. 773—80th Congress; 15 U.S.C. §§ 8–11 (1970)]

An Act to reduce taxation, to provide revenue for the Government, and for other purposes.

Be it enacted by the Senate and House of Representatives of the United States of America in Congress assembled, that

Sec. 73. Every combination, conspiracy, trust, agreement, or contract is declared to be contrary to public policy, illegal, and void when the same is made by or between two or more persons or corporations, either of whom, as agent or principal, is engaged in importing any article from any foreign country into the United States, and when such combination, conspiracy, trust, agreement, or contract is intended to operate in restraint of lawful trade, or free competition in lawful trade or commerce, or to increase the market price in any part of the United States of any article or articles imported or intended to be imported into the United States, or of any manufacture into which such imported article enters or is intended to enter. Every person who shall be engaged in the importation of goods or any commodity from any foreign country in violation of this section of this Act, who shall combine or conspire with another to violate the same, is guilty of a misdemeanor, and on conviction thereof in any court of the United States such person shall be fined in a sum not less than one hundred dollars and not exceeding five thousand dollars, and shall be further punished by imprisonment, in the discretion of the court, for a term not less than three months nor exceeding twelve months.

Sec. 74. The several district courts of the United States are invested with jurisdiction to prevent and restrain violations of section seventy-three of this Act; and it shall be the duty of the several United States attorneys, in their respective districts, under the direction of the Attorney General, to institute proceedings in equity to prevent and restrain such violations. Such proceedings may be by way of petitions setting forth the case and praying that such violations shall be enjoined or otherwise prohibited. When the parties complained of shall have been duly notified of such petition the court shall proceed, as soon as may be, to the hearing and determination of the case; and pending such petition and before final decree, the court may at any time make such temporary restraining order or prohibition as shall be deemed just in the premises.

Sec. 75. Whenever it shall appear to the court before which any proceeding under the seventy-fourth section of this Act may be pending, that the ends of justice require that other parties should be brought before the court, the court may cause them to be summoned, whether they reside in the district in which the court is held or not; and subpoenas to that end may be served in any district by the marshall thereof.

Sec. 76. Any property owned under any contract or by any combination, or pursuant to any conspiracy, and being the subject thereof, mentioned in section seventy-three of this Act, imported into and being within the United States or being in the course of transportation from one State to another, or to or from a Territory or the District of Columbia, shall be forfeited to the United States, and may be seized and condemned by like proceedings as those provided by law for the forfeiture, seizure, and condemnation of property imported into the United States contrary to law.

Sec. 77. That any person who shall be injured in his business or property by any other person or corporation by reason of anything forbidden or declared to be unlawful by this Act may sue therefor in any [district] [1] court of the United States in the district in which the defendant resides or is found, without respect to the amount in controversy, and shall recover threefold the damages by him sustained, and the costs of suit, including a reasonable attorney's fee.

Approved August 27, 1894
Amended March 3, 1911
February 12, 1913
June 25, 1948

---

[1] The circuit courts were abolished by Section 289 of the Judicial Code of 1911, Public No. 475—61st Congress, and their jurisdiction was transferred to the district courts by Section 291. Section 77 of the Wilson Tariff Act was never included in the United States Code.

CLAYTON ACT
(INCLUDING THE ROBINSON–PATMAN AMENDMENT)

[Public No. 212—63d Congress, As Amended by Public No. 692–74th Congress,[1] Public No. 899—81st Congress and Public No. 86–107, 86th Congress; 15 U.S.C. §§ 12–27 (1970)]

An Act to supplement existing laws against unlawful restraints and monopolies, and for other purposes

Be it enacted by the Senate and House of Representatives of the United States of America in Congress assembled,

"antitrust laws," as used herein, includes the Act entitled "An Act to protect trade and commerce against unlawful restraints and monopolies," approved July second, eighteen hundred and ninety; sections seventy-three to seventy-seven, inclusive, of an Act entitled "An Act to reduce taxation, to provide revenue for the Government, and for other purposes," of August twenty-seventh, eighteen hundred and ninety-four; an Act entitled "An Act to amend sections seventy-three and seventy-six of the Act of August twenty-seventh, eighteen hundred and ninety-four, entitled 'An Act to reduce taxation, to provide revenue for the Government, and for other purposes,' " approved February twelfth, nineteen hundred and thirteen; and also this Act.

"Commerce," as used herein, means trade or commerce among the several States and with foreign nations, or between the District of Columbia or any Territory of the United States and any State, Territory or foreign nation, or between any insular possessions or other places under the jurisdiction of the United States, or between any such possession or place and any State or Territory of the United States or the District of Columbia or any foreign nation, or within the District of Columbia or any Territory or any insular possession or other place under the jurisdiction of the United States: *Provided*, That nothing in this Act contained shall apply to the Philippine Islands.

The word "person" or "persons" wherever used in this Act shall be deemed to include corporations and associations existing under or authorized by the laws of either the United States, the laws of any of the Territories, the laws of any State, or the laws of any foreign country.

Sec. 2. (a) That it shall be unlawful for any person engaged in commerce, in the course of such commerce, either directly or indirectly, to discriminate in price between different purchasers of commodities of like grade and quality, where either or any of the purchases involved in such discrimination are in commerce, where such commodities are sold for use, consumption, or resale within the United States or any Territory thereof or the District of Columbia

---

[1] The Robinson-Patman Act (see footnote 2). See also footnote 5 and footnote 10, with respect to the repeal of Section 9, Section 17 in part, Sections 18 and 19, and Sections 21-25, inclusive, by two acts of June 25, 1948, namely, C. 645 (62 Stat. 683) and C. 646 (62 Stat. 896); and footnotes 4 and 6 concerning the amendment of Sections 7 and 11 by act of December 29, 1950, C. 1184 (64 Stat. 1125).

or any insular possession or other place under the jurisdiction of the United States, and where the effect of such discrimination may be substantially to lessen competition or tend to create a monopoly in any line of commerce, or to injure, destroy, or prevent competition with any person who either grants or knowingly receives the benefit of such discrimination, or with customers of either of them: *Provided*, That nothing herein contained shall prevent differentials which make only due allowances for differences in the cost of manufacture, sale, or delivery resulting from the differing methods or quantities in which such commodities are to such purchasers sold or delivered: *Provided, however,* That the Federal Trade Commission may, after due investigation and hearing to all interested parties, fix and establish quantity limits, and revise the same as it finds necessary, as to particular commodities or classes of commodities, where it finds that available purchasers in greater quantities are so few as to render differentials on account thereof unjustly discriminatory or promotive of monopoly in any line of commerce; and the foregoing shall then not be construed to permit differentials based on differences in quantities greater than those so fixed and established: *And provided further,* That nothing herein contained shall prevent persons engaged in selling goods, wares, or merchandise in commerce from selecting their own customers in bona fide transactions and not in restraint of trade: *And provided further,* That nothing herein contained shall prevent price changes from time to time where in response to changing conditions affecting the market for or the marketability of the goods concerned, such as but not limited to actual or imminent deterioration of perishable goods, obsolescence of seasonal goods, distress sales under court process, or sales in good faith in discontinuance of business in the goods concerned.[2]

(b) Upon proof being made, at any hearing on a complaint under this section, that there has been discrimination in price or services or facilities furnished, the burden of rebutting the prima facie case thus made by showing justification shall be upon the person charged with a violation of this section, and unless justification shall be affirmatively shown, the Commission is authorized to issue an order terminating the discrimination: *Provided, however,* That nothing herein contained shall prevent a seller rebutting the prima facie case thus made by showing that his lower price or the furnishing of services or facilities to any purchaser or purchasers was made in good faith to meet an equally low price of a competitor, or the services or facilities furnished by a competitor.

(c) That it shall be unlawful for any person engaged in commerce, in the course of such commerce, to pay or grant, or to receive or accept, anything of

[2] Sections 2(a)–(f) of the Clayton Act contain the provisions of the Robinson-Patman Anti-Discrimination Act, approved June 19, 1936, amending Section 2 of the original Clayton Act, approved October 15, 1914.

Section 4 of said Act provides that nothing therein "shall prevent a cooperative association from returning to its members, producers or consumers the whole, or any part of, the neat earnings or surplus resulting from its trading operations, in proportion to their purchases or sales from, to, or through the association."

Public No. 550, 75th Congress, approved May 26, 1938, to amend the said Robinson-Patman Act, further provides that nothing therein "shall apply to purchases of their supplies for their own use by schools, colleges, universities, public libraries, churches, hospitals, and charitable institutions not operated for profit."

value as a commission, brokerage, or other compensation, or any allowance or discount in lieu thereof, except for services rendered in connection with the sale or purchase of goods, wares, or merchandise, either to the other party to such transaction or to an agent, representative, or other intermediary therein where such intermediary is acting in fact for or in behalf, or is subject to the direct or indirect control, of any party to such transaction other than the person by whom such compensation is so granted or paid.

(d) That it shall be unlawful for any person engaged in commerce to pay or contract for the payment of anything of value to or for the benefit of a customer of such person in the course of such commerce as compensation or in consideration for any services or facilities furnished by or through such customer in connection with the processing, handling, sale, or offering for sale of any products or commodities manufactured, sold, or offered for sale by such person, unless such payment or consideration is available on proportionally equal terms to all other customers competing in the distribution of such products or commodities.

(e) That it shall be unlawful for any person to discriminate in favor of one purchaser against another purchaser or purchasers of a commodity bought for resale, with or without processing, by contracting to furnish or furnishing, or by contributing to the furnishing of, any services or facilities connected with the processing, handling, sale, or offering for sale of such commodity so purchased upon terms not accorded to all purchasers on proportionally equal terms.

(f) That it shall be unlawful for any person engaged in commerce, in the course of such commerce, knowingly to induce or receive a discrimination in price which is prohibited by this section.

Sec. 3. That it shall be unlawful for any person engaged in commerce, in the course of such commerce, to lease or make a sale or contract for sale of goods, wares, merchandise, machinery, supplies or other commodities, whether patented or unpatented, for use, consumption or resale within the United States or any Territory thereof or the District of Columbia or any insular possession or other place under the jurisdiction of the United States, or fix a price charged therefor, or discount from, or rebate upon, such price, on the condition, agreement, or understanding that the lessee or purchaser thereof shall not use or deal in the goods, wares, merchandise, machinery, supplies, or other commodities of a competitor or competitors of the lessor or seller, where the effect of such lease, sale, or contract for sale or such condition, agreement or understanding may be to substantially lessen competition or tend to create a monopoly in any line of commerce.

Sec. 4. That any person who shall be injured in his business or property by reason of anything forbidden in the antitrust laws may sue therefor in any district court of the United States in the district in which the defendant resides or is found or has an agent, without respect to the amount in controversy, and shall recover threefold the damages by him sustained, and the cost of suit, including a reasonable attorney's fee.

Sec. 4A. Whenever the United States is hereafter injured in its business or property by reason of anything forbidden in the antitrust laws it may sue therefor in the United States district court for the district in which the defendant resides or is found or has an agent, without respect to the amount in controversy, and shall recover actual damages by it sustained and the cost of suit.[3]

Sec. 4B. Any action to enforce any cause of action under Section 4 or 4A shall be forever barred unless commenced within four years after the cause of action accrued. No cause of action barred under existing law on the effective date of this Act shall be revived by this Act.

Sec. 5. (a)   A final judgment or decree heretofore or hereafter rendered in any civil or criminal proceeding brought by or on behalf of the United States under the antitrust laws to the effect that a defendant has violated said laws shall be prima facie evidence against such defendant in any action or proceeding brought by any other party against such defendant under said laws or by the United States under section 4A of this Act, as to all matters respecting which said judgment or decree would be an estoppel as between the parties thereto: *Provided*, That this section shall not apply to consent judgments or decrees entered before any testimony has been taken or to judgments or decrees entered in actions under section 4A of this Act.

(b) Whenever any civil or criminal proceeding is instituted by the United States to prevent, restrain, or punish violations of any of the antitrust laws, but not including an action under section 4a of this Act, the running of the statute of limitations in respect of every private right of action arising under said laws and based in whole or in part on any matter complained of in said proceeding shall be suspended during the pendency thereof and for one year thereafter: *Provided, however*, That whenever the running of the statute of limitations in respect of a cause of action arising under section 4 of this Act is suspended hereunder, any action to enforce such cause of action shall be forever barred unless commenced either within the period of suspension or within four years after the cause of action accrued.

Sec. 6. That the labor of a human being is not a commodity or article of commerce. Nothing contained in the antitrust laws shall be construed to forbid the existence and operation of labor, agricultural, or horticultural organizations, instituted for the purposes of mutual help, and not having capital stock or conducted for profit, or to forbid or restrain individual members of such organizations from lawfully carrying out the legitimate objects thereof; nor shall such organizations, or the members thereof, be held or construed to be illegal combinations or conspiracies in restraint of trade, under the antitrust laws.

Sec. 7. That no corporation engaged in commerce shall acquire, directly or indirectly, the whole or any part of the stock or other share capital and no corporation subject to the jurisdiction of the Federal Trade Commission shall acquire the whole or any part of the assets of another corporation engaged also in commerce, where in any line of commerce in any section of the country, the effect of such acquisition may be substantially to lessen competition, or to tend to create a monopoly.

No corporation shall acquire, directly or indirectly, the whole or any part of the stock or other share capital and no corporation subject to the jurisdiction of the Federal Trade Commission shall acquire the whole or any part of the assets of one or more corporations engaged in commerce, where in any line of

---

[3] Sec. 4A, 4B, 5(a) and 5(b) were added by Pub. Law 137, approved July 7, 1955, 69 Stat. 282, 283.

commerce in any section of the country, the effect of such acquisition, of such stocks or assets, or of the use of such stock by the voting or granting of proxies or otherwise, may be substantially to lessen competition, or to tend to create a monopoly.

This section shall not apply to corporations purchasing such stock solely for investment and not using the same by voting or otherwise to bring about, or in attempting to bring about, the substantial lessening of competition. Nor shall anything contained in this section prevent a corporation engaged in commerce from causing the formation of subsidiary corporations for the actual carrying on of their immediate lawful business, or the natural and legitimate branches or extensions thereof, or from owning and holding all or a part of the stock of such subsidiary corporations, when the effect of such formation is not to substantially lessen competition.

Nor shall anything herein contained be construed to prohibit any common carrier subject to the laws to regulate commerce from aiding in the construction of branches or short lines so located as to become feeders to the main line of the company so aiding in such construction or from acquiring or owning all or any part of the stock of such branch lines, nor to prevent any such common carrier from acquiring and owning all or any part of the stock of a branch or short line constructed by an independent company where there is no substantial competition between the company owning the branch line so constructed and the company owning the main line acquiring the property or an interest therein, nor to prevent such common carrier from extending any of its lines through the medium of the acquisition of stock or otherwise of any other common carrier where there is no substantial competition between the company extending its lines and the company whose stock, property, or an interest therein is so acquired.

Nothing contained in this section shall be held to affect or impair any right heretofore legally acquired: *Provided*, That nothing in this section shall be held or construed to authorize or make lawful anything heretofore prohibited or made illegal by the antitrust laws, nor to exempt any person from the penal provisions thereof or the civil remedies therein provided.

Nothing contained in this section shall apply to transactions duly consummated pusuant to authority given by the Civil Aeronautics Board, Federal Communications Commission, Federal Power Commission, Interstate Commerce Commission, the Securities and Exchange Commission in the exercise of its jurisdiction under section 79J of this title [15 U.S.C. §79J], the United States Maritime Commission, or the Secretary of Agriculture under any statutory provision vesting such power in such Commission, Secretary, or Board.[4]

Sec. 8. No private banker or director, officer, or employee of any member bank of the Federal Reserve System or any branch thereof shall be at the same time a director, officer, or employee of any other bank, banking association, savings bank, or trust company organized under the National Bank Act or organized under the laws of any State or of the District of Columbia, or any branch thereof, except that the Board of Governors of the Federal Reserve

---

[4] This section, and also section 11, which amend the respective sections of the Clayton Act, were enacted by Act of Dec. 29, 1950 (P.L., 899; 64 Stat. 1125; 15 U.S.C. 18).

System may by regulation permit such service as a director, officer, or employee of not more than one other such institution or branch thereof; but the foregoing prohibition shall not apply in the case of any one or more of the following or any branch thereof:

(1) A bank, banking association, savings bank, or trust company, more than 90 per centum of the stock of which is owned directly or indirectly by the United States or by any corporation of which the United States directly or indirectly owns more than 90 per centum of the stock.

(2) A bank, banking association, savings bank, or trust company which has been placed formally in liquidation or which is in the hands of a receiver, conservator, or other official exercising similar functions.

(3) A corporation, principally engaged in international or foreign banking or banking in a dependency or insular possession of the United States which has entered into an agreement with the Board of Governors of the Federal Reserve System pursuant to section 601 to 604A of Title 12.

(4) A bank, banking association, savings bank, or trust company, more than 50 per centum of the common stock of which is owned directly or indirectly by persons who own directly or indirectly more than 50 per centum of the common stock of such member bank.

(5) A bank, banking association, savings bank, or trust company not located and having no branch in the same city, town, or village as that in which such member bank or any branch thereof is located, or in any city, town, or village contiguous or adjacent thereto.

(6) A bank, banking association, savings bank, or trust company not engaged in a class or classes of business in which such member bank is engaged.

(7) A mutual savings bank having no capital stock.

Until February 1, 1939, nothing in this section shall prohibit any director, officer, or employee of any member bank of the Federal Reserve System, or any branch thereof, who is lawfully serving at the same time as a private banker or as a director, officer, or employee of any other bank, banking association, savings bank, or trust company, or any branch thereof, on the date of enactment of the Banking Act of 1935, from continuing such service.

The Board of Governors of the Federal Reserve System is authorized and directed to enforce compliance with this section, and to prescribe such rules and regulations as it deems necessary for that purpose.

No person at the same time shall be a director in any two or more corporations, any one of which has capital, surplus, and undivided profits aggregating more than $1,000,000, engaged in whole or in part in commerce, other than banks, banking associations, trust companies, and common carriers subject to the Act to regulate commerce, approved February fourth, eighteen hundred and eighty-seven, if such corporations are or shall have been theretofore, by virtue of their business and location of operation, competitors, so that the elimination of competition by agreement between them would constitute a violation of any of the provisions of any of the antitrust laws. The eligibility of a director under the foregoing provision shall be determined by the aggregate amount of the capital, surplus, and undivided profits, exclusive of dividends declared but not paid to stockholders, at the end of the fiscal year of said corporation next preceding the election of directors, and when a director has been elected in accordance with the provisions of this Act it shall be lawful for him to continue as such for one year thereafter.

When any person elected or chosen as a director or officer or selected as an employee of any bank or other corporation subject to the provisions of this Act is eligible at the time of his election or selection to act for such bank or other corporation in such capacity his eligibility to act in such capacity shall not be affected and he shall not become or be deemed amenable to any of the provisions hereof by reason of any change in the affairs of such bank or other corporation from whatsoever cause, whether specifically excepted by any of the provisions hereof or not, until the expiration of one year from the date of his election or employment.

Sec. 9. Every president, director, officer or manager of any firm, association or corporation engaged in commerce as a common carrier, who embezzles, steals, abstracts or willfully misapplies, or willfully permits to be misapplied, any of the moneys, funds, credits, securities, property, or assets of such firm, association, or corporation, arising or accuring from, or used in, such commerce, in whole or in part, or willfully and knowingly converts the same to his own use or to the use of another, shall be deemed guilty of a felony and upon conviction shall be fined not less than $500 or confined in the penitentiary not less than one year nor more than ten years, or both, in the discretion of the court.

Prosecutions hereunder may be in the district court of the United States for the district wherein the offense may have been committed.

That nothing in this section shall be held to take away or impair the jurisdiction of the courts of the several States under the laws thereof; and a judgement of conviction or acquittal on the merits under the laws of any State shall be a bar to any prosecution hereunder for the same act or acts.[5]

Sec. 10. No common carrier engaged in commerce shall have any dealings in securities, supplies, or other articles of commerce, or shall make or have any contracts for construction or maintenance of any kind, to the amount of more than $50,000, in the aggregate, in any one year, with another corporation, firm, partnership, or association when the said common carrier shall have upon its board of directors or as its president, manager, or as its purchasing or selling officer, or agent in the particular transaction, any person who is at the same time a director, manager, or purchasing or selling officer of, or who has any substantial interest in, such other corporation, firm, partnership, or association, unless and except such purchases shall be made from, or such dealings shall be with, the bidder whose bid is the most favorable to such common carrier, to

---

[5] Repealed by Act of June 25, 1948, c. 645 (62 Stat. 683), which revised, codified and enacted into "positive law" Title 18 of the Code (Crimes and Criminal Procedure). Said act reenacted said matter as to substance, as 18 U.S.C., Sec. 660 (62 Stat. 730).

be ascertained by competitive bidding under regulations to be prescribed by rule or otherwise by the Interstate Commerce Commission. No bid shall be received unless the name and address of the bidder or the names and addresses of the officers, directors, and general managers thereof, if the bidder be a corporation, or of the members, if it be a partnership or firm, be given with the bid.

Any person who shall, directly or indirectly, do or attempt to do anything to prevent anyone from bidding, or shall do any act to prevent free and fair competition among the bidders or those desiring to bid, shall be punished as prescribed in this section in the case of an officer or director.

Every such common carrier having any such transactions or making any such purchases shall, within thirty days after making the same, file with the Interstate Commerce Commission a full and detailed statement of the transaction showing the manner of the competitive bidding, who were the bidders, and the names and addresses of the directors and officers of the corporations and the members of the firm or partnership bidding; and whenever the said commission shall, after investigation or hearing, have reason to believe that the law has been violated in and about the said purchases or transactions, it shall transmit all papers and documents and its own views or findings regarding the transaction to the Attorney General.

If any common carrier shall violate this section, it shall be fined not exceeding $25,000; and every such director, agent, manager, or officer thereof who shall have knowingly voted for or directed the act constituting such violation, or who shall have aided or abetted in such violation, shall be deemed guilty of a misdemeanor and shall be fined not exceeding $5,000 or confined in jail not exceeding one year, or both, in the discretion of the court.

Sec. 11. (a) That authority to enforce compliance with sections 2, 3, 7, and 8 of this Act by the persons respectively subject thereto is vested in the Interstate Commerce Commission where applicable to common carriers subject to the Interstate Commerce Act, as amended; in the Federal Communications Commission where applicable to common carriers engaged in wire or radio communication or radio transmission of energy; in the Civil Aeronautics Board where applicable to air carriers and foreign air carriers subject to the Civil Aeronautics Act of 1938; in the Federal Reserve Board where applicable to banks, banking associations, and trust companies; and in the Federal Trade Commission where applicable to all other character of commerce to be exercised as follows:[6]

(b) Whenever the Commission or Board vested with jurisdiction thereof shall have reason to believe that any person is violating or has violated any of the provisions of sections 2, 3, 7 and 8 of this Act, it shall issue and serve upon such person and the Attorney General a complaint stating its charges in that respect, and containing a notice of hearing upon a day and at a place therein fixed at least thirty days after the service of said complaint. The person so complained of shall have the right to appear at the place and time so fixed and show cause why an order should not be entered by the Commission or Board requiring such person to cease and desist from the violation of the law

[6] This section, and also section 7, which amend the respective sections of the Clayton Act, were enacted by Act of Dec. 29, 1950. (P.L. 899; 64 Stat. 1125; 15 U.S.C. §21.)

so charged in said complaint. The Attorney General shall have the right to intervene and appear in said proceeding and any person may make application, and upon good cause shown may be allowed by the Commission or Board, to intervene and appear in said proceeding by counsel or in person. The testimony in any such proceeding shall be reduced to writing and filed in the office of the Commission or Board. If upon such hearing the Commission or Board, as the case may be, shall be of the opinion that any of the provisions of said sections have been or are being violated, it shall make a report in writing, in which it shall state its findings as to the facts, and shall issue and cause to be served on such person an order requiring such person to cease and desist from such violations, and divest itself of the stock, or other share capital, or assets, held or rid itself of the director chosen contrary to the provisions of sections 7 and 8 of this Act, if any there be, in the manner and within the time fixed by said order. Until the expiration of the time allowed for filing a petition for review, if no such petition has been duly filed within such time, or, if a petition for review has been filed within such time then until the record in the proceeding has been filed in a court of appeals of the United States, as hereinafter provided, the Commission or Board may at any time, upon such notice and in such manner as it shall deem proper, modify or set aside, in whole or in part, any report or any order made or issued by it under this section. After the expiration of the time allowed for filing a petition for review, if no such petition has been duly filed within such time, the Commission or Board may at any time, after notice and opportunity for hearing, reopen and alter, modify, or set aside, in whole or in part, any report or order made or issued by it under this section, whenever in the opinion of the Commission or Board conditions of fact or of law have so changed as to require such action or if the public interest shall so require: *Provided,* however, That the said person may, within sixty days after service upon him or it of said report or order entered after such a reopening, obtain a review thereof in the appropriate court of appeals of the United States, in the manner provided in subsection (c) of this section.[7]

(c) Any person required by such order of the commission or board to cease and desist from any such violation may obtain a review of such order in the court of appeals of the United States for any circuit within which such violation occurred or within which such person resides or carries on business, by filing in the court, within sixty days after the date of the service of such order, a written petition praying that the order of the commission or board be set aside. A copy of such petition shall be forthwith transmitted by the clerk of the court to the commission or board, and thereupon the commission or board shall file in the court the record in the proceeding, as provided in section 2112 of Title 28.

---

[7] Parts of paragraphs two, three, four and five of this section were amended by Public Law 85–791, 85th Con., H.R. 6788, approved August 28, 1958, 72 Stat. 943.

The first and second paragraphs of this section were redesignated as subsections (a) and (b), the last sentence of subsection (b) was amended, and the third, fourth, fifth, sixth and seventh paragraphs were amended by Public Law 86–107, 86th Cong., S. 726, approved July 23, 1959, 73 Stat. 243–246.

The amendments so made do not apply to any proceeding initiated before the date of enactment of that Act under the third or fourth paragraph of section 11. Each such proceeding continues to be governed by the provisions of such section as they existed on the day preceding the date of enactment of Public Law 86–107.

Upon such filing of the petition the court shall have jurisdiction of the proceeding and of the question determined therein concurrently with the commission or board until the filing of the record, and shall have power to make and enter a decree affirming, modifying, or setting aside the order of the commission or board, and enforcing the same to the extent that such order is affirmed, and to issue such writs as are ancillary to its jurisdiction or are necessary in its judgment to prevent injury to the public or to competitors pendente lite. The findings of the commission or board as to the facts, if supported by substantial evidence, shall be conclusive. To the extent that the order of the commission or board is affirmed, the court shall issue its own order commanding obedience to the terms of such order of the commission or board. If either party shall apply to the court for leave to adduce additional evidence, and shall show to the satisfaction of the court that such additional evidence is material and that there were reasonable grounds for the failure to adduce such evidence in the proceeding before the commission or board, the court may order such additional evidence to be taken before the commission or board, and to be adduced upon the hearing in such manner and upon such terms and conditions as to the court may seem proper. The commission or board may modify its findings as to the facts, or make new findings, by reason of the additional evidence so taken, and shall file such modified or new findings, which, if supported by substantial evidence, shall be conclusive, and its recommendation, if any, for the modification or setting aside of its original order, with the return of such additional evidence. The judgment and decree of the court shall be final, except that the same shall be subject to review by the Supreme Court upon certiorari, as provided in section 1254 of Title 28.

(d) Upon the filing of the record with it the jurisdiction of the court of appeals to affirm, enforce, modify, or set aside orders of the commission or board shall be exclusive.

(e) Such proceedings in the court of appeals shall be given precedence over other cases pending therein, and shall be in every way expedited. No order of the commission or board or judgment of the court to enforce the same shall in anywise relieve or absolve any person from any liability under the antitrust laws.

(f) Complaints, orders, and other processes of the commission or board under this section may be served by anyone duly authorized by the commission or board, either (1) by delivering a copy thereof to the person to be served, or to a member of the partnership to be served, or to the president, secretary, or other executive officer or a director of the corporation to be served; or (2) by leaving a copy thereof at the residence or the principal office or place of business of such person; or (3) by mailing by registered or certified mail a copy thereof addressed to such person at his or its residence or principal office or place of business. The verified return by the person so serving said complaint, order, or other process setting forth the manner of said service shall be proof of the same, and the return post office receipt for said complaint, order, or other process mailed by registered or certified mail as aforesaid shall be proof of the service of the same.

(g) Any order issued under subsection (b) of this section shall become final—

(1) upon the expiration of the time allowed for filing a petition for review, if no such petition has been duly filed within such time; but the commission or board may thereafter modify or set aside its order to the extent provided in the last sentence of subsection (b) of this section; or

(2) upon the expiration of the time allowed for filing a petition for certiorari, if the order of the commission or board has been affirmed, or the petition for review has been dismissed by the court of appeals, and no petition for certiorari has been duly filed; or

(3) upon the denial of a petition for certiorari, if the order of the commission or board has been affirmed or the petition for review has been dismissed by the court of appeals; or

(4) upon the expiration of thirty days from the date of issuance of the mandate of the Supreme Court, if such Court directs that the order of the commission or board be affirmed or the petition for review be dismissed.

(h) If the Supreme Court directs that the order of the commission or board be modified or set aside, the order of the commission or board rendered in accordance with the mandate of the Supreme Court shall become final upon the expiration of thirty days from the time it was rendered, unless within such thirty days either party has instituted proceedings to have such order corrected to accord with the mandate, in which event the order of the commission or board shall become final when so corrected.

(i) If the order of the commission or board is modified or set aside by the court of appeals, and if (1) the time allowed for filing a petition for certiorari has expired and no such petition has been duly filed, or (2) the petition for certiorari has been denied, or (3) the decision of the court has been affirmed by the Supreme Court, then the order of the commission or board rendered in accordance with the mandate of the court of appeals shall become final on the expiration of thirty days from the time such order of the commission or board was rendered, unless within such thirty days either party has instituted proceedings to have such order corrected so that it will accord with the mandate, in which event the order of the commission or board shall become final when so corrected.

(j) If the Supreme Court orders a rehearing; or if the case is remanded by the court of appeals to the commission or board for a rehearing, and if (1) the time allowed for filing a petition for certiorari has expired, and no such petition has been duly filed, or (2) the petition for certiorari has been denied, or (3) the decision of the court has been affirmed by the Supreme Court, then the order of the commission or board rendered upon such rehearing shall become final in the same manner as though no prior order of the commission or board had been rendered.

(k) As used in this section the term "mandate," in case a mandate has been recalled prior to the expiration of thirty days from the date of issuance thereof, means the final mandate.

(l) Any person who violates any order issued by the commission or board under subsection (b) of this section after such order has become final, and while such order is in effect, shall forfeit and pay to the United States a civil penalty of not more than $5,000 for each violation, which shall accrue to the United States and may be recovered in a civil action brought by the United States. Each separate violation of any such order shall be a separate offense, except that in the case of a violation through continuing failure or neglect to obey a final order of the commission or board each day of continuance of such failure or neglect shall be deemed a separate offense.

Sec. 12. That any suit, action, or proceeding under the antitrust laws against a corporation may be brought not only in the judicial district whereof it is an inhabitant, but also in any district wherein it may be found or transacts business; and all process in such cases may be served in the district of which it is an inhabitant, or wherever it may be found.

Sec. 13. That in any suit, action, or proceeding brought by or on behalf of the United States subpoenas for witnesses who are required to attend a court of the United States in any judicial district in any case, civil or criminal, arising under the antitrust laws may run into any other district: *Provided,* That in civil cases no writ of subpoena shall issue for witnesses living out of the district in which the court is held at a greater distance than one hundred miles from the place of holding the same without the permission of the trial court being first had upon proper application and cause shown.

Sec. 14. That whenever a corporation shall violate any of the penal provisions of the antitrust laws, such violation shall be deemed to be also that of the individual directors, officers, or agents of such corporation who shall have authorized, ordered, or done any of the acts constituting in whole or in part such violation, and such violation shall be deemed a misdemeanor, and upon conviction therefor of any such director, officer, or agent he shall be punished by a fine of not exceeding $5,000 or by imprisonment for not exceeding one year, or by both, in the discretion of the court.

Sec. 15. That the several district courts of the United States are invested with jurisdiction to prevent and restrain violations of this Act, and it shall be the duty of the several United States attorneys, in their respective districts, under the direction of the Attorney General, to institute proceedings in equity to prevent and restrain such violations. Such proceedings may be by way of petition setting forth the case and praying that such violation shall be enjoined or otherwise prohibited. When the parties complained of shall have been duly notified of such petition, the court shall proceed, as soon as may be, to the hearing and determination of the case; and pending such petition, and before final decree, the court may at any time make such temporary restraining order or prohibition as shall be deemed just in the premises. Whenever it shall appear to the court before which any such proceeding may be pending that the ends of justice require that other parties should be brought before the court, the court may cause them to be summoned whether they reside in the district in which the court is held or not, and subpoenas to that end may be served in any district by the marshal thereof.

Sec. 16. That any person, firm, corporation, or association shall be entitled to sue for and have injunctive relief, in any court of the United States having jurisdiction over the parties, against threatened loss or damage by a violation of the antitrust laws, including sections 2, 3, 7, and 8 of this Act, when and under the same conditions and principles as injunctive relief against threatened conduct that will cause loss or damage is granted by courts of equity, under the rules governing such proceedings, and upon the execution of proper bond against damages for an injunction improvidently granted and a showing that the danger of irreparable loss or damage is immediate, a preliminary injunction may issue: *Provided,* That nothing herein contained shall be construed to entitle any person, firm, corporation, or association, except the United States, to bring suit in equity for injunctive relief against any common carrier subject to the provisions of the Act to regulate commerce, approved February fourth, eighteen hundred and eighty-seven, in respect of any matter subject to the regulation, supervision, or other jurisdiction of the Interstate Commerce Commission.

Sec. 17. That no preliminary injunction shall be issued without notice to the opposite party.[8]

No temporary restraining order shall be granted without notice to the opposite party unless it shall clearly appear from specific facts shown by affidavit or by the verified bill that immediate and irreparable injury, loss, or damage will result to the applicant before notice can be served and a hearing had thereon. Every such temporary restraining order shall be endorsed with the date and hour of issuance, shall be forthwith filed in the clerk's office and entered of record, shall define the injury and state why it is irreparable and why the order was granted without notice, and shall by its terms expire within such time after entry, not to exceed ten days, as the court or judge may fix, unless within the time so fixed the order is extended for a like period for good cause shown, and the reasons for such extensions shall be entered of record. In case a temporary restraining order shall be granted without notice in the contingency specified, the matter of the issuance of a preliminary injunction shall be set down for a hearing at the earliest possible time and shall take precedence of all matters except older matters of the same character; and when the same comes up for hearing the party obtaining the temporary restraining order shall proceed with the application for a preliminary injunction, and if he does not do so the court shall dissolve the temporary restraining order. Upon two days' notice to the party obtaining such temporary restraining order the opposite party may appear and move the dissolution or modification of the order, and in that event the court or judge shall proceed to hear and determine the motion as expeditiously as the ends of justice may require.

Section two hundred and sixty-three of an Act entitled "An Act to codify, revise, and amend the laws relating to the judiciary," approved March third, nineteen hundred and eleven, is hereby repealed.

Nothing in this section contained shall be deemed to alter, repeal, or amend section two hundred and sixty-six of an Act entitled "An Act to codify, revise, and amend the laws relating to the judiciary," approved March third, nineteen hundred and eleven.

Sec. 18. That, except as otherwise provided in section 26 of this title [15 U.S.C. §26], no restraining order or interlocutory order of injunction shall issue, except upon the giving of security by the applicant in such sum as the court or judge may deem proper, conditioned upon the payment of such costs

---

[8] See second paragraph of footnote 11.

and damages as may be incurred or suffered by any party who may be found to have been wrongfully enjoined or restrained thereby.[9]

Sec. 19. That every order of injunction or restraining order shall set forth the reasons for the issuance of the same, shall be specific in terms, and shall describe in reasonable detail, and not by reference to the bill of complaint or other document, the act or acts sought to be restrained, and shall be binding only upon the parties to the suit, their officers, agents, servants, employees and attorneys, or those in active concert or participating with them, and who shall, by personal service or otherwise, have received actual notice of the same.

Sec. 20. That no restraining order or injunction shall be granted by any court of the United States, or a judge or the judges thereof, in any case between an employer and employees, or between employers and employees, or between employees, or between persons employed and persons seeking employment, involving, or growing out of, a dispute concerning terms or conditions of employment, unless necessary to prevent irreparable injury to property, or to a property right of the party making the application, for which injury there is no adequate remedy at law, and such property or property right must be described with particularity in the application which must be in writing and sworn to by the applicant or by his agent or attorney.

And no such restraining order or injunction shall prohibit any person or persons, whether singly or in concert, from terminating any relation of employment, or from ceasing to perform any work or labor, or from recommending, advising, or persuading others by peaceful means so to do; or from attending at any place where any such person or persons may lawfully be, for the purpose of peacefully obtaining or communicating information, or from peacefully persuading any person to work or to abstain from working; or from ceasing to patronize or to employ any party to such dispute, or from recommending, advising, or persuading others by peaceful and lawful means so to do; or from paying or giving to, or withholding from, any persons engaged in such dispute, any strike benefits or other moneys or things of value; or from peaceably assembling in a lawful manner, and for lawful purposes; or from doing any act or thing which might lawfully be done in the absence of such dispute by any party thereto; nor shall any of the acts specified in this paragraph be considered or held to be violations of any law of the United States.

Sec. 21. That any person who shall willfully disobey any lawful writ, process, order, rule, decree, or command of any district court of the United States or any court of the District of Columbia by doing any act or thing therein, or thereby forbidden to be done by him, if the act or thing so done by him be of such character as to constitute also a criminal offense under any statute of the United States, or under the laws of any State in which the act was committed, shall be proceeded against for his said contempt hereinafter provided.[10]

Sec. 22. That whenever it shall be made to appear to any district court or judge thereof, or to any judge therein sitting, by the return of a proper officer or lawful process, or upon the affidavit of some credible person, or by information filed by any district attorney, that there is reasonable ground to believe

[9] See second paragraph of footnote 11.
[10] See footnote 11.

that any person has been guilty of such contempt, the court or judge thereof, or any judge therein sitting, may issue a rule requiring the said person so charged to show cause upon a day certain why he should not be punished therefor, which rule, together with a copy of the affidavit or information, shall be served upon the person charged, with sufficient promptness to enable him to prepare for and make return to the order at the time fixed therein. If upon or by such return, in the judgment of the court, the alleged contempt be not sufficiently purged, a trial shall be directed at a time and place fixed by the court: *Provided, however,* That if the accused, being a natural person, fail or refuse to make return to the rule to show cause, an attachment may issue against his person to compel an answer, and in case of his continued failure or refusal, or if for any reason it be impracticable to dispose of the matter on the return day, he may be required to give reasonable bail for his attendance at the trial and his submission to the final judgment of the court. Where the accused is a body corporate, an attachment for the sequestration of its property may be issued upon like refusal or failure to answer.

In all cases within the purview of this Act such trial may be by the court, or, upon demand of the accused, by a jury; in which latter event the court may impanel a jury from the jurors then in attendance, or the court or the judge thereof in chambers may cause a sufficient number of jurors to be selected and summoned, as provided by law, to attend at the time and place of trial, at which time a jury shall be selected and impaneled as upon trial for misdemeanor; and such trial shall conform, as near as may be, to the practice in criminal cases prosecuted by indictment or upon information.

If the accused be found guilty, judgment shall be entered accordingly, prescribing the punishment, either by fine or imprisonment, or both, in the discretion of the court. Such fine shall be paid to the United States or to the complainant or other party injured by the act constituting the contempt, or may, where more than one is so damaged, be divided or apportioned among them as the court may direct, but in no case shall the fine to be paid to the United States exceed, in case the accused is a natural person, the sum of $1,000, nor shall such imprisonment exceed the term of six months: *Provided,* That in any case the court or a judge thereof may, for good cause shown, by affidavit or proof taken in open court or before such judge and filed with the papers in the case, dispense with the rule to show cause, and may issue an attachment for the arrest of the person charged with contempt; in which event such person, when arrested, shall be brought before such court or a judge thereof without unnecessary delay and shall be admitted to bail in a reasonable penalty for his appearance to answer to the charge or for trial for the contempt; and thereafter the proceedings shall be the same as provided herein in case the rule had issued in the first instance.

Sec. 23. That the evidence taken upon the trial of any persons so accused may be preserved by bill of exceptions, and any judgment of conviction may be reviewed upon writ of error in all respects as now provided by law in criminal cases, and may be affirmed, reversed, or modified as justice may require. Upon the granting of such writ of error, execution of judgment shall be stayed, and the accused, if thereby sentenced to imprisonment, shall be admitted to bail in such reasonable sum as may be required by the court, or by any justice or any judge of any district court of the United States or any court of the District of Columbia.[11]

Sec. 24. That nothing herein contained shall be construed to relate to contempts committed in the presence of the court, or so near thereto as to obstruct the administration of justice, nor to contempts committed in disobedience of any lawful writ, process, order, rule, decree, or command entered in any suit or action brought or prosecuted in the name of, or on behalf of, the United States, but the same, and all the other cases of contempt not specifically embraced within section twenty-one of this Act, may be punished in conformity to the usages at law and in equity now prevailing.

Sec. 25. That no proceeding for contempt shall be instituted against any person unless begun within one year from the date of the act complained of; nor shall any such proceeding be a bar to any criminal prosecution for the same act or acts; but nothing herein contained shall affect any proceedings in contempt pending at the time of the passage of this Act.

Sec. 26. If any clause, sentence, paragraph, or part of this Act shall, for any reason, be adjudged by any court of competent jurisdiction to be invalid, such judgment shall not affect, impair, or invalidate the remainder thereof, but shall be confined in its operation to the clause, sentence, paragraph, or part thereof directly involved in the controversy in which such judgment shall have been rendered.

Approved, October 15, 1914.

[11] Sections 21 to 25, inclusive, were repealed by Act of June 25, 1948, c. 645 (62 Stat. 683), which revised, codified and enacted into "positive law," Title 18 of the Code (Crimes and Criminal Procedure). Said act reenacted said matter, excluding Section 23, as to substance, as 18 U.S.C., Section 402 (as amended by Public Law 72, May 21, 1949, 81st Congress), 18 U.S.C., Section 3285 and 18 U.S.C., Section 3691. Section 23 was omitted as no longer required in view of the civil and criminal rules promulgated by the Supreme Court.

The Act of June 25, 1948, c. 646 (62 Stat. 869), which revised, codified and enacted into law, Title 28 of the Code (Judicial Code and Judiciary), repealed the first, second, and fourth pars. of Sec. 17, and repealed Secs. 18 and 19, in view of Rule 65, Federal Rules of Civil Procedure, which covers the substance of the matter involved.

FEDERAL TRADE COMMISSION ACT[1]

[Public No. 203—63d Congress, as amended by Public No. 477—75th Congress, as amended by Public No. 459—81st Congress, as amended by Public No. 542—82d Congress, as amended by Public No. 85—791—85th Congress, as amended by Public No. 85–909—85th Congress, as amended by Public No. 93–153—93d Congress; 15 U.S.C. §§ 41–58 (1970)] [1]

An Act to create a Federal Trade Commission, to define
its powers and duties, and for other purposes

Be it enacted by the Senate and House of Representatives of the United States of America in Congress assembled, That a commission is hereby created and established, to be known as the Federal Trade Commission (hereinafter referred to as the Commission), which shall be composed of five Commissioners, who shall be appointed by the President, by and with the advice and consent of the Senate. Not more than three of the Commissioners shall be members of the same political party. The first Commissioners appointed shall continue in office for terms of three, four, five, six, and seven years, respectively, from September 26, 1914, the term of each to be designated by the President, but their successors shall be appointed for terms of seven years, except that any person chosen to fill a vacancy shall be appointed only for the unexpired term of the Commissioner whom he shall succeed: *Provided, however,* That upon the expiration of his term of office a Commissioner shall continue to serve until his successor shall have been appointed and shall have qualified. The President shall choose a chairman from the Commission's membership.[2] No Commissioner shall engage in any other business, vocation, or employment. Any Commissioner may be removed by the President for inefficiency, neglect of duty, or malfeasance in office. A vacancy in the Commission shall not impair the right of the remaining Commissioners to exercise all the powers of the Commission.

With the exception of the secretary, a clerk to each Commissioner, the tation of itemized vouchers therefor approved by the Commission.

The Commission shall have an official seal, which shall be judicially noticed.

---

[1] The Act is published as also amended by Public No. 706, 75th Congress, and by Public No. 542, 82d Congress (see footnote 7), and as further amended, as above noted, by Public No. 459, 81st Congress. Ch. 61, 2d Session. H.R. 2023 (An Act to regulate oleomargarine, etc.), approved March 16, 1950, and effective July 1, 1950, and by Public No. 93–153, 93d Congress (Alaska pipeline, etc.).

[2] Under the provisions of Section 3 of Reorganization Plan No. 8 of 1950, effective May 24, 1950 (as published in the Federal Register for May 25, 1950, at page 3175) the functions of the Commission with respect to choosing a chairman from among the membership of the Commission was transferred to the President. Under said plan, prepared by the President and transmitted to the Senate and House on March 13, 1950, pursuant to the provisions of the Reorganization Act of 1949, approved June 20, 1949, there were also transferred to the Chairman of the Commission, subject to certain limitations, "the executive and administrative functions of the Commission, including functions of the Commission with respect to (1) the appointment and supervision of personnel employed under the Commission, (2) the distribution of business among such personnel and among administrative units of the Commission, and (3) the use and expenditure of funds."

Sec. 2. The Commission shall appoint a secretary, who shall receive a salary, payable in the same manner as the salaries of the judges of the courts of the United States, and it shall have authority to employ and fix the compensation of such attorneys, special experts, examiners, clerks and other employees as it may from time to time find necessary for the proper performance of its duties and as may be from time to time appropriated for by Congress.

With the exception of the secretary, a clerk to each Commissioner, the attorneys, and such special experts and examiners as the Commission may from time to time find necessary for the conduct of its work, all employees of the Commission shall be a part of the classified civil service, and shall enter the service under such rules and regulations as may be prescribed by the commission and by the Civil Service Commission.

All of the expenses of the Commission, including all necessary expenses for transportation incurred by the Commissioners or by their employees under their orders, in making any investigation, or upon official business in any other places than in the city of Washington, shall be allowed and paid on the presentation of itemized vouchers therefor approved by the Commission.

Until otherwise provided by law, the Commission may rent suitable offices for its use.

The Auditor for the State and Other Departments shall receive and examine all accounts of expenditures of the Commission.[3]

Sec. 3. The principal office of the Commission shall be in the city of Washington, but it may meet and exercise all its powers at any other place. The Commission may, by one or more of its members, or by such examiners as it may designate, prosecute any inquiry necessary to its duties in any part of the United States.

Sec. 4. The words defined in this section shall have the following meaning when found in this Act, to wit:

"Commerce" means commerce among the several States or with foreign nations, or in any Territory of the United States or in the District of Columbia, or between any such Territory and another, or between any such Territory and any State or foreign nation, or between the District of Columbia and any State or Territory or foreign nation.

"Corporation" shall be deemed to include any company, trust, so-called Massachusetts trust, or association, incorporated or unincorporated, which is organized to carry on business for its own profit or that of its members, and has shares of capital or capital stock or certificates of interest, and any company, trust, so-called Massachusetts trust, or association, incorporated or unincorporated, without shares of capital or capital stock or certificates of interest, except partnerships, which is organized to carry on business for its own profit or that of its members.

"Documentary evidence" includes all documents, papers, correspondence, books of account, and financial and corporate records.

"Acts to regulate commerce" means the Act entitled "An Act to regulate commerce," approved February 14, 1887, and all Acts amendatory thereof

[3] Auditing of accounts was made a duty of the General Accounting Office by the Act of June 10, 1921, 42 Stat. 24.

and supplementary thereto and the Communications Act of 1934 and all Acts amendatory thereof and supplementary thereto.

"Antitrust Acts" means the Act entitled "An Act to protect trade and commerce against unlawful restraints and monopolies," approved July 2, 1890; also sections 73 to 77 of an Act entitled "An Act to reduce taxation, to provide revenue for the Government, and for other purposes," approved August 27, 1894; also the Act entitled "An Act to amend sections 73 and 76 of the Act of August 27, 1894, entitled 'An Act to reduce taxation, to provide revenue for the Government, and for other purposes,'" approved February 12, 1913; and also the Act entitled "An Act to supplement existing laws against unlawful restraints and monopolies, and for other purposes," approved October 15, 1914.

Sec. 5. (a) (1) Unfair methods of competition in commerce, and unfair or deceptive acts or practices in commerce are declared unlawful.

(2) Nothing contained in this section or in any of the Antitrust Acts shall render unlawful any contracts or agreements prescribing minimum or stipulated prices, or requiring a vendee to enter into contracts or agreements prescribing minimum or stipulated prices, for the resale of a commodity which bears, or the label or container of which bears, the trade-mark, brand, or name of the producer or distributor of such commodity and which is in free and open competition with commodities of the same general class produced or distributed by others, when contracts or agreements of that description are lawful as applied to intrastate transactions under any statute, law, or public policy now or hereafter in effect in any State, Territory, or the District of Columbia in which such resale is to be made, or to which the commodity is to be transported for such resale.

(3) Nothing contained in this section or in any of the Antitrust Acts shall render unlawful the exercise or the enforcement of any right or right of action created by any statute, law, or public policy now or hereafter in effect in any State, Territory, or the District of Columbia, which in substance provides that willfully and knowingly advertising, offering for sale, or selling any commodity at less than the price or prices prescribed in such contracts or agreements whether the person so advertising, offering for sale, or selling is or is not a party to such a contract or agreement, is unfair competition and is actionable at the suit of any person damaged thereby.

(4) Neither the making of contracts or agreements as described in paragraph (2) of this subsection, nor the exercise or enforcement of any right or right of action as described in paragraph (3) of this subsection shall constitute an unlawful burden or restraint upon, or interference with, commerce.

(5) Nothing contained in paragraph (2) of this subsection shall make lawful contracts or agreements providing for the establishment or maintenance of minimum or stipulated resale prices on any commodity referred to in paragraph (2) of this subsection, between manufacturers, or between producers, or between wholesalers, or between brokers, or between factors, or between retailers, or between persons, firms, or corporations in competition with each other.

(6) The Commission is empowered and directed to prevent persons, partnerships, or corporations, except banks, common carriers subject to the Acts to regulate commerce, air carriers and foreign air carriers subject to the

Federal Aviation Act of 1958, and persons, partnerships, or corporations insofar as they are subject to the Packers and Stockyards Act, 1921, as amended, except as provided in section 406(b) of said Act, from using unfair methods of competition in commerce and unfair or deceptive acts or practices in commerce.[4]

(b) Whenever the Commission shall have reason to believe that any such person, partnership, or corporation has been or is using any unfair method of competition or unfair or deceptive act or practice in commerce, and if it shall

---

[4] Public No. 542, 82d Cong., Ch. 745, 2d Session, H.R. 5767, approved July 14, 1952 (the McGuire Act, 15 U.S.C. §45, 66 Stat. 631), amended Sec. 5 (a) of this Act, by inserting in lieu thereof Sec. 5(a) (1) through (6).

Therefore, by subsection (f) of Section 1107, of the "Civil Aeronautics Act of 1938," approved June 23, 1938, Public No. 706, 75th Congress, Ch. 601, 3d Sess., S. 3845, 52 Stat. 1028, the language of former Sec. 5 (a) was amended by inserting immediately following the words "to regulate commerce," the words "air carriers and foreign air carriers subject to the Civil Aeronautics Act of 1938," as above set out in Sec. 5 (a) (6).

Public No. 85–909, 85th Cong., H.R. 9020, approved September 2, 1958, amended the Packers and Stockyards Act, 1921, as amended (7 U.S.C. §§226, 227 and 72 Stat. 1749, 1750) by striking out subsection (b) of Section 406 and inserting in lieu thereof the following:

"(b) The Federal Trade Commission shall have power and jurisdiction over any matter involving meat, meat food products, livestock products in unmanufactured form or poultry products, which by this Act is made subject to the power or jurisdiction of the Secretary, as follows:

"(1) When the Secretary in the exercise of his duties requests of the Commission that it make investigations and reports in any case.

"(2) In any investigation of, or proceeding for the prevention of, an alleged violation of any act administered by the Commission, arising out of acts or transactions involving meat, meat products, livestock products in unmanufactured form, or poultry products, if the Commission determines that effective exercise of its power or jurisdiction with respect to retail sales of any such commodities is or will be impaired by the absence of power or jurisdiction over all acts or transactions involving such commodities in such investigation or proceeding. In order to avoid unnecessary duplication of effort by the Government and burdens upon the industry, the Commissioner shall notify the Secretary of such determination, the reasons therefor, and the acts or transactions involved, and shall not exercise power or jurisdiction with regard to acts or transactions (other than retail sales) involving such commodities if the Secretary within ten days from the date of receipt of the notice notifies the Commission that there is pending in his Department an investigation of, or proceeding for the prevention of, an alleged violation of this Act involving the same subject matter.

"(3) Over all transactions in commerce in margarine or oleomargarine and over retail sales of meat, meat food products, livestock products in unmanufactured form, and poultry products.

"(c) The Federal Trade Commission shall have no power or jurisdiction over any matter which by this Act is made subject to the jurisdiction of the Secretary, except as provided in subsection (b) of this section."

*   *   *   *   *   *

The same Public Law also amended Subsection 6 of section 5(a) of the Federal Trade Commission Act (15 U.S.C. §45(a)(6) and 38 Stat. 719) by substituting "persons, partnerships, or corporations insofar as they are subject to the packers and Stockyards Act, 1921, as amended, except as provided in section 406(b) of said Act" for "persons, partnerships, or corporations subject to the Packers and Stockyards Act, 1921, except as provided in section 406(b) of said Act."

appear to the Commission that a proceeding by it in respect thereof would be to the interest of the public, it shall issue and serve upon such person, partnership, or corporation a complaint stating its charges in that respect and containing a notice of a hearing upon a day and at a place therein fixed at least thirty days after the service of said complaint. The person, partnership, or corporation so complained of shall have the right to appear at the place and time so fixed and show cause why an order should not be entered by the Commission requiring such person, partnership, or corporation to cease and desist from the violation of the law so charged in said complaint. Any person, partnership, or corporation may make application, and upon good cause shown may be allowed by the Commission to intervene and appear in said proceeding by counsel or in person. The testimony in any such proceeding shall be reduced to writing and filed in the office of the Commission. If upon such hearing the Commission shall be of the opinion that the method of competition or the act or practice in question is prohibited by this Act, it shall make a report in writing in which it shall state its findings as to the facts and shall issue and cause to be served on such person, partnership, or corporation an order requiring such person, partnership, or corporation to cease and desist from using such method of competition or such act or practice. Until the expiration of the time allowed for filing a petition for review, if no such petition has been duly filed within such time, or, if a petition for review has been filed within such time then until the record in the proceedings has been filed in a court of appeals of the United States, as hereinafter provided, the Commission may at any time, upon such notice and in such manner as it shall deem proper, modify or set aside, in whole or in part, any report or any order made or issued by it under this section.[5] After the expiration of the time allowed for filing a petition for review, if no such petition has been duly filed within such time, the Commission may at any time, after notice and opportunity for hearing, reopen and alter, modify, or set aside, in whole or in part, any report, or order made or issued by it under this section, whenever in the opinion of the Commission conditions of fact or of law have so changed as to require such action or if the public interest shall so require: *Provided, however,* That the said person, partnership, or corporation may, within sixty days after service upon him or it of said report or order entered after such a reopening, obtain a review thereof in the appopriate court of appeals of the United States, in the manner provided in subsection (c) of this section.

(c) Any person, partnership, or corporation required by an order of the Commission to cease and desist from using any method of competition or act or practice may obtain a review of such order in the court of appeals of the United States, within any circuit where the method of competition or the act or practice in question was used or where such person, partnership, or corporation resides or carries on business, by filing in the court, within sixty days [6]

[5] This sentence was amended by Public Law 85–791, 85th Cong., H.R. 6788, approved August 28, 1958, 72 Stat. 942.

[6] Section 5(a) of the amending Act of 1938 provides:

Sec. 5. (a) In case of an order by the Federal Trade Commission to cease and desist, served on or before the date of the enactment of this Act, the sixty-day period referred to in sections 5(c) of the Federal Trade Commission Act, as amended by this Act, shall begin on the date of the enactment of this Act.

from the date of the service of such order, a written petition praying that the order of the Commission be set aside. A copy of such petition shall be forthwith transmitted by the clerk of the court to the Commission, and thereupon the Commission shall file in the court the record in the proceeding, as provided in section 2112 of Title 28. Upon such filing of the petition the court shall have jurisdiction of the proceeding and of the question determined therein concurrently with the Commission until the filing of the record and shall have power to make and enter a decree affirming, modifying, or setting aside the order of the Commission, and enforcing the same to the extent that such order is affirmed and to issue such writs as are ancillary to its jurisdiction or are necessary in its judgment to prevent injury to the public or to competitors pendente lite.[7] The findings of the Commission as to the facts, if supported by evidence, shall be conclusive. To the extent that the order of the Commission is affirmed, the court shall thereupon issue its own order commanding obedience to the terms of such order of the Commission. If either party shall apply to the court for leave to adduce additional evidence, and shall show to the satisfaction of the court that such additional evidence is material and that there were reasonable grounds for the failure to adduce such evidence in the proceeding before the Commission, the court may order such additional evidence to be taken before the Commission and to be adduced upon the hearing in such manner and upon such terms and conditions as to the court may seem proper. The Commission may modify its findings as to the facts, or make new findings, by reason of the additional evidence so taken, and it shall file such modified or new findings, which, if supported by evidence, shall be conclusive, and its recommendation, if any, for the modification or setting aside of its original order, with the return of such additional evidence. The judgment and decree of the court shall be final, except that the same shall be subject to review by the Supreme Court upon certiorari, as provided in section 347 of Title 28.

(d) Upon the filing of the record with it the jurisdiction of the court of appeals of the United States to affirm, enforce, modify, or set aside orders of the Commission shall be exclusive.[8]

(e) Such proceedings in the court of appeals shall be given precedence over other cases pending therein, and shall be in every way expedited. No order of the Commission or judgment of court to enforce the same shall in anywise relieve or absolve any person, partnership, or corporation from any liability under the Antitrust Acts.

(f) Complaints, orders, and other processes of the Commission under this section may be served by anyone duly authorized by the Commission, either (a) by delivering a copy thereof to the person to be served, or to a member of the partnership to be served, or the president, secretary, or other executive officer or a director of the corporation to be served; or (b) by leaving a copy thereof at the residence or principal office or place of business of such person, partnership, or corporation; or (c) by mailing a copy thereof by registered mail or by certified mail addressed to such person, partnership, or corporation at his or its residence or principal office or place of business. The verified return by the person so serving said complaint, order, or other process setting forth the

[7] The above two sentences were also amended by Public Law 85–791.
[8] The above section was also amended by Public Law 85–791.

manner of said service shall be proof of the same, and the return post office receipt for said complaint, order, or other process mailed by registered mail or by certified mail as aforesaid shall be proof of the service of the same.

(g) An order of the Commission to cease and desist shall become final—

(1) Upon the expiration of the time allowed for filing a petition for review, if no such petition has been duly filed within such time; but the Commission may thereafter modify or set aside its order to the extent provided in the last sentence of subsection (b); or

(2) Upon the expiration of the time allowed for filing a petition for certiorari, if the order of the Commission has been affirmed, or the petition for review dismissed by the court of appeals, and no petition for certiorari has been duly filed; or

(3) Upon the denial of a petition for certiorari, if the order of the Commission has been affirmed or the petition for review dismissed by the court of appeals; or

(4) Upon the expiration of thirty days from the date of issuance of the mandate of the Supreme Court, if such Court directs that the order of the Commission be affirmed or the petition for review dismissed.

(h) If the Supreme Court directs that the order of the Commission be modified or set aside, the order of the Commission rendered in accordance with the mandate of the Supreme Court shall become final upon the expiration of thirty days from the time it was rendered, unless within such thirty days either party has instituted proceedings to have such order corrected to accord with the mandate, in which event the order of the Commission shall become final when so corrected.

(i) If the order of the Commission is modified or set aside by the court of appeals, and if (1) the time allowed for filing a petition for certiorari has expired and no such petition has been duly filed, or (2) the petition for certiorari has been denied, or (3) the decision of the court has been affirmed by the Supreme Court, then the order of the Commission rendered in accordance with the mandate of the court of appeals shall become final on the expiration of thirty days from the time such order of the Commission was rendered, unless within such thirty days either party has instituted proceedings to have such order corrected so that it will accord with the mandate, in which event the order of the Commission shall become final when so corrected.

(j) If the Supreme Court orders a rehearing; or if the case is remanded by the court of appeals to the Commission for a rehearing, and if (1) the time allowed for filing a petition for certiorari has expired, and no such petition has been duly filed, or (2) the petition for certiorari has been denied, or (3) the decision of the court has been affirmed by the Supreme Court, then the order of the Commission rendered upon such rehearing shall become final in the same manner as though no prior order of the Commission had been rendered.

(k) As used in this section the term "mandate," in case a mandate has been recalled prior to the expiration of thirty days from the date of issuance thereof, means the final mandate.

(1) Any person, partnership, or corporation who violates an order of the Commission after it has become final, and while such order is in effect, shall forfeit and pay to the United States a civil penalty of not more than $10,000 for each violation, which shall accrue to the United States and may be recovered in a civil action brought by the Attorney General of the United States. Each separate violation of such an order shall be a separate offense, except that in the case of a violation through continuing failure to obey or neglect to obey a final order of the Commission, each day of continuance of such failure or neglect shall be deemed a separate offense. In such actions, the United States district courts are empowered to grant mandatory injunctions and such other and further equitable relief as they deem appropriate in the enforcement of such final orders of the Commission.

(m) Whenever in any civil proceeding involving this Act the Commission is authorized or required to appear in a court of the United States, or to be represented therein by the Attorney General of the United States, the Commission may elect to appear in its own name by any of its attorneys designated by it for such purpose, after formally notifying and consulting with and giving the Attorney General 10 days to take the action proposed by the Commission.[9]

Sec. 6. The Commission shall also have power[10]—

(a) To gather and compile information concerning, and to investigate from time to time the organization, business, conduct, practices, and management of any corporation engaged in commerce, excepting banks and common carriers subject to the Act to regulate commerce, and its relation to other corporations and to individuals, associations, and partnerships.

(b) To require, by general or special orders, corporations engaged in commerce, excepting banks and common carriers subject to the Act to regulate commerce, or any class of them, or any of them, respectively, to file with the Commission in such form as the Commission may prescribe annual or special, or both annual and special, reports or answers in writing to specific questions, furnishing to the Commission such information as it may require as to the organization, business, conduct, practices, management, and relation to other corporations, partnerships, and individuals of the respective corporations filing such reports or answers in writing. Such reports and answers shall be made under oath, or otherwise, as the Commission may prescribe, and shall be filed with the Commission within such reasonable period as the Commission may prescribe, unless additional time be granted in any case by the Commission.

(c) Whenever a final decree has been entered against any defendant corporation in any suit brought by the United States to prevent and restrain any violation of the antitrust Acts, to make investigation, upon its own initiative, of the manner in which the decree has been or is being carried out, and upon the application of the Attorney General it shall be its duty to make such

---

[9] Section 5(1) was amended and 5(m) added by Public Law 93–153, 93d Cong., approved November 16, 1973.

[10] Public No. 78, 73d Cong., approved June 16, 1933, making appropriations for the fiscal year ending June 30, 1934, for the "Executive Office and sundry independent bureaus, boards, commissions," etc., made the appropriation for the Commission contingent upon the provision (48 Stat. 291; 15 U.S.C.A., Sec. 46a) that "hereafter no new investigations shall be initiated by the Commission as the result of a legislative resolution, except the same be a concurrent resolution of the two Houses of Congress."

investigation. It shall transmit to the Attorney General a report embodying its findings and recommendations as a result of any such investigation, and the report shall be made public in the discretion of the Commission.

(d) Upon the direction of the President or either House of Congress to investigate and report the facts relating to any alleged violations of the antitrust Acts by any corporation.

(e) Upon the application of the Attorney General to investigate and make recommendations for the readjustment of the business of any corporation alleged to be violating the antitrust Acts in order that the corporation may thereafter maintain its organization, management, and conduct of business in accordance with law.

(f) To make public from time to time such portions of the information obtained by it hereunder, except trade secrets and names of customers, as it shall deem expedient in the public interest; and to make annual and special reports to the Congress and to submit therewith recommendations for additional legislation; and to provide for the publication of its reports and decisions in such form and manner as may be best adapted for public information and use.

(g) From time to time to classify corporations and to make rules and regulations for the purpose of carrying out the provisions of this Act.

(h) To investigate, from time to time, trade conditions in and with foreign countries where associations, combinations, or practices of manufacturers, merchants, or traders, or other conditions, may affect the foreign trade of the United States, and to report to Congress thereon, with such recommendations as it deems advisable.

Provided, That the exception of "banks and common carriers subject to the Act to regulate commerce" from the Commission's powers defined in clauses (a) and (b) of this section, shall not be construed to limit the Commission's authority to gather and compile information, to investigate, or to require reports or answers from, any such corporation to the extent that such action is necessary to the investigation of any corporation, group of corporations, or industry which is not engaged or is engaged only incidentally in banking or in business as a common carrier subject to the Act to regulate commerce.[11]

Sec. 7. In any suit in equity brought by or under the direction of the Attorney General as provided in the antitrust Acts, the court may, upon the conclusion of the testimony therein, if it shall be then of opinion that the complainant is entitled to relief, refer said suit to the Commission, as a master in chancery, to ascertain and report an appropriate form of decree therein. The Commission shall proceed upon such notice to the parties and under such rules of procedure as the court may prescribe, and upon the coming in of such report such exceptions may be filed and such proceedings had in relation thereto as upon the report of a master in other equity causes, but the court may adopt or reject such report, in whole or in part, and enter such decree as the nature of the case may in its judgment require.

Sec. 8. The several departments and bureaus of the Government when directed by the President shall furnish the Commission, upon its request, all

[11] This proviso was added by Public Law 93–153, 93d Cong., approved November 16, 1973.

records, papers, and information in their possession relating to any corporation subject to any of the provisions of this Act, and shall detail from time to time such officials and employees to the Commission as he may direct.

Sec. 9. For the purposes of this Act the Commission, or its duly authorized agent or agents, shall at all reasonable times have access to, for the purpose of examination, and the right to copy any documentary evidence of any corporation being investigated or proceeded against; and the Commission shall have power to require by subpoena the attendance and testimony of witnesses and the production of all such documentary evidence relating to any matter under investigation. Any member of the Commission may sign subpoenas, and members and examiners of the Commission may administer oaths and affirmations, examine witnesses, and receive evidence.

Such attendance of witnesses, and the production of such documentary evidence, may be required from any place in the United States, at any designated place of hearing. And in case of disobedience to a subpoena the Commission may invoke the aid of any court of the United States in requiring the attendance and testimony of witnesses and the production of documentary evidence.

Any of the district courts of the United States within the jurisdiction of which such inquiry is carried on may, in case of contumacy or refusal to obey a subpoena issued to any corporation or other person, issue an order requiring such corporation or other person to appear before the Commission, or to produce documentary evidence if so ordered, or to give evidence touching the matter in question; and any failure to obey such order of the court may be punished by such court as a contempt thereof.

Upon the application of the Attorney General of the United States, at the request of the Commission, the district courts of the United States shall have jurisdiction to issue writs of mandamus commanding any person or corporation to comply with the provisions of this Act or any order of the Commission made in pursuance thereof.

The Commission may order testimony to be taken by deposition in any proceeding or investigation pending under said sections at any stage of such proceeding or investigation. Such depositions may be taken before any person designated by the Commission and having power to administer oaths. Such testimony shall be reduced to writing by the person taking the deposition, or under his direction, and shall then be subscribed by the deponent. Any person may be compelled to appear and depose and to produce documentary evidence in the same manner as witnesses may be compelled to appear and testify and produce documentary evidence before the Commission as hereinbefore provided.

Witnesses summoned before the Commission shall be paid the same fees and mileage that are paid witnesses in the courts of the United States, and witnesses whose depositions are taken, and the persons taking the same shall severally be entitled to the same fees as are paid for like services in the courts of the United States.

Sec. 10. Any person who shall neglect or refuse to attend and testify, or to answer any lawful inquiry, or to produce documentary evidence, if in his power to do so, in obedience to the subpoena or lawful requirement of the Commission, shall be guilty of an offense and upon conviction thereof by a court of competent jurisdiction shall be punished by a fine of not less than $1,000 nor more than $5,000, or by imprisonment for not more than one year, or by both such fine and imprisonment.

Any person who shall willfully make, or cause to be made, any false entry or statement of fact in any report required to be made under this Act, or who shall willfully make, or cause to be made, any false entry in any account, record, or memorandum kept by any corporation subject to this Act, or shall willfully neglect or fail to make, or cause to be made, full, true, and correct entries in such accounts, records, or memoranda of all facts and transactions appertaining to the business of such corporation, or who shall willfully remove out of the jurisdiction of the United States, or willfully mutilate, alter, or by any other means falsify any documentary evidence of such corporation, or who shall willfully refuse to submit to the Commission or to any of its authorized agents, for the purpose of inspection and taking copies, and documentary evidence of such corporation in his possession or within his control, shall be deemed guilty of an offense against the United States of competent jurisdiction, to a fine of not less than $1,000 nor more than $5,000 or to imprisonment for a term of not more than three years, or to both such fine and imprisonment.

If any corporation required by this Act to file any annual or special report shall fail so to do within the time fixed by the Commission for filing the same, and such failure shall continue for thirty days after notice of such default, the corporation shall forfeit to the United States the sum of $100 for each and every day of the continuance of such failure, which forfeiture shall be payable into the Treasury of the United States, and shall be recoverable in a civil suit in the name of the United States brought in the district where the corporation has its principal office or in any district in which it shall do business. It shall be the duty of the various United States attorneys, under the direction of the Attorney General of the United States, to prosecute for the recovery of forfeitures. The costs and expenses of such prosecution shall be paid out of the appropriation for the expenses of the courts of the United States.

Any officer or employee of the Commission who shall make public any information obtained by the Commission without its authority, unless directed by a court, shall be deemed guilty of a misdemeanor, and, upon conviction thereof, shall be punished by a fine not exceeding $5,000, or by imprisonment not exceeding one year, or by fine and imprisonment, in the discretion of the court.

Sec. 11. Nothing contained in this Act shall be construed to prevent or interfere with the enforcement of the provisions of the antitrust Acts or the Acts to regulate commerce, nor shall anything contained in the Act be construed to alter, modify, or repeal the said antitrust Acts or the Acts to regulate commerce or any part or parts thereof.

Sec. 12 (a) It shall be unlawful for any person, partnership, or corporation to disseminate, or cause to be disseminated, any false advertisement—

(1) By United States mails, or in commerce by any means, for the purpose of inducing, or which is likely to induce, directly or indirectly the purchase of food, drugs, devices or cosmetics; or

(2) By any means, for the purpose of inducing, or which is likely to induce, directly or indirectly, the purchase in commerce of food, drugs, devices, or cosmetics.

(b) The dissemination or the causing to be disseminated of any false advertisement within the provisions of subsection (a) of this section shall be an unfair or deceptive act or practice in commerce within the meaning of section 5.

Sec. 13. (a) Whenever the Commission has reason to believe—

(1) that any person, partnership, or corporation is engaged in, or is about to engage in, the dissemination or the causing of the dissemination of any advertisement in violation of section 12, and

(2) that the enjoining thereof pending the issuance of a complaint by the Commission under section 5, and until such complaint is dismissed by the Commission or set aside by the court on review, or the order of the Commission to cease and desist made thereon has become final within the meaning of section 5, would be to the interest of the public,

the Commission by any of its attorneys designated by it for such purpose may bring suit in a district court of the United States or in the United States court of any Territory, to enjoin the dissemination or the causing of the dissemination of such advertisement. Upon proper showing a temporary injunction or restraining order shall be granted without bond. Any such suit shall be brought in the district in which such person, partnership, or corporation resides or transacts business.

(b) Whenever the Commission has reason to believe—

(1) that any person, partnership, or corporation is violating, or is about to violate, any provision of law enforced by the Federal Trade Commission, and

(2) that the enjoining thereof pending the issuance of a complaint by the Commission and until such complaint is dismissed by the Commission or set aside by the court on review, or until the order of the Commission made thereon has become final, would be in the interest of the public—

the Commission by any of its attorneys designated by it for such purpose may bring suit in a district court of the United States to enjoin any such act or practice. Upon a proper showing that, weighing the equities and considering the Commission's likelihood of ultimate success, such action would be in the public interest, and after notice to the defendant, a temporary restraining order or a preliminary injunction may be granted without bond: *Provided, however*, That if a complaint is not filed within such period (not exceeding 20 days) as may be specified by the court after issuance of the temporary restraining order or preliminary injunction, the order or injunction shall be dissolved by the court and be of no further force and effect: *Provided further*, That in proper cases the Commission may seek, and after proper proof, the court may issue, a permanent injunction. Any such suit shall be brought in the district in which such person, partnership, or corporation resides or transacts business.[12]

(c) Whenever it appears to the satisfaction of the court in the case of a newspaper, magazine, periodical, or other publication, published at regular intervals—

[12] Subsection (b) was added by Public Law 93–153, 93d Cong., approved November 16, 1973. Former subsection (b) was redesignated as (c).

(1) that restraining the dissemination of a false advertisement in any particular issue of such publication would delay the delivery of such issues after the regular time therefor, and

(2) that such delay would be due to the method by which the manufacture and distribution of such publication is customarily conducted by the publisher in accordance with sound business practice, and not to any method or device adopted for the evasion of this section or to prevent or delay the issuance of an injunction or restraining order with respect to such false advertisement or any other advertisement,

the court shall exclude such issue from the operation of the restraining order or injunction.

Sec. 14. (a) Any person, partnership, or corporation who violates any provision of section 12(a) shall, if the use of the commodity advertised may be injurious to health because of results from such use under the conditions prescribed in the advertisement thereof, or under such conditions as are customary or usual, or if such violation is with intent to defraud or mislead, be guilty of a misdemeanor, and upon conviction shall be punished by a fine of not more than $5,000 or by imprisonment for not more than six months, or by both such fine or imprisonment, except that if the conviction is for a violation committed after a first conviction of such person, partnership, or corporation, for any violation of such section, punishment shall be by a fine of not more than $10,000 or by imprisonment for not more than one year, or by both such fine and imprisonment: *Provided*, That for the purposes of this section meats and meat food products duly inspected, marked, and labeled in accordance with rules and regulations issued under the Meat Inspection Act shall be conclusively presumed not injurious to health at the time the same leave official "establishments." [13]

(b) No publisher, radio-broadcast licensee, or agency or medium for the dissemination of advertising, except the manufacturer, packer, distributor, or seller of the commodity to which the false advertisement relates, shall be liable under this section by reason of the dissemination by him of false advertisement, unless he has refused, on the request of the Commission, to furnish the Commission the name and post-office address of the manufacturer, packer, distributor, or advertising agency, residing in the United States, who caused him to disseminate such advertisement. No advertising agency shall be liable under this section by reason of the causing by it of the dissemination of any false advertisement, unless it has refused, on the request of the Commission, to furnish the Commission the name and post-office address of the manufacturer, packer, distributor, or seller, residing in the United States, who caused it to cause the dissemination of such advertisement.

Sec. 15. For the purposes of sections 12, 13, and 14—

(a) (1) The term "false advertisement" means an advertisement, other than labeling, which is misleading in a material respect; and in determining

[13] Section 5 (b) of the amending Act of 1938 provides:

Sec. 5. (b) Section 14 of the Federal Trade Commission Act, added to such Act by section 4 of this Act, shall take effect on the expiration of sixty days after the date of the enactment of this Act.

whether any advertisement is misleading, there shall be taken into account (among other things) not only representations made or suggested by statement, word, design, device, sound, or any combination thereof, but also the extent to which the advertisement fails to reveal facts material in the light of such representations or material with respect to consequences which may result from the use of the commodity to which the advertisement relates under the conditions prescribed in said advertisement, or under such conditions as are customary or usual. No advertisement of a drug shall be deemed to be false if it is disseminated only to members of the medical profession, contains no false representation of a material fact, and includes, or is accompanied in each instance by truthful disclosure of, the formula showing quantitatively each ingredient of such drug.

(2) In the case of oleomargarine or margarine an advertisement shall be deemed misleading in a material respect if in such advertisement representations are made or suggested by statement, word, grade designation, design, device, symbol, sound, or any combination thereof, that such oleomargarine or margarine is a dairy product, except that nothing contained herein shall prevent a truthful, accurate, and full statement in any such advertisement of all the ingredients contained in such oleomargarine or margarine.[14]

(b) The term "food" means (1) articles used for food or drink for man or other animals, (2) chewing gum, and (3) articles used by components of any such article.

(c) The term "drug" means (1) articles recognized in the official United States Pharmacopoeia, official Homoeopathic Pharmacopoeia of the United States, or official National Formulary, or any supplement to any of them; and (2) articles intended for use in the diagnosis, cure, mitigation, treatment, or prevention of disease in man or other animals; and (3) articles (other than food) intended to affect the structure or any function of the body of man or other animals; and (4) articles intended for use as a component of any article specified in clause (1), (2), or (3); but does not include devices or their components, parts, or accessories.

(d) The term "device" (except when used in subsection (a) of this section) means instruments, apparatus, and contrivances, including their parts and accessories, intended (1) for use in the diagnosis, cure, mitigation, treatment, or prevention of disease in man or other animals; or (2) to affect the structure or any function of the body of man or other animals.

(e) The term "cosmetic" means (1) articles to be rubbed, poured, sprinkled, or sprayed on, introduced into, or otherwise applied to the human body or any part thereof intended for cleansing, beautifying, promoting attractiveness, or altering the appearance, and (2) articles intended for use as a component of any such article; except that such term shall not include soap.

(f) For the purposes of this section and section 347 of Title 21, the term "oleomargarine" or "margarine" includes—

(1) all substances, mixtures, and compounds known as oleomargarine or margarine;

---

[14] Subsection (a) of Sec. 4 of Public No. 459, 81st Congress (see footnote 1), amended sec. 15 of this Act by inserting "(1)" after the letter "(a)" in subsection (a) above, and by adding at the end of such subsection new paragraph (2), above set out.

(2) all substances, mixtures, and compounds which have a consistence similar to that of butter and which contain any edible oils or fats other than milk fat if made in imitation or semblance of butter.[15]

Sec. 16. Whenever the Federal Trade Commission has reason to believe that any person, partnership, or corporation is liable to a penalty under section 14 or under subsection (1) of section 5 of this Act, it shall—

(a) certify the facts to the Attorney General, whose duty it shall be to cause appropriate proceedings to be brought for the enforcement of the provisions of such section or subsection; or

(b) after compliance with the requirements with section 5(m), itself cause such appropriate proceedings to be brought.[16]

Sec. 17. If any provision of this Act, or the application thereof to any person, partnership, corporation, or circumstance, is held invalid, the remainder of the said sections, and the application of such provision to any other person, partnership, corporation, or circumstance, shall not be affected thereby.

Sec. 18. This Act may be cited as the "Federal Trade Commission Act."
Original approved September 26, 1914.
Amended and approved March 21, 1938.
Amended and approved November 16, 1973.

---

[15] Subsection (b) of Sec. 4 of Public No. 459, 81st Congress (see footnote 1) further amended sec. 15 of this Act, by adding at the end thereof the new subsection (f) as above set out.

[16] Section 16 was amended by Public Law 93–153, 93d Cong., approved November 16, 1973.

WEBB–POMERENE ACT

[Public No. 126—65th Congress, as amended by Public No. 773—80th Congress; 15 U.S.C. §§ 61–65 (1970)]

An Act to promote export trade, and for other purposes.

Be it enacted by the Senate and House of Representatives of the United States of America in Congress assembled, that

Sec. 1. The words "export trade" wherever used in this Act mean solely trade or commerce in goods, wares, or merchandise exported, or in the course of being exported from the United States or any Territory thereof to any foreign nation; but the words "export trade" shall not be deemed to include the production, manufacture, or selling for consumption or for resale, within the United States or any Territory thereof, of such goods, wares, or merchandise, or any act in the course of such production, manufacture, or selling for consumption or for resale.

The words "trade within the United States" wherever used in this Act mean trade or commerce among the several States or in any Territory of the United States or in the District of Columbia, or between any such Territory and another, or between any such Territory or Territories and any State or States or the District of Columbia, or between the District of Columbia and any State or States.

The word "association" wherever used in this Act means any corporation or combination, by contract or otherwise, of two or more persons, partnerships, or corporations.

Sec. 2. Nothing contained in the Act entitled "An Act to protect trade and commerce against unlawful restraints and monopolies," approved July second, eighteen hundred and ninety, [Sherman Act] shall be construed as declaring to be illegal an association entered into for the sole purpose of engaging in export trade and actually engaged solely in such export trade, or an agreement made or act done in the course of export trade by such association, provided such association, agreement, or act is not in restraint of trade within the United States, and is not in restraint of the export trade of any domestic competitor of such association: *Provided*, That such association does not, either in the United States or elsewhere, enter into any agreement, understanding, or conspiracy, or do any act which artificially or intentionally enhances or depresses prices within the United States of commodities of the class exported by such association, or which substantially lessens competition within the United States or otherwise restrains trade therein.

Sec. 3. Nothing contained in section seven of the Act entitled "An Act to supplement existing laws against unlawful restraints and monopolies, and for other purposes," [Clayton Act] approved October fifteenth, nineteen hundred and fourteen, shall be construed to forbid the acquisition or ownership by any corporation of the whole or any part of the stock or other capital of any corporation organized solely for the purpose of engaging in export trade, and actually engaged solely in such export trade, unless the effect of such acquisition or ownership may be to restrain trade or substantially lessen competition within the United States.

Sec . 4. The prohibition against "unfair methods of competition" and the remedies provided for enforcing said prohibition contained in the Act entitled "An Act to create a Federal Trade Commission, to define its powers and duties, and for other purposes," [Federal Trade Commission Act] approved September twenty-sixth, nineteen hundred and fourteen, shall be construed as extending to unfair methods of competition used in export trade against competitors engaged in export trade, even though the acts constituting such unfair methods are done without the territorial jurisdiction of the United States.

Sec. 5. Every association which engages solely in export trade, within thirty days after its creation, shall file with the Federal Trade Commission a verified written statement setting forth the location of its offices or places of business and the names and addresses of all its officers and of all its stockholders or members, and if a corporation, a copy of its certificate or articles of incorporation and bylaws, and if unincorporated, a copy of its articles or contract of association, and on the 1st day of January of each year every association engaged solely in export trade shall make a like statement of the location of its offices or places of business and the names and addresses of all its officers and of all its stockholders or members and of all amendments to and changes in its articles or certificate of incorporation or in its articles or contract of association. It shall also furnish to the commission such information as the commission may require as to its organization, business, conduct, practices, management, and relation to other associations, corporations, partnerships, and individuals. Any association which shall fail so to do shall not have the benefit of the provisions of section two and section three of this Act, and it shall also forfeit to the United States the sum of $100 for each and every day of the continuance of such failure, which forfeiture shall be payable into the Treasury of the United States, and shall be recoverable in a civil suit in the name of the United States brought in the district where the association has its principal office, or in any district in which it shall do business. It shall be the duty of the various United States attorneys, under the direction of the Attorney General of the United States, to prosecute for the recovery of the forfeiture. The costs and expenses of such prosecution shall be paid out of the appropriation for the expenses of the courts of the United States.

Whenever the Federal Trade Commission shall have reason to believe that an association or any agreement made or act done by such association is in restraint of trade within the United States or in restraint of the export trade of any domestic competitor of such association, or that an association either in the United States or elsewhere has entered into any agreement, understanding, or conspiracy, or done any act which artificially or intentionally enhances or depresses prices within the United States of commodities of the class exported by such association, or which substantially lessens competition within the United States or otherwise restrains trade therein, it shall summon such association, its officers, and agents to appear before it, and thereafter conduct an investigation into the alleged violations of law. Upon investigation, if it shall conclude that the law has been violated, it may make to such association recommendations for the readjustment of its business, in order that it may thereafter maintain its organization and management and conduct its business in accordance with law. If such association fails to comply with the recommendations of the Federal Trade Commission, said commission shall refer its findings and recommendations to the Attorney General of the United States for such action thereon as he may deem proper.

For the purpose of enforcing these provisions the Federal Trade Commission shall have all the powers, so far as applicable, given it in "An Act to create a Federal Trade Commission, to define its powers and duties, and for other purposes" [Federal Trade Commission Act].

Approved April 10, 1918
Amended June 25, 1948

SECTION 337, TARIFF ACT OF 1930

[Public No. 361—71st Congress, as amended by Pres. Proc. No. 2695, July 4, 1946, as amended by Public No. 686—85th Congress; 19 U.S.C. § 1337 (1970)]

Be it enacted by the Senate and House of Representatives of the United States of America in Congress assembled, that

Sec. 337(a). Unfair methods of competition and unfair acts in the importation of articles into the United States, or in their sale by the owner, importer, consignee, or agent of either, the effect or tendency of which is to destroy or substantially injure an industry, efficiently and economically operated, in the United States, or to prevent the establishment of such an industry, or to restrain or monopolize trade and commerce in the United States, are declared unlawful, and when found by the President to exist shall be dealt with, in addition to any other provisions of law, as hereinafter provided.

(b) To assist the President in making any decisions under this section the commission [U. S. Tariff Commission] is authorized to investigate any alleged violation hereof on complaint under oath or upon its initiative.

(c) The commission shall make such investigation and give such notice and afford such hearing, and when deemed proper by the commission such rehearing, with opportunity to offer evidence, oral or written, as it may deem sufficient for a full presentation of the facts involved in such investigation. The testimony in every such investigation shall be reduced to writing, and a transcript thereof with the findings and recommendation of the commission shall be the official record of the proceedings and findings in the case, and in any case where the findings in such investigation show a violation of this section, a copy of the findings shall be promptly mailed or delivered to the importer or consignee of such articles. Such findings, if supported by evidence, shall be conclusive, except that a rehearing may be granted by the commission and except that, within such time after said findings are made and in such manner as appeals may be taken from decisions of the United States Customs Court, an appeal may be taken from said findings upon a question or questions of law only to the United States Court of Customs and Patent Appeals by the importer or consignee of such articles. If it shall be shown to the satisfaction of said court that further evidence should be taken, and that there were reasonable grounds for the failure to adduce such evidence in the proceedings before the commission, said court may order such additional evidence to be taken before the commission in such manner and upon such terms and conditions as to the court may seem proper. The commission may modify its findings as to the facts or make new findings by reason of additional evidence, which, if supported by evidence, shall be conclusive as to the facts except that within such time and in such manner an appeal may be taken as aforesaid upon a question or questions of law only. The judgment of said court shall be final.

(d) The final findings of the commission shall be transmitted with the record to the President.

(e) Whenever the existence of any such unfair method or act shall be established to the satisfaction of the President he shall direct that the articles concerned in such unfair methods or acts, imported by any person violating the provisions of this Act, shall be excluded from entry into the United States, and upon information of such action by the President, the Secretary of the Treasury shall, through the proper officers, refuse such entry. The decision of the President shall be conclusive.

(f) Whenever the President has reason to believe that any article is offered or sought to be offered for entry into the United States in violation of this section but has not information sufficient to satisfy him thereof, the Secretary of the Treasury shall, upon his request in writing, forbid entry thereof until such investigation as the President may deem necessary shall be completed; except that such articles shall be entitled to entry under bond prescribed by the Secretary of the Treasury.

(g) Any refusal of entry under this section shall continue in effect until the President shall find and instruct the Secretary of the Treasury that the conditions which led to such refusal of entry no longer exist.

(h) When used in this section and in sections 338 and 340, the term "United States" includes the several States and Territories, the District of Columbia, and all possessions of the United States except the Virgin Islands, American Samoa, and the Island of Guam.

SECTION 337a, TARIFF ACT OF 1930
[Added by Public No. 710—76th Congress; 19 U.S.C. § 1337a (1970)]

The importation for use, sale, or exchange of a product made, produced, processed, or mined under or by means of a process covered by the claims of any unexpired valid United States letters patent, shall have the same status for the purposes of section 337 of the Tariff Act of 1930 as the the importation of any product or article covered by the claims of any unexpired valid United States letters patent.

Approved June 17, 1930
Amended July 4, 1946
July 2, 1940
August 20, 1958

appendix III

U.S. Justice Department
Merger Guidelines

1. *Purpose*. The purpose of these guidelines is to acquaint the business community, the legal profession, and other interested groups and individuals with the standards currently being applied by the Department of Justice in determining whether to challenge corporate acquisitions and mergers under Section 7 of the Clayton Act. (Although mergers or acquisitions may also be challenged under the Sherman Act, commonly the challenge will be made under Section 7 of the Clayton Act and, accordingly, it is to this provision of law that the guidelines are directed.) The responsibilities of the Department of Justice under Section 7 are those of an enforcement agency, and these guidelines are announced solely as a statement of current Department policy, subject to change at any time without prior notice, for whatever assistance such statement may be in enabling interested persons to anticipate in a general way Department enforcement action under Section 7. Because the statements of enforcement policy contained in these guidelines must necessarily be framed in rather general terms, and because the critical factors in any particular guideline formulation may be evaluated differently by the Department than by the parties, the guidelines should not be treated as a substitute for the Deparment's business review procedures, which make available statements of the Department's present enforcement intentions with regard to particular proposed mergers or acquisitions.

2. *General Enforcement Policy*. Within the over-all scheme of the Department's antitrust enforcement activity, the primary role of Section 7 enforcement is to preserve and promote market structures conducive to competition. Market

structure is the focus of the Department's merger policy chiefly because the conduct of the individual firms in a market tends to be controlled by the structure of that market, *i.e.*, by those market conditions which are fairly permanent or subject only to slow change (such as, principally, the number of substantial firms selling in the market, the relative sizes of their respective market shares, and the substantiality of barriers to the entry of new firms into the market). Thus, for example, a concentrated market structure, where a few firms account for a large share of the sales, tends to discourage vigorous price competition by the firms in the market and to encourage other kinds of conduct, such as use of inefficient methods of production or excessive promotional expenditures, of an economically undesirable nature. Moreover, not only does emphasis on market structure generally produce economic predictions that are fully adequate for the purposes of a statute that requires only a showing that the effect of a merger "may be substantially to lessen competition, or to tend to create a monopoly," but an enforcement policy emphasizing a limited number of structural factors also facilitates both enforcement decision-making and business planning which involves anticipation of the Department's enforcement intent. Accordingly, the Department's enforcement activity under Section 7 is directed primarily toward the identification and prevention of those mergers which alter market structure in ways likely now or eventually to encourage or permit non-competitive conduct.

In certain exceptional circumstances, however, the structural factors used in these guidelines will not alone be conclusive, and the Department's enforcement activity will necessarily be based on a more complex and inclusive evaluation. This is sometimes the case, for example, where basic technological changes are creating new industries, or are significantly transforming older industries, in such fashion as to make current market boundaries and market structure of uncertain significance. In such unusual transitional situations application of the normal guideline standards may be inappropriate; and on assessing probable future developments, the Department may not sue despite nominal application of a particular guideline, or it may sue even though the guidelines, as normally applied, do not require the Department to challenge the merger. Similarly, in the area of conglomerate merger activity, the present incomplete state of knowledge concerning structure-conduct relationships may preclude sole reliance on the structural criteria used in these guidelines, as explained in paragraphs 17 and 20 below.

3. *Market Definition.* A rational appraisal of the probable competitive effects of a merger normally requires definition of one or more relevant markets. A market is any grouping of sales (or other commercial transactions) in which each of the firms whose sales are included enjoys some advantage in competing with those firms whose sales are not included. The advantage need not be great, for so long as it is significant it defines an area of effective competition among the included sellers in which the competition of the excluded sellers is, *ex hypothesi*, less effective. The process of market definition may result in identification of several appropriate markets in which to test the probable competitive effects of a particular merger.

A market is defined both in terms of its "product dimension" ("line of commerce") and its "geographic dimension" ("section of the country").

(i) *Line of commerce*. The sales of any product or service which is distinguishable as a matter of commercial practice from other products or services will ordinarily constitute a relevant product market, even though, from the standpoint of most purchasers, other products may be reasonably, but not perfectly, interchangeable with it in terms of price, quality, and use. On the other hand, the sales of two distinct products to a particular group of purchasers can also appropriately be grouped into a single market where the two products are reasonably interchangeable for that group in terms of price, quality, and use. In this latter case, however, it may be necessary also to include in that market the sales of one or more other products which are equally interchangeable with the two products in terms of price, quality, and use from the standpoint of that group of purchasers for whom the two products are interchangeable.

The reasons for employing the foregoing definitions may be stated as follows. In enforcing Section 7 the Department seeks primarily to prevent mergers which change market structure in a direction likely to create a power to behave noncompetitively in the production and sale of any particular product, even though that power will ultimately be limited, though not nullified, by the presence of other similar products that, while reasonably interchangeable, are less than perfect substitutes. It is in no way inconsistent with this effort also to pursue a policy designed to prohibit mergers between firms selling distinct products where the result of the merger may be to create or enhance the companies' market power due to the fact that the products, though not perfectly substitutable by purchasers, are significant enough alternatives to constitute substantial competitive influences on the production, development or sale of each.

(ii) *Section of the Country*. The total sales of a product or service in any commercially significant section of the country (even as small as a single community), or aggregate of such sections, will ordinarily constitute a geographic market if firms engaged in selling the product make significant sales of the product to purchasers in the section or sections. The market need not be enlarged beyond any section meeting the foregoing test unless it clearly appears that there is no economic barrier (*e.g.*, significant transportation costs, lack of distribution facilities, customer inconvenience, or established consumer preference for existing products) that hinders the sale from outside the section to purchasers within the section; nor need the market be contracted to exclude some portion of the product sales made inside any section meeting the foregoing test unless it clearly appears that the portion of sales in question is made to a group of purchasers separated by a substantial economic barrier from the purchasers to whom the rest of the sales are made.

Because data limitations or other intrinsic difficulties will often make precise delineation of geographic markets impossible, there may often be two or more groupings of sales which may reasonably be treated as constituting a relevant geographic market. In such circumstances, the Department believes it to be ordinarily most consistent with the purposes of Section 7 to challenge any merger which appears to be illegal in any reasonable geographic market, even though in another reasonable market it would not appear to be illegal.

The market is ordinarily measured primarily by the dollar value of the sales or other transactions (*e.g.*, shipments, leases) for the most recent twelve month period for which the necessary figures for the merging firms and their competitors are generally available. Where such figures are clearly unrepresentative, a different period will be used. In some markets, such as commercial banking, it is more appropriate to measure the market by other indicia, such as total deposits.

I. Horizontal Mergers

4. *Enforcement Policy*. With respect to mergers between direct competitors (*i.e.*, horizontal mergers), the Department's enforcement activity under Section 7 of the Clayton Act has the following interrelated purposes: (i) preventing elimination as an independent business entity of any company likely to have been a substantial competitive influence in a market; (ii) preventing any company or small group of companies from obtaining a position of dominance in a market; (iii) preventing significant increases in concentration in a market; and (iv) preserving significant possibilities for eventual deconcentration in a concentrated market.

In enforcing Section 7 against horizontal mergers, the Department accords primary significance to the size of the market share held by both the acquiring and the acquired firms. ("Acquiring firm" and "acquired firm" are used herein, in the case of horizontal mergers, simply as convenient designations of the firm with the larger market share and the firm with the smaller share, respectively, and do not refer to the legal form of the merger transaction.) The larger the market share held by the acquired firm, the more likely it is that the firm has been a substantial competitive influence in the market or that concentration in the market will be significantly increased. The larger the market share held by the acquiring firm, the more likely it is that an acquisition will move it toward, or further entrench it in, a position of dominance or of shared market power. Accordingly, the standards most often applied by the Department in determining whether to challenge horizontal mergers can be stated in terms of the sizes of the merging firms' market shares.

5. *Market Highly Concentrated*. In a market in which the shares of the four largest firms amount to approximately 75% or more, the Department will ordinarily challenge mergers between firms accounting for, approximately, the following percentages of the market:

Acquiring Firm	Acquired Firm
4%	4% or more
10%	2% or more
15% or more	1% or more

(Percentages not shown in the above table should be interpolated proportionately to the percentages that are shown.)

6. *Market Less Highly Concentrated*. In a market in which the shares of the four largest firms amount to less than approximately 75%, the Department will ordinarily challenge mergers between firms accounting for, approximately, the following percentages of the market:

Acquiring Firm	Acquired Firm
5%	5% or more
10%	4% or more
15%	3% or more
20%	2% or more
25% or more	1% or more

(Percentages not shown in the above table should be interpolated proportionately to the percentages that are shown.)

7. *Market With Trend Toward Concentration.* The Department applies an additional, stricter standard in determining whether to challenge mergers occurring in any market, not wholly unconcentrated, in which there is a significant trend toward increased concentration. Such a trend is considered to be present when the aggregate market share of any grouping of the largest firms in the market from the two largest to the eight largest has increased by approximately 7% or more of the market over a period of time extending from any base year 5–10 years prior to the merger (excluding any year in which some abnormal fluctuation in market shares occurred) up to the time of the merger. The Department will ordinarily challenge any acquisition, by any firm in a grouping of such largest firms showing the requisite increase in market share, of any firm whose market share amounts to approximately 2% or more.

8. *Non-Market Share Standards.* Although in enforcing Section 7 against horizontal mergers the Department attaches primary importance to the market shares of the merging firms, achievement of the purposes of Section 7 occasionally requires the Department to challenge mergers which would not be challenged under the market share standards of Paragraphs 5, 6, and 7. The following are the two most common instances of this kind in which a challenge by the Department can ordinarily be anticipated:

(a) acquisition of a competitor which is a particularly "disturbing," "disruptive," or otherwise unusually competitive factor in the market; and

(b) a merger involving a substantial firm and a firm which, despite an insubstantial market share, possesses an unusual competitive potential or has an asset that confers an unusual competitive advantage (for example, the acquisition by a leading firm of a newcomer having a patent on a significantly improved product or production process).

There may also be certain horizontal mergers between makers of distinct products regarded as in the same line of commerce for reasons expressed in Paragraph 3(i) where some modification in the minimum market shares subject to challenge may be appropriate to reflect the imperfect substitutability of the two products.

9. *Failing Company.* A merger which the Department would otherwise challenge will ordinarily not be challenged if (i) the resources of one of the merging firms are so depleted and its prospects for rehabilitation so remote that the firm faces the clear probability of a business failure, and (ii) good faith efforts by the failing firm have failed to elicit a reasonable offer of acquisition more consistent with the purposes of Section 7 by a firm which intends to keep the

failing firm in the market. The Department regards as failing only those firms with no reasonable prospect of remaining viable; it does not regard a firm as failing merely because the firm has been unprofitable for a period of time, has lost market position or failed to maintain its competitive position in some other respect, has poor management, or has not fully explored the possibility of overcoming its difficulties through self-help.

In determining the applicability of the above standard to the acquisition of a failing division of a multi-market company, such factors as the difficulty in assessing the viability of a portion of a company, the possibility of arbitrary accounting practices, and the likelihood that an otherwise healthy company can rehabilitate one of its parts, will lead the Department to apply this standard only in the clearest of circumstances.

10. *Economies.* Unless there are exceptional circumstances, the Department will not accept as a justification for an acquisition normally subject to challenge under its horizontal merger standards the claim that the merger will produce economies (*i.e.,* improvements in efficiency) because, among other reasons, (i) the Department's adherence to the standards will usually result in no challenge being made to mergers of the kind most likely to involve companies operating significantly below the size necessary to achieve significant economies of scale; (ii) where substantial economies are potentially available to a firm, they can normally be realized through internal expansion; and (iii) there usually are severe difficulties in accurately establishing the existence and magnitude of economies claimed for a merger.

II.   Vertical Mergers

11. *Enforcement Policy.* With respect to vertical mergers (*i.e.,* acquisitions "backward" into a supplying market or "forward" into a purchasing market), the Department's enforcement activity under Section 7 of the Clayton Act, as in the merger field generally, is intended to prevent changes in market structure that are likely to lead over the course of time to significant anticompetitive consequences. In general, the Department believes that such consequences can be expected to occur whenever a particular vertical acquisition, or series of acquisitions, by one or more of the firms in a supplying or purchasing market, tends significantly to raise barriers to entry in either market or to disadvantage existing non-integrated or partly integrated firms in either market in ways unrelated to economic efficiency. (Barriers to entry are relatively stable market conditions which tend to increase the difficulty of potential competitors' entering the market as new sellers and which thus tend to limit the effectiveness of the potential competitors both as a restraint upon the behavior of firms in the market and as a source of additional actual competition.)

Barriers to entry resting on such factors as economies of scale in production and distribution are not questionable as such. But vertical mergers tend to raise barriers to entry in undesirable ways, particularly the following: (i) by foreclosing equal access to potential customers, thus reducing the ability of non-integrated firms to capture competitively the market share needed to achieve an efficient level of production, or imposing the burden of entry on an integrated basis (*i.e.,* at both the supplying and purchasing levels) even though entry at a single level would permit efficient operation; (ii) by foreclosing equal access to potential suppliers, thus either increasing the risk of a price or supply squeeze on the new entrant or imposing the additional burden of entry as an integrated firm; or (iii) by facilitating promotional product differentiation, when the merger involves a manufacturing firm's acquisition of firms at the retail level. Besides impeding the entry of new sellers, the foregoing consequences of vertical mergers, if present, also artificially inhibit the expansion of presently competing sellers by conferring on the merged firm competitive advantages, unrelated to real economies of production or distribution, over non-integrated or partly integrated firms. While it is true that in some instances vertical integration may raise barriers to entry or disadvantage existing competitors only as the result of the achievement of significant economies of production or distribution (as, for example, where the increase in barriers is due to achievement of economies of integrated production through an alteration of the structure of the plant as well as of the firm), integration accomplished by a large vertical merger will usually raise entry barriers or disadvantage competitors to an extent not accounted for by, and wholly disproportionate to, such economies as may result from the merger.

It is, of course, difficult to identify with precision all circumstances in which vertical mergers are likely to have adverse effects on market structure of the kinds indicated in the previous paragraph. The Department believes, however, that the most important aims of its enforcement policy on vertical mergers can be satisfactorily stated by guidelines framed primarily in terms of the market shares of the merging firms and the conditions of entry which already exist in the relevant markets. These factors will ordinarily serve to identify most of the situations in which any of the various possible adverse effects of vertical mergers may occur and be of substantial competitive significance. With all vertical mergers it is necessary to consider the probable competitive consequences of the merger in both the market in which the supplying firms sells and the market in which the purchasing firm sells, although a significant adverse effect in either market will ordinarily result in a challenge by the Department. ("Supplying firm" and "purchasing firm," as used herein, refer to the two parties to the vertical merger transaction, the former of which sells a product in a market in which the latter buys that product.)

12. *Supplying Firm's Market.* In determining whether to challenge a vertical merger on the ground that it may significantly lessen existing or potential competition in the supplying firm's market, the Department attaches primary significance to (i) the market share of the supplying firm, (ii) the market share of the purchasing firm or firms, and (iii) the conditions of entry in the purchasing firm's market. Accordingly, the Department will ordinarily challenge a merger or series of mergers between a supplying firm, accounting for approximately 10% or more of the sales in its market, and one or more purchasing firms, accounting *in toto* for approximately 6% or more of the total purchases in that market, unless it clearly appears that there are no significant barriers to entry into the business of the purchasing firm or firms.

13. *Purchasing Firm's Market.* Although the standard of paragraph 12 is designed to identify vertical mergers having likely anticompetitive effects in the supplying firm's market, adherence by the Department to that standard will also

normally result in challenges being made to most of the vertical mergers which may have adverse effects in the purchasing firm's market (*i.e.*, that market comprised of the purchasing firm and its competitors engaged in resale of the supplying firm's product or in the sale of a product whose manufacture requires the supplying firm's product) since adverse effects in the purchasing firm's market will normally occur only as the result of significant vertical mergers involving supplying firms with market shares in excess of 10%. There remain, however, some important situations in which vertical mergers which are not subject to challenge under paragraph 12 (ordinarily because the purchasing firm accounts for less than 6% of the purchases in the supplying firm's market) will nonetheless be challenged by the Department on the ground that they raise entry barriers in the purchasing firm's market, or disadvantage the purchasing firm's competitors, by conferring upon the purchasing firm a significant supply advantage over unintegrated or partly integrated existing competitors or over potential competitors. The following paragraph sets forth the enforcement standard governing the most common of these situations.

If the product sold by the supplying firm and its competitors is either a complex one in which innovating changes by the various suppliers have been taking place, or is a scarce raw material or other product whose supply cannot be readily expanded to meet increased demand, the merged firm may have the power to use any temporary superiority, or any shortage, in the product of the supplying firm to put competitors of the purchasing firm at a disadvantage by refusing to sell the product to them (supply squeeze) or by narrowing the margin between the price at which it sells the product to the purchasing firm's competitors and the price at which the end-product is sold by the purchasing firm (price squeeze). Even where the merged firm has sufficient market power to impose a squeeze, it may well not always be economically rational for it actually to do so; but the Department believes that the increase in barriers to entry in the purchasing firm's market arising simply from the increased risk of a possible squeeze is sufficient to warrant prohibition of any merger between a supplier possessing significant market power and a substantial purchaser of any product meeting the above description. Accordingly, where such a product is a significant feature or ingredient of the end-product manufactured by the purchasing firm and its competitors, the Department will ordinarily challenge a merger or series of mergers between a supplying firm, accounting for approximately 20% or more of the sales in its market, and a purchasing firm or firms, accounting *in toto* for approximately 10% or more of the sales in the market in which it sells the product whose manufacture requires the supplying firm's product.

14. *Non-market Share Standards.* (a) Although in enforcing Section 7 against vertical mergers the Department attaches primary importance to the market shares of the merging firms and the conditions of entry in the relevant markets, achievement of the purposes of Section 7 occasionally requires the Department to challenge mergers which would not be challenged under the market share standards of paragraphs 12 and 13. Clearly the most common instances in which challenge by the Department can ordinarily be anticipated are acquisitions of suppliers or customers by major firms in an industry in which (i) there has been, or is developing, a significant trend toward vertical integration by merger such that the trend, if unchallenged, would probably raise barriers to

entry or impose a competitive disadvantage on unintegrated or partly integrated firms, and (ii) it does not clearly appear that the particular acquisition will result in significant economies of production or distribution unrelated to advertising or other promotional economies.

(b) A less common special situation in which a challenge by the Department can ordinarily be anticipated is the acquisition by a firm of a customer or supplier for the purpose of increasing the difficulty of potential competitors in entering the market of either the acquiring or acquired firm, or for the purpose of putting competitors of either the acquiring or acquired firm at an unwarranted disadvantage.

15. *Failing Company.* The standards set forth in paragraph 9 are applied by the Department in determining whether to challenge a vertical merger.

16. *Economies.* Unless there are exceptional circumstances, and except as noted in paragraph 14(a), the Department will not accept as a justification for an acquisition normally subject to challenge under its vertical merger standards the claim that the merger will produce economies, because, among other reasons, (i) where substantial economies of vertical integration are potentially available to a firm, they can normally be realized through internal expansion into the supplying or purchasing market, and (ii) where barriers prevent entry into the supplying or purchasing market by internal expansion, the Department's adherence to the vertical merger standards will in any event usually result in no challenge being made to the acquisition of a firm or firms of sufficient size to overcome or adequately minimize the barriers to entry.

III.   Conglomerate Mergers

17. *Enforcement Policy.* Conglomerate mergers are mergers that are neither horizontal nor vertical as those terms are used in sections I and II, respectively, of these guidelines. (It should be noted that a market extension merger, *i.e.,* one involving two firms selling the same product, but in different geographic markets, is classified as a conglomerate merger.) As with other kinds of mergers, the purpose of the Department's enforcement activity regarding conglomerate mergers is to prevent changes in market structure that appear likely over the course of time to cause a substantial lessening of the competition that would otherwise exist or to create a tendency toward monopoly.

At the present time, the Department regards two categories of conglomerate mergers as having sufficiently identifiable anticompetitive effects as to be the subject of relatively specific structural guidelines: mergers involving potential entrants (Paragraph 18) and mergers creating a danger of reciprocal buying (Paragraph 19).

Another important category of conglomerate mergers that will frequently be the subject of enforcement action—mergers which for one or more of several reasons threaten to entrench or enhance the market power of the acquired firm —is described generally in Paragraph 20.

As Paragraph 20 makes clear, enforcement action will also be taken against still other types of conglomerate mergers that on specific analysis appear anticompetitive. The fact that, as yet, the Department does not believe it useful to describe such other types of mergers in terms of a few major elements of market structure should in no sense be regarded as indicating that enforcement action will not be taken. Nor is it to be assumed that mergers of the type described in Paragraphs 18 and 19, but not covered by the specific rules thereof, may not be the subject of enforcement action if specific analysis indicates that they appear anticompetitive.

18. *Mergers Involving Potential Entrants.* (a) Since potential competition (*i.e.,* the threat of entry, either through internal expansion or through acquisition and expansion of a small firm, by firms not already or only marginally in the market) may often be the most significant competitive limitation on the exercise of market power by leading firms, as well as the most likely source of additional actual competition, the Department will ordinarily challenge any merger between one of the most likely entrants into the market and:

(i) any firm with approximately 25% or more of the market;

(ii) one of the two largest firms in a market in which the shares of the two largest firms amount to approximately 50% or more;

(iii) one of the four largest firms in a market in which the shares of the eight largest firms amount to approximately 75% or more, provided the merging firm's share of the market amounts to approximately 10% or more; or

(iv) one of the eight largest firms in a market in which the shares of these firms amount to approximately 75% or more, provided either (A) the merging firm's share of the market is not insubstantial and there are no more than one or two likely entrants into the market, or (B) the merging firm is a rapidly growing firm.

In determining whether a firm is one of the most likely potential entrants into a market, the Department accords primary significance to the firm's capability of entering on a competitively significant scale relative to the capability of other firms (*i.e.,* the technological and financial resources available to it) and to the firm's economic incentive to enter (evidenced by, for example, the general attractiveness of the market in terms of risk and profit; or any special relationship of the firm to the market; or the firm's manifested interest in entry; or the natural expansion pattern of the firm; or the like).

(b) The Department will also ordinarily challenge a merger between an existing competitor in a market and a likely entrant, undertaken for the purpose of preventing the competitive "disturbance" or "disruption" that such entry might create.

(c) Unless there are exceptional circumstances, the Department will not accept as a justification for a merger inconsistent with the standards of this paragraph 18 the claim that the merger will produce economies, because, among other reasons, the Department believes that equivalent economies can be normally achieved either through internal expansion or through a small firm acquisition or other acquisition not inconsistent with the standards herein.

19. *Mergers Creating Danger of Reciprocal Buying.* (a) Since reciprocal buying (*i.e.,* favoring one's customer when making purchases of a product which is sold by the customer) is an economically unjustified business practice

which confers a competitive advantage on the favored firm unrelated to the merits of its product, the Department will ordinarily challenge any merger which creates a significant danger of reciprocal buying. Unless it clearly appears that some special market factor makes remote the possibility that reciprocal buying behavior will actually occur, the Department considers that a significant danger of reciprocal buying is present whenever approximately 15% or more of the total purchases in a market in which one of the merging firms ("the selling firm") sells are accounted for by firms which also make substantial sales in markets where the other merging firm ("the buying firm") is both a substantial buyer and a more substantial buyer than all or most of the competitors of the selling firm.

(b) The Department will also ordinarily challenge (i) any merger undertaken for the purpose of facilitating the creation of reciprocal buying arrangements, and (ii) any merger creating the possibility of any substantial reciprocal buying where one (or both) of the merging firms has within the recent past, or the merged firm has after consummation of the merger, actually engaged in reciprocal buying, or attempted directly or indirectly to induce firms with which it deals to engage in reciprocal buying, in the product markets in which the possibility of reciprocal buying has been created.

(c) Unless there are exceptional circumstances, the Department will not accept as a justification for a merger creating a significant danger of reciprocal buying the claim that the merger will produce economies, because, among other reasons, the Department believes that in general equivalent economies can be achieved by the firms involved through other mergers not inconsistent with the standards of this paragraph 19.

20. *Mergers Which Entrench Market Power and Other Conglomerate Mergers.* The Department will ordinarily investigate the possibility of anticompetitive consequences, and may in particular circumstances bring suit, where an acquisition of a leading firm in a relatively concentrated or rapidly concentrating market may serve to entrench or increase the market power of that firm or raise barriers to entry in that market. Examples of this type of merger include: (i) a merger which produces a very large disparity in absolute size between the merged firm and the largest remaining firms in the relevant markets, (ii) a merger of firms producing related products which may induce purchasers, concerned about the merged firm's possible use of leverage, to buy products of the merged firm rather than those of competitors, and (iii) a merger which may enhance the ability of the merged firm to increase product differentiation in the relevant markets.

Generally speaking, the conglomerate merger area involves novel problems that have not yet been subjected to as extensive or sustained analysis as those presented by horizontal and vertical mergers. It is for this reason that the Department's enforcement policy regarding the foregoing category of conglomerate mergers cannot be set forth with greater specificity. Moreover, the conglomerate merger field as a whole is one in which the Department considers it necessary, to a greater extent than with horizontal and vertical mergers, to carry on a continuous analysis and study of the ways in which mergers may have significant anticompetitive consequences in circumstances beyond those covered by these guidelines. For example, the Department has used Section 7 to prevent mergers which may diminish long-run possibilities of enhanced competition resulting from technological developments that may increase interproduct competition between industries whose products are presently relatively imperfect substitutes. Other areas where enforcement action will be deemed appropriate may also be identified on a case-by-case basis; and as the result of continuous analysis and study the Department may identify other categories of mergers that can be the subject of specific guidelines.

21. *Failing Company*. The standards set forth in paragraph 9 are normally applied by the Department in determining whether to challenge a conglomerate merger, except that in marginal cases involving the application of Paragraph 18(a)(iii) and (iv) the Department may deem it inappropriate to sue under Section 7 even though the acquired firm is not "failing" in the strict sense.

appendix IV

European Economic Community: Articles 85 & 86, Regulation No. 17

Articles 85 & 86, Treaty Establishing the European Economic Community

[European Communities, Treaties Establishing the European Communities pt. EEC, pp. 245-247 (1973); Vol. 1 Commerce Clearing House, Common Market Reporter ¶¶2005–2111 (1973); Vol. 298 United Nations Treaty Series pp. 47–49; Vol. IV Organization for Economic Co-operation and Development, Guide to Legislation on Restrictive Business Practices pt. EEC, sec 1 (Supp. 1, 1972).]

ARTICLE 85

1. The following shall be deemed to be incompatible with the Common Market and shall hereby be prohibited: any agreement between enterprises, any decisions by associations of enterprises and any concerted practices which are likely to affect trade between the Member States and which have as their object or result the prevention, restriction or distortion of competition within the Common Market, in particular those consisting in:

(a) the direct or indirect fixing of purchase or selling prices or of any other trading conditions;

363

(b) the limitation or control of production, markets, technical development or investment;

(c) market-sharing or the sharing of sources of supply;

(d) the application to parties to transactions of unequal terms in respect of equivalent supplies, thereby placing them at a competitive disadvantage; or

(e) the subjecting of the conclusion of a contract to the acceptance by a party of additional supplies which, either by their nature or according to commercial usage, have no connection with the subject of such contract.

2.   Any agreements or decisions prohibited pursuant to this Article shall be null and void.

3.   Nevertheless, the provisions of paragraph 1 may be declared inapplicable in the case of:

—any agreements or classes of agreements between enterprises,

—any decisions or classes of decisions by associations of enterprises, and

—any concerted practices or classes of concerted practices

which contribute to the improvement of the production or distribution of goods or to the promotion of technical or economic progress while reserving to users an equitable share in the profit resulting therefrom, and which:

(a) neither impose on the enterprises concerned any restrictions not indispensable to the attainment of the above objectives;

(b) nor enable such enterprises to eliminate competition in respect of a substantial proportion of the goods concerned.

ARTICLE 86

To the extent to which trade between any Member States may be affected thereby, action by one or more enterprises to take improper advantage of a dominant position within the Common Market or within a substantial part of it shall be deemed to be incompatible with the Common Market and shall hereby be prohibited.

Such improper practices may, in particular, consist in:

(a) the direct or indirect imposition of any inequitable purchase or selling prices or of any other inequitable trading conditions;

(b) the limitation of production, markets or technical development to the prejudice of consumers;

(c) the application to parties to transactions of unequal terms in respect of equivalent supplies, thereby placing them at a competitive disadvantage; or

(d) the subjecting of the conclusion of a contract to the acceptance, by a party, of additional supplies which, either by their nature or according to commercial usage, have no connection with the subject of such contract.

Approved March 25, 1957
Effective January 1, 1958

Regulation No. 17 of the Council of 6 February 1962

First Regulation Implementing Articles 85 and 86 of the EEC Treaty

[Official Journal of the European Economic Community [O.J.E.E.C.] No. 13, p. 204 (Feb. 21, 1962), as amended by O.J.E.E.C. No. 56, p. 1655 (July 10, 1962), as amended by O.J.E.E.C. No. 162, p. 2696 (Nov. 7, 1963), as amended by O.J.E.E.C. No. L 285, p. 49 (Dec. 29, 1971), as amended by O.J.E.E.C. No. L 173, p. 92 (Mar. 27, 1972); Vol. 1 Commerce Clearing House, Common Market Reporter ¶ ¶2401– 2634 (1973); Vol. IV Organization for Economic Co-operation and Development, Guide to Legislation on Restrictive Business Practices pt. EEC, sec. 1.1 (Supp. 1, 1972).]

The Council of the European Economic Community,
Having regard to the Treaty establishing the European Economic Community, and in particular Article 87 thereof;
Having regard to the proposal from the Commission;
Having regard to the Opinion of the Economic and Social Committee;
Having regard to the Opinion of the European Parliament;
Whereas, in order to establish a system ensuring that competition shall not be distorted in the common market, it is necessary to provide for balanced application of Articles 85 and 86 in a uniform manner in the Member States;
Whereas in establishing the rules for applying Article 85(3) account must be taken of the need to ensure effective supervision and to simplify administration to the greatest possible extent;
Whereas it is accordingly necessary to make it obligatory, as a general principle, for undertakings which seek application of Article 85(3) to notify to the Commission their agreements, decisions and concerted practices;
Whereas, on the one hand, such agreements, decisions and concerted practices are probably very numerous and cannot therefore all be examined at the same time and, on the other hand, some of them have special features which may make them less prejudicial to the development of the common market;
Whereas there is consequently a need to make more flexible arrangements for the time being in respect of certain categories of agreement, decisions and concerted practices without prejudging their validity under Article 85;
Whereas it may be in the interest of undertakings to know whether any agreements, decisions or practices to which they are party, or propose to become party, may lead to action on the part of the Commission pursuant to Article 85(1) or Article 86;
Whereas, in order to secure uniform application of Articles 85 and 86 in the common market, rules must be made under which the Commission, acting in close and constant liaison with the competent authorities of the Member States, may take the requisite measures for applying those Articles;
Whereas for this purpose the Commission must have the cooperation of the competent authorities of the Member States and be empowered, throughout the common market, to require such information to be supplied and to undertake such investigations as are necessary to bring to light any agreement, decision or concerted practice prohibited by Article 85(1) or any abuse of a dominant position prohibited by Article 86;

Whereas in order to carry out its duty of ensuring that the provisions of the Treaty are applied the Commission must be empowered to address to undertakings or associations of undertakings recommendations and decisions for the purpose of bringing to an end infringements of Articles 85 and 86;

Whereas compliance with Articles 85 and 86 and the fulfillment of obligations imposed on undertakings and associations of undertakings under this Regulation must be enforceable by means of fines and periodic penalty payments;

Whereas undertakings concerned must be accorded the right to be heard by the Commission, third parties whose interests may be affected by a decision must be given the opportunity of submitting their comments beforehand, and it must be ensured that wide publicity is given to decisions taken;

Whereas all decisions taken by the Commission under this Regulation are subject to review by the Court of Justice under the conditions specified in the Treaty; whereas it is moreover desirable to confer upon the Court of Justice, pursuant to Article 172, unlimited jurisdiction in respect of decisions under which the Commission imposes fines or periodic penalty payments;

Whereas this Regulation may enter into force without prejudice to any other provisions that may hereafter be adopted pursuant to Article 87;

Has adopted this regulation:

Article 1

Basic Provision

Without prejudice to Articles 6, 7 and 23 of this Regulation, agreements, decisions and concerted practices of the kind described in Article 85(1) of the Treaty and the abuse of a dominant position in the market, within the meaning of Article 86 of the Treaty, shall be prohibited, no prior decision to that effect being required.

Article 2

Negative Clearance

Upon application by the undertakings or associations of undertakings concerned, the Commission may certify that, on the basis of the facts in its possession, there are no grounds under Article 85(1) or Article 86 of the Treaty for action on its part in respect of an agreement, decision or practice.

Article 3

Termination of Infringements

1. Where the Commission, upon application or upon its own initiative, finds that there is infringement of Article 85 or Article 86 of the Treaty, it may by decision require the undertakings or associations of undertakings concerned to bring such infringement to an end.

2. Those entitled to make application are:

    (a) Member States;

    (b) natural or legal persons who claim a legitimate interest.

3. Without prejudice to the other provisions of this Regulation, the Commission may, before taking a decision under paragraph 1, address to the undertakings or associations of undertakings concerned recommendations for termination of the infringement.

Article 4

Notification of New Agreements, Decisions and Practices

1. Agreements, decisions and concerted practices of the kind described in Article 85(1) of the Treaty which come into existence after the entry into force of this Regulation and in respect of which the parties seek application of Article 85(3) must be notified to the Commission. Until they have been notified, no decision in application of Article 85(3) may be taken.

2. Paragraph 1 shall not apply to agreements, decisions or concerted practices where:

(1) the only parties thereto are undertakings from one Member State and the agreements, decisions or practices do not relate either to imports or to exports between Member States;

(2) not more than two undertakings are party thereto, and the agreements only:

(a) restrict the freedom of one party to the contract in determining the prices or conditions of business upon which the goods which he has obtained from the other party to the contract may be resold; or

(b) impose restrictions on the exercise of the rights of the assignee or user of industrial property rights—in particular patents, utility models, designs or trade marks—or of the person entitled under a contract to the assignment, or grant, of the right to use a method of manufacture or knowledge relating to the use and to the application of industrial processes;

(3) they have as their sole object:

(a) the development or uniform application of standards or types; or

(b) joint research for improvement of techniques.

(c) specialisation in the manufacture of products, including agreements necessary for achieving this,

—where the products which are the subject of specialisation do not, in a substantial part of the common market, represent more than 15% of the volume of business done in identical products or those considered by consumers to be similar by reason of their characteristics, price and use, and

—where the total annual turnover of the participating undertakings does not exceed 200 million units of account.

These agreements, decisions and practices may be notified to the Commission.

Article 5

Notification of Existing Agreements, Decisions and Practices

1. Agreements, decisions and concerted practices of the kind described in Article 85(1) of the Treaty which are in existence at the date of entry into force of this Regulation and in respect of which the parties seek application of Article 85(3) shall be notified to the Commission before 1 August 1962. However notwithstanding the foregoing provisions any agreements, decisions and concerted practice to which not more than two undertakings are party shall be notified before 1 February 1963.
2. Paragraph 1 shall not apply to agreements, decisions or concerted practices falling within Article 4(2); these may be notified to the Commission.

Article 6

Decisions Pursuant to Article 85(3)

1. Whenever the Commission takes a decision pursuant to Article 85(3) of the Treaty, it shall specify therein the date from which the decision shall take effect. Such date shall not be earlier than the date of notification.
2. The second sentence of paragraph 1 shall not apply to agreements, decisions or concerted practices falling within Article 4(2) and Article 5(2), nor to those falling within Article 5(1) which have been notified within the time limit specified in Article 5(1).

Article 7

Special Provisions for Existing Agreements, Decisions and Practices

1. Where agreements, decisions and concerted practices in existence at the date of entry into force of this Regulation and notified before 1 August 1962 do not satisfy the requirements of Article 85(3) of the Treaty and the undertakings or associations of undertakings concerned cease to give effect to them or modify them in such manner that they no longer fall within the prohibition contained in Article 85(1) or that they satisfy the requirements of Article 85(3), the prohibition contained in Article 85(1) shall apply only for a period fixed by the Commission. A decision by the Commission pursuant to the foregoing sentence shall not apply as against undertakings and associations of undertakings which did not expressly consent to the notification.
2. Paragraph 1 shall apply to agreements, decisions and concerted practices falling within Article 4(2) which are in existence at the date of entry into force of this Regulation if they are notified before 1 January 1964.

Article 8

Duration and Revocation of Decisions Under Article 85(3)

1. A decision in application of Article 85(3) of the Treaty shall be issued for a specified period and conditions and obligations may be attached thereto.

2.   A decision may on application be renewed if the requirements of Article 85(3) of the Treaty continue to be satisfied.

3.   The Commission may revoke or amend its decision or prohibit specified acts by the parties:

(a) where there has been a change in any of the tests which were basic to the making of the decision;

(b) where the parties commit a breach of any obligation attached to the decision;

(c) where the decision is based on incorrect information or was induced by deceit;

(d) where the parties abuse the exemption from the provisions of Article 85(1) of the Treaty granted to them by the decision.

In cases to which subparagraphs (b), (c) or (d) apply, the decision may be revoked with retroactive effect.

Article 9

Powers

1.   Subject to review of its decision by the Court of Justice, the Commission shall have sole power to declare Article 85(1) inapplicable pursuant to Article 85(3) of the Treaty.

2.   The Commission shall have power to apply Article 85(1) and Article 86 of the Treaty; this power may be exercised notwithstanding that the time limits specified in Article 5(1) and in Article 7(2) relating to notification have not expired.

3.   As long as the Commission has not initiated any procedure under Articles 2, 3 or 6, the authorities of the Member States shall remain competent to apply Article 85(1) and Article 86 in accordance with Article 88 of the Treaty; they shall remain competent in this respect notwithstanding that the time limits specified in Article 5(1) and in Article 7(2) relating to notification have not expired.

Article 10

Liaison with the Authorities of the Member States

1.   The Commission shall forthwith transmit to the competent authorities of the Member States a copy of the applications and notifications together with copies of the most important documents lodged with the Commission for the purpose of establishing the existence of infringements of Articles 85 or 86 of the Treaty or of obtaining negative clearance or a decision in application of Article 85(3).

2.   The Commission shall carry out the procedure set out in paragraph 1 in close and constant liaison with the competent authorities of the Member States; such authorities shall have the right to express their views upon that procedure.

3.   An Advisory Committee on Restrictive Practices and Monopolies shall be

consulted prior to the taking of any decision following upon a procedure under paragraph 1, and of any decision concerning the renewal, amendment or revocation of a decision pursuant to Article 85(3) of the Treaty.

4. The Advisory Committee shall be composed of officials competent in the matter of restrictive practices and monopolies. Each Member State shall appoint an official to represent it who, if prevented from attending, may be replaced by another official.

5. The consultation shall take place at a joint meeting convened by the Commission; such meeting shall be held not earlier than fourteen days after dispatch of the notice convening it. The notice shall, in respect of each case to be examined, be accompanied by a summary of the case together with an indication of the most important documents, and a preliminary draft decision.

6. The Advisory Committee may deliver an opinion notwithstanding that some of its members or their alternates are not present. A report of the outcome of the consultative proceedings shall be annexed to the draft decision. It shall not be made public.

Article 11

Requests for Information

1. In carrying out the duties assigned to it by Article 89 and by provisions adopted under Article 87 of the Treaty, the Commission may obtain all necessary information from the Governments and competent authorities of the Member States and from undertakings and associations of undertakings.

2. When sending a request for information to an undertaking or association of undertakings, the Commission shall at the same time forward a copy of the request to the competent authority of the Member State in whose territory the seat of the undertaking or association of undertakings is situated.

3. In its request the Commission shall state the legal basis and the purpose of the request and also the penalties provided for in Article 15(1)(b) for supplying incorrect information.

4. The owners of the undertakings or their representatives and, in the case of legal persons, companies or firms, or of associations having no legal personality, the persons authorised to represent them by law or by their constitution, shall supply the information requested.

5. Where an undertaking or association of undertakings does not supply the information requested within the time limit fixed by the Commission, or supplies incomplete information, the Commission shall by decision require the information to be supplied. The decision shall specify what information is required, fix an appropriate time limit within which it is to be supplied and indicate the penalties provided for in Article 15(1)(b) and Article 16(1)(c) and the right to have the decision reviewed by the Court of Justice.

6. The Commission shall at the same time forward a copy of its decision to the competent authority of the Member State in whose territory the seat of the undertaking or association of undertakings is situated.

Article 12

Inquiry into Sectors of the Economy

1. If in any sector of the economy the trend of trade between Member States, price movements, inflexibility of prices or other circumstances suggest that in the economic sector concerned competition is being restricted or distorted within the common market, the Commission may decide to conduct a general inquiry into that economic sector and in the course thereof may request undertakings in the sector concerned to supply the information necessary for giving effect to the principles formulated in Articles 85 and 86 of the Treaty and for carrying out the duties entrusted to the Commission.
2. The Commission may in particular request every undertaking or association of undertakings in the economic sector concerned to communicate to it all agreements, decisions and concerted practices which are exempt from notification by virtue of Article 4(2) and Article 5(2).
3. When making inquiries pursuant to paragraph 2, the Commission shall also request undertakings or groups of undertakings whose size suggests that they occupy a dominant position within the common market or a substantial part thereof to supply to the Commission such particulars of the structure of the undertakings and of their behaviour as are requisite to an appraisal of their position in the light of Article 86 of the Treaty.
4. Article 10(3) to (6) and Articles 11, 13 and 14 shall apply correspondingly.

Article 13

Investigations by the Authorities of the Member States

1. At the request of the Commission, the competent authorities of the Member States shall undertake the investigations which the Commission considers to be necessary under Article 14(1), or which it has ordered by decision pursuant to Article 14(3). The officials of the competent authorities of the Member States responsible for conducting these investigations shall exercise their powers upon production of an authorization in writing issued by the competent authority of the Member State in whose territory the investigation is to be made. Such authorization shall specify the subject matter and purpose of the investigation.
2. If so requested by the Commission or by the competent authority of the Member State in whose territory the investigation is to be made, the officials of the Commission may assist the officials of such authority in carrying out their duties.

Article 14

Investigating Powers of the Commission

1. In carrying out the duties assigned to it by Article 89 and by provisions adopted under Article 87 of the Treaty, the Commission may undertake all necessary investigations into undertakings and associations of undertakings. To this end the officials authorized by the Commission are empowered:

(a) to examine the books and other business records;

(b) to take copies of or extracts from the books and business records;

(c) to ask for oral explanations on the spot;

(d) to enter any premises, land and means of transport of undertakings.

2.   The officials of the Commission authorized for the purpose of these investigations shall exercise their powers upon production of an authorization in writing specifying the subject matter and purpose of the investigation and the penalties provided for in Article 15(1)(c) in cases where production of the required books or other business records is incomplete. In good time before the investigation, the Commission shall inform the competent authority of the Member State in whose territory the same is to be made of the investigation and of the identity of the authorized officials.

3.   Undertakings and associations of undertakings shall submit to investigations ordered by decision of the Commission. The decision shall specify the subject matter and purpose of the investigation, appoint the date on which it is to begin and indicate the penalties provided for in Article 15(1)(c) and Article 16(1)(d) and the right to have the decision reviewed by the Court of Justice.

4.   The Commission shall take decisions referred to in paragraph 3 after consultation with the competent authority of the Member State in whose territory the investigation is to be made.

5.   Officials of the competent authority of the Member State in whose territory the investigation is to be made may, at the request of such authority or of the Commission, assist the officials of the Commission in carrying out their duties.

6.   Where an undertaking opposes an investigation ordered pursuant to this Article, the Member State concerned shall afford the necessary assistance to the officials authorized by the Commission to enable them to make their investigation. Member States shall, after consultation with the Commission, take the necessary measures to this end before 1 October 1962.

Article 15

Fines

1.   The Commission may by decision impose on undertakings or associations of undertakings fines of from one hundred to five thousand units of account where, intentionally or negligently:

(a) they supply incorrect or misleading information in an application pursuant to Article 2 or in a notification pursuant to Articles 4 or 5; or

(b) they supply incorrect information in response to a request made pursuant to Article 11(3) or (5) or to Article 12, or do not supply information within the time limit fixed by a decision taken under Article 11(5); or

(c) they produce the required books or other business records in incomplete form during investigations under Article 13 or 14, or refuse to submit to an investigation ordered by decision issued in implementation of Article 14(3).

2. The Commission may by decision impose on undertakings or associations of undertakings fines of from one thousand to one million units of account, or a sum in excess thereof but not exceeding ten per cent of the turnover in the preceding business year of each of the undertakings participating in the infringement where, either intentionally or negligently:

(a) they infringe Article 85(1) or Article 86 of the Treaty; or

(b) they commit a breach of any obligation imposed pursuant to Article 8(1).

In fixing the amount of the fine, regard shall be had both to the gravity and to the duration of the infringement.

3. Article 10(3) to (6) shall apply.

4. Decisions taken pursuant to paragraphs 1 and 2 shall not be of a criminal law nature.

5. The fines provided for in paragraph 2(a) shall not be imposed in respect of acts taking place:

(a) after notification to the Commission and before its decision in application of Article 85(3) of the Treaty, provided they fall within the limits of the activity described in the notification;

(b) before notification and in the course of agreements, decisions or concerted practices in existence at the date of entry into force of this Regulation, provided that notification was effected within the time limits specified in Article 5(1) and Article 7(2).

6. Paragraph 5 shall not have effect where the Commission has informed the undertakings concerned that after preliminary examination it is of opinion that Article 85(1) of the Treaty applies and that application of Article 85(3) is not justified.

Article 16

Periodic Penalty Payments

1. The Commission may by decision impose on undertakings or associations of undertakings periodic penalty payments of from fifty to one thousand units of account per day, calculated from the date appointed by the decision, in order to compel them:

(a) to put an end to an infringement of Article 85 or 86 of the Treaty, in accordance with a decision taken pursuant to Article 3 of this Regulation;

(b) to refrain from any act prohibited under Article 8(3);

(c) to supply complete and correct information which it has requested by decision taken pursuant to Article 11(5);

(d) to submit to an investigation which it has ordered by decision taken pursuant to Article 14(3).

2. Where the undertakings or associations of undertakings have satisfied the obligation which it was the purpose of the periodic penalty payment to enforce, the Commission may fix the total amount of the periodic penalty payment at a lower figure than that which would arise under the original decision.
3. Article 10(3) to (6) shall apply.

Article 17

Review by the Court of Justice

The Court of Justice shall have unlimited jurisdiction within the meaning of Article 17 of the Treaty to review decisions whereby the Commission has fixed a fine or periodic penalty payment; it may cancel, reduce or increase the fine or periodic penalty payment imposed.

Article 18

Unit of Account

For the purposes of applying Articles 15 to 17 the unit of account shall be that adopted in drawing up the budget of the Community in accordance with Articles 207 and 209 of the Treaty.

Article 19

Hearing of the Parties and of Third Persons

1. Before taking decisions as provided for in Articles 2, 3, 6, 7, 8, 15 and 16, the Commission shall give the undertakings or associations of undertakings concerned the opportunity of being heard on the matters to which the Commission has taken objection.
2. If the Commission or the competent authorities of the Member States consider it necessary, they may also hear other natural or legal persons. Applications to be heard on the part of such persons shall, where they show a sufficient interest, be granted.
3. Where the Commission intends to give negative clearance pursuant to Article 2 or take a decision in application of Article 85(3) of the Treaty, it shall publish a summary of the relevant application or notification and invite all interested third parties to submit their observations within a time limit which it shall fix being not less than one month. Publication shall have regard to the legitimate interest of undertakings in the protection of their business secrets.

Article 20

Professional Secrecy

1. Information acquired as a result of the application of Articles 11, 12, 13 and 14 shall be used only for the purpose of the relevant request or investigation.

2. Without prejudice to the provisions of Articles 19 and 21, the Commission and the competent authorities of the Member States, their officials and other servants shall not disclose information acquired by them as a result of the application of this Regulation and of the kind covered by the obligation of professional secrecy.

3. The provisions of paragraphs 1 and 2 shall not prevent publication of general information or surveys which do not contain information relating to particular undertakings or associations of undertakings.

Article 21

Publication of Decisions

1. The Commission shall publish the decisions which it takes pursuant to Articles 2, 3, 6, 7 and 8.

2. The publication shall state the names of the parties and the main content of the decision; it shall have regard to the legitimate interest of undertakings in the protection of their business secrets.

Article 22

Special Provisions

1. The Commission shall submit to the Council proposals for making certain categories of agreement, decision and concerted practice falling within Article 4(2) or Article 5(2) compulsorily notifiable under Article 4 or 5.

2. Within one year from the date of entry into force of this Regulation, the Council shall examine, on a proposal from the Commission, what special provisions might be made for exempting from the provisions of this Regulation agreements, decisions and concerted practices falling within Article 4(2) or Article 5(2).

Article 23

Transitional Provisions Applicable to Decisions of Authorities of the Member States

1. Agreements, decisions and concerted practices of the kind described in Article 85(1) of the Treaty to which, before the entry into force of this Regulation, the competent authority of a Member State has declared Article 85(1) to be inapplicable pursuant to Article 85(3) shall not be subject to compulsory notification under Article 5. The decision of the competent authority of the Member State shall be deemed to be a decision within the meaning of Article 6; it shall cease to be valid upon expiration of the period fixed by such authority but in any event not more than three years after the entry into force of this Regulation. Article 8(3) shall apply.

2. Applications for renewal of decisions of the kind described in paragraph 1 shall be decided upon by the Commission in accordance with Article 8(2).

Article 24

Implementing Provisions

The Commission shall have power to adopt implementing provisions concerning the form, content and other details of applications pursuant to Articles 2 and 3, and of notifications pursuant to Articles 4 and 5, and concerning hearings pursuant to Article 19(1) and (2).

This Regulation shall be binding in its entirety and directly applicable in all Member States.

Article 25

[Accession Agreements]

1.   As regards agreements, decisions and concerted practices to which Article 85 of the Treaty applies by virtue of accession, the date of accession shall be substituted for the date of entry into force of this Regulation in every place where reference is made in this Regulation to this latter date.

2.   Agreements, decisions and concerted practices existing at the date of accession to which Article 85 of the Treaty applies by virtue of accession shall be notified pursuant to Article 5(1) or Article 7(1) and (2) within six months from the date of accession.

3.   Fines under Article 15(2) (a) shall not be imposed in respect of any act prior to notification of the agreements, decisions and practices to which paragraph 2 applies and which have been notified within the period therein specified.

4.   New Member States shall take the measures referred to in Article 14(6) within six months from the date of accession after consulting the Commission.

Approved February 6, 1962
Effective March 13, 1962
Amended July 10, 1962
November 7, 1963
December 29, 1971
March 27, 1972

Index

Abuse of Dominant Position, in Common Market, 221–24

Acquisitions, mergers, and joint ventures in foreign commerce, 118–38

"Act-of-state" doctrine, 31, 32

Act of state, compelling, 264

Acte clair theory, 227

Activity, continuous and systematic, alien corporations and, 38–39

Advertising
comity and (*Holophane* case), 66, 67
deceptive and misleading, in Canada, 250–51
foreign, in U.S. (*De Beers* case), 39
FTC and, 109

Agency for International Development (AID), 24, 25 (*Pacific Seafarers* case)
in export trade, 182 (*Concentrated Phosphate* case)

Agreements
in Common Market, 195
exclusive-distribution, 204
new, old, and accession, 202–203
and practices prohibited, 208–19
specialization, 204–206
definition of, in United Kingdom, 231
know-how and export, in United Kingdom, 236
restrictive, *see* Restrictive agreements

Alcoa case, *see U.S.* v. *Aluminum Co. of America*

Alexander Report, 170–71

Alfred Bell & Co. v. *Catalda Fine Arts,* 81

Aliens
foreign trade and, 22
U.S. antitrust laws and, 26–29
venue law and, 42–44
See also Person, foreign

Alien corporations
in continuous and systematic activity in U.S., 38–39
with U.S. subsidiaries, 36–37
with U.S. parents, 37–38
See also Foreign companies

Alkasso case, *see U.S.* v. *U.S. Alkali Export Ass'n.*

Aloha Airlines, Inc. v. *Hawaiian Airlines, Inc.,* 188

American Banana Co. v. *United Fruit Co.,* 22–24, 29, 32

American Society of Mechanical Engineers (ASME), 83–84

Anti-Combines Law of Canada, 246–52

Antimonopoly Act of Japan, 253–59

Antitrust Civil Process Act, 48, 49

Antitrust decrees on licensing agreements, 162–65

Antitrust Division of Department of